ITALIAN VIOLIN MAKERS

KAREL JALOVEC

ITALIAN VIOLIN MAKERS

PAUL HAMLYN · LONDON

Designed and produced by Artia
for Paul Hamlyn Ltd
Westbook House · Fulham Broadway · London

First published 1958
Revised edition 1964
Printed in Czechoslovakia
S 1584

INTRODUCTION

The study of old instruments can give us much knowledge that is important and interesting about the history of music. Though the general falling into disuse and consequent unavailability of some once common instruments necessitates the music written for them being played nowadays on other instruments related to or evolved from the originals, familiarity with the instruments for which the music was originally written can give us considerable enlightenment and often a revelation of the composer's intentions. Moreover, through the evocation of the music of the past which the study of old instruments permits we are able to understand better the thoughts and emotions which affected our ancestors, whether this be in the field of formal music-making or of folk-music and song.

There are other reasons for recommending this book which deals with the finest specimens of what is without doubt the most popular and important family of instruments — the violin family. Firstly, the difficulties of distinguishing the false from the genuine are such that only an expert treatise such as the present one can enable one to pursue one's studies with any assurance. Secondly, the book is more than a mere compilation: it is critical in mood and attempts to acquaint the public with what should be considered the proofs of genuineness.

While it would be false to claim that many modern instruments are not of outstanding quality, it is also true that for all intents and purposes most of the stringed instruments achieved their final form long ago (there has been little evolution since) and that they achieved a state of perfection at the hands of the great violin makers which has never been surpassed.

From many points of view, then, this book can fairly claim to be of the utmost value and importance in the study of music.

In conclusion I wish it every success on its journey.

PROFESSOR L. ZELENKA

CONTENTS

LIST OF ILLUSTRATIONS

PROFESSOR DR. J. B. KOZÁK

ON THE EVALUATION OF STRINGED INSTRUMENTS

Those who wish to understand the peculiar relation of the performing artist and connoisseur to his stringed instrument must learn to regard the violin and its larger relatives as works of art. The feelings of pride and partiality, of extreme fondness and love that certain instruments evoke, even the regret, when some quality is lacking or destroyed, can be understood only if this artistic approach is used. The original invariably is of a much higher price and value than copies made by the dozen, and the work of the creative master is superior to that of his followers, even though they are endowed with a part of his excellence and a reflection of his glory.

Like a picture, an instrument to be a work of art must be genuine, original, accomplished and in its own way beautiful. Although old it must be well preserved and as nearly as possible in its original condition. This analogy with pictures will be helpful to us in assessing qualities, for, as with pictures, in this line there also existed schools: schools of instrument-making. Here, too, some sort of hierarchy of artists is recognized and, as in plastic art, there have been changes in taste and judgement. Several fashions have come and gone, and often what is best liked and most valued today was misunderstood and unrecognized in the past and had to force its way to success.

The matter, however, is more complicated than in the case of pictures. The aesthetic function of pictures is visual, meaningful and often historical, but except for being looked at or preserved nothing is, or should be, done with them. In their own way stringed instruments are works of art, but their primary function is musical.

Today the role of the violin or 'cello is different and considerably greater than was the case in the past. Before Beethoven, when delicate compositions and graceful minuets were played in the salons of the nobles, tenderness of tone and a flute-like timbre were valued most highly. Instruments made by Jacob Stainer were endowed with these qualities to perfection. This accounts for their popularity in the past, as well as for their innumerable imitations. The German masters of the eighteenth century mostly endeavoured to attain the same goal: they sought for the required tone, raising the archings of instruments and complying with the current tastes even as far as colouring was concerned. Nowadays such instruments are not in very great favour; even when new they often appeared as though tarnished by smoke, and grew darker still with age; their tone generally falls short of the increased orchestral and particularly solo requirements. In modern performances, conducted in large halls and accompanied by powerful orchestras, resiliency and strength of tone are required. Thus musical development itself has brought to the fore instruments of a different build, which formerly had been considered by the public fit chiefly for a large church. First among these new favourites were the Italian instruments, whose power and clearness, even when the swiftest passages are executed, are a veritable miracle.

It was only in the nineteenth century that Italian instruments achieved international fame. The masters of the Amati family, it is true, had been famous before that time, mostly because of the delicately subdued, silvery sound of their instruments which vied with that of Stainer; Stradivari likewise had been admired during his lifetime and had noble, rich customers. His works, however, had still to come out of the castles and churches in order to reach the general public. With feudalism giving way to the middle classes, the musical public underwent a change in its structure.

The great soloists of the first half of the past century revealed the excellence of these Italian instruments to their audiences, who were enraptured by the richness and carrying power of the tone. Paganini directed public attention to Joseph Guarneri del Gesù. The collector Tarisio sought and gathered precious originals throughout Italy, taking them to Paris. On Tarisio's death they made J. B. Vuillaume, an excellent violin maker and an even better businessman, a rich man. The sudden rise in the prices of these makes is not explained by the interest of performers alone. Collecting began to spread and became a considerable fashion in the rich industrial countries. Many a marvellous instrument was condemned to temporary silence, only to appear later on the market in an excellent state of preservation, sometimes even with a complete list of its previous owners.

But the tone of a stringed instrument, although astoundingly persistent and improved by playing, is not everlasting. The number of old, even classical, violins worn out by constant use over a period of centuries, is rapidly growing. What used to be an acoustic marvel, will grow old and deteriorate, though ever so slowly. The number of perfect old specimens is diminishing and their prices keep growing. Often the tone of a wonderful fiddle becomes too soft and smooth and loses the ability to dominate a large orchestra. And it goes without saying that the times are gone when it was possible to discover an Italian rarity in some forgotten attic. The artist and even the fancier has to rest satisfied with something less spectacular, just as he cannot adorn his home with a Raphael or a Rembrandt.

The increasing price and diminishing number of first-class originals directed public attention first to the minor Italian masters. Many uncommonly good, almost perfect, specimens were found among them. A number of old Italian instruments measure up in tone to the great masters of the Cremona school. Today we appreciate their originality and do not consider them inferior, if their style of workmanship differs from Stradivari. On the contrary, we like them.

Unfortunately this appreciation has in many cases come too late. Thousands of originals have been rechristened after greater names. The label inside is in itself no proof of origin. There are, of course, methods for distinguishing a genuine label from a fake and, even more important, for discovering the real craftsman. An instrument, like a picture, should itself reveal its identity. But it must not be "repainted", i. e. revarnished, substantially altered or fitted with incongruent new parts. If the instrument is in a fairly original state, the maker can often be discovered and the school to which he belonged almost unmistakably ascertained. And even when the school cannot be determined, the value of an excellent nondescript instrument cannot be denied, for it is obviously the work of skilled hands. Some old violin makers have been greatly wronged: we know little about them, but their instruments are in use, sailing under false colours.

Because of the slow but inevitable decay of stringed instruments, violins of the oldest school of Brescia (Gasparo da Salò, G. P. Maggini, etc.) are extremely rare. We seldom have an opportunity to see and hear them. There are in existence more violas of that time, partly because violins were then a novelty and violas were more common, partly because violas last longer and are less played. However, fate will inevitably one day overtake (although not soon, because of the great care bestowed upon them), the famous instruments of the Cremona school also. The time will come when they will be worn out; cracks will appear and they will become rare relics in the hands of collectors and in the glass cases of museums. At the present time, those that have fortunately survived the vicissitudes of two and sometimes even more centuries are still in full splendour. Their high price, however, and the knowledge that they are past their prime, cause musicians, amateurs and collectors to direct their attention to the masters of the nineteenth century. An exacting musician or listener can be fully satisfied with a beautiful instrument by Pressenda or Rocca, and there is quite a number of such names. If such makes were passed as being those with a more popular name they would enrapture the listener even more, for suggestion and illusion play a role which is only too well known.

This shift in the interest in old instruments is basically correct. It has led to a fair evaluation and admiring appreciation of great French masters (N. Lupot, J. B. Vuillaume, etc.) and of other makers, among whom the outstanding Czechs, particularly those of Prague, will, we hope, attain the distinction they deserve.

It is impossible to explain the acoustic value of stringed instruments without bringing to mind a truism which is nevertheless often overlooked. The instrument does not play itself. What we hear is the interplay of the instrument and the performer. The same violin has a different value in different hands. Not even a Guarnerius can make good the deficiencies of an unskilful hand and many a great artist works miracles on an instrument which is not extremely precious. Although stringed instruments really gain by playing, especially in that they speak more easily and develop a more supple tone — a fact which is no illusion, particularly to the performer — the process of maturing can be fairly rapid and may be at its end within a few decades. There is no lack of modern instruments acoustically excellent, with a fresh, full, and yet soft tone.

The acoustic side, however, of these works of art is not the only basis for their evaluation. As early as the first half of the seventeenth century, as we know from the correspondence of Galileo Galilei, they began to be regarded as works of fine art. The masters of the Brescia school sought, above all, a solemn and sonorous tone, whereas in Cremona they put stress on a graceful appearance; the sound of the latter was at first somewhat small and more melodious than powerful. Sometimes, probably on the demand of customers, the instruments were provided with artistic tarsia adornments. The inlaid instruments by Stradivari are famous, and we know similar though less beautiful ones by other masters. Such adornment, however, was exceptional. On the whole the Italian masters remained true to aesthetically sober and functional principles, proving thereby, it would seem, a still higher degree of taste. Stress remained on the gracefulness of shapes, beauty of material, careful workmanship, and colour appearance. What matters nowadays was also important in the past, viz. how much the client would and could pay for the instrument. The reader should look at the old instrument makers realistically, in the social position and circumstances in which they probably had to make their living. Very few of them were of patrician origin or well-to-do men. For the most part they were humble artisans who were content to work anonymously in what would today be called the *atelier* of a prominent or enterprising master. The number of makers to whom only one or a couple of instruments can be attributed is so great that it cannot be always ascribed to price-raising practices, although we know that these practices occurred in the seventeenth and eighteenth centuries, sometimes with the connivance of the makers themselves. Nor could the mortality of fiddles of minor makers have been much greater than that of expensive specimens. Some of these artisans probably but seldom got an order, and if they did they had to put up with a low price. The provincial maker had mostly provincial customers, communications were slow and Italy was divided into a number of territories. The plain appearance and less careful finish of an old instrument does not therefore mean that the maker knew no better. Even so, some of these instruments have a wonderful tone. Sometimes one of the minor masters suddenly produced an instrument of stunning perfection and there are certainly precious specimens in which only the salient traits and finish are the work of the master whose name we read inside.

Sometimes the makers even dispensed with the purfling of the back, since the back is hard, is not taken off like the belly and therefore requires strengthening to a lesser degree. Instead of it we find two lines branded about the edges by means of hot iron points. The backs of 'cellos even by good masters are sometimes made of poplar wood. Both these peculiarities, for instance, characterize certain products of the Milanese Testore family, particulary of Paolo Antonio Testore.

It is the beauty and perfection of the specimen, therefore, which counts most in its evaluation. What counts further is the name, state of preservation, and only in the last place the tone. A beautiful undamaged instrument by a good master nearly always sounds well; moreover, the owner will take a liking to it even if its tone is more sweet and harmonious than powerful. The artist appreciates, of course, above all, the acoustic qualities.

The number of factors that must be considered in appraising stringed instruments as works of art is so great that, in the aggregate, the presence of all these factors in a given specimen is sufficient to render it rare, even though it is not distinguished by age.

An instrument lacking good, matured, acoustical wood, or careful, strong, light, correct build, may have a nice appearance, but falls short of the requirements of music, particularly on the concert platform and in chamber music. None of these conditions is isolated. Much was written once about the tuning of the belly and back, that their upper tones should blend harmoniously so as to produce that complicated mixture of sounds which combines softness with carrying power, strength with easy resonance, song with brilliance, and has in the individual strings the peculiar colour required for interpretation. This question remains open and it is not difficult to understand why. It is impossible to determine the conditions of vibration on detached parts: they are different in an instrument firmly glued together and exposed to the heavy pull of the strings.

It seems more probable that knowledge gained from constructive statics will throw some light on the problem. If we know the coefficient of elasticity of pine and maple wood, the height and shape of arching, the strength of pull of the strings and that of the pressure on the bridge, the maximum and minimum thickness of the belly and back, we shall perhaps be able to figure out how and where the thickness has to be diminished gradually towards the edges.

Such calculations were actually undertaken about 40 years ago by a member of the Czech Institute of Technology; the curves connecting the points of equal thickness were, strange to say, similar to those found in Italian masterpieces. In these calculations, however, the basic data had been given by practical experience of the makers. Most important was the maximum and minimum thickness of belly and back. But this difference varies; it is greater in hard woods: that is, the bellies are more uniform in thickness. For these reasons mathematical computations are by themselves not revealing. Moreover, what has been discovered, or rather confirmed, by calculation can be no mechanical guidance to an experienced instrument maker. In individual cases he alters the models and arching and conforms to the inequalities of the material. He feels by means of his tools what sort of material he has in his hands. He studies the acoustic materials and knows how much he is allowed to take off in order to achieve the best results. He is aware that a thin-profiled instrument has no brilliant prospects and that many a good old instrument has been hopelessly spoiled by scraping the plates in order to endow them with a "finer" sound.

Tradition, example and experience guide the violin maker. He can achieve fine results by carefully imitating outstanding patterns. We realize that those who did pioneer work in this field were endowed with great power of observation and creative genius. It is remarkable that instruments by the same distinguished master almost always embody some special quality of their own, i.e. the same peculiar colour of the individual strings, even if the model of the sounding body is altered. This is true of Stradivari, whose successive models — amatisé, allongé, period of glory and that of old age — are very similar in tone. It is still more striking with Joseph Guarneri del Gesù, who in his early years made daring experiments with the shape of his instruments. We have already mentioned the tone of the instruments by the masters of the Amati family, but this applies more or less to all superior violin makers, with some exceptions of course, for even they did not succeed in all their designs.

"Violin varnish" has been much written about, and much research has been done in this field. The secret of the old Cremona varnish, once apparently prepared of common ingredients and accessible even to cabinet makers, seems to have got lost about 1780. After that the varnish deteriorates, perhaps for the reason that other kinds dried faster. But some schools, e.g., that of Naples, used a drier, less supple, though also fine-looking varnish even before that date. Chemical analyses of varnish, after two or more centuries of exposure to air and sunlight, have thrown little light on this matter. Is seems that individual violin makers had their own methods of colouring and applying; they used either to combine coats of different colours or to choose merely different shades. Sometimes they would add colouring matter of a vegetable nature — not, of course, the modern chemical colours of today; at other times they shaded off in varying degrees the ground tone, perhaps by boiling the varnish. The Cremona varnish is not the only type that stands out singularly. Just as beautiful, although in a different way, are the instruments of the Venetian school, the products of the masters of Naples and Turin; even those of Milan were not much inferior, although they did not succeed in achieving the same sweet golden appearance and fire. Some varnish of the nineteenth century, such as that of Pressenda, Vuillaume, etc., justly arouses admiration in this respect. The old "secret" need not be lost forever; it may even be surpassed with modern means. But it is essential to know what is being sought. The grounding of the famous Italian varnish sank into and united with the wood; this is evident from the fact that even in places where it is completely worn off there remained the coloured ground, which may again be brought to a soft lustre by gentle rubbing. The varnish forms with the wood an acoustic unity. It never chipped off, but was merely wiped off gradually. It not only protected the wood, which, had it not been for the varnish, would have fallen into decay a long time ago, but it also made the tone fine and mellow. The ingredients used in the varnish remained as a rule moderately soft. The surface in uninjured sections feels smooth as butter, in other places like velvet. Its transparency is practically absolute, showing quite clearly all fibres of the grain and the reflexes of the material. At the same time it has an apparent depth which seems incredible considering the very thin coat. The colours were selected very tastefully, from deep yellow to orange, golden-brown, pinkish brown, reaching up to dark red. When light falls upon them, they will scintillate. Originally the colouring of the old Italian instruments was more lively than it is today; a little of the colour was taken away by the sun and the varnish became somewhat brown. The darkening of the old wood has contributed to this change in colour, so that at a distance one always gets the impression of a brownish shade.

These hues are sometimes as beautiful as those of pictures. Where the upper coats of colouring are already worn off, figures have appeared that enhance the beauty of the whole. This "face" of old originals (particularly visible in red varnish with underlying golden-yellow ground) has been imitated for a long time. But an imitation is always recognizable; a connoisseur discovers even the most cunning imitation, if it is not itself old and the work of a maker who almost equals his paragon. Real age cannot be imitated even by staining the wood without betraying the fake. Moreover, it is known that the surface of old maplewood (on the backs and sides), may get slightly warped into undulations because of shrinking, so that it has an uneven mother-of-pearl appearance. The waves follow the curl marked by the structure of the material. As a rule the general impression is enchanting and utterly different from the flat appearance of "paint" with which cheap new instruments are provided.

The originals we admire are, it is true, children of the Italian sun. But they are, above all, works of patient men. A thing of beauty always requires patience.

It is incredible how much individuality the old masters were able to embody in every detail, although they worked within the scope of their own school and as a rule departed only gradually from the patterns on which they based their craftsmanship. Sometimes there are only shades of difference, which require a well-trained and experienced eye, but on the whole they almost remind one of a characteristic handwriting.

The scroll of the old school of Brescia has half a turn less than the scrolls of a later period. In scrolls there is much variety: they may be perfect, but in other cases poor, carved without patience, somewhat small in proportion to the whole, narrow or massive, having the axis of symmetry either horizontal (when the instrument is held in a vertical position) or somewhat inclined downward, etc. Nowadays the best patterns are imitated with an extraordinary precision, and yet the product lacks the softness of the old original, which looks almost as if it had grown up organically. Likewise, the shape of the sound-holes has become to a great extent stereotyped. These sound-holes are nearly always the same accurately redrawn, elegant shapes of the well-known works of Guarneri and Stradivari. But their contemporaries and fellow countrymen always had something new in their shape and position and even the slightest modification can be seen and forms a part of their originality.

The outlines of Italian instruments developed within two generations and attained its peak of elegance in the works of those to whom pre-eminence was awarded for other reasons as well. The figure of the wood was made use of with refined taste; the backs and sides of better specimens are beautifully streaked, broad or narrow flames flash forth from the centre, opalescing when the instrument is moved. In other specimens these flames reach across the whole back, if it is made of one piece, and they are often aslant. At times they continue aslant even on the sides, and sometimes — particularly in the instruments by some of the Cremona masters — this impression is further increased by the fact that the hatching is reversed in the middle bouts. On the other hand it seems that some masters, e. g. Goffredo Cappa and his disciples, stressed the design so that it would be horizontal when the instrument is held straight up.

The purfling which lines the edges likewise tells a story. Tommaso Balestrieri, one of the really great masters, whose instruments shine both in colour and tone, often failed in this one point. Perhaps he was an amateur, or his hand was less sure. The latter is pathetically true of Stradivari himself, when he was ninety-three years old (a violin bearing a label written with his own hand and stating his age when the instrument was made, has been preserved).

A perfect purfling is almost a matter of course today, the modern purfling is even more accurate than that of the old masters, who had to make this part themselves. It consists of three strips glued together, the two outer strips being black and the middle one white. But nowadays the production looks as though a print had been made, not a manuscript carefully brought into completion. The purfling has lost its personal character.

Less attention is paid by the uninitiated observer to the rounding of the edges and the shape of the corners. Such things are, however, very typical, and even good instrument-makers have failed in this respect.

All these individual factors are intermixed in various ways. This brings about a play of art and creativeness that is almost as interesting as the study and appreciation of pictures. At times one is moved to exclaim, "What a pity that it has not got a better scroll". At another time, "It's a pity that the instrument is not broader — what tone that would bring about", etc.

Another important question that must be considered is the state of preservation of the old originals. They have hardly ever been handed down to us in an unchanged state. Pegs, tailpieces, bridges, finger-boards, necks are exchanged. Complete originals are great rarities. Stringed instruments of the seventeenth and eighteenth centuries had the necks fixed in a straight position — often traces can be seen showing how the instrument rocked on its back when it was laid down. An angle was of course even then necessary because the finger-board (which was then shorter) and the strings had to slant upwards to the bridge (which was low). This was originally accomplished by a wedge put under the fingerboard. Later it was done by tilting back the neck and the head, and today we can hardly imagine it otherwise. An original neck is a rare item. It has usually been replaced by a new one, because nowadays necks must be longer. This obviously need not be considered a corruption of originality. We also know that the old violins were held differently from the manner common nowadays. Formerly the player's chin rested on the tailpiece, or even slightly to the right of it, evidence thereof being the traces visible on many old violins. Development of new techniques, quick changes of position, etc., brought about a change in the manner of holding the violin and inaugurated the use of chin-rests, which were originally primitive and did not protect the belly.

This brief explanation ought to be sufficient to put an end to some popular naïveties. To these belong "the tsigane violin, highly improved by playing", for to acquire a rare instrument from such a source is about as probable as to buy a thoroughbred horse from the same hands. Because it happened that someone had a broken fiddle repaired by a violin maker, which resulted in its having a better tone than before, some people concluded that smashing a violin improves the tone. And so on. To this same category belongs the scraping out of instruments. It is a pity that such stories still have credence and remain in circulation.

Cracks in the wood are usually due to injuries against which these delicate instruments should be carefully protected. However, cracks also appear spontaneously because of age. If they are short, small in number and not under the bridge, they can be repaired easily and do not cause any particular depreciation of value. The original varnish, however, should be preserved under all conditions. Even mere traces of the original varnish are better than retouches. Even a colourless coating is undesirable, although at times unavoidable because of repairs. It corrupts the original structure of the surface, which may be evidence of originality, and in addition grows more characteristic with the patina of age.

Interferences of this kind, although unnoticeable by daylight, may be detected by ultraviolet rays. These rays also accelerate the maturation of the wood. However, an old instrument cannot endure such experimentation, and woe to the owner of a modern one who subjects it to such abuse. It will crack all over, the reaction being violent. It may be worth while trying when using unfinished wood — but everything in moderation.

We have already said that from the musical point of view the old instruments can be equalled. Coming centuries will bring to light new values and it is possible that some day a further change in musical demands will bring about greater power or a different colour of tone. For instruments are intimately connected with the development of music. There have been changes in tuning, which is much higher now than it used to be. The original makers would undoubtedly shake their heads at the high-pitched, "piercing" tone and at all that a virtuoso demands of his fiddle today.

Within the limits of these new developments and the predilections connected with them we are still conservative. Violin making is no field for new inventions, on the one hand because the visual impression of a differently constructed body is different — usually inferior — and on the other because we feel that it sounds "different from a violin". If the time comes, however, when new qualities will be required, masters will arise to meet that demand. At the present time imitation, perhaps a little biased, prevails and there are too many of those ever-recurring patterns of Stradivari and Guarneri.

A genuine work of art created by a craftsman must be internally homogeneous. It is impossible to use formal elements which do not belong together. Those who are able to look at instruments with a loving eye — and this is what as a rule musicians do — will also appreciate the harmony of the whole. It may not always be perfect. How to look at it and to judge it will be explained in detail by Mr. Jalovec.*

Pronounced Yalovets.

KAREL JALOVEC

ITALIAN VIOLIN MAKERS

This book does not deal only with violin makers, although, we admit, they are more in the spotlight than makers of the lutes, guitars, mandolins and other instruments of the kind, who are also included. It is difficult to find a comprehensive title for a work of this kind. The title *Violin Makers* is too narrow; expressions like "makers of stringed instruments played with the bow" are not nice; and it would go too far to speak of stringed instruments in general, for we do not include harps, pianos and the like. The Italian word *liutajo* and the French *luthier* would do, for they include the violin makers, but other languages use the corresponding words in a less ancient and more accurate sense. The title *Lute and Violin Makers* might be the most pardonable of all combinations. Both words must, however, be taken in a broader meaning, the first including producers of lutes, guitars and mandolins, the second makers of violins, violas, 'cellos and contrabasses, in both cases with occasional glances at instruments which have gone out of use.

The origins of the most important stringed instrument played with the bow, the violin, are wrapped in darkness. We only know for certain that it developed out of the viola. The latter had been in use for a considerable time before, and though it was in many ways more primitive and of a very variable size, it did not differ essentially from its present form and was tuned as it is now, though to a much lower pitch. As early as 1449 Giovanni Kerlino is said to have built violas not only with a bridge, but with an arched belly, and about 1500 Pietro Dardelli of Mantua, a contemporary of Leonardo da Vinci, built violas convex on both sides. Half a century later the treble viol, tuned in fifths, but a quint higher, made its appearance — the violin. Many conjectures have been made concerning the inventor: authors of three nations have tried to confer the honour on this or that of their countrymen. It seems, however, probable that it was developed gradually and in a groping way, in obvious co-operation with and at the behest of musicians. There was growing demand for an instrument with a soprano voice, whereas the viola da braccio (i. e. held in hand and under the chin, not between the knees like the viola da gamba) represented the alto, and quite successfully at that.

The crescent-like soundholes of violas from the previous period appear definitely changed into their present *f*-like shape in the works of *Gasparo Bertolotti*, known as *Gasparo da Salò* who was born in 1542 at Salò on Lake Garda and worked in Brescia where he died in 1609. He also adopted the arching introduced by his predecessors. The most remarkable feat of Gasparo da Salò was not the "invention" of the violin, but the fact that it sounded so well. His violins were less refined in appearance than the works of the Cremona masters who began to appear practically in the same generation, but a century later, when the development of music and performances in churches and larger halls called for a more voluminous tone, the leading masters of the craft began to wind their way back to Gasparo da Salò and the other great Brescians in order to find a synthesis of the melodious sweetness — the ideal of the Cremonese Amatis and Jacob Stainer — with their powerful carrying tone. The true miracle of the invention lies in the fact that the viola and violin have not been changed in any essential way since the time of Gasparo da Salò and G. P. Maggini. Masterpieces of later origin are more elegant, more carefully finished than the fiddles they could produce (and sell), but as regards the tone the Brescians have set one of the chief standards of beauty and expression.

Few ingenious creations, if any, have withstood the impact of innovations so steadfastly as the violin. And yet musicians and experts insist that it was due to their intrinsic worth; they are by no means conservative with regard to many other instruments. To the uninitiated the importance ascribed in this work to slight differences in arching, to the position of the sound-holes and the bridge and similar trifles may appear all but ridiculous. But violins, although they differ quite visibly in outlines, sound-holes, scrolls and colours, differ very little in build. Thicknesses vary but slightly — a trifle less and the results may be distressing. Certain proportions, expressible, as we are convinced, in numerical relations, appear to have been an iron rule, at least in genuine Italian fiddles.

Of course, it has not been possible to preserve them in their original condition, even if they had the good (and rare) luck to be in the hands of people endowed with due respect for originality. The development of violin play has necessitated longer necks tilted back the way we are now familiar with, higher bridges, chin-rests, etc. Most important is the distance from the middle of the sound-holes to the upper end of the belly (or of the length of strings to the total length of the body of the instrument). The former proportion seems to be set "for good" and without it no artist today can handle his instrument with assurance. Inside the instruments of the violin family only the bass-bar has been almost always replaced by a stronger one. All other alterations are detrimental, to old instruments always, to new ones usually.

Several schools have successively or simultaneously held sway in Italy. They have their characteristics, but individual masters, especially the great ones, did not hesitate to borrow this or that particular they liked from other quarters. There was plenty of emulation among the leaders of the craft, but no mechanical imitation.

The school of *Brescia*, headed by *Gasparo da Salò* and *G. P. Maggini*, built instruments which are characterized by relatively low, but broad, archings which reach almost to the edges. They form low convex curves in all directions. The corners are short and mostly rather pointed. The purfling is often double and sometimes forms, particularly at a later period, interlaced ornaments on the back. The sides are low; the scroll, which looks old-fashioned, has half a turn less than the scrolls of later schools. Sometimes the instruments have instead of a scroll a carved human or animal head. The wide-open sound-holes are in an almost upright position, practically parallel, in other specimens sharply inclined; their upper and lower openings are of the same diameter. The belly has regular grain, the bass-bar often forms one piece with the belly. The back is usually carved out of one slab of wood taken from the outside of a maple-tree and is as a rule without curl. The Brescia makers made the backs, sides and scrolls of their instruments also of other kinds of wood.

They used a varnish ranging from dark yellow to dark brown. They applied it in rather thick coats and it is not so transparent as the Cremonese.

The tone of these instruments is sonorous; the violins sound on the D and G strings a little like violas. The violas and contrabasses are often superior to the violins and particularly to the 'cellos. Originally these instruments were rather thick in wood and many specimens have been spoiled by scraping out in the hope that they would get a "finer" tone.

The Brescian school flourished in the years 1558-1620.

From 1560 to c. 1740 the *Cremona* school was at its best and at the head of the Italian violincraft. The founder of this school was *Andrea Amati* who was long considered as a disciple of Gasparo da Salò. His father Gotardo, who died in 1553, seems to have been a lute maker — he was called Maestro Gotardo Amati. But Andrea, although probably apprenticed by his father and without being a direct pupil of Casparo da Salò, turned towards violin making. However, with regard to tone, he followed another ideal then popular in higher circles. According to another version he was pupil of a Marco del Busetto who lived in Cremona from 1540 to 1580. But this is improbable, for Andrea Amati was an independent craftsman as early as 1546.

The Cremona school gave to the world masters unsurpassed to this day. It is, however, not sharply circumscribed. This is due partly to its very excellence, for it inspired imitation. It is consequently not easy to formulate the criteria of the Cremonese style. A number of outstanding masters who belong to the school lived outside Cremona, others, like Alessandro Gagliano, started in Cremona and founded a new school elsewhere; after Lorenzo Storioni, roughly since the end of the 18th century, even very good masters in Cremona were mere followers. Nor does meticulous copying constitute a Cremonese trait, not to speak of later imitations — their number has been mounting for over a century and they may be as soulless as cheap prints.

The masters of Cremona worked very carefully. The instruments have graceful outlines, the corners rather protruding, but rounded off with fine taste; the edges have a profile regularly executed all the way around the instrument. The Amatis and other early masters took the arching rather high and roof-like, i.e., flat (even slightly hollow) near the edges and rising rather suddenly towards the middle line. Later the instruments become flatter, the construction perceptibly stronger. The scrolls, at first somewhat small, since Stradivari larger, but not massive, are never standardized. The sound-holes have the upper openings smaller than the lower ones. The back of a 'cello or contrabass may be of poplar wood, but even here maple is the rule and the smaller instruments are always made of light regular pinewood and carefully selected maplewood, the latter as a rule with beautiful curl.

The varnish of the true Cremonese masters is supple, soft and persistent at the same time, transparent, underneath yellow and variously coloured in hues ranging from bright yellow which suggests the idea of liquid gold, to amber-yellow and orange and again from pale red to deep red; transitions and mixtures of these tints occur in the works of the same makers; only neutral brown is seldom found. The varnish is carefully applied in thin coats. When pressed with a warm finger for some time, it retains a trace which then slowly disappears by itself. And it can never be rubbed off entirely, for the grounding is united with the wood and some of its lustre can be even then renewed by careful rubbing (not without some oil).

The schools of *Naples* and *Milan* represent transitions between the former two. They produced finer instruments than the Brescian makers, but did not reach the Cremona level. The masters of Naples generally followed some of the later models of Stradivari, while the Milanese leaned towards the Guarneri patterns. Low archings are the rule. The Neapolitan makers used a varnish which has sometimes a magnificent appearance, but is less supple and slightly inferior to that of Cremona.

These two schools flourished for a long time, from c. 1680 to 1800.

The schools of *Florence*, *Rome* and *Bologna* were less creative; they borrowed traits from other, even from Tyrolese masters, altered the archings, not always in an elegant manner; their sound-holes are less ornamental, especially if they cut across a suddenly rising arching and appear too open. Most masters in Rome adopted Jacob Stainer's shape of sound-holes, short and with circular ends. The makers of Bologna at first followed the Cremona masters, then reverted to Brescian examples. They employed a yellow or brown, exceptionally also dark-red varnish. In composition the varnish of all these schools is almost as good as that of Cremona, but it deteriorates after 1760, for these cities had their best violin makers from 1680 to c. 1760.

The school of *Venice* flourished from 1690 to 1764. In the 17th century it was even superior to the Brescian school. Venice, a sea port, was frequented by foreigners; it had favourable conditions for sale and special orders; there are consequently specimens from Venice which almost equal those of the best Cremonese masters. At first the craftsmen of Venice followed the larger patterns of Nic. Amati, making the well-designed sound-holes slightly shorter; later they lowered the archings according to the models of Stradivari and of the members of the Guarneri family, one of whom lived and died in the city.

Besides these schools there were masters who cannot be simply assigned to any of them and are sometimes not only individual but really outstanding. On the other hand there were places where one finds quite interesting blends of styles. This is true e.g. of Goffredo Cappa and his pupils in Saluzzo and Turin. Turin was at times a famous centre of violin making, for several Cremonese masters established themselves in the city and even in the first half of the 19th century F. Pressenda and his school almost revived the glory of the preceding century. In Pisa, Livorno (Leghorn), Genoa, Piacenza and several other towns one comes across makers in whom fluctuating influences almost obliterated each other. Much of this blending must be attributed to the migrations of makers from different parts of Italy.

Italian violin making flourished for almost 250 years. After 1850 it was almost extinct, and before it took a new breath, Italy, the cradle of the famous craft, depended on the importation of instruments from abroad.

Some information concerning the materials employed in violin making may be useful. The bellies are made of pine or fir wood with grain of varying breadth, but it is seldom excessively close in genuine Italian violins. The backs, sides, necks and scrolls are mostly, not always, of maplewood. The best pine and maplewood came from the southern slopes of the Alps, from present-day Yugoslavia and the eastern Carpathians. The Brescian makers nearly always used maple wood cut on the slab, i.e. from outside planks. Later the makers proceeded towards the middle of the trunk, and finally they made, of course not always, the backs from wedges reaching to the middle.

Wood from outside planks is plain, without curl; further inside figures begin to appear, first in concentric lines (fig. 1), then in the form of curl which then reaches right across the instrument, either horizontally or in slanting direction (fig. 2). Backs made from wedges (generally in two pieces) show clear "flames" which seem to be moving when we incline the instrument. These can be arranged horizontally (fig. 3) or in a roof (fig. 4) or reversely (fig. 5). Wood from near the roots of the tree has a marble-like appearance (fig. 6). So called bird's eye maple (fig. 7), popular beyond the Alps, was seldom used in Italy. There are, of course, instruments with combined figures, the upper part striped, the lower part marbled, etc. It is difficult to state the time when the makers departed from outside slabs. Much depended on the material at hand, and even when the latter two ways began to predominate makers sometimes reverted to plain slabs which were cheaper. On the other hand Stradivari used the combination method as early as 1690. From the very beginning of the 17th century there are Amati instruments with a fine curl. The sides and head should be, and in better instruments generally are, of the same wood as the back.

If you have a fine instrument of the violin family, keep it clean and have it cleaned from time to time, not too often. Do not gather experience with bridges and the soundpost at the expense of your fiddle. Have these delicate operations always made by an expert — very much depends on it, including "your tone", if you are an artist. And bear in mind that lack of knowledge has only too often led to financial losses when instruments were bought from unscrupulous persons.

Many inquiries are made concerning the varnish of the classical instruments. To see miracles in the composition of the old Italian varnish is erroneous. It was actually superseded by other compositions some time before the end of the eighteenth century, but some modern masters equal the old ones in this respect. Impatience with the length of the drying period may have been one of the chief reasons of deterioration. But violin varnish is basically more a question of taste, patience and careful execution than a secret. Since it is going to be dealt with in a special booklet, we limit our remarks to a few essentials.

Before applying the varnish it is necessary to clean the instrument of the remainders of glasspaper, dust and stains; impurities in the air are also harmful. The pores of the wood must then be filled with a suitable substance able to yield to the vibrations, to prevent resins from sinking into the wood and to unite the varnish with the grounding. If this is done effectually, the problem is all but solved. But it should be borne in mind that the ingredients themselves should be of a kind which never hardens too

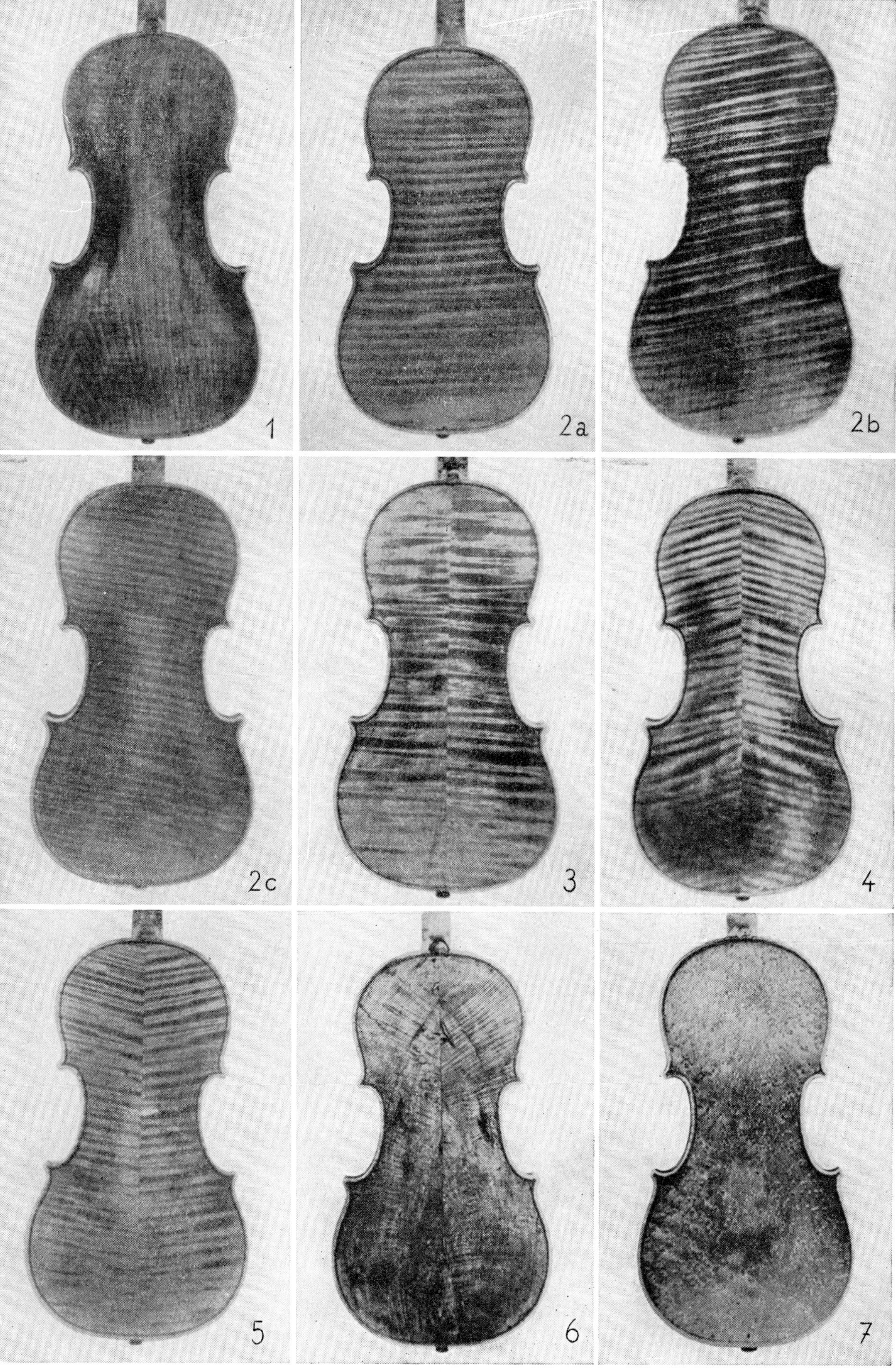
1
2a
2b
2c
3
4
5
6
7

much. For this reason shellac is not to be recommended. Before applying each additional coating the surface should be well polished. If these rules are observed, the solvent is not of paramount importance; all solvents must evaporate or oxydize sooner or later. But alcohol varnish, having the tendency to eat into a softer ground, leads to the use of harder ingredients and to hasty work: both influences combine to produce a dry, too compact, even glassy surface and may have a bad effect on tone. Varnish with linseed oil dries very slowly and must not be too fat, but a number of volatile oils can also be used as solvents. A varnish which does not thicken under the brush can be spread without haste, more thinly and evenly, which afterwards aids refraction and adds to the fire of the varnish. A new instrument treated in this manner has a strong lustre which softens in the course of time, but can be revived to a certain extent by cleaning and gentle rubbing. Also the colours get subdued; if this is imitated when the instruments are new, they may have too little colour to start with. Insofar as the choice and order of the coloured layers are concerned, it is a matter of personal taste and tradition. The old masters apparently had many individual methods. Only colours of vegetable origin should be used — no aniline dyes.

About twenty years ago attention was drawn, e. g. by Dr. P. W. Philipp in Döbeln, in a review for beekeepers, to the propolis or bee-glue, a substance with which bees stop crevices in the hives, fix and protect the honeycombs. The discovery was not new. Properly dissolved — the methods have yet be studied — it possesses all the required qualities and has a pleasing golden-yellow hue. The shades depend largely on the treatment and vary without addition of colours, but the propolis blends with colouring ingredients very well. It can be given various degrees of consistency, for which reason it is admirably suited to form a gradual transition from the grounding to the upper coatings. We share the opinion that it was widely in use in Italy for over three centuries, and not only by instrument-makers, since it is very common.

The literature on our subject is copious and of unequal value. Some publications repeat what has been published before. Original and very valuable are the works of the Hill Brothers of London — William Ebsworth Hill: *Antonio Stradivari*, 1907; W. H. Hill, A. F. Hill, and W. E. Hill: *Antonio Stradivari*, 1922; *The Makers of the Guarneri Family*, 1931; all these works are written with the responsibility of first-class experts. Of permanent value is the great work of Louis A. Vidal, *Les instruments á archet, les faiseurs, les joueurs d'instruments, leur histoire sur le continent européen, suivi d'un catalogue général de la musique de chambre* (3 vols. 1876—1878).

The large work in two volumes *Die Geigen- und Lautenmacher vom Mittelalter bis zur Gegenwart* by F. L. von Lüttgendorff was compiled with the help of several violin makers and experts, which increases its value. Lüttgendorff himself has done a great deal of original research, especially about the German makers, but some of his information concerning Italian and other masters must nowadays be revised.

To these important works one must add the interesting volume by Friedr. Hamma, the Stuttgart violin-dealer and maker, which contains very good pictures, but little reading, and deals chiefly with Italian masters. The small book by F. Farga, provided with photographs by the violin maker Hugo, is not complete. The *Dictionnaire universel des Luthiers* by René Vannes is at its best where it deals with the Italian and French makers, includes contemporary ones, but contains errors elsewhere, e.g. where Czechs and other Mid-Europeans are concerned. A similar older *Dictionnaire des Luthiers* by Henri Poidras falls short of the preceding works both in text and illustrations. Apart from the above-named we have used a number of other sources, e.g. a Czech book on the technology of wood by J. Antoš; A. Bagatella: *Regeln zur Verfertigung von Violinen* (transl. from Italian — see Bagatella); J. J. Baumann (a Czech book on the violin and its construction); F. J. Fétis: *Ant. Stradivari, luthier célèbre;* Fétis—Gallay: *Stradivarius;* Hill and Sons: *The Salabue Violin — Le Messie;* G. Kinsky: *Musikhistorisches Museum von W. Heyer in Köln;* O. Möckel: *Die Kunst des Geigenbaues;* J. Mařák (a Czech book *The Violin and its Construction*)*;* A. Fuchs: *Streichinstrumenten-Taxe;* Paul de Witt: *Geigenzettel alter Meister;* finally a number of smaller publications, some magazines and catalogues. The Chicago firm Lewis and Sons has published two books by E. N. Doring: *How many Strads?* and *The Violin Makers of the Guadagnini Family*. We do not know them, but are using this opportunity to call attention to them.

This author has been gathering information and first-hand experience concerning violin makers for almost thirty years. His work on the makers who lived on the territory of present-day Czechoslovakia, which he takes the liberty herewith to announce, has had predecessors. Mr. Lev Kůs, a notable student of music and its history, intended to publish a book on the Czech violin makers, but he died prematurely during the German occupation. Some of his fine photographs could be utilized; they were put at our disposal by the courtesy of his widow. The violin maker E. E. Homolka, who had had the same intention, also died, in 1928, before he could finish his work. Much of it had to be done anew and much left unexplored.

As far as this volume on the Italian masters is concerned, we hesitated a long time, originally intending to publish it in Czech only. It appeared, however, in Czech and English and the decision proved a happy one. The response was favourable, and it sold well despite the deficiencies of the first edition of which we are only too conscious.

This edition, which appears in separate English and German versions, is considerably enlarged and thoroughly revised.

May it attain its modest goal. But above all we should appreciate the co-operation of other experts. We have done our best to study as many instruments as was humanly possible in our circumstances, but others, who have been more fortunate in some respect or other, might send in their contributions, photographs of guaranteed specimens, and their critical remarks to our statements. Joint authorship seems to us to be the only way to a really authoritative work; one man's efforts do not suffice. It would be an honour to us to see other names join that of this author, should a new edition, or a supplement to this volume, come under consideration.

The prices given are to be taken as mere hints; since they are outdated, they should be adapted with regard to the present conditions, at the rate of about Kč 200 to the £. Violas are cheaper than violins, 'cellos more expensive. All other conditions and qualities being similar, the ratio is roughly 2 : 3 : 5. Where we say that the 'cellos of a certain master are more valuable than his violins, it means that they exceed this normal ratio. Exceptionally beautiful instruments in a perfect state of preservation fetch, of course, exceptional prices. On the other hand, prices of instruments which have grown too old — many of them of Brescian origin — are falling, unless they reach collectors' and museum prices, in which case the reverse is true.

Readers will notice that we are often reserved in assessing the respective merits of violin makers, especially the modern ones. Many of them have yet to prove their mettle and all modern instruments must stand the test of time. We are slow to leave the ground of direct experience, but as each individual experience is necessarily limited one must rely on authorities. We do so when it can be reasonably supposed that the authors did not pretend to know more than they could answer for. The dates indicate the actual length of life only, if it is expressly stated; otherwise they indicate the years when the person was already and still alive; they refer to the productive years, or to the years from which genuine, or at least guaranteed instruments have come down to us, or the approximate time. If only one or two definite years are given, they refer to isolated labelled instruments known to exist, which is surprisingly often the case — we have already touched upon this point. Experts who agree with these principles are requested to keep their own notes for private or public use. We hope they will be charitable, if they feel obliged to correct some error of ours.

STRADIVARI

FRANCIA
SVIZZERA
UNGHERIA
JUGOSLAVIA
ALBANIA
TUNISIA
Corsica
Sardegna
Sicilia
MAR LIGURE
MARE ADRIATICO
MARE TIRRENO
MARE MEDITERRANEO
MAR IONIO
Golfo di Gaëta
Golfo di Taranto
Danubio
Po
Adige
Arno
Tevere
L. Maggiore
L. di Como
L. di Garda
Berna
Ginevra
Innsbruck
Brennero
Vienna
Budapest
Belgrado
Bolzano
Trento
Udine
Bergamo
Brescia
Milano
Torino
Pavia
Verona
Padova
Venezia
Trieste
Fiume
Abazzia
Pola
Zara
Cremona
Mantua
Alessandria
Piacenza
Parma
Modena
Ferrara
Reggio
Genova
Spezia
San Remo
Carrara
Bologna
Pistoja
Rimini
Lucca
Pisa
Firenze
Ravenna
Livorno
Arezzo
Siena
Ancona
Elba
Perugia
Tivoli
Roma
Littoria
Foggia
Skutari
Durazzo
Tirana
Elbasan
Capua
Napoli
Vesuvio
Ischia
Salerno
Capri
Bari
Brindisi
Taranto
Otranto
Cagliari
Cosenza
Stromboli
Isole Lipari
Palermo
Trapani
Marsala
Termini
Messina
Reggio
Etna
Catania
Siracusa
Modica
Biserta
Tunisi
Pantelleria
Malta (brit.)
Lampedusa
1
2
3
4
5
6
7
8
9
10
11
12
13
14
0
100
200
300 km

A

Abbate Alessandro, Naples. 1890—1899. Son and probably also pupil of Alfonso Abbate; mandolin-producer.

Abbate Alfonso, Naples. Ca 1845. Violin maker; but devoted himself more to the making of lutes and mandolins.

Abbate Luigi, Naples. Ca 1860. Son, disciple and successor of Alfonso Abbate.

Abbati Giambattista, Modena. 1755—1795. Disciple of Antonio Cassini: worked on the latter's high model. There are known, however, works of lower arching, too, in the style of Amati and the older instruments of Stradivari. He worked conscientiously and genuine instruments are beautiful. Although he made besides violins also 'cellos, violas and contrabasses of strong build, there are but few of those instruments left. All possess a good tone; particularly his contrabasses are of excellent quality.

Hamma valued a violin by Abbati at between 25.000 to 35.000 Kčs.

Abrotano Marco, Florence. 1861. Died 1876.

Accardi Antonio, Rome. 1880. Died 1900.

Aceldero Giovanni Tonio, Venice. 1870—1876. Worked after Guarneri del Gesù. Red and brown-red varnish.

Acevo (Acero?) Saluzzo, allegedly born at Cremona. (1620—1690). According to R. Vannes the very name rests on a misunderstanding which gave rise to fictitious labels and fakes.

Achille Vinaccia, Neapel. See *Vinaccia* Achille.

Acimen Tomas, Como. 1705—1714. Used beautiful wood and red-brown varnish. He also made good bows.

Adam Abele, Turin. About 1712. Made various instruments, even spinets. Violins, etc., bearing his name come almost certainly from various makers, so different are they in character and quality.

Adani Pancrazio, Modena. 1770—1830. Made violins and 'celli on Stradivari's model. He worked conscientiously; the wood is of medium quality. His purflings are of outstanding beauty. The instruments sound well. Price valued by Hamma at 25.000 Kč., 'cellos even more.

Aglio Giuseppe Dall I, Mantua. 1723—1775. Probably father of Joseph Dall 'Aglio II. He used brown varnish.

Agostinelli Luigi. Turin, Kenya. Born Jan. 26 1891 in Gubio. Musician and amateur violin-maker who worked after the Cremonese school. He returned to Italy in 1948 and worked in Torre Pellice (Turin).

LUIGI AGOSTINELLI da Gubbio
in TORRE PELLICE - Anno 1949

Agostini Sante, Palermo. 1822. Little known as violin maker, but renowned for his repairs.

Agostino Nicolo, Palermo. Violin and lute maker of the 19th century.

Aiodante Nero, Asti. 1870—1890. He was a direct pupil of Gianfrancesco Pressenda in Turin. Besides labels he also branded his initials N. A.

Airaghi Cesare, Milan. 1885—1916. Violin maker of high repute. Brown varnish.

Alagio Niccolo, Lauria (Potenza). Born May 11, 1879 in Lauria Superiore, was a self-taught violin maker, but won distinction at expositions with instruments of an individual model. Oil varnish of brick-red colour. Good repairer.

Aisele Michel, Brescia, see Eisele Michel.

Albanesi Sebastiano, Cremona. 1720—1762. Disciple of Carlo Bergonzi. Although his instruments are made of fine wood, their finish is less good: they are valued for their good tone, but do not stand comparison with the work of his master. He rather worked in the style of the Milanese school, but applied the same varnish as the masters of Cremona. His instruments have a low arching. The prices of his violins fluctuate between 12.000 to 16.000 Kčs.

Albani Filippo, Bologna. 1773. — Instruments by him are not known. There exists but a label.

FILIPPO ALBANI FECIT
ANNO 1777

Albani Giuseppe, Milan. Born 1684. D. 1718. Son and probably also pupil of Matthias Albani of Bolzano (Tyrolese school). At the age of 21 he worked in Italy; employed German and Italian labels. His golden-yellow and brown varnish is of good quality.

Albani Giuseppe Paolo. Bolzano, Milano. 1710—1758.

Names beginning with Da, Dall', De, Di (not, however, those followed by d', de) come under D.

Albani Leopoldo, Ancona. 1883. Violin maker who devoted most of his time to repairs of old instruments.

Albani Leopoldo restaurò
in Ancona 27 decembre 1883.

Albani Michele, Palermo. 18th century. Son of Paolo Albani. Little known, violin maker.

Albani Nicolo, Mantua, Milan. 1763—1770. He imitated Tommaso Balestriri's large, broad and flat pattern. The belly is wide-grained; the sound-holes are cut after Stainer's fashion. He applied a beautiful, predominantly deep-red varnish. The tone is good and strong. The price amounts to 40.000 Kčs and more.

Nicolas Albani fecit Mantua 1763	Nicolaus Albani fatte Milano 1770.

Albani Paolo, Palermo, Rome, Cremona. 1630—1695. He was a disciple of Nic. Amati and worked on the latter's "grand pattern". His work is good, the tone fine and powerful. Red varnish. Price of violin 25 to 30.000 Kč.

Albani Giuseppe Paolo. Bolzano. 1710—1755. Probably also worked in Palermo and a relative of Signor Albani.

Alberti Adalberto, Pavia. 1915—1920.

Alberti Ferdinando, Milan 1730—1769. Disciple of Nic. Amati. His workmanship reminds of that of Giov. Bapt. Grancino, after whose death he took over the workshop and trade-mark (a crown — Segno della Corona). Some of his instruments are quite good, made of fine wood, well built on a large model. He applied good yellow, red-yellow, and red varnish. The scrolls are large, flat, their cut is not bad. The instruments sound well.
Price of violins 15—20.000 Kčs, outstanding specimens more.

Alberti Giorgio, Rome. Died in 1624. Son and perhaps pupil of Pietro Alberto.

Alberti Giovanni I, Rome. Died 1600. Little is known about him and other bearers of the name, their works having probably been provided with faked labels of better known masters.

Alberti Giovanni II, Rome. 1656.

Alberti Giovanni Giorgio, Rome. Died 1617.

Alberti Guglielmo, Arezzo (1877).

Guglielmo Alberti
fece Arezzo Anno 18..

Albertini Carlo, Milan. B. 1866, d. 1940. Only guitars and mandolins with his name are known.

Albertis Peter de, called Pietro Alberto, Rome. 1578. Died 1598.
Lute maker, known only from labels which have survived their instruments.

Petrus Albertus faciebat R.	Petrus Albertus 1598.

Alberto Andrea di, Rome 1608. D. 1649. Lived in the street Via dei Liutari. Otherwise unknown.

Albinus. Ancient lute maker of the 14th century. Mere name.

Aldovrandi Emilio, Bologna. 1850—1882. Maker of mediocre skill: for the most part he occupied himself with repairs.

Alessandro surnamed "il Veneziano", Venice. Ca 1540. Of his instruments only one viola survives today; a lute of his making was exhibited at Turin in 1880.

Allegretti Massimiliano (surnamed Monferino), Soliera (Modena). 1873—1883. Assiduous violin maker whose instruments are of medium quality.

Allegri Giovanni, Milan. 1708—1725. Little known, though the few specimens extant are said to be excellent.

Allessandroni Paolo, Rome. 1850—1880. Beautiful model, deeply carved heads.

Aloy Dario, Rome. Born 1902 in Rome. Studied violin-playing with Jan Mařák in Prague. He devoted himself mainly to the making of guitars.

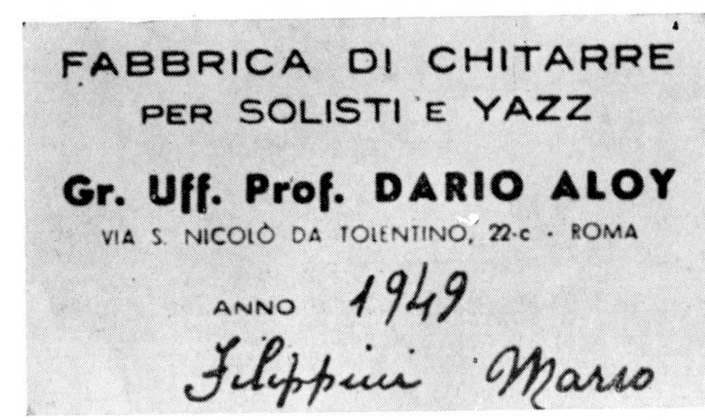

Altavia Armando, Naples. 1923.

Alvi Carlo and Dario, Rome. 1930.

Alvani Francesco, Cremona. 1840—1850. Used beautiful red-brown varnish.

Alvani Gaetano, Turin. 1870—1880. Excellent imitations of Stradivari, Amati and Guarneri. He used red varnish.

Alvani Paolo, Cremona. 1750—1755. Perhaps a son or grandson of Paolo Albani. He imitated Giuseppe Guarneri and Amati, used beautiful wood and a fine yellow varnish.

Amaglioni. 19th cent. Reported to have worked on the Stradivari model. Otherwise little known.

Genealogy of the Amati family

Maestro Gotardo Amati
d. ca 1553

Andrea Amati b. 1535 d. 1611	Nicolo Amati I 1568-1620	
Antonio Amati b. 1555—1560 d. ca 1640	Hieronymus I. Amati b. ca 1556 d. 2. 11. 1636	
Nicolo Amati II 1644—1662	Nicolo Amati III b. 1596 d. 1684	
D. Nicolo Amati (?) 1731	Hieronymus II Amati b. Feb. 26, 1649 d. Feb. 21, 1740.	Nicolo Amati IV 1691—1730

Amati Andrea, Cremona. Born about 1535, died after 1611. Reportedly a disciple of Gasparo da Salò. He married at the age of 19 in the year 1554. By his first wife he had three children: Antonio, Girolamo (Hieronymus I.) — the name of the third child is unknown. Both his sons became violin makers and worked jointly with their father. After 1601 the instruments bear the names of his sons. He is considered as one of the founders of the Cremona violin-craft.

The belly is of pine-wood with close grain, the sound-holes are medium-sized, open, in a vertical position, gracefully cut, with a shape only slightly reminiscent of Gasp. da Salò. The upper parts of the sound-holes are at a distance of 38 mm. from each other. The arching of the belly is of the same height as the model of Gasparo da Salò, i. e. 16 mm. The purfling is wide and executed in a masterly manner. The back is usually made of maple-wood, sometimes of platan or pear-wood. The arching of the back is 14 mm. high. The sides are always of maple wood, 28—30 mm. high, the scroll also of maple wood, rather large, gracefully cut.

Andrea Amati built violins in various sizes, in most instances, however, of rather small pattern. He used to apply, in strong coats and most carefully, a golden-brown, golden-yellow or amber varnish. The tone of his instruments is wonderful, but not strong; Hamma calls it hard. For the king of France, Charles IX, he made 12 violins on the small, 12 violins on the large model, 6 violas, and 8 contrabasses.

His instruments are rare relics, worth 200.000 Kč, and more. The firm of Hamma & Co. of Stuttgart bought one of his violins in Southern France c. 1880 at the price of 30.000 M.

Dimensions of violins and 'celli

	Violin	Violin	'Cello
Length of belly and back	353	353	730 mm
Upper width	164	163	340 mm
Middle width	106	—	230 mm
Lower width	197	202	430 mm
Top sides	—	29	120 mm
Bottom sides	—	30	120 mm
Length of sound-holes	—	—	140 mm

Andrea Amati in
Cremona MDLXXII

Andrea Amati Cremonensis fecit anno 1546

AN.... AMA.. FE.. .IC.....A .NC.....A
AN.. 1555

(ANdrea AMAti FEce dI CremonA iN CremonA
ANno 1555)

Amati Antonio, Cremona. Born about 1555, died 1649. Elder son of Andrea Amati, and his disciple. He worked jointly with his father and brother. After his brother's death (i.e. 1630) he marked the instruments with his own name only. His instruments have a rather high arching, with slim, narrow sound-holes. He used a cherry-red varnish, later a varnish of a fine orange or golden-yellow colour. (See Amati Antonius and Hieronymus.)

For the court-orchestra of Henry IV, king of France, he made fine instruments of small pattern.

Amati D. Nicolaus, Bologna (1723—1737). A monk and amateur. Little known. Price 30.000 Kč.

D. Nicolaus Amati
Fecit Bononiae Apud
SS. Cosma, et Damiani m.

Amati Francesco, Cremona, 1640. Almost unknown. In the cloister of Kremsmünster there is a violin of the year 1640 with the label:

Francesco Amati in Cremona 1640

Amati Hieronymus (I), Cremona. Born about 1556, died Nov. 2, 1630. Younger son of Andrea Amati. He worked in company with his brother Antonio and was more skilled than the latter. His instruments are of outstanding qualities both in finish and in tone (see Amati Antonius and Hieronymus).

Amati Hieronymus (II) Cremona. Born Feb. 26, 1649, d. Feb. 21, 1740. Son and pupil of Nicolo Amati. According to Hill Bros. he was a very outstanding artist who worked according to his father's style, but his violins are of a larger size. Many instruments of his making bear the label of his father, others seem to have been "rechristened" for still greater names (perhaps even Stradivari). Price of violin 60.000 Kč. Rare.

Hieronimus Amati Cremonensis
Fecit Anno Salutis 1697

Amati Antonius and Hieronymus, Cremona. 1555—1630. Name of the common workshop of the two sons, disciples and collaborators of Andrea Amati. After their father's death, they worked and labelled their instruments jointly until the death of Hieronymus. Antonio is said not to have worked with such a light touch as Hieronymus. Nevertheless, their creations are so alike that it is almost impossible to tell them apart. They worked on their father's pattern which they adapted and perfected.

Lower arching and the improved shape are evidence of the two brothers' ingenuity. They used well seasoned maple-wood with small curl and old pine-wood. The back is often made of one piece, the purfling wonderfully finished, reaching almost to the ends of the corners. The edges are rounded off in a handsome and uniform way, the scrolls wonderfully carved and elegant. They used a fine varnish of yellow, yellow-red, golden-red and amber colour. The varnish is applied in a masterly way, is transparent and possesses a wonderful lustre. The instruments sound very well, the softness of tone is marvellous. The harmonics, natural as well as artificial, give a pure and clear sound. Best sound the strings E, A, D, whereas the G-string does not possess the desirable timbre. The violins are not so well fitted for concert halls as the 'celli and violas which have great carrying power and speak easily.

A violin made in the year 1626 measures as follows: length 352, upper width 165, centre width 109, lower width 207, height of top sides 28, bottom sides 30, length of sound-holes 74, length of scroll 102 mm. For comparison we give the dimensions of other instruments.

		Width		Sides	
	Length	upper	lower	upper	lower
Violin	352	165	207	28	30
Violin	350	165	205	27	29
Viola	450	220	268	39	41
Viola	411	197	247	33	34
'Cello	752	330	450	118	118

Price 150.000 Kč and more.

Antonius Hieronymus Fr. Amati
Cremonen Andreae fil. F. 1630

Antonius & Hieronym. Fr. Amati
Cremonen. Andreae Al. F. 1630

Antonius & Hieronimus Fr.
Amati Cremonen Andreae F. 16..

Antonius, & Hieronymus Fr Amati
Cremonen Andreæ fil. F. 1630

Antonius, & Hieronym. Fr. Amati
Cremonen. Andreæ F 1630

Antonius, & Hieronimus Fr.
Amati Cremonen. AndreæF 16

Amati Nicolo I, Cremona. 1568—1620. Could have been a brother of Andrea Amati. He devoted himself to the making of double-basses and small violins (320—340 mm) probably for pupils.

Amati Nicolo II, Cremona. 1644. Son of Antonio. Violin-maker of little importance.

Nicolaus Amatus Cremonen. Hieronymi
Fil. ac Antonij Nepos Fecit. 1677

Amati Nicolo III, Cremona. Born Dec. 3, 1596, died Apr. 12, 1684. Son and disciple of Girolamo Amati (I). He worked at first on the model of his father; besides violins he made violas, 'celli, contrabasses, and bass-viols. The most outstanding master of the family. He had 9 children of whom only Girolamo II became a violin maker.

The elegant shape of all his instruments gives proof of this great master's skill. The scroll, of the peculiar Amati type, is sometimes (not always), large in size, beautifully cut. The purfling is executed in a delicate way. The sound-holes are tastefully cut and enhance the beauty of the instrument. He used a brilliant varnish in shades from yellow-brown to golden-red. Excellent is his so-called "grand pattern", a number of violins which are excellent concert instruments with a tone of great carrying power. The 'cellos were built by him in two sizes; their tone is magnificent. One fine cello with a beautiful tone has the following dimensions: Length 730, lower width 440, upper width 360, centre width 250, sides 120, scroll 200, sound-holes 130 mm long: yellow-golden varnish.

Amati instruments were valued, in 1930—1935, at 320—350.000 Kč.

His last labels are from the year 1684; he worked to the last.

Dimensions of some instruments

	Made in	Length	Top	Width centre	Width bottom	Total height of plates and sides	Distance of corners	Sides top	Sides bottom
Violin	1645	353	160	109	199.5	60	78/78	—	—
,,	1648	355	172	—	210	—	—	28	29.5
,,	1658	355	168	—	208	—	—	29.5	29.5
,,	1663	358	172	—	214	—	—	26.5	28

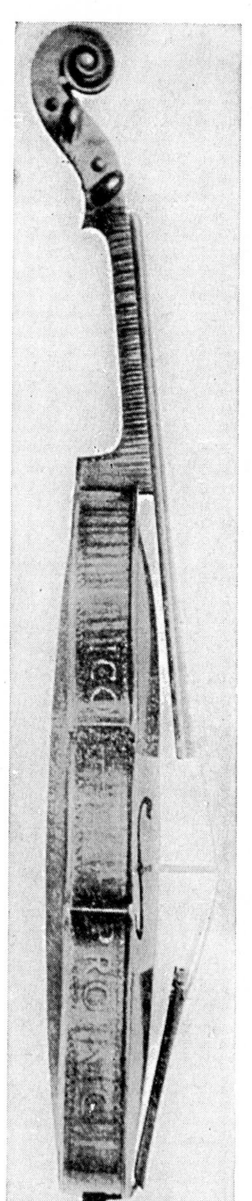
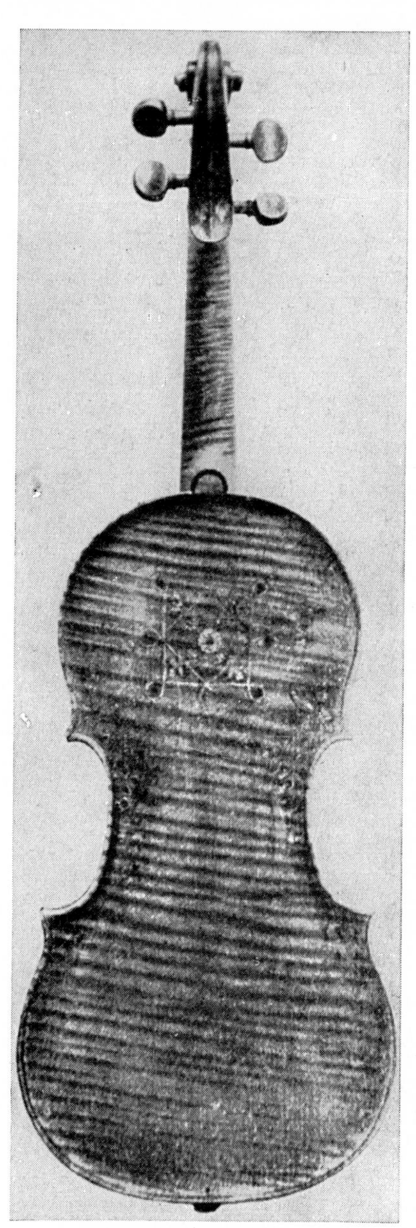

1. Amati Andrea, Cremona 1574

2. Amati D. Nicolo, Bologna 1720
Photo Hamma & Co

3. Amati Antonio & Hieronymo, Cremona
Photo Hamma & Co

4. Amati Antonio & Hieronymo, Cremona
Photo Hamma & Co

5. Amati Antonio & Hieronymo, Cremona 1606 (VIOLA)
Photo Hamma & Co

6. Amati Antonio & Hieronymo, Cremona 1609

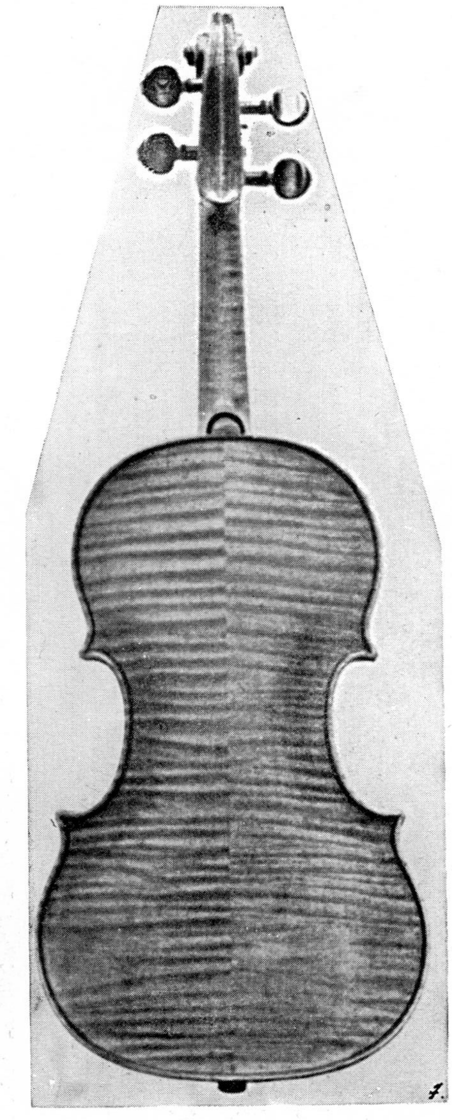

7. Amati Antonio & Hieronymo, Cremona 1620

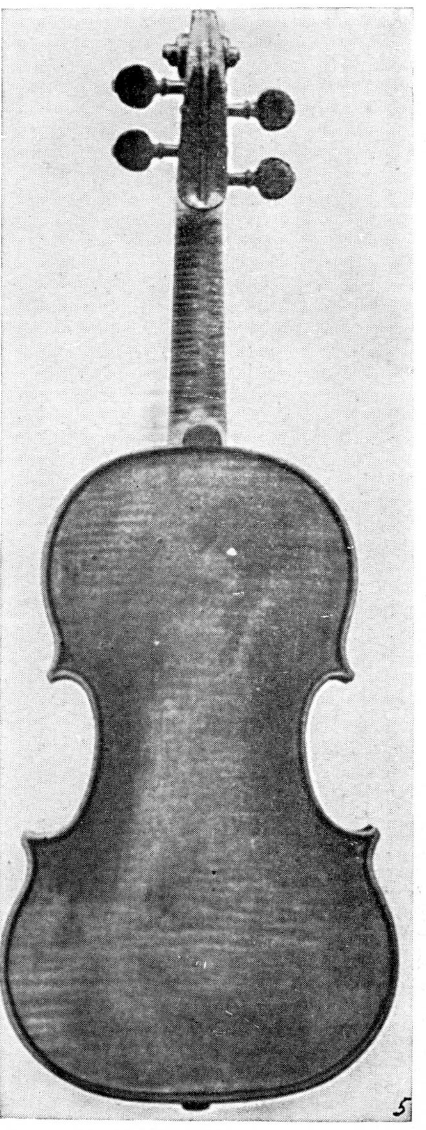

8. Amati Antonio & Hieronymo, Cremona 1605

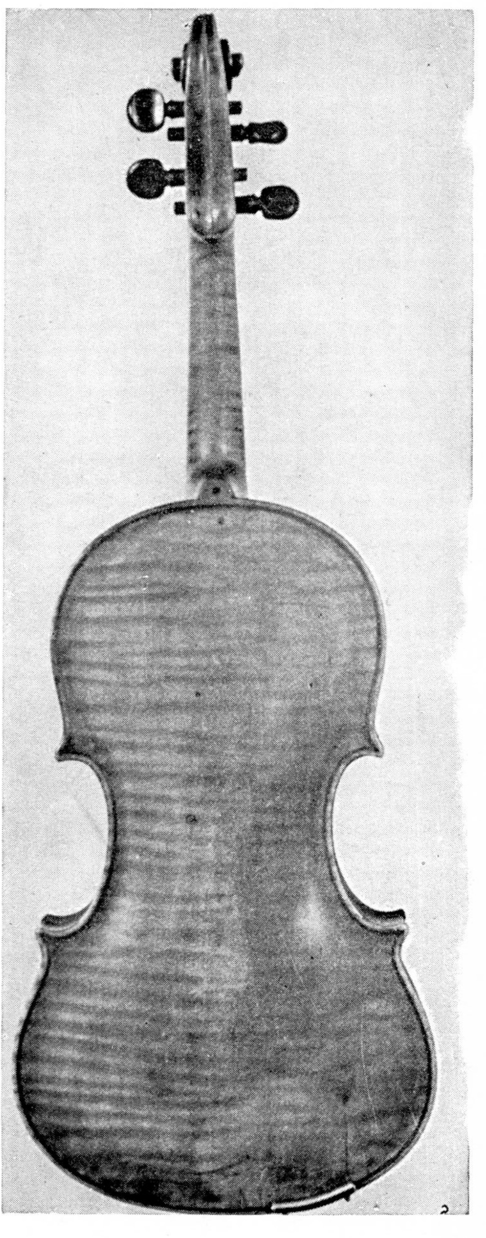

9. Amati Hieronymo, Cremona

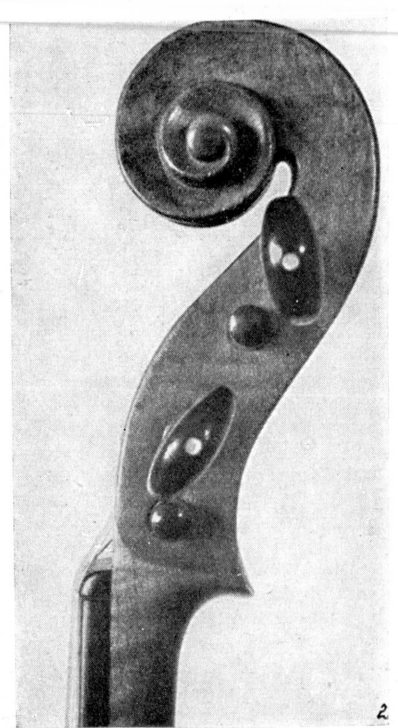

10. Amati Hieronymo, Cremona

11. Amati Hieronymo fil. Nicolo, Cremona 1710

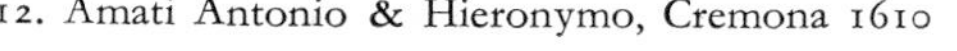

12. Amati Antonio & Hieronymo, Cremona 1610

13. Amati Nicolo, Cremona 1636
Photo Hamma & Co

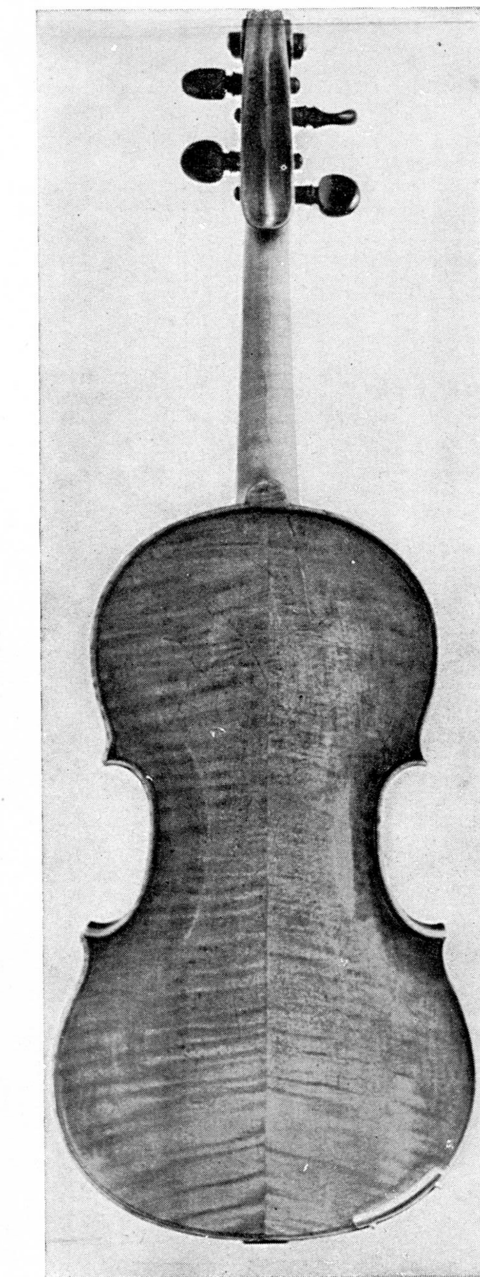

14. Amati Nicolo, Cremona 16..

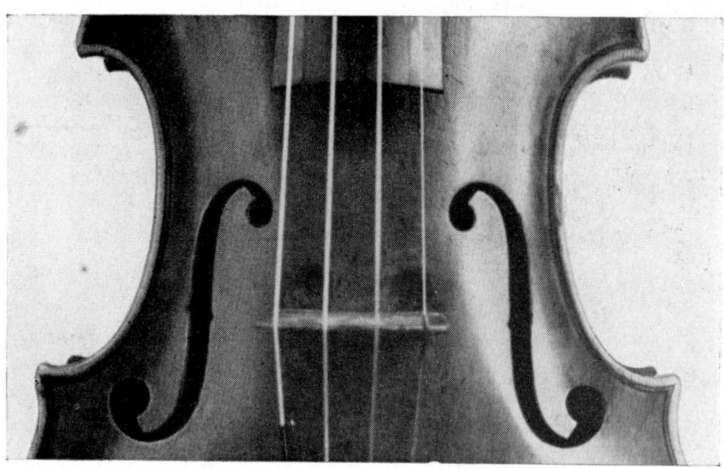

15. Amati Nicolo, Cremona 16..

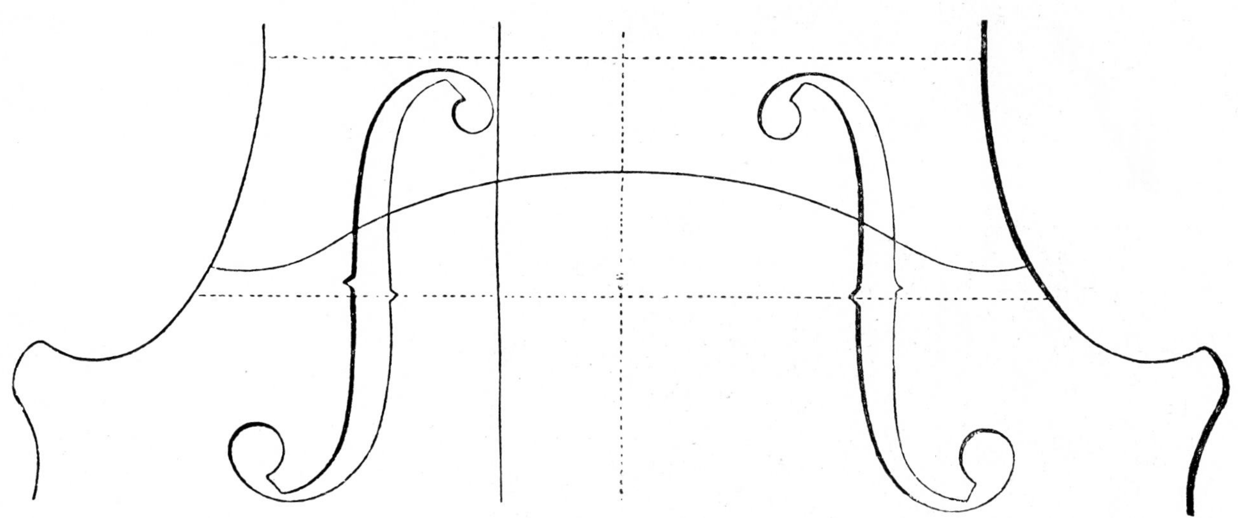

16. Amati Nicolo, Cremona 1653

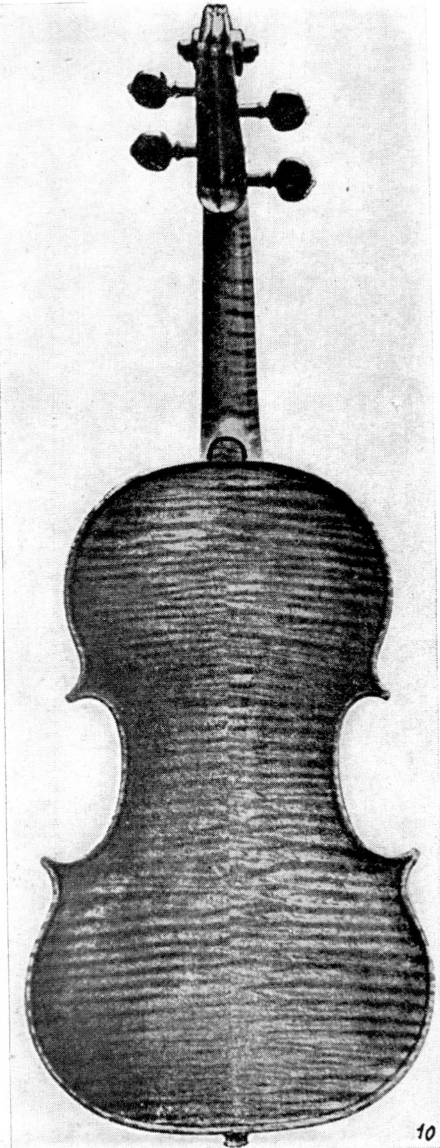

17. Amati Nicolo, Cremona 1645

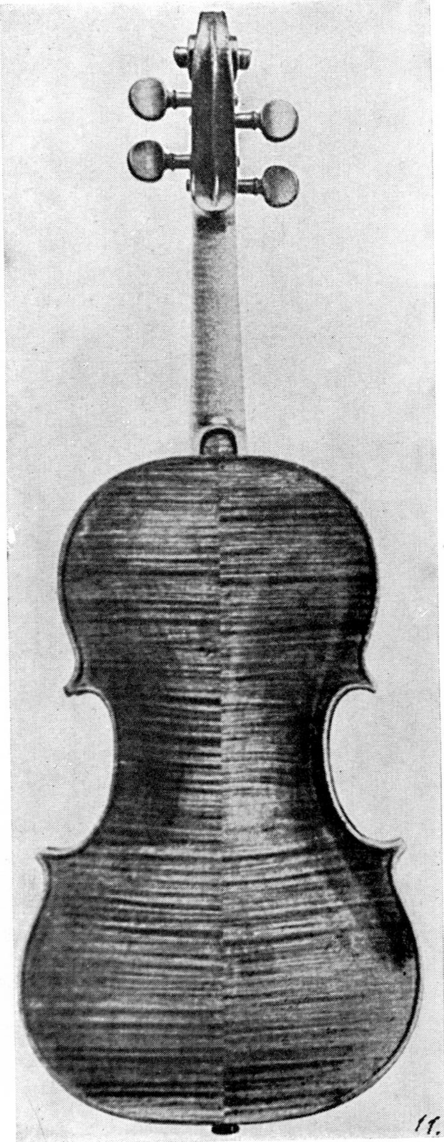

18. Amati Nicolo, Cremona 1662

19. Amati Nicolo, Cremona 1660
Photo Hamma & Co

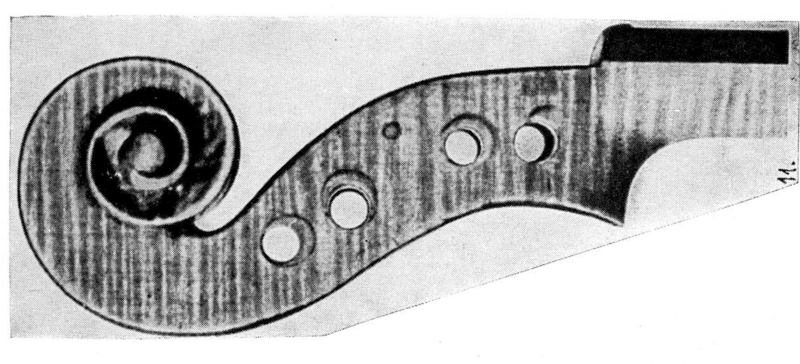

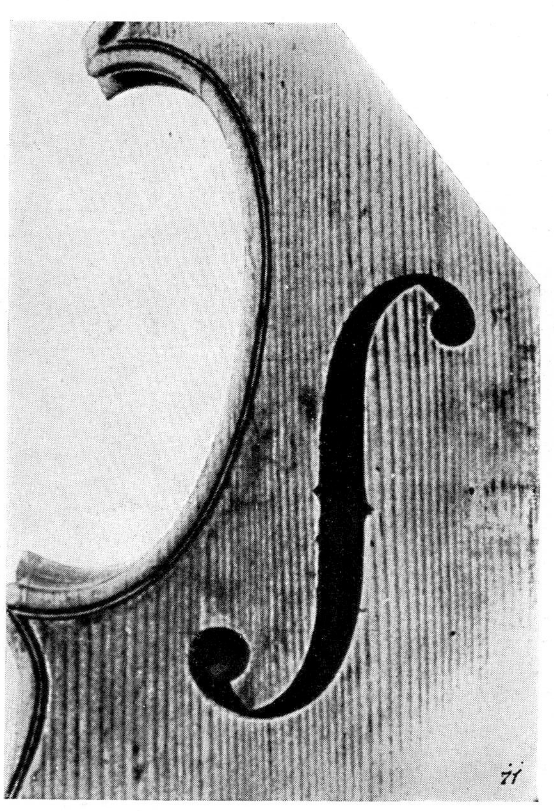

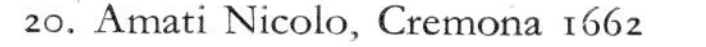

20. Amati Nicolo, Cremona 1662

21. Amati Nicolo, Cremona 1681 (CELLO)
Photo Hamma & Co

22. Baierhoff Giorgio, Napoli
Photo Hamma & Co

23. Baldantoni Joseph, Ancona 1817

24. Balestrieri Tomasso, Mantova 1733
Photo Hamma & Co

25. Balestrieri Tomasso, Mantova 1752
Photo Hamma & Co

26. Balestrieri Tomasso, Mantova 1756
Photo Hamma & Co

27. Balestrieri Tomasso, Mantova 1752

28. Balestrieri Tomasso, Mantova 1760

	Made in	Length	Top	Width centre	Width bottom	Total height of plates and sides	Distance of corners	Sides top	Sides bottom
Violin	1673	354	167	109	206	65	75/75	—	—
,,	1683	355	168	108	206	66	78/79	—	—
,, med. shape		354	165	—	204	—	—	30	30
,, small ,,		352	162	—	202	—	—	28.5	29.5
'Cello		783	368	—	474	—	—	114	114

Nicolaus Amatus Cremonen Hieronymi
Fil. ac Antonij Nepos Fecit 1677

Nicolaus Amatus Cremonę &
Hieronymi filii fecit. An 1651

Sub difciplina Nicolai Amati
in eius Officina Cremonæ.

Amati Nicolo IV, Cremona. 1691—1730.

Nicolo Amati fecit Cremona
Sub titulo Santa Teresia 1727

C. Nicolaus Amati fecit
Bonomæ 17

Amati Pietro, Naples. 1581—1627. Probably only a coincidence of names, for he did not belong to the Cremonese family of violin-makers.

Amatis Giambattista, Venice. 1677. Violin maker. His works are lost.

Amberton Laurentius, Turin.

Laurentius Amberton Torino 1756.

Ambrogi Pietro, Brescia, Rome. 1712—1748. He worked in Rome after 1745. His violins are good, but not outstanding. He imitated Balestrieri and applied dark varnish. His 'celli sound best. Price 20.000 Kč.

Petrus Ambrogi Crem. fecit Romae
an 17..

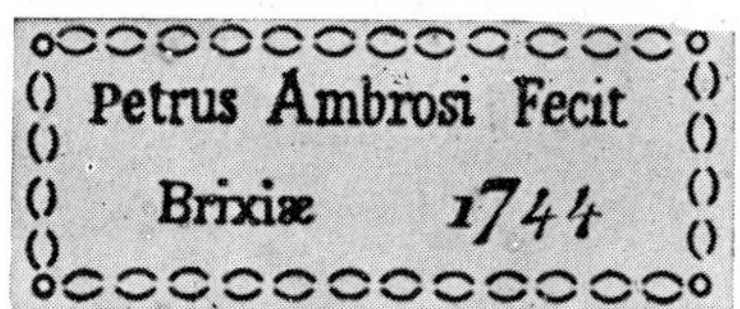

Ambrosio Antonio d', Naples. 1810—1825. Worked after the Naples school. He made mainly guitars.

Amici Luigi, Rome. 1780—1800. Apart from violins, violoncellos and guitars he made also mandolins. His violins are narrow resembling the small model of Nicolo Amati III, his violoncellos have flat backs with no arching at all. Narrow heads of instruments. Golden-yellow varnish.

Amighetti Giacomo, Lovere. 1890—1914.

Amore Giuseppe d'. Rome. 1930.
He tried to imitate the Cremonese masters.

Anderlini Giuseppe, Spilamberto (Modena) 1860. Built violins in his earlier years; later he ran a factory.

Andina Francesco, Poggio (Lugano). B. 1891, was an amateur who worked on the model of Stradivari and applied a dark brown oil varnish, result of his own experiments.

Angiello Luigi fu Giacinto, Milan, 20th century. In 1937, he exhibited a string quartet at Cremona.

Andrea Giovanni, Rome 1606. In 1606 he is known to have worked for Visconte Bruto in Piperna. Otherwise unknown, but for the following rhyme:

Con Andrea, luitar poi siate pratico
perche non voglio piu la sua amicizia
ne, la mattina, ber secco il alliatico.*
(Quoted by Valdrighi)

Andrea Pietro, Venice. 1650—1700. Instruments of high arching, red varnish.

Andreas Joannes, Verona, Venice. 1511. In a museum of Vienna there is a lyre bearing the following label:

Johannes Andreas Veronen
adi 12 Agosto 1511.

Andreolo, Venice. 1359. The oldest lute maker mentioned by Valdrighi.

Andrès Domenico, Bologna. 1736—1744. An amateur known only from one handwritten label:

Dominicus Andres
Bollognensis Diletante
Fecit a. Domini 1740.

Angelin Dominici, Naples. 1625—1630. He worked after the Gagliani model.

Angelis de Vitus, Bologna. 1609. Lute and violin maker known only by name.

Angeloni Sigismondo, Venice. 1846—1859. He worked after Nicolo Amati and used golden-yellow varnish.

* Be careful with Andrea the lute maker, for I don't care for his friendship — as little as for sour Alliatico (a wine-sort) in the morning.

Annarumma Vincenzo, Salerno. Born Feb. 4, 1892.

rividuto da
VINCENZO ANNARUMMA
l'anno 1943 N. 16-4

VINCENZO ANNARUMMA
fece in Salerno
Salerno il 18-3 1937

No 57
ANNARUMA
SALERNO

Anselmo Pietro, Cremona, Florence, Venice. 1730—1760. — His work is beautiful, following the pattern of Francesco Rugieri, whose pupil he may have been. He used a wonderful yellow varnish, applying it in rather thick coats. For his work he chose the best wood. His violins are usually rather small. His 'cellos are best. The value of his violins is 30.000 Kč and more.

Ansoldo Rocco, Genoa. 1752—1760. He imitated J. B. Guadagnini's work.

Antegnati Giov. Francesco, Brescia. 1535. He belongs to a family of organ-builders. He was a composer of sacred music and a good lute maker.

Antolini Francesco, Milan, 19th century.

Francesco Antolini Fece Milano 1857

Antoniazzi Gaetano I, Cremona. 1810.

Antoniazzi Gaetano, Cremona. Born Aug. 7, 1823, died Aug. 1, 1897 at Milan. His products are good imitations of old masters.

Antoniazzi Gregorio, Colle near Bergamo. 1732—1750. A disciple of Domenico Montagnana whose labels he is said to have put into instruments of his own making. There exist only few specimens marked with his own name.

It is difficult to distinguish his work from that of Montagnana.

Antoniazzi used fine wide-grained wood. His workmanship is most conscientious, his varnish beautiful, matching the best Cremona varnish. His instruments possess a wonderful tone of a quite peculiar silky timbre and a good carrying power.

Value of violin 120.000 Kč and more.

Gregorio
Antoniazzi
in Colle 1738.

Antoniazzi Riccardo, Milan. B. 1858, d. 1910. Brother of Romeo Antoniazzi. He worked for a long time in Leonardo Bisiachi's workshop at Milan.

Antoniazzi Riccardo di Cremona
figlio di Gaetano fece Milano
l'anno 1904

Riccardo Antoniazzi Cremonese
fece in Milano l'anno 1887 A+R

Ricardo Antoniazzi Cremonese
fece in Milano l'anno 1899

Riccardo Antoniazzi Cremonese
fece in Milano l'anno 1887 AR

Riccardo Antoniazzi Cremonese
fece in Milano l'anno 1899

Antoniazzi Riccardo di Cremona
figlio di Gaetano fece in Milano
l'anno 1904

Antoniazzi Romeo, Cremona, Milan. Born May 4, 1862 at Cremona. Son and disciple of Gaetano Antoniazzi. His violins are good.

Antoniazzi Romeo di Cremona
fece in Cremona l'anno....

Antoniazzi Romeo Cremonese
fece a Cremona l'anno 19..

Antoniazzi Romeo Cremonese
fece a Cremona l'anno 19..

Antonij (Antony) Girolamo, Cremona 1750—1780. His workmanship is not of the best, the acoustic quality of his instruments good, his varnish comely yellow.

Hieronimus Antonij
Cremonae Anno 17..

Antonio. Bologna. 1550. He made violas. We know of one of his violas da gamba.

Antonio dai Liuti, Ferrara. 1475. Lute maker. His true name is unknown, people called him "Maestro Antonio dai Liuti" (Master Anthony, lute maker).

Antonio di Ancona, Ancona. 1723.

Antonio Maestro, Venice. 16th century. — A lute maker and according to Valdrighi a lyre maker.

Arassi Enzo, Milan. Born 1889 in Trieste. Violin maker and able violinist, too. He founded an instrument-workshop in Milan. Worked after the pattern of Emiliani, using beautiful golden-rose and golden-brown varnish. His workmanship was conscientious; his instruments, having very good tone, are in great demand.

Arcangoli Ulderico, Morciano di Romagna (Forli). B. 1889. — In 1937 he exhibited three violins and a viola at Cremona.

Arcangioli Lorenzo, Florence. 1825—1849. Instruments of medium quality.

Lorenzo Arcangeli
fece in Arezzo nell'anno 1844

Arcangoli Udelrico, Morciano di Romagna. Born 1889. Artistic cabinet-maker working in ebony who devoted himself to the making of violins, violas and violoncellos. He used thin golden-yellow varnish coating.

Arcellaschi Galileo, Como. B. 1910. Good 'cellos.

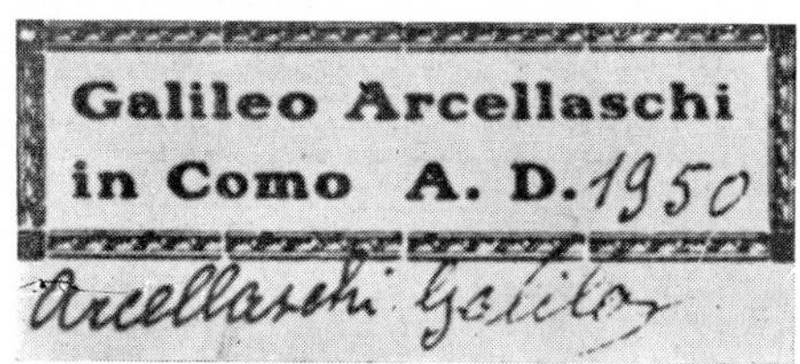

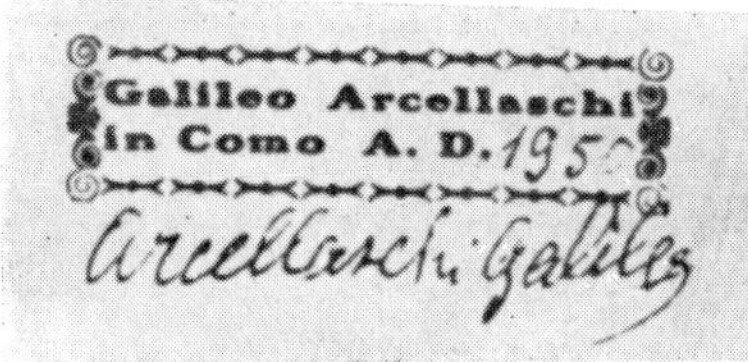

Ardeli Angelo, Sesto Calende. B. Apr. 23, 1929.

Arezzo Nicolo, Naples. 20th century.

Arienti Carlo Giuseppe, Milan. 1810—1863. The Milan conservatory of music possesses a three-quarter contrabass, varnished brown-yellow, labelled:

Carlo Giuseppe Arienti
Fece in Milano, nella
Contrada Ponte Vetro
num. 1863. Anno 1810.

Arnaldus Joannes Aloysius. Ca 1584. Mr. Alfred Keil of Lisbon owned a seven-stringed guitar marked with the above given name, the label bearing the date of 25th October 1584. The work is of Italian origin. Otherwise unknown.

Arnoldi Carlo, Anagni, Rome. 1790. Mediocre instruments.

Arpino Felice, producer of mandolins.

Artalli Giuseppe Antonio, Milan. 1759—1768. Little known violin maker who worked on C. A. Testore's model.

Artioli Antonio, Milan. 1880 was valued for repairs.

Artioli Antonio
riparò l'anno 1880.

Artmann H., Capri. 19th century. He made good mandolins.

Capri
H. Artmann.

Assalone Gasparo d', Pesaro, Rome. 1690—1740. He constructed instruments on the highly arched models of Amati and Gaspar da Salò and used a good yellow varnish. He did not work with sufficient conscientiousness; nevertheless, his work was often counterfeited and labelled:

Gasparo d'Assalone

Who made the imitations, is not known. Price of a genuine violin 12.000 Kč.

Attore Michele, Padua, Venice. 1583—1620. Little known violin and lute maker.

Michele Attore Fece
1620 Venezia

Auciello Luigi, Milan. Born 1881 in Molfetta (Bari). He established himself in 1935.

LUIGI AUCIELLO
15 Via P. Sarpi :: MILANO Anno 1941

C. AUCIELLO

Aurelli Aurelio, Rome. Born 1870 in Rome, d. Apr. 20,1925. Distinctions were conferred on him for his careful imitations of great Italian masters. Varnish deep yellow or red.

Aureli Auriolio
Romano
Fece in Roma nell anno 1921. N. 32

Auria Fratelli di Milano. Mandolin producers. Undated labels.

AURIA Fratelli d'Milano.

Autiero Giuseppe. B. 1858 in Teano, d. March 9, 1919 in Avignon, France. Son and pupil of Paride Autiero.

Autiero Paride, Teano. 1860—1870.

Paride Autiero
fecit Teano 1867

Avellano e figlio, Naples 1870—1896.

Avenia Carlo d', Naples. 1780—1810. He worked after Gagliani using golden-yellow varnish. He also made guitars and mandolins.

Avenia d', L., Naples. 1888. A skilful mandolin maker.

Averna Alfonso (and son), producers of mandolins in Palermo, Sicily. 1925.

Averna Alfredo, Palermo, b. March 12, 1902 in Caltanissetta, Sicily, pupil of his brother Alfonso and uncle Gesualdo. Violin maker. He exhibited a violin at Cremona in 1937.

Alfredo Averna

Averna Alfredo
me Fecit Palermo 19..

Averna Alfredo
me Fecit Palermo 1947

Averna Enrico, Palermo. Died. Sept. 15, 1960. He exhibited a violin at Cremona in 1937.

Averna Gesualdo, Caltanissetta. B. 1875. Careful workmanship on classical patterns. Exhibited two violins at Cremona in 1937.

Azzola Luigi, Turin. Born in Venice 1883. Imitator of Pressenda. Crimson varnish.

LUIGI AZZOLA fece in TORINO
Anno Domini 19..

AZZOLA ALOYSIUS
venetianus
fecit
AUGUSTAE TAURINORUM
ANNO DOMINI 947

B

Bachetta Giuseppe, Cremona, Mantua. 1730—1780. Some of his instruments, insofar as we have seen them, are no masterpieces.

Badalassi Pietro Valentino di. Pisa. Born June 29, 1915. He worked after Antonio Stradivari and won a diploma at the Cremona Exhibition of 1937.

Riparato in Pisa
da Piero Badalassi
19..

Piero Badalassi in Pisa
Faceva l'Anno 19..

Badarello Carlo, Turin. Born 1885. Died 1931. He worked after the Cremona school. His violins and violoncellos are very good.

Baffo Antonio, Venice. Ancient instrument maker, born about 1490, allegedly still alive in 1581, was a lute and harp maker and cannot have made violins, at most some old-type violas.

Antonius Baffo Venetus fecit.

Bagatella Antonio I, Padua. Born Feb. 4, 1716, died Feb. 1806. Son of Gaetano Bagatella and Catharina née Coppo-Scanferle. Violin maker and musicologist. Between 1740 and 1770 he worked for Giuseppe Tartini*. Author of *Regole per la constructione dei violini, violoncelli e violiny*, which was awarded an Academy prize in Padua. He worked skilfully after the Guarneri model and used golden-brown or red varnish. His instruments are of a medium height with short sound-holes placed parallel to the middle bouts. The edges of his violins are flat and the corners are small. Length 353 mm, upper width 169 mm, middle width 107 mm, lower width 204 mm, measure 192 mm.

Antonio Bagatella fecit
Patavij D', 1753

Antonius Bagatella delectens
fecit Patavij. Anno 1794.

Bagatella Antonio II, Padua. B. Feb. 21, 1755, d. Feb. 25, 1829. Probably son of Pietro Bagatella, usually mistaken for Antonio I. Allegedly worked with Giuseppe Tartini 1740—1770, which is impossible because he was not born until 1775.

Bagatella Pietro, Padua. 1712—1760. Father of Antonio Bagatella: his own violins are highly arched and rather dark.

Bagillo Gaetano, Ancona. 1770—1776. He worked after Stradivari and Amati. The backs are usually made of one slab of beautiful maple-wood.

Bagnini Orazio, Florence. 1661—1667. Lute maker, little known.

Bagoletto A., Padua 1782. According to some identical with Bagatella, perhaps merely a corruption of the latter name. The specimen adduced is in the style of Guarneri del Gesù.

Antonio Bagoletto
in Padua 1782.

Bairhoff Giorgio, Naples. 1740—1790. He was employed in Nicolo Gagliano's workshop. Worked on the pattern of Gennaro and Nicolo Gagliano. His instruments are outstanding for their beautiful flat shape, faultless wood, gracefully carved scrolls, and careful workmanship. He often made instruments of middle size.

Giorgio Bairhoff Fecit
Neapoli 1757.

Giorgio Bairhoff Fecit
Napoli 1757 . GB

Bajoni Luigi, Milan. Born 1838 in Milan. Was already dead in 1878. Instruments of medium quality. He worked after Nicolo Amati's small model.

* Guiseppe Tartini (1692—1770), famous violinist, composer, and theorist, who compiled the famous "Tartini's Rules of Art" with instructions on how to handle the bow.

LUIGI BAJONI
FECE
L'ANNO 1854
MILANO

Balcaini, Milan, 1750. Very good workmanship, brown varnish. Price 10.000 Kč.

Baldantoni Giuseppe, Ancona. Born March 19, 1784, died Jan. 5, 1873. Built flat instruments and did not use the best wood; the sound-holes are cut on the pattern of Stradivari, the scrolls are neatly carved, purfling broad. Yellow-brown varnish, applied in thin coats. Besides violins he also built violas, 'cellos and contrabasses. Only a few violins survive. Into some of his instruments he put labels antedated by a hundred years (1734). Price 12—16.000 K.

Joseph Baldantony
Anconae fecit anno 1834

Josephus Baldantonus Anconiae
fecit Anno 1839.

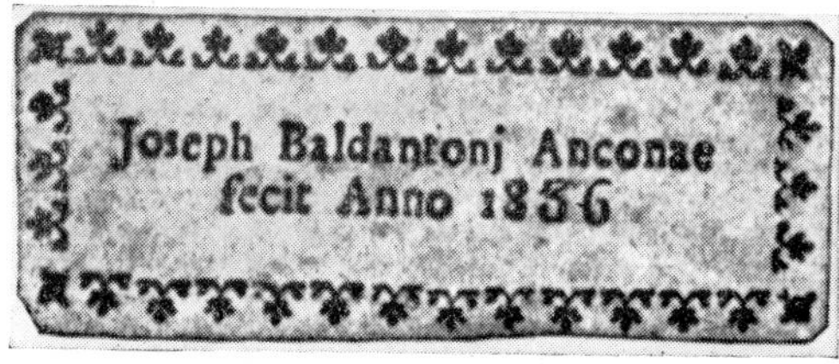

Baldini Ugo, Faenza. B. 1878. An amateur who specialized in guitars. He published a work on guitar-making (1934/35).

Balestrieri Pietro, Cremona. 1725—1740. Brother of Tommaso Balestrieri, disciple of A. Stradivari. Good workmanship. Orange or brown-yellow varnish. Price 25——40.000 Kč.

Petrus Balestrien alummus Antonii
Stradivarii fecit Cremonae, anno 17..

Pietro Balestrieri
fece in Cremona 17..

Balestrieri Tommaso, Mantua. 1720—1795. Brother of Pietro B. Balestrieri, pupil of Pietro I Guarneri. Worked at Cremona and Mantua. He imitated his master so well that his instruments are often sold as instruments by P. Guarneri. His products are masterpieces. It is possible to distinguish them from P. Guarneri's works by the purfling, scrolls, sound-holes and broad pattern. Balestrieri's scrolls are of a rather deep cut, his sound-holes broader and more erect than those of Guarneri's instruments. Sound-holes cut by Guarneri are more pleasing to the eye and finished in a more delicate fashion.

Balestrieri's varnish, very similar to that used by P. Guarneri, is yellow, orange or red. The violoncellos are the best of his instruments. Only the purfling is less perfect and belongs to the distinguishing marks of this master. Price of violins 120—160.000 Kč, 'cellos more.

Size of Violin:

Length of belly and back	355 mm
Upper width	165.5 mm
Middle width	110 mm
Lower width	207 mm
Total height under the bridge (sides, belly and back)	68 mm
Distance of corners of belly and back	75/72 mm
Thickness of belly and back:	
Belly:	
under the bridge	3.3 mm
between the bridge and the lower block	2.9 mm
between the bridge and the upper block	2.5 mm
on the upper edge	2.2—2.5 mm
on the lower edge	2.4 mm
on the edge	2.7—3.2 mm
along the sound-holes	2.9—3.1 mm
Back:	
under the bridge	4.7 mm
between the sound-post and the lower block	2.5 mm
between the sound-post and the upper block	2.8 mm
on the upper edge	1.9—2 mm
on the lower edge	2 —2.2 mm
on the edge	2.6—3 mm
between the bouts	2.2—2.5 mm

Dimensions of his violins in mm:

year	1752	1753
length	356	357
upper width	162	165
centre width	110	110
lower width	208	203

Tomaso Balestrieri
fece in Mantova 1735.

Thomas Balestrieri Cremonensis
fecit Mantuae 1775.

Thomas Baleftrieri Cremonenfis
Fecit Mantuæ Anno 1771

Thomas Baleſtrieri
Cremonenſis
Fecit Mantuæ anno 1759

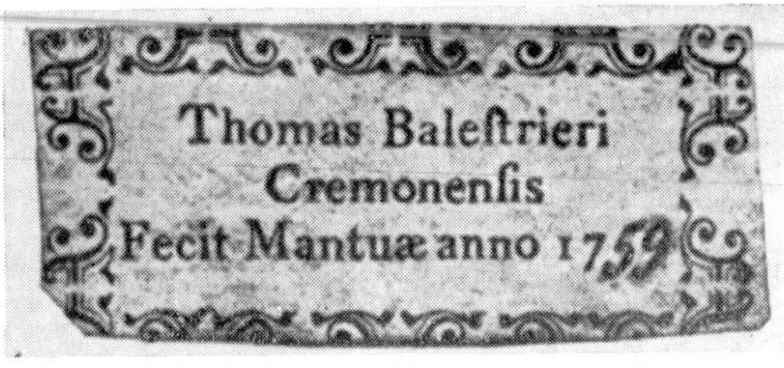

Ballarini Santo, Rimini, Terni, Rome. 1740—1781. Worked on the pattern of Andrea Gisalberti, whose pupil he may have been.

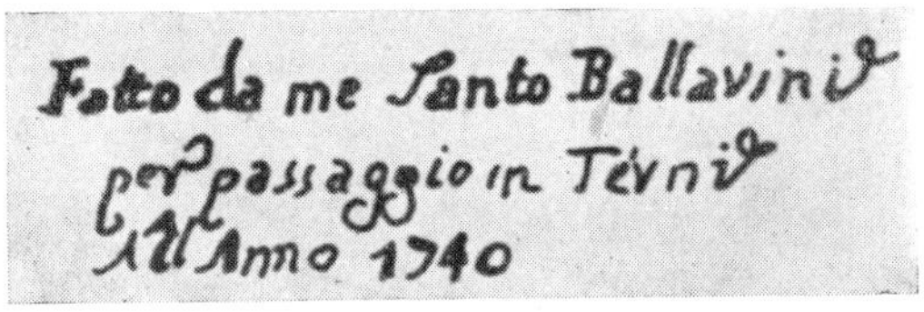

Fatto da me Santo-Ballarini
per passagio in Terni

Nel Anno 1740.
Sanct Ballarini
fece in Roma 1780

Fatto da me Santo Ballarini
per passaggio in Terni
Nel Anno 1740

Ballerini Pietro, Florence. 1900. He took over the musical instrument and string factory from Castellani & Figlio.

Ballini Paolo, Brescia. 1840—1860. Worked skilfully on the pattern of Stradivari and Guarneri. Red varnish.

Baltus Nicolo, Catania. 1788. His narrow shape is reminiscent of the violins by Pietro Guarneri III of Mantua. He used red varnish. His instruments have an equal, though slender tone.

Banni Giuseppe, Rapallo (Genoa). 1940.

Barabas, Cremona, 1793. A Munich painter, Kraus, owned a viola d'amore made by Barabas in 1793.

Baracchi Venerio, S. Martino d'Este (Modena). 1829. Built fairly good instruments.

Baraldi Alfonso, Modena, Bomporto. 1879—1891. Mediocre violin maker.

Baraldi Giovanni, San Felice (Modena). 1760—1766. Known from a surviving 'cello which bears a curious label:

Fece questo Vio
loncello il Giouan
Baroldi di S. D.
Lanno del Signo re 1766.

Barbanti Silvio Francesco, Corregio. 1847—1850. Good workmanship, particularly his violoncellos are masterpieces. Orange-red varnish. Price 10.000 Kč.

Barbi Michele, Venice. 1748.

Michael Barbi, flor. fecit Venetiis A 1748.

Barbier Michel, Palermo. 1870.

Barbieri Armando, Forli, Via S. Martino, Strada 1/1. Born 1893 in Asti and he established himself in 1925. He exhibited a violin and a viola at Cremona in 1937. He works after Stradivari, Guarneri and an original model.

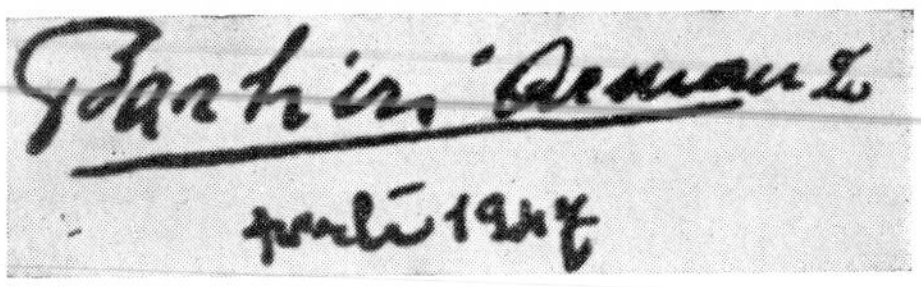

Barbieri Francesco, Verona. Mantua. 1695—1750. Worked on Andrea Guarneri's model. He built violins of large shape. Light-red varnish. Good workmanship. Price 12—15.000 Kč and more. Alfred Keil of Lisbon possessed a viola da gamba of his making of the year 1697.

Barbieri Giuseppe, Poggio (Mantua). 1876—1896. He was a good hand at repairs and built also new instruments.

Barbieri Giuseppe liutaio e reparatore Poggio 1885.

Barbieri Paolo (de), Genoa. Born 1889, pupil of Cesare Candi in Genoa; Stradivari and Guarneri patterns, red varnish.

PAOLO BARBIERI-GENOVA
Fece nell'anno 19 PD

Barbieri Pietro, Mantua. 1821—1864. Imitations of the Cremonese school. Several of his instruments are modelled on Pietro Guarneri of Mantua and are very good. He used Guarnerian orange varnish. His violins are very good concert instruments.

Barbieri R., Genoa. He devoted himself more to the building of mandolins than to the making of violins.

Bardollo Gino Silvio, Cavarzere (Venice), Via Bosco Chiaro. 20th century. He exhibited two violins at Cremona in 1937.

Bargazo Francesco. Padua. 17th century. Run-of-the-mill instruments.

Bargelli Giuseppe di Saladino. Born Apr. 15, 1886 at Vecchio di Mugello near Florence and established himself in Florence. He made violins, violas, violoncellos and double-basses.

GIUSEPPE BARGELLI
fece in
FIRENZE ANNO 1948

Bargelli Giuseppe
fece in Firenze anno 19..

GIUSEPPE BARGELLI
FIRENZE ANNO 19

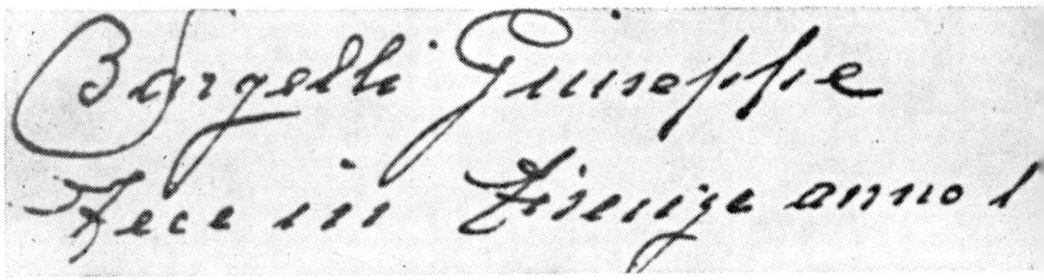

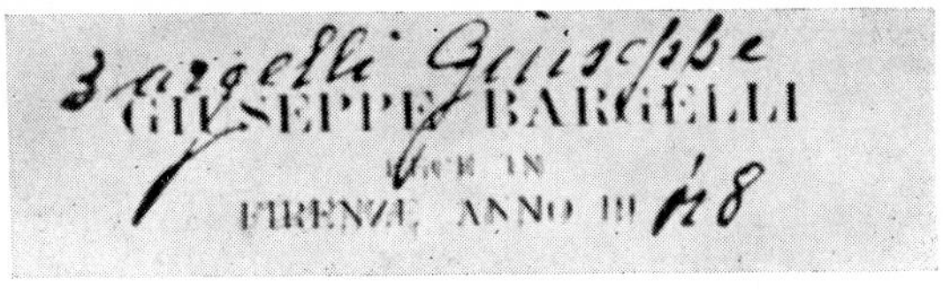

Barnia Fedele, Venice 1745—1780. He came from Milan, where he was born. Worked in the style of the Milanese school and on the pattern of Pietro Guarneri. Skilful master of conscientious workmanship. The scrolls of his violins are tastefully carved; beautiful outlines. He used a yellow or reddish varnish. Price 12—16.000 Kč.

Fedele Barnia Milanese
fece in Venezia l'anno 1761.

Baroldi Giovanni, San Felice (Modena). 1766. Known by a 'cello with this label:

Fece questo Vio
loncello il Giovan
Baroldi di S. D.
L anno del Signo
re 1766

Baroncini Giuseppe, Pistoia. 19th century. His instruments are of large shape, sound-holes beautifully cut. Yellow varnish. Tone not outstanding.

Baroncini Giuseppe
Pistoja 1..

Baroncini Michele, Lodi. Violin maker.

Barrata Ermentoli, Padua. 1564. Was not a violin maker. A label in an ancient-looking instrument reads as follows:

Barrata Ermentoli facebit in Padoua, anno Dominum 1564.

Barranti Silvio Francesco, Correggio, 1850. Made good 'celli.

Bartoli Giuseppe, Venice. 1899. Disciple of Eug. Degani.

Bartolini M., Rome, 19th century.

Barzellini Aegidius, Cremona. 1670—1720. Disciple of Amati, worked on the pattern of Hieron. Amati, using beautiful wood. The back of his instruments is less arched than the belly, the sound-holes rather open and aslant. Price 12.000 Kč.

AEgidius Barzellini fecit
Ecolle Amatius Cremonen 1680.

Bassi Leandro, Rome, Milan. 1900—1920. Imitations of old masterpieces. His own model is without personal characteristics.

Bassani Giuseppe, Brescia. 1678. Known only from a pochette.

Josef Bassani
fecit in Brescia
Anno 1678.

Bassi A., Scandiano (Modena). 19th century. Little known, violin maker.

Bassiano, Rome, 1666. Lute maker, who labelled his instruments as follows:

Bassiano liuttaro in Roma 1666.

Bastiano (Bastiano da Verona) Verona. 15th — 16th century. Made lutes, violas, lyres, flutes, bugle-horns and harps, but no specimens of his work seem to have been preserved.

Bastogi Gaetano, Leghorn. 18th century. Built lutes and guitars.

Batiazza Antonio Maria, Milan. 1707. Worked on the pattern of the Milanese masters.

Antonio Maria Batiazza
fece in Milano in Contrada
Larga 1707.

Battaglio Antonio, Milan. 1757—1766. Violin and lute maker.

Antonio Battaglia
Fabbricatore de Salterij
nella Streta del Mangano
vicino a S. Maria Segreta
in Milano.
* F * S

Antonio Battaglia
fece nell' anno 1766
Nella stretta del Mangano
Dirimpetto a Santa Maria Secreta
Vicino a Cordusio
in Milano.

Battani Antonio, Frassinoro, 19th century. Devoted himself to the repairing of instruments.

Batti Antonio, Arezzo, 1660—1691. Made chiefly spinets.

Antonio Batti Arezzo 1691

Battioni Alberto, Foligno and after 1885 Ferrara. Son and pupil of Marc-Antonio Battioni in Foligno.

Battioni Marc-Antonio. Foligno. 1850. Born in Foligno.

Bausch Emanuele, Florence. 19th century (?). Probably of German extraction. He worked after Stradivari using brown varnish on yellow ground.

Beccani Stefano, Mantua. 1890. Good instruments, labelled under the lower sound-holes curve.

Becchini Renzo, Leghorn. Born 1911 in Pisa. He worked after Stradivari and established himself in 1932. Yellow-red varnish.

Bedocchi Mario, Reggio Emilia, Corso Garibaldi 40. Born Dec. 13, 1880. He exhibited three violins and a viola at Cremona in 1937.

MARIO BEDOCCHI
FECE
Anno 19.. in Reggio E.

Mario Bedocchi
fece
l'anno 19.. in Regio Emilia

MARIO BEDOCCHI
FECE
Anno 19..... in Reggio-E.

Mario Bedocchi fece BM.
l'anno 19... in Reggio Emilia

Belacqua, Florence. 13th century lute maker, friend of Dante.

Belcioni Antonio di Stefano, Modena. 1663—1673. He used yellow-brown varnish.

Bellafontana Lorenzo, Genoa, Via Davide Chiassone 8/9. Born July 15, 1906. Pupil of Cesari Candi and an excellent violinist. He worked after Stradivari and Guarneri using red varnish on a yellow ground. He also made bows. In 1937 he exhibited a violin, a viola and a quartet at Cremona in 1937.

LAURENTIUS BELLAFONTANA
Fecit Genua L. B.
A. D. 1937 N G.
Laurentius Bellafontana fecit
Genuae Anno Domini 1948

L. BELLAFONTANA
GENOVA
Laurentius Bellafontana
fecit Genuae 1949
N. 76

Laurentius Bellafontana fecit Ve ra L B G
Genuae Anno Domini 1948
Bellafontana

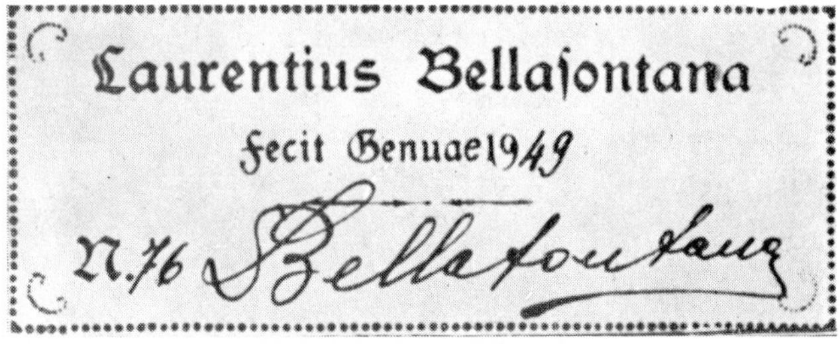
Laurentius Bellafontana
fecit Genuae 1949
N. 76 LBellafontana

L. BELLAFONTANA
GENOVA

Ballarini Santo, Torino. 1749—1781.

Bellarosa Riccardo, Naples. Born 1871. Died 1941. He worked after the Cremonese and Naples school using orange varnish.

Bellarosa Vittorio, Naples. Born 1907. Apprenticed since 1922. Later he worked in Mittenwald and Rome and established himself in Naples. His favourite model is Januarius Gagliano whom he imitates to the last detail. He uses orange or golden-yellow and golden-red varnish.

Vittorio Bellarosa
Napoli Anno 1950
Via Michele Cammarano N. 10
Vittorio Bellarosa

Bellinazzi Giuseppe, Bonferraro (Verona). 20th century violin maker, exhibited a violin at Cremona in 1937.

Bellone Pietro Antonio, surnamed Il Pescorino, Milan. 1691—1708. Clean workmanship, brown-red varnish, long sound-holes. His instruments, finished in a masterly manner, possess a beautiful tone and are in great demand. Hamma valued them as works ranking between those of Landolfi and Guadagnini. He seems to have been a Frenchman by birth.

Pietro Antonio Bellone detto il
Pescorino fece in Contrada,
Larga in Milano 1691 al Se-
gno di S. Antonio da Padoua.

Bell' Orsi Michel Angelo, Turin. 1675—1684. Violin maker, who used labels as follows:

Michel Angelo Bell' Orsi
fece in Torino
l'anno 1681.

Bellosio Anselmo, Venice. 1715—1889. Probably son of Giovanni Bellosio. He was a pupil of Serafino Santo and imitated the latter's style. His instruments are of rather full arching and have strong edges. He used beautiful, rather heavy wood, applied in thin coats, wonderful yellow-red varnish, superior in colour and lustre even to that of Santo Serafino. His instruments, though of good tone, are not strong enough. Best are his 'cellos. Price 100.000 Kč, 'cellos more.

Anselmij Bellosij
Fecit Venetijs 17..

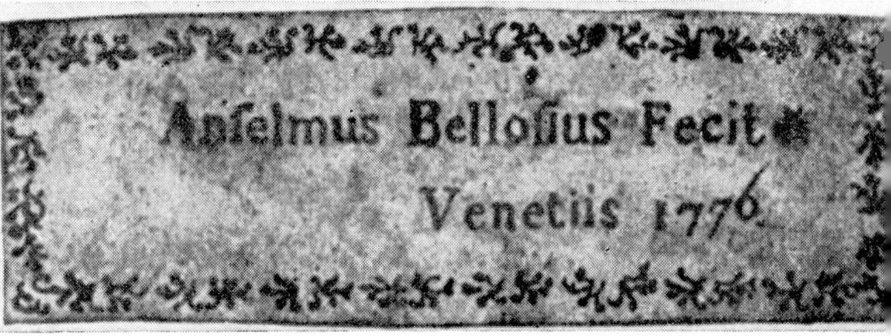
Anselmus Bellosius Fecit
Venetiis 1776

Anselmus Bellosius Fecit
Venetiis 1783

Bellosio Giovanni, Venice. 1730—1740. Father of Anselm Bellosio, pupil of Domenico Montagnano. He worked after the Cremonese school, mainly after the large Stradivari. He varnished his violins, built after Giuseppe Guarneri del Gesù, by an orange varnish.

Belluomini Maurizio, Pisa. 1884—1890. He worked after Stradivari using golden-yellow and yellow-red varnish. The details of his instruments are carefully worked out.

Belosi Antonio, Venice. 1734. He worked after the Venetian school with small sound-holes and carefully worked edges.

Beltrami Giuseppe, Vescovato (Cremona). 1870—1881. Imitations of Cremonese school. He used red-brown varnish.

Belveglieri Gregorio, Bologna. 1742—1772. Violin maker of no particular merit. Best are his violas. Price 16.000 Kč.

Gregorius Bilveglieri fecit
Bologniae villa Bononice

Bendini Giambattista, Milan. 1665—1672.

Benedetti Giuseppe, Piacenza. 1700, 1727. The violins and violas of his making are not of the best quality. Golden-yellow varnish. Price 10—12.000 Kč.

Benedecti de Donato, Cremona. 1679.

Bennettini Milan. 1868—1890. He made good double-basses. He modelled his instruments on Stradivari. Red-brown varnish.

Benito Antonio J., Milan. 1664. A violin of his making, inlaid with tortoise-shell, its head provided with a well carved lion's head, survives. The label quoted below is almost illegible.

B. Lüttgendorff doubts its genuineness and even A. J. Antoni's existence.

A. J. Antoni Benito
Milan 1664.

Benti Matteo, Brescia. Born 1580, died after 1637. Lute and violin maker, built instruments of large shape with somewhat high arching on the pattern of Gasparo da Salò. The virtuoso A. Genz of Berlin owned a viola made by Benti in 1630. The violinists Ole Bull and W. Burmester possessed violins of his making.

Matteo Bente
fecit Bresciae 1580.
Matteo Benti
fecit Bresciae 1601.

Benozzati Girolamo, Cittadella (Pavia). 1860. Pupil of Eugenio Degani from Venice. He worked after the models by Italian masters. Towards the end of his life he lived in Rome.

Benvenuti Joseph Maria, Borgo. 1690—1710. Rare instruments of excellent qualities, good golden-yellow varnish.

Benvenuti Paolo, Pisa. 18th century (in San Lorenzo). Named by Valdrighi; works lost.

Benvenuti Silvio, Ancona. B. March 13, 1904 in Pergola. Died 1948. He exhibited one of his violins at Cremona in 1937.

Silvio Benvenuti
Liutario pergolese faceva in Ancona
l'anno 19..

Berardi Pasquale, Imola, Modena. Born 1807. Died 1896 in Alassio. He used yellow-brown varnish.

Berati, Imola (Bologna). 1760—1784.

Berera Giov. Antonio, Trente. 1745—1770. Current workmanship of no particular interest.

Johannes Antonius
Berera
Faciebat Tridenti Anno 1760.

Joannes Antonius Brera [sic]
fecit Tridente Anno 1745.

Beretta Felice, Como. 1760—1789. Disciple of Giuseppe Guadagnini: imitated his master's and J. B. Guadagnini's style. Instruments of his making are often believed to be works produced by Giuseppe and J. B. Guadagnini (II.); they differ from those of the masters Guadagnini by their rough edges, which are not cleaned up outside; the wide purfling is less good-looking; less shapely sound-holes, wide, rather untastefully cut scroll. In spite of all these small defects, the instruments have a good tone. Deep-yellow varnish. Price 40.000 Kč, and more.

Felice Beretta alievo di Giuseppe Guadagnino
fece in Como l'Anno 1770

Bergamo Domenico fu Giacomo, Padua, Via Allessandrio Poerio 15 A. 20th century. Exhibited a violin of his making at Cremona in 1937.

Bergonzi Benedetto, Cremona. Born 1790; d. at Cremona in 1840. The last member of a family of violin makers who devoted himself to the repairing of instruments.

Bergonzi Carlo, Cremona. B. 1676, d. 1747. Disciple of Joseph Guarneri fil. Andreae. He also worked in the workshop of Antonio Stradivari in whose house he lived after 1746. Carlo Bergonzi's violins stand on account of their beauty and also of the quality of their tone midway between those of Antonio Stradivari and Joseph Guarneri del Gesù. They are of superb workmanship, made of beautiful wood and covered with a brilliant varnish, red, brown-red, golden-yellow or amber coloured, similar to that of Stradivari. Carlo Bergonzi built violins of large pattern and low arching, sometimes also on a smaller model. The scrolls are wonderfully cut, with protruding ends; the sound-holes, the cut of which recalls partly Stradivari, partly Guarneri del Gesù, are placed a little lower than usual, as is also the case in many works of his first teacher. Carlo Bergonzi belongs to the Cremonese classics and experts place his best work on a par with those of Antonio Stradivari and Guarneri del Gesù. His 'celli and contrabasses do not measure up to his violins. His oldest violin of 1696 bears a handwritten label on parchment. The elegance and finish of Bergonzi's works is reflected in their prices — 320.000 Kč, and more. They are coveted as concert instruments, for they fulfil the ideal of a magnificent, carrying and brilliant, yet liquid and mellow tone.

Carlo Bergonzi fece in Cremona
anno 1737.

Anno 17.. Reuisto e corretto da me
Carlo Bergonzi Cremona

Sizes of violins:

Violin made in	1722	1723	1735	1737	1737	1742
Length of back	353	353	354	355	352	352 mm
Width of top	166	166	166	164	165	163 mm
Width of centre	105	106	108	106	107	105 mm
Width of bottom	202	203	205	203.5	208	204 mm
Height of body (with sides)	—	—	61	61	62	64 mm

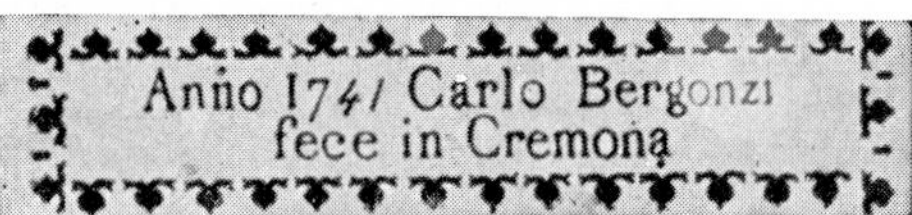

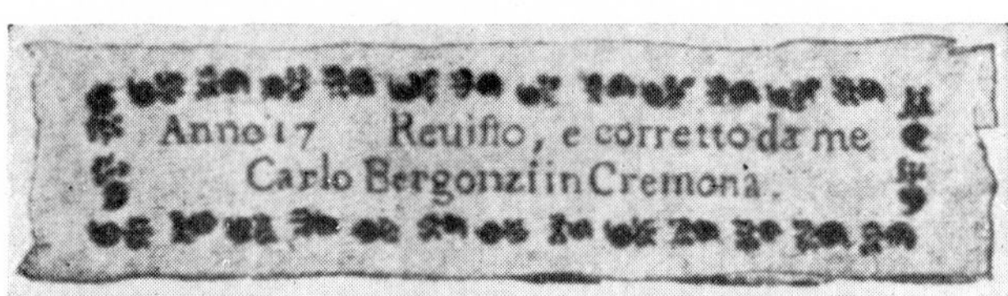

Bergonzi Carlo (II), Cremona. Born 1780. Died 1820. Third son of Michel Angiolo Bergonzi. Violin-maker who devoted himself to the repairing of instruments. His own creations, varnished red-brown or brown, are not of best quality.

Besides violins he also built guitars and mandolins. Length of violin: 350 mm.

Bergonzi Francesco, Cremona. 1687. Considered to be father of Carlo Bergonzi.

Bergonzi Giuseppe, Cremona. 1740.

Bergonzi Lodovico, Cremona. 1741.
Cousin of Michael Angelo Bergonzi. He made violins of large shape.

Bergonzi Michel Angiolo, Cremona. Born 1722. Died 1770. Son and pupil of Carlo Bergonzi and after the latter's death his successor. Worked on various models: built for the most part smaller-sized instruments on the pattern of Carlo Bergonzi, but they lack the conscientious and accurate workmanship of his father. He is also known to have worked on the large model of Stradivari. His instruments often have a wide, flat edge. Very fine wood, wonderful red-yellow varnish of excellent quality. His instruments are outstanding for their smooth and powerful tone: best are his contrabasses. Price 100—120.000 Kč.

Michel'Angelo Bergonzi figlio di Carlo
fece in Cremona 17..

Michel Angelo Bergonzi
figlio di Carlo fece in
Cremona l'Anno 1749.

Michel-Angelo Bergonzi
figlio di Carlo
fece in Cremona l'anno 1755.

Michelangelus Bergonzi
fecit Cremonae 17..

Bergonzi Nicolo, Cremona. 1749—1782. Elder son of Michel Angiolo Bergonzi, his successor and probably his pupil, too. Worked on his father's pattern of broad, flat shape. His workmanship is not of the best, but he was able; some instruments show very good workmanship and a carefully chosen wood.

His violins are of good tone, yet the wood is not always of the best: orange-yellow varnish of brilliant lustre. The scroll is not delicately cut. Handsome specimens fetch prices of 140—160.000 Kč.

Nicolaus Bergonzi
Cremonensis faciebat
Anno 1765

---

* Carlo Bergonzi is the oldest and greatest master of the Bergonzi family. Francesco, his contemporary (1687), was perhaps his brother. With two other violin makers of the family, Guiseppe (1740) and Lodovico (1741) it is impossible to determine the descent. Michel Angiolo Bergonzi (1715—1765) was son of Carlo, while Nicolò (1749—1782), Zosimo (1750—1777) and Carlo II (1780—1820) were sons of Michel Angiolo.

Nicolaus Bergonzi
Cremonenſis faciebat
Anno 17 60

Bergonzi Zosimo, Cremona. 1750—1777. Second son of Michel Angiolo Bergonzi, and perhaps also his pupil. Somewhat heavy and not so skilled as his brother Nicolo. But few of his instruments survive. He devoted himself mostly to the making of 'cellos and contrabasses; they are of very good tone. Price of violins 30—50.000 Kč, 'celli more.

Fatto da me Zosimo Bergonzi
L'anno 1771. Cremonae.

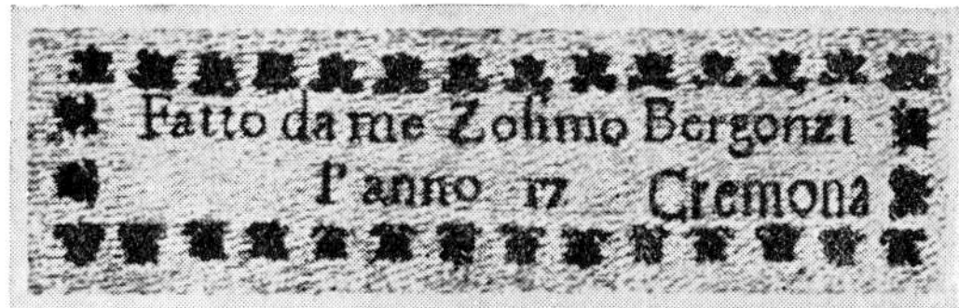

Berretta Adolfa, Turin. 1860—1880. Pale-brown varnish on golden-yellow ground.

Bertani, Modena. 1880. Made also flutes and English horns besides violins.

Bertani Vito, Cesena. 1922.

Bertasio Luigi, Piadena. 1795—1820.

Bertassi Ambrogio, Piadena. 1712—1730. Good workmanship. Violins of his making are valued at 12.000 Kč.

Berti Antonio, Cortona (Tosca) 1721. Violin and lute maker.

Berti Giuseppe, called "Giusino", Fumalba (Modena). 19th century. Inferior instruments.

Bertini Vincenzo, Rome 1914. Mandolin maker.

Bertolazzi Giacinto. Milan. Born June 14, 1910. Died 1956. Pupil of Euro Peluzzi in Milan. Originally a violinist who worked after the Cremonese school.

Bertoletti Antonio, Brescia. 1790—1800. Only one violoncello which is not of superior quality, survives. Golden-yellow varnish.

Antonio Bertoleti
Fece in Brescid. 1796.

Bertolini Angelo, Reggio, Emilia. B. May 1, 1881, violin maker, exhibited a violin of his making at Cremona in 1937.

Bertolotti Francesco, called "Violino", Polpenaza, 16th century. Son of Santino Bertolotti and father of Gasparo da Salò. Originally he was a painter and became a viol maker at a later age. A Santino Bertolotti was a native of Polpenazza and lived in the 16th century. Also Francesco stayed in Polpenazza, but Gasparo da Salò moved to Brescia, a large town, where he died, leaving his workshop to his son Francesco (1564—1614).

Bertolotti Francesco, Brescia. Born at Brescia in March 1564, still lived in 1614. Son and pupil of Gasparo da Salò. Less skilled and diligent than his father. He sold the workshop, which he had taken over from his father, to Paolo Maggini and moved to Galvanese near Lake Garda in 1614, where his father had bought some land.

D. Francesco f. Gaspar da Salò in Brescia.

Bertolotti Gasparo, called "Gasparo da Salò", Brescia. Born at Salò near Lake Garda on May 20, 1540, died at Brescia Apr. 14, 1609; his burying-place is St. Joseph's Church of Brescia. Son of Francesco Bertolotti: pupil of his grandfather Santino Bertolotti at Polpenazza and disciple of Girolamo da Virchi at a later time. In 1565 he became independent violin maker. He gave the violin its modern shape. Gasparo da Salò built violins of moderately arched shape, using strong wood for the belly and back; the outlines of his instruments are not symmetrical enough: the long, large, wide-open sound-holes are mostly upright; the belly is of pine with very regular wide grain; for the back he used mostly the outside-planks of poplar trunks, for the large, roughly carved scrolls maple and sometimes even pear-wood. The brown varnish, applied in thin coats, is of wonderful lustre like polished agate; Hamma calls it "a handsome tarry hue"; it is of good quality. He built instruments both of small and large pattern; both have a good tone. Gasparo da Salò was the best violin maker of his time and is the founder of the Brescian School. His violas, gambas and contrabasses are good masterworks; their backs and sides were often made of pear-wood. Very few of his violins survive, mostly those made in 1601—1603. In the appendix will be found outlines of violins in real size and three-quarter contrabasses.

Price of violin 150.000 Kč, and more — collectors' prices.

Sizes of instruments:

	Length	Width		Sides	
		upper	lower	upper	lower
Violin, small pattern . . .	351	160	200	—	— mm
Violin, large pattern . . .	364	176	216	27	28 mm
	365	155	208	—	— mm
Viola	443	220	257	38	40 mm
Contrabass	1080	544	660	—	— mm

(A gigantic three-stringed contrabass is exposed in the Kensington Museum in London.)

Gasparo da Salò, In Brescia.

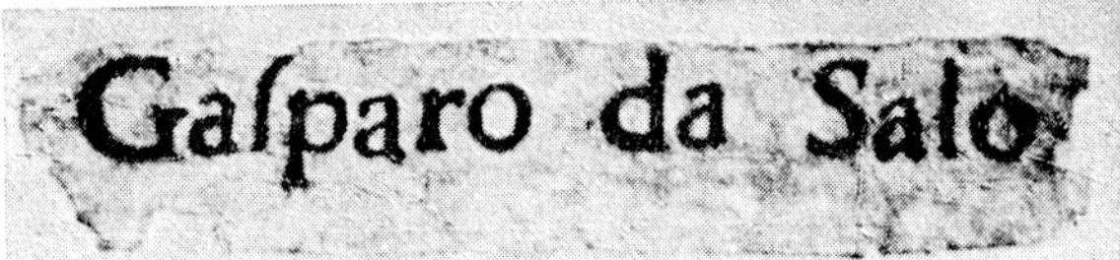
Gasparo da Salò

Bertolotti Santino, Polpenazza. 16th century. Lute maker, grandfather of Gasparo da Salò.

Bertozzi Alfredo, fu Giuseppe, Ripa Saravezza (Lucca). Via di Mignano. 20th century. Exhibited a violin and a viola at Cremona in 1937.

Bertucci Costantino, Pesare. Born 1860 in Rome, d. 1930, specialized in the construction of guitars and mandolins; he was also an outstanding performer.

Chitarra Classica
Modello BERTUCCI
anno

Bertucci D. Giuseppe, Mont-Orsello. 1748—1777.

Bertucci Fausto Maria, Rome. Born in Rome on June 25, 1897. Worked on the pattern of Stradivari, used a varnish of the colour of old gold. His instruments show careful workmanship and are included among the best creations of the violin makers of his time.

F. M. BERTUCCI e A. GONZALES
Fecero in ROMA nel 1928

Lavorazione
F. M. B. VIOLINI ITALIANI
Roma 1949

F. M. BERTUCCI
LIUTAIO
ROMA - Via dei Greci N. 27
N. 46 Anno 26

Bianchi Giovanni, Florence. 1746—1757. Worked on the pattern of Stainer. His workmanship lacks carefulness, only the scrolls are neatly carved: large sound-holes, unevenly executed purfling. Yellow varnish. The instruments are of good tone, particularly his 'cellos are excellent. Price 20—25.000 Kč, 'cello more.

Giovanni Bianchi Fece
In Firenze, anno 1746.

Bianchi Nicolo, Aix, Paris, Genoa, Nice. Born in Genoa 1796. Died in Nice 1881. Worked mostly on the pattern of Guarneri, made good copies and repaired excellently the instruments of old masters. The varnish he used is of wonderful lustre. Some of his instruments are quite outstanding in shape and tone. Price 16.000 Kč (average).

Réparé par Bianchi Nicolo
Luthier decoré
A Parigi 1851.

RÉPARÉ PAR
BIANCHI NICOLO,
Luthier décoré
A 1846

Nicolo Bianchi

Bianchini Secondo Castel Vetro (Pisa). B. Oct. 3, 1928 at Castelvetro Piacentino, productive violin maker active in his birthplace and (for some time) at Salò Guarneri pattern, also developed his own model.

Bianchini Secondo
fecit Cremona 1948

Bianchini Secondo
fecit Salò 1949

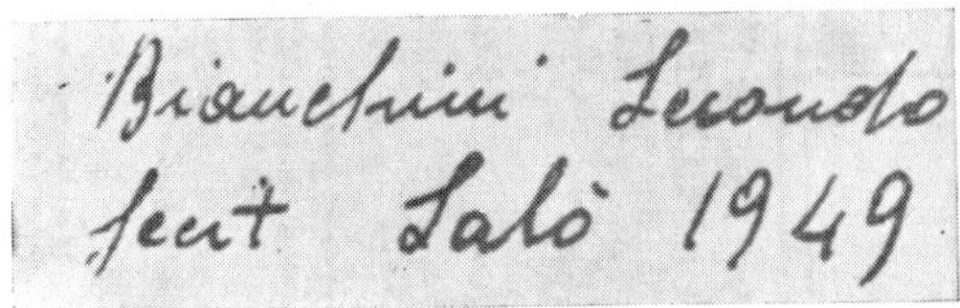
Bianchini Secondo
fecit Salò 1949

Bianchini Vincenzo. ?

Biasio Carlo de. Sottoguda (Rocca Pistore). Born 1909 in Sottoguda. Pupil of Luigi Contavalli. He established himself in 1937. Golden-red varnish.

Bignani Otello, Bologna. Born 1914 in Bologna. Pupil of Giuseppe Bonora. He used amber-coloured varnish.

Bimbi Bartolomeo, Siena. 1750—1769. Built, in the style of Gabrielli, mostly instruments of small pattern with high and full arching. Careful workmanship, wonderful transparent golden-yellow, orange-red or red varnish. Price 20—40.000 Kč according to the state of preservation.

Bartolomeo Bimbi Fiorentino
Fecit Lanno 1760

Birlotti Giovanni, Venice. Died 1920. Pupil of Gaetano Sgarabotto.

Birmetti Giambattista, Florence. 1770—1775. Large pattern, wonderful bright red varnish.

Bisiach Andrea, Milan. Born 1890 in Milan. More an author than a violin maker.

Bisiach Carlo, Florence, Via Puccinotti 72. Born Mar. 9, 1892; exhibited five violins at Cremona in 1937.

Carlo Bisiach di Leandro
Milanese fece in
Firenze l'Anno 1948 + C B

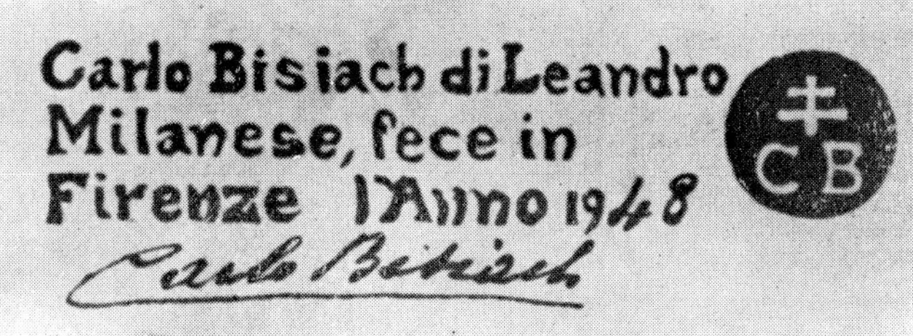

Bisiach Giacomo, Milan, Corso Magenta 27. B. Nov. 28, 1900 exhibited four violins at Cremona in 1937.

Giacomo e Leandro Bisiach
Fecero in Milano l'A 1947

Bisiach Leandro I, Milan. Born May 15, 1864, died 1946. Pupil of Gaetano Antonioazzi II in Cremona who devoted himself mainly to the study of classical Cremonese instruments. All parts of his instruments were made in his workshop. Excellent repairs. In 1922, together with his son Leandro II, he repaired classical instruments of Count Guido Chigi Saracini. The repairs were finished in 1924. He worked with his son Leandro who was his pupil.

Bisiach Leandro II, Milan. Born Feb. 29, 1904. Son and pupil of Leandro Bisiach I. He became apprenticed to him at a very early age and worked at his school. In 1922 he left with his father for Sienna where they repaired instruments in the collection of Count Guido Chigi Saracini. At present he works with his brother Giaccomo. He took part in various exhibitions and is the ANLAI violin expert. He usually employs the Stradivari model, using varnish made of natural resins and volatile oils. The story according to which his father acquired Stradivari's tools and a photograph of Stradivari's recipe for varnish cannot be proved.

Biza Giovanni Battista, Treviso. 1770—1790. Little known.

Bizzi Egidio fu Giovanni, Finale Emilia (Modena) Via A. Costa 1. 20th century. Exhibited two violins at Cremona in 1937.

Leandro Bisiach da Milano
Fece l'Anno 1922 LB

iacomo e Leandro Bisiach
I Fecero in Milano l'A 1947

Leandro Bisiach da Milano
Fece l'Anno 1922
Leandro Bisiach

LEANDRO BISIACH della Scuola Cremonese
fece in Milano 1896 Piazza del Duomo
Leandro Bisiach

Blasich Louis, Terst. 1881. Amateur violin-maker.

Blasio Raffaele di, Naples. 1780. He worked after the Gagliano model using yellow-brown varnish.

Bobbi Giuseppe, Milan. Born 1891.

Boccaber Matteo, Rome. 1592—1619. Excellent lute-maker.

Boccaccini Giuseppe, Pistoia (Florence). Born 1836. Double-bass player who made low-arched double-basses.

Bodeni Luigi, Venice. 1719. Skilled amateur of repute but nowadays almost unknown.

Bodiani — never existed: the instruments marked with this name are fakes, unsuccessful besides, and seem to have impaired the reputation of the violin maker Giovita Rodiani (Brescia, 1580—1630). The fakes have a glassy yellow varnish.

Bodio Gennaro, Venice. Ca 1740. Price of instruments ca 16.000 Kč. He worked after Italian school.

Bodio Giambattista, Venice. 1790—1832. Son and disciple of Gennaro Bodio. Built, on the pattern of Dom. Montagnana, flat-shaped wide-edged instruments with wide purfling. Yellow or yellow-red hard varnish. The instruments have a hard, rather powerless tone. Price 10—16.000 Kč.

Boldrini Ovidio, Salò. 1864. Little known master.

Bolelli Pietro, Bologna. 19th century.

Bolli III. Naples. 1897—1906. Assiduous violin-maker. Orange varnish.

Bolondi Odoastro, Reggio Emilia. Born 1906. Amateur violin-maker who made violins and double-basses.

Bomberghi Lorenzo, Florence. 1680—1710. Son of Giovanni B. Devoted himself mostly to the building of violas. Price of violin 10.000 Kč.

Bombirio Domenico, Villafranca (Piedmont), 1720—1730. Perhaps pupil of Goffredo Cappa, unfortunately little known.

Bomini Carlo, Cremona 1715. Adherent of Antonio Stradivari, worked on the latter's pattern. Applied a golden-yellow varnish of excellent quality. Good workmanship, beautiful tone.

Carolus Bomini Discipulus
Antonij Stradivarij Cremona

Bonardi Domenico, Modena. 1728. Devoted himself mostly to the repairing of instruments.

Bondanelli Chiarissimo, Novara. Born 1910 in Venice. Chemist. Golden-yellow alcohol or turpentine varnish.

Bono Gaetano, Venice. 1730—1740. Good workmanship; quite rare.

Bonoris Cesare, Mantua. 1568. Built excellent violas of which only a few survive.

Cesare Bonoris
di Mantova 1568

Bonozzati Girolamo, Venice. 1899.

Bonvincini Filippo. Spilamberto. 1790—1796. He made violins and violoncellos after Amati using yellow-brown varnish.

Bora Eugen, Naples. 1905.

Borani A., Naples. 1873. He made violins and violoncellos.

Borelli Andrea, Parma. 1720—1746. Worked on the large pattern of Stradivari, yet his workmanship lacks carefulness. Upright sound-holes after the fashion of Lorenzo Guadagnini: glassy yellow, brown-yellow or brown varnish. The instruments, however, sound well, particularly the 'cellos are good so far as their shape and tone are concerned. Price 25—30.000 Kč, 'cellos more. In 1912—14 violins were sold at 1000 and 'cellos at 1500 M.

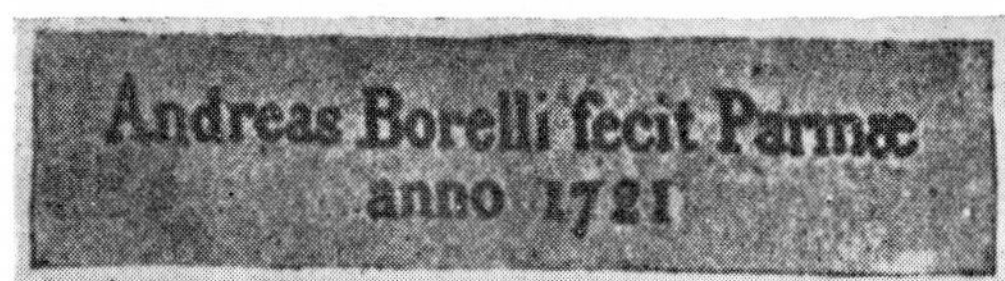
Andreas Borelli fecit Parmæ
anno 1721

Borelli Antonio, Cesare, Parma. 1785—1794. Son of Andrea Borelli. Built violins of large pattern. Applied an agate-coloured yellow-brown varnish.

Borgelli Giuseppe di Saladino, Florence. Died 1886.

Borghi Francesco, Milan. Died 1956.

Borghi Pietro, Modena. B. 1892, d. 1957, was a wood carver or cabinet maker and at the same time amateur violin maker worthy of notice. He worked in the style of Andrea Guarneri and applied a rather thick rose or bright brown varnish. Fine finish.

Borgia Antonio, Milan. 1765—1772. Worked on the pattern of Testori. Price 12.000 Kč.

Antonius Borgia me fecit
in Milano, anno 1769

Borgognoni — Senigallia (Ancona). 1840. Amateur violin-maker who made double-basses.

Boriero Alfonso, Malo (Vicenza). 19th century.

Borio Francesco Antonio, Asti a Cuneo (Coni). 1737. Instruments of inferior quality.

Borrerio Francesco, Padua. 1834. He used yellow-brown varnish.

Bortolotti Giovanni, Verica (Frignano). 1884—1894. He made excellent double-basses.

Bortolotti Luigi I, Milan. 1810—1830. He branded his instruments, yellow or reddish brown in colour.

Luigi Bortolotti
1815

Bortolotti Luigi II, Milan. 1860—1875. Maker of violas and violoncellos.

Boselli Alfredo, Florence. 1925.

Bosi Carlo, Cremona, Via S. Bernardo 5. B. 1873, d. 1940. Exhibited a violin, a real masterpiece, at Cremona in 1937.

Bossi Floriano di, Bologna. 1756—1782. Built lutes and mandolins and violas d'amore. He made only few violins (360 mm.).

Florianus Bosi in via
S. Mamola Bononiae
fecit 1756

Bossi Giuseppe, Stradella (Pavia). 1900. Died 1944.

Botte, Brescia. 1760—1790. He worked after the large Maggini model using golden-yellow and brown varnish.

Botello Angelo, Naples. 1857—1860. Assiduous violin-maker who worked after the Neapolitan school.

Bottari Ferdinando, Pisa. 1849. Guitar-maker.

Botti Antonio, Sassuolo (Modena). 19th century. Built good double-basses.

Botturi Benvenuto, Brescia. Born Nov. 27, 1882 in Gambera (Brescia). Pupil of Luigi Digiuni in Cremona. He worked in Brescia after Stradivari between 1929 and 1941. He used red-brown varnish. His two violins and a viola were exhibited at Cremona in 1937.

Bozzi Raffaele, Milan. Born 1905 in Milan. He worked after the large Stradivari model using golden-yellow varnish. Bows after French patterns (Lama, Sartory, Tourte a. o.).

Bozzolo Pietro, born at Milan about 1830, died in St. Petersburg 9. 7. 1907. Went to St. Petersburg as member of the Italian opera chorus in 1862 and stayed there until his death. Repaired excellently instruments of old masters and founded, in St. Petersburg, a large business dealing in Italian musical instruments.

Braglia Antonio, Modena. 1790—1820. Specialized in bow-making but he made also double-basses.

Braidi Geminiano, Modena. 1794—1805. Son of Giovanni Braidi. Specialized only in making stringed instruments.

Braidi Giovanni, Modena. 1766. His workmanship is not of the best.

Johannes Braidi protomagister
violae majoris in C. S.^{mi} ducis
Mutinae fecit a. 1766.

Bran Marsino, Roveredo in Piano (Udina). Born 1909. D. Sept. 5, 1960. Pupil of Iginio Siega. Original instruments after Italian school.

Brandilioni Filippo, Brescia. 1790. Worked on the pattern of Amati, but more in the style of the Tyrolese school.

Brandini . . . . . , Pesaro c. 1660, is renowned for his 'celli.

Brandini Fausto, Pisa c. 1777. A minor master whose violins, made after Amati, may fetch from 10 to 12.000 Kč.

Brandini Jacopo, Pisa. 1765—1807. His violins sound well and are made of good material; the varnish, of good quality, is chestnut brown, but the outline inelegant. Price 10—12.000 Kč.

Branzo Francesco Barbaro, Padua. 1620—1660.

Branzo Francesco Barbaro
ai Padova Anno 1620.

Branza Francesco BARBARO.

Bratti Cesare, Florence, 1830.

Premiata fabbrica
strumenti a corda
e corde armoniche
Bratti & Co.
7 Via dei Martinelli 7
Firenze anno 1830.

Brensio Antonio, Bologna. 1592. Made mainly excellent 'cellos.

Antonius Brensius Bononi
Antonius Bononiensis (written)
Antonius Bononiensis
Antonio Brensius Bononi.

1592.
Antonius Brenſius Bonon

Brensio Girolamo, Bologna. 16th century. A few 'cellos of his making are known.

Heronymus Brenſius Bonon.

Brenzoni Pietro, 1902.

Bresa Francesco, Milan. 1700—1716. Instruments of medium quality. Orange-red varnish. Price 15.000 Kč.

Francesco Bresa fecit
alla scala in Mi... 1708.

Bressano Battista, Bologna. 1590—1600.

Briani Cipriani Vicentino, Milan. Died 1920. Pupil of Leandro Bisiacha. He worked after Italian classics.

Brizano Vincenzo, Foggia. 1840—1860. Built good violins. His true name might have been *Buzano* or *Busan*.

Brocca Gentilino, Lugano. 1680—1710. He worked after Gasparo da Salò.

Broga Francesco, Milan. 1710—1740. Skilled amateur, little known, yet remarkable. Worked in the style of Andrea Guarneri and applied a light brown or pink varnish.

Brosa Francesco, Milan. See Broga F.

Broschi Carlo, Parma. 1730—1744. Violins of his making are of small shape, made on the pattern of N. Amati; his workmanship is not of the best; beautifully cut sound-holes and scrolls. Price 12.000 Kč.

Carlo Broschi
in Parma fecit 1732.

Bruno Carlo Colombo, Turin. Born May 16, 1872 in Caltanisetta (Sicily). He established himself in Turin in 1890. He worked after the large Stradivari model and small model by Nicolo Amati using red-brown or orange varnish. His instruments have a beautiful tone. Best are his violoncellos and mandolins.

CARLO BRVNO
Fabbricante d'istrvmenti mvsicali a corda
Fece anno 190 in TORINO

Bruno Nicolo, Bologna. 1727—1730. He worked together with Georg Klotz and his instruments distinctly bear traces of the Tyrolese school. He used golden-yellow varnish.

Nicolo Bruno e Giorgio Klotz
nella Strada delli Maestri di Legnani
in Bologna 1726

Brusaterra Mariano, Vicenza. Born 1927. Pupil of Giuseppe Zamberti. It is said that he made his first violin at the age of 17. He worked after the Cremonese school, varnishing his instruments golden-yellow.

Bucci Mariano, Rome. 19th century. He was a craftsman, but not a master, who made violins and guitars.

Bucchenberg Matthias, Rome. 1597—1619. Lute-maker who came originally from Germany.

Budiani Giovita, Brescia. 1580. *See* Rodiani.

Buonarotti, Rome. 1735—1755. Violins of narrow shape with high arching. Yellow varnish.

Buonfigliuoli Pier Francesco, Florence. 17th century.

Busan Domenico, Vicenza, Venice. 1740—1780. Built instruments on the patterns of the Venetian school. Best are his contrabasses.

Price of violin c. 20.000 Kč.

Domenicus Busan
Venetus fecit
anno 1746.
Domenicus Busan
fecit Venetiis 1761.

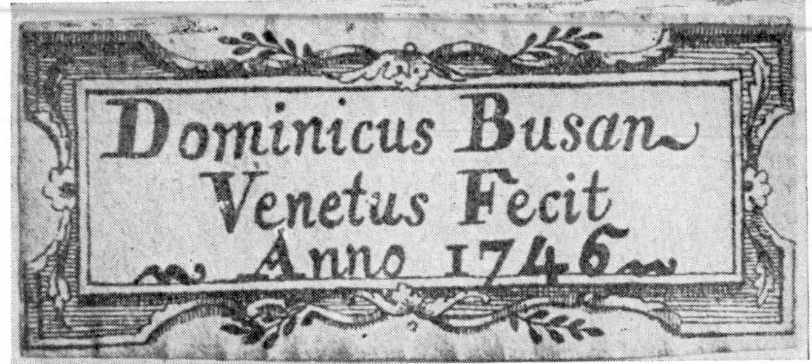

Buseto Giovanni Maria del, Cremona, Brescia, 1640—1681. He is often said, by mistake, to have lived from 1540—1580.

Built mostly instruments of large shape with rather high arching on the pattern of G. P. Maggini. The wood, particularly that of the belly, is not always of best quality, sound-holes open at the top. Applied dark-yellow or brown varnish. Large-shaped and high arched violins of powerful, yet hollow tone. Rare instruments, only a few survive. Price 25—35.000 Kč. Collectors, however, pay still more.

Gio. Maria del Busetto
fece in Cremona. 1660

Buti Antonio, Albano, Archi. 1756. Violin maker from Albano. Little known.

Antonio Buti d'Albano Archi
Fece l'anno 1756.

C

Cabroli Lorenzo, Milan. 1716—1720. Built violins of average quality, applied, however, excellent yellow or orange varnish. Price 12.000 Kč.

Cacchioni e Figli, Rome, 1920.

Caeste Gaetano, Cremona. 1660—1689. Mere name.

Perhaps a member of the Costa family.

Caesto (Caesta) Pietro Antonio della. Treviso. 1660—1680. He worked after Amati's medium and large models.

Caffarata Luigi. 1850. Known by a guitar with the following label:

Luigi Caffarata 1850

Caimi Arturo, Milan. Died ca 1935. Violin maker who made mainly guitars.

Caistemel Paolo, Cremona. 1763. He worked after Stradivari and Amati.

Calabri Pier Vittorio di, Ferrara. 1549—1551. Musician who also made lyres.

Calace Antonio, Naples. B. 1828, d. ca 1875. Maker of guitars and mandolins.

Antonio Calace
Fabbricante di chitare
Strada Mezzo—Canone No 32.

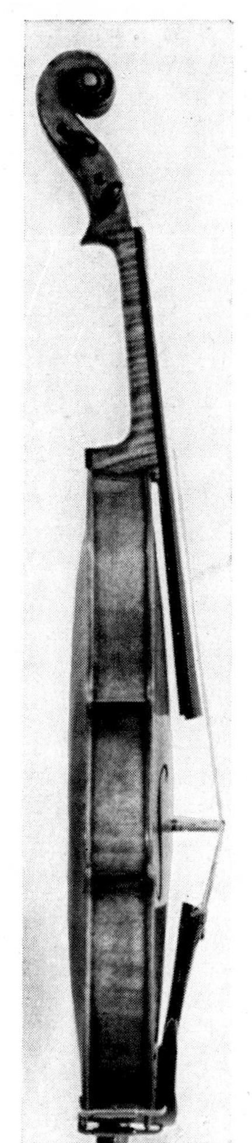
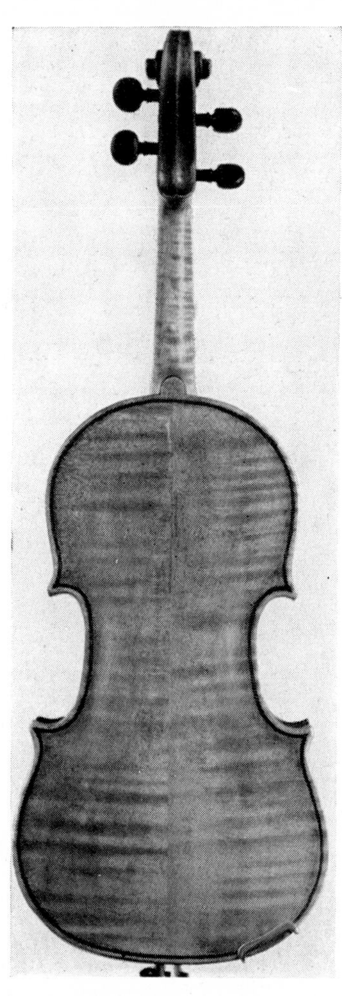

29. Balestrieri Tomasso, Mantova 1762

30. Balestrieri Tomasso, Mantova 1763
Photo Hamma & Co

31. Balestrieri Tomasso, Mantova 1764

32. Balestrieri Tomasso, Mantova 1765

33. Balestrieri Tomasso, Mantova 1770

34. Balestrieri Tomasso, Mantova 17..

35. Balestrieri Tomasso, Mantova 1795
Photo Hamma & Co

36. Barbieri Paolo de, Genova 1948

37. Barbieri Paolo de, Genova 1948 (VIOLA)
Photo Hamma & Co

38. Barbieri Paolo de, Genova 1948 (CELLO)

39. Bellone Antonio, Milano 1693 (CELLO)

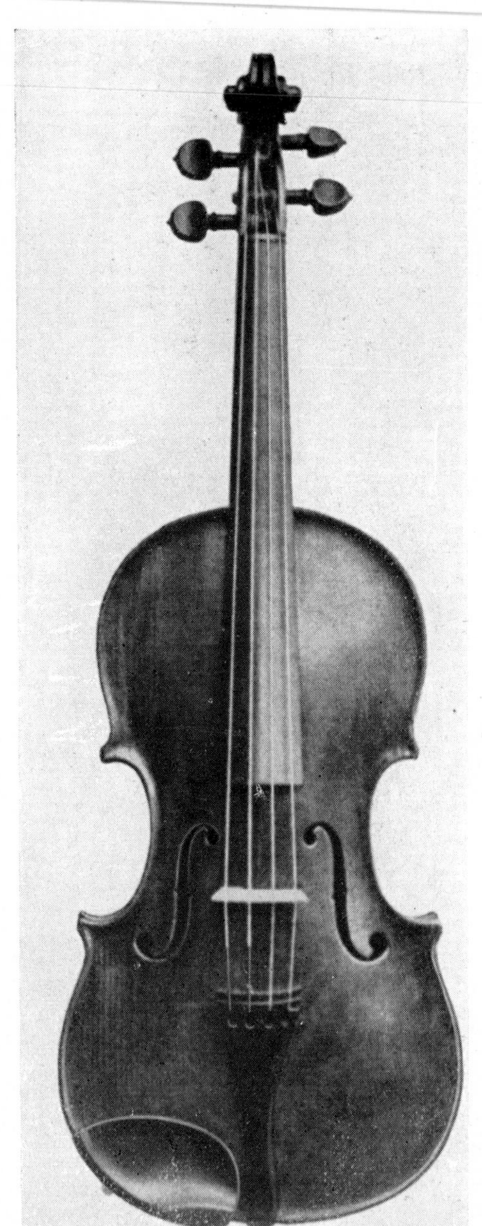

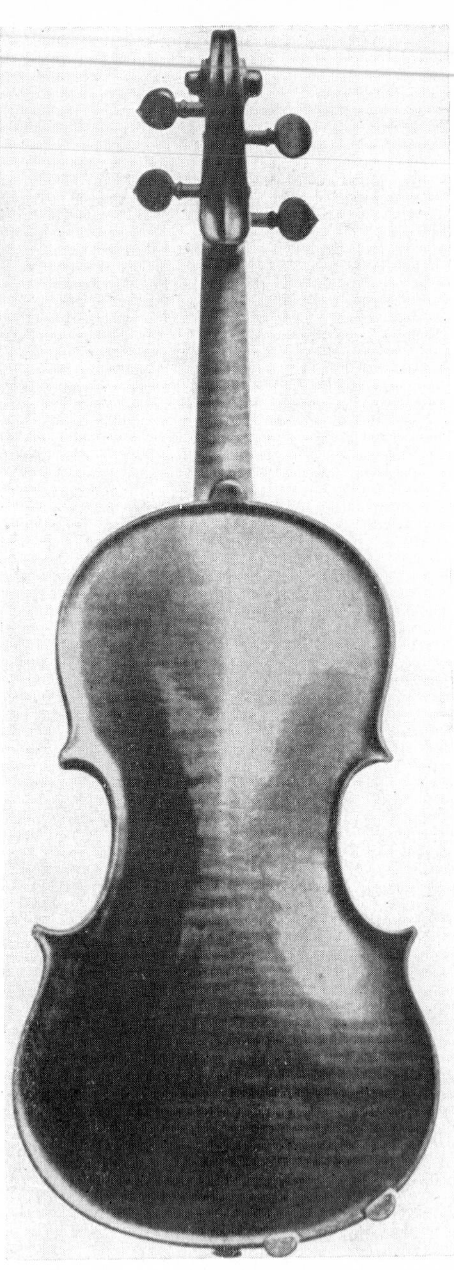

40. Bellosio Anselmo, Venezia 1780

41. Bergonzi Carlo, Cremona 1737

42. Bergonzi Carlo, Cremona 17 . .

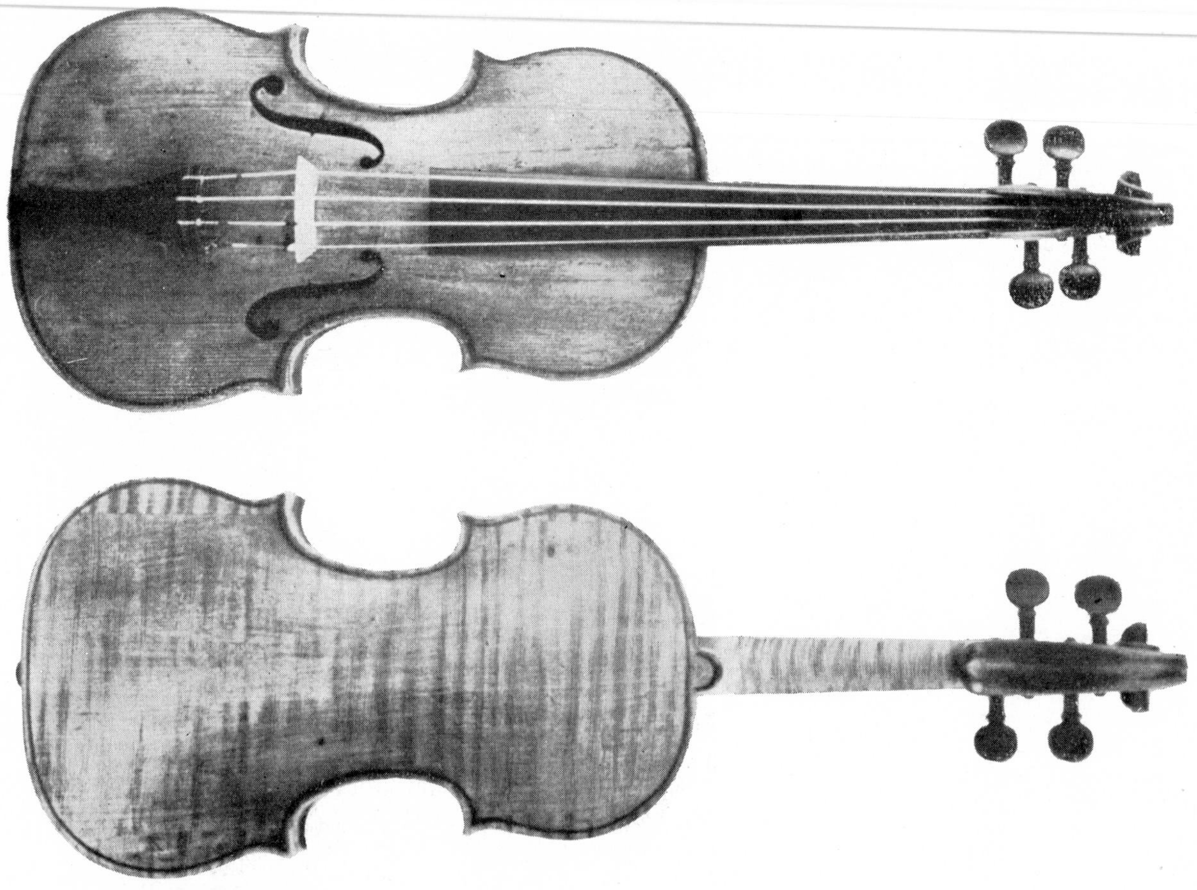

43. Bergonzi Carlo, Cremona 1722

44. Bergonzi Carlo, Cremona 1733

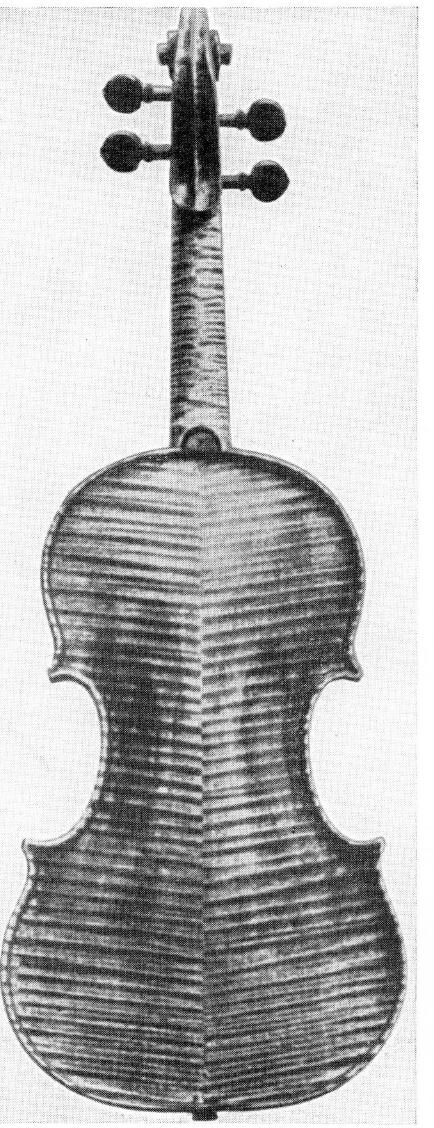

45. Bergonzi Carlo, Cremona 1742

46. Bergonzi Carlo, Cremona 1740

47. Bergonzi Carlo, Cremona 1723
Photo Hamma & Co

48. Bergonzi Michelangelo, Cremona 1732

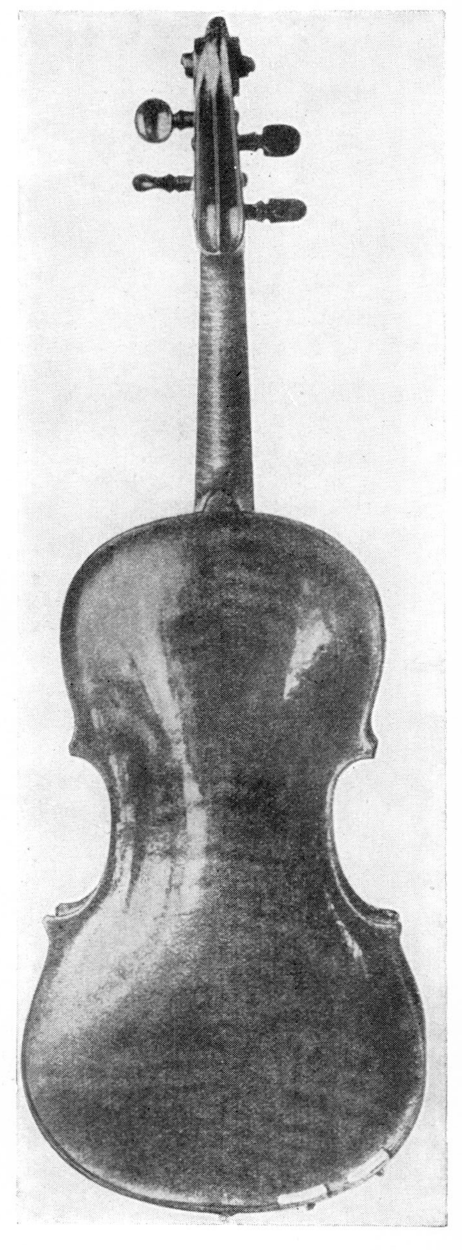

49. Bergonzi Nicolo, Cremona 178.

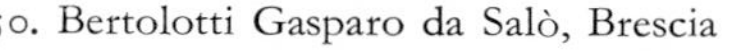

50. Bertolotti Gasparo da Salò, Brescia

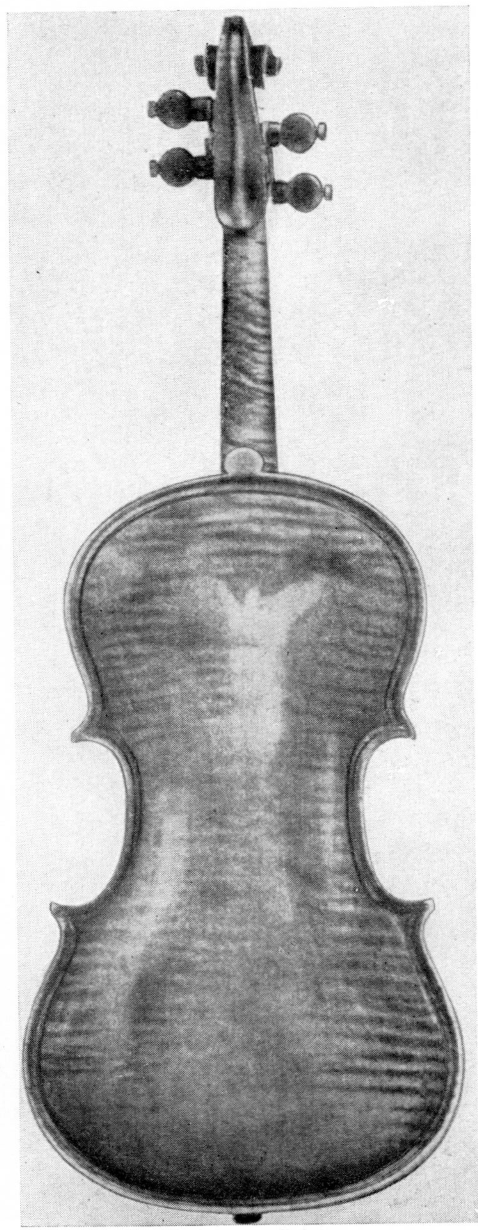

51. Bertolotti Gasparo da Salò, Brescia

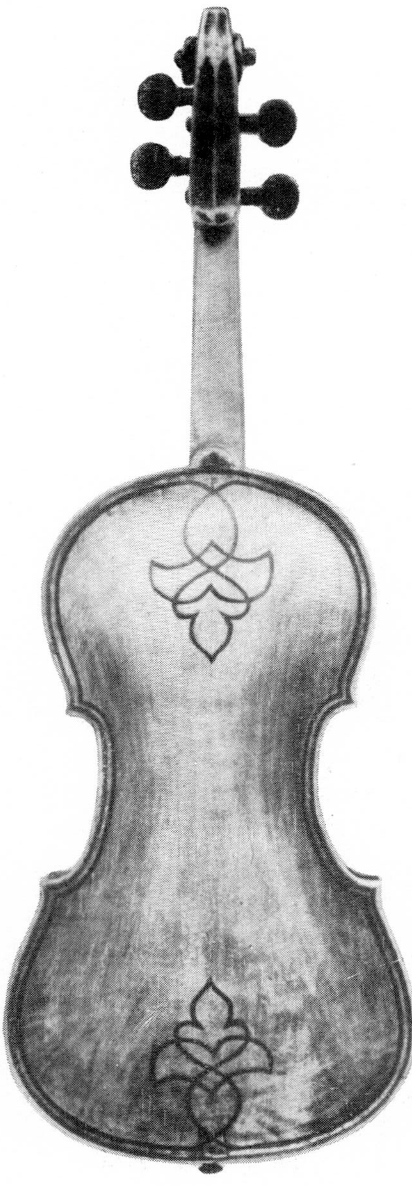

52. Bertolotti Gasparo da Salò, Brescia
Photo Hamma & Co

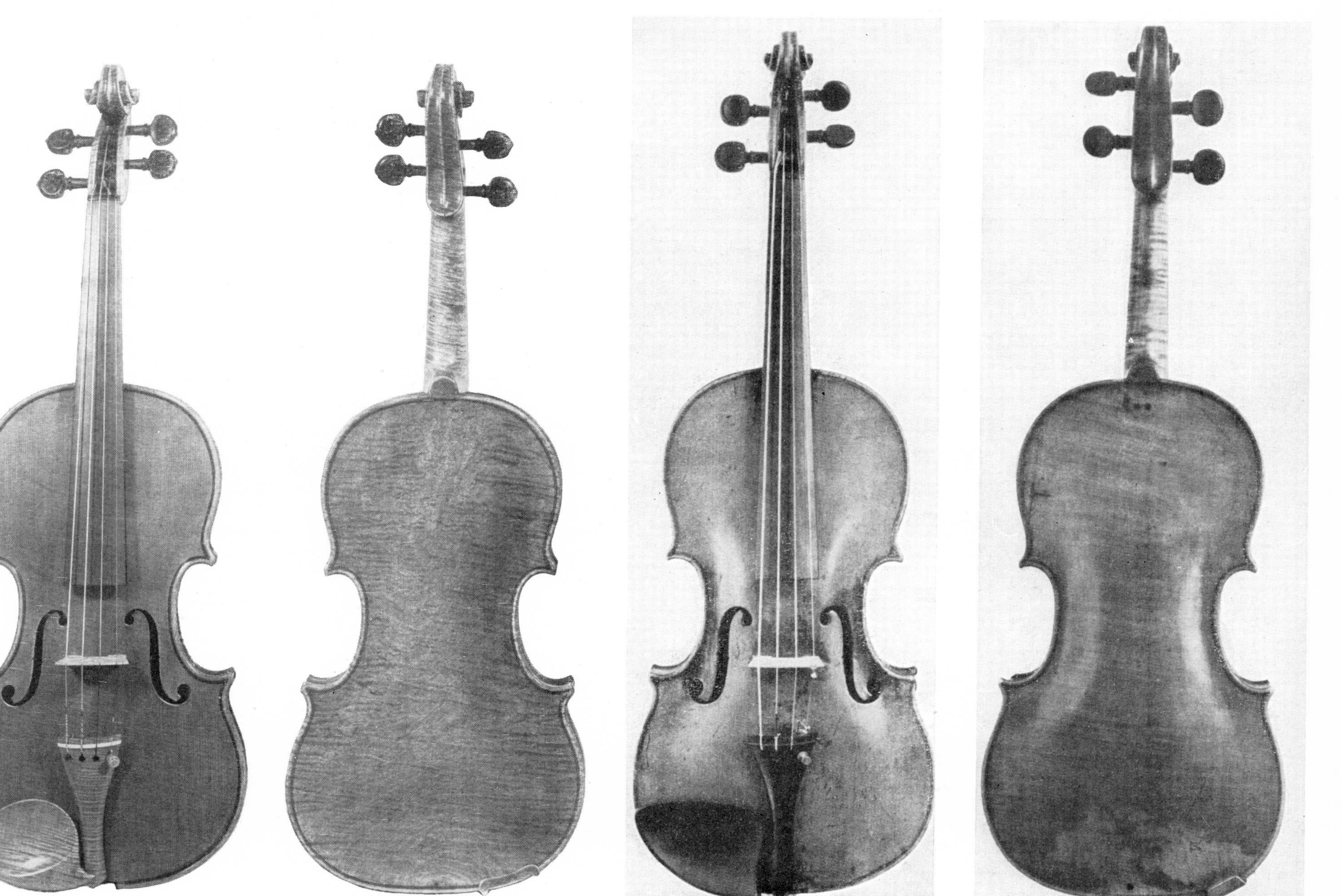

53. Bisiach Carlo, Firenze 1949

54. Brandini Jacopo, Pisa 1797

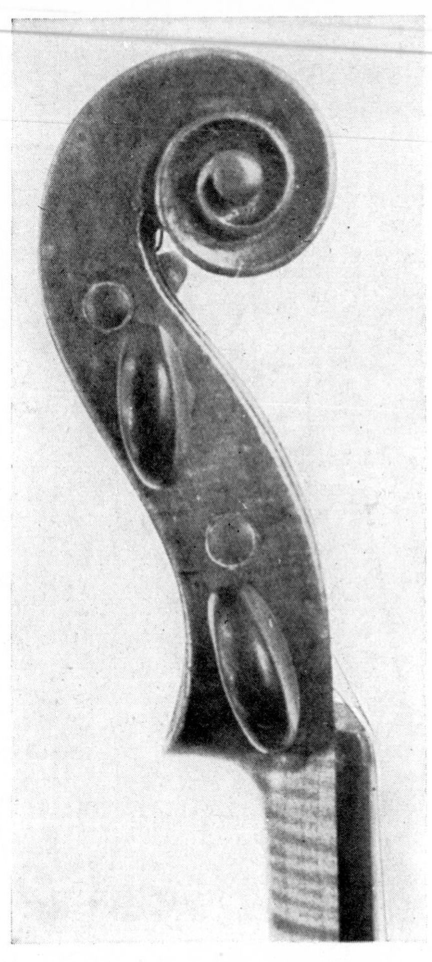

55. Brandini Jacopo, Pisa 1797

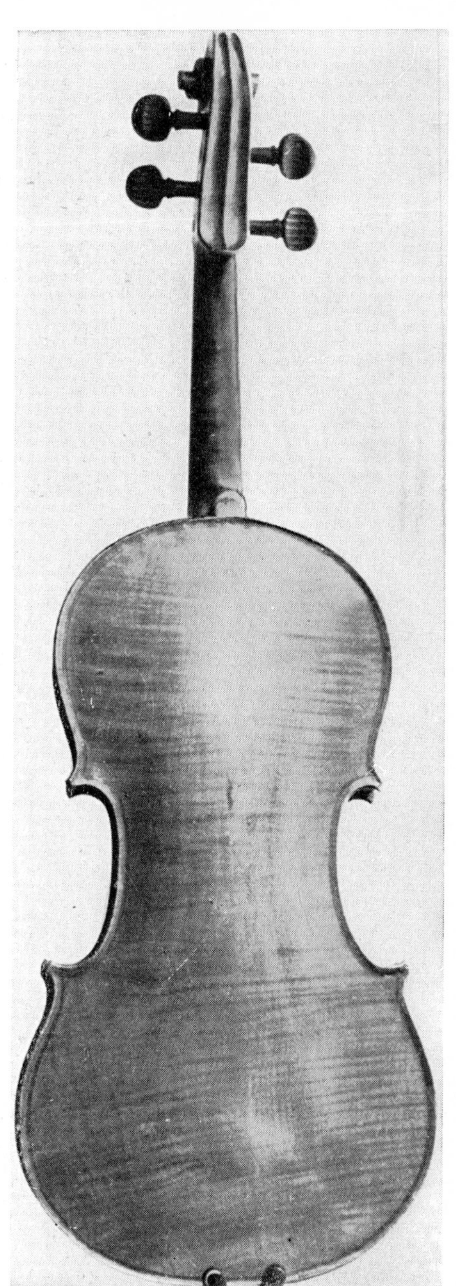

56. Bruno Carlo, Torino 1901

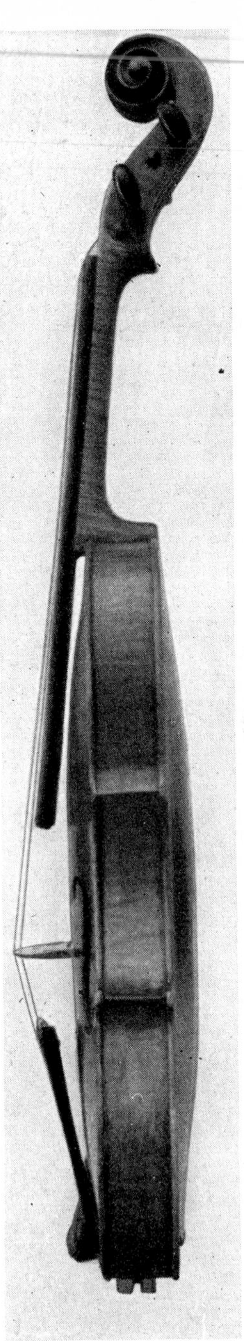
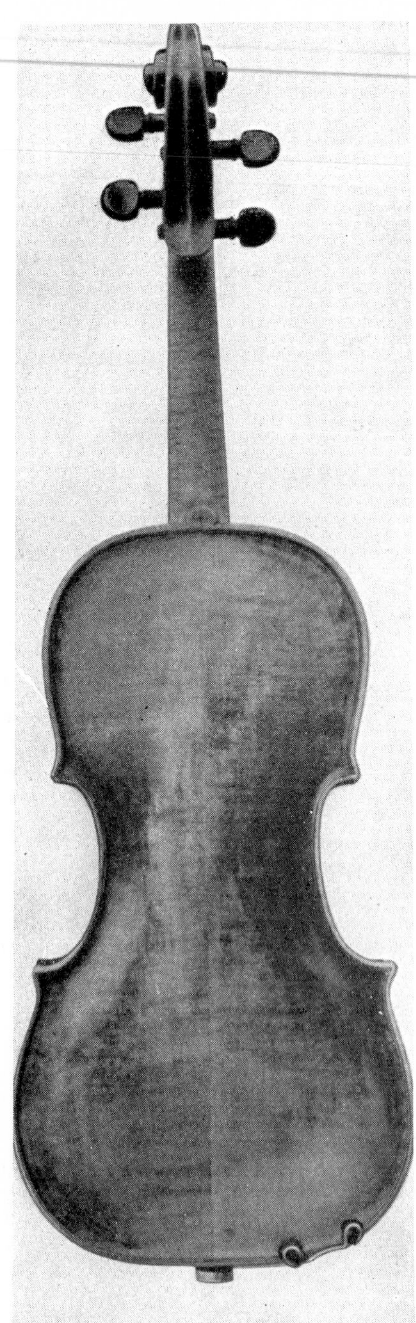

57. Busan Domenico, Vicenza

58. Calcagni Bernardo, Genova 1738

59. Calcagni Bernardo, Genova 1738

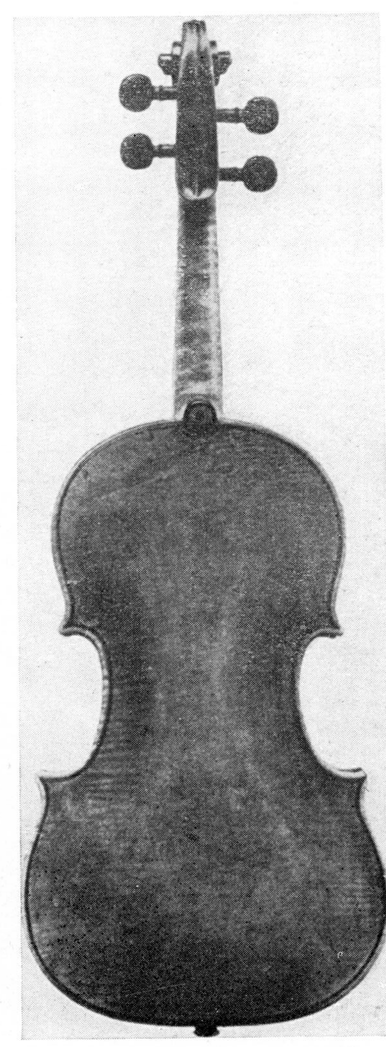

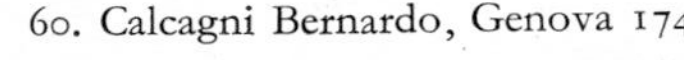

60. Calcagni Bernardo, Genova 1744

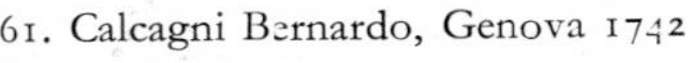

61. Calcagni Bernardo, Genova 1742

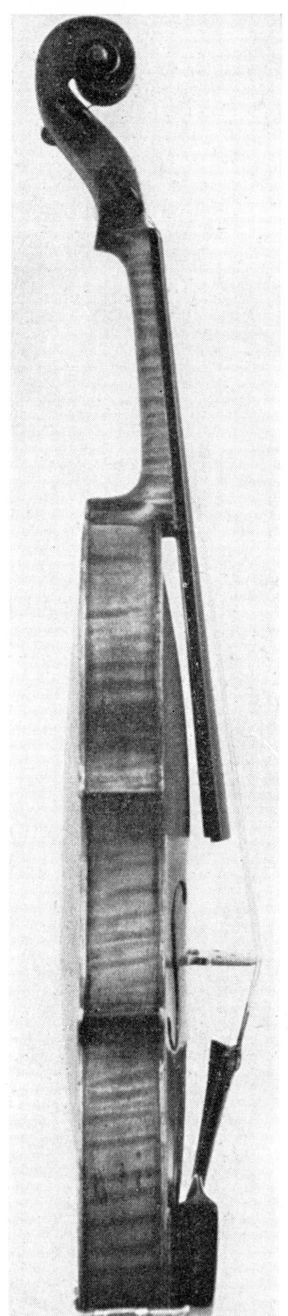
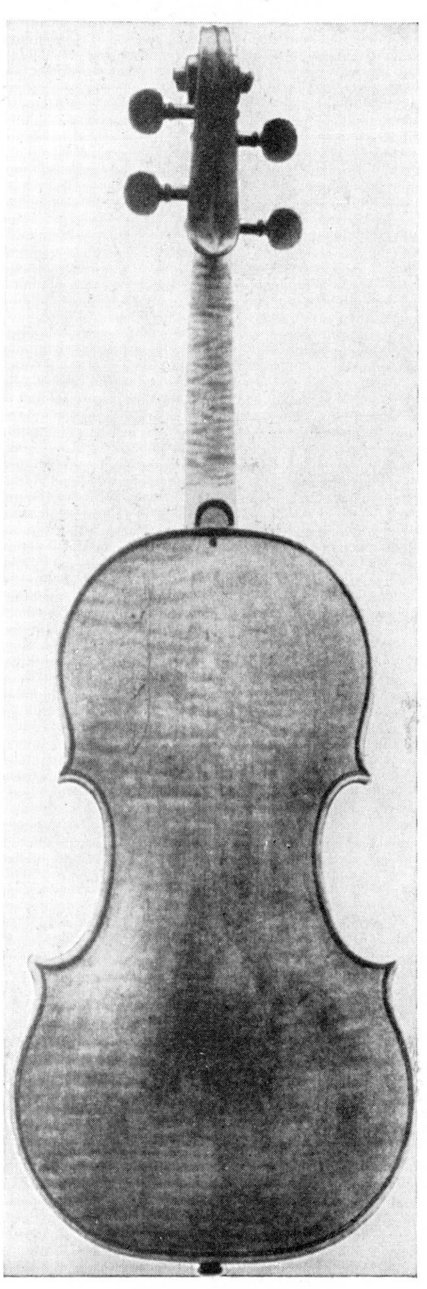
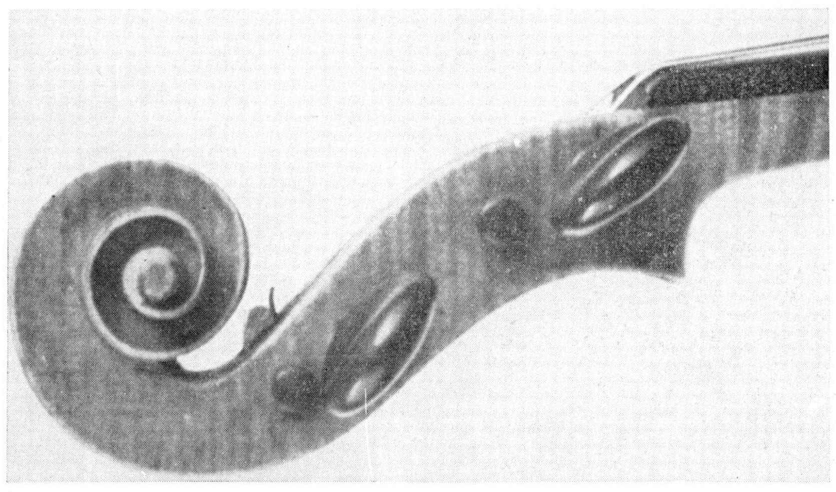

62. Camilli Camillus, Mantova

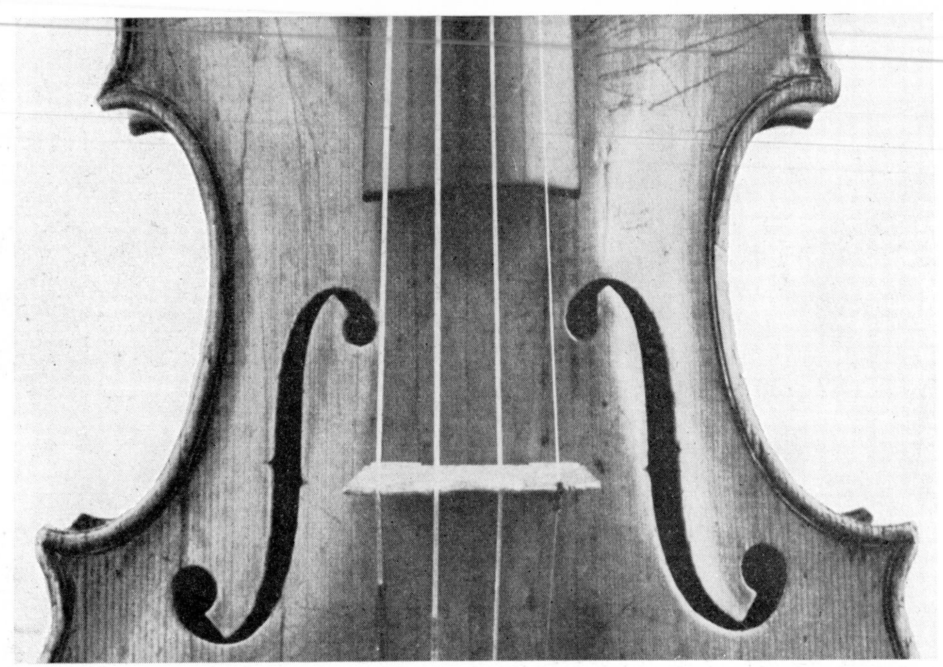

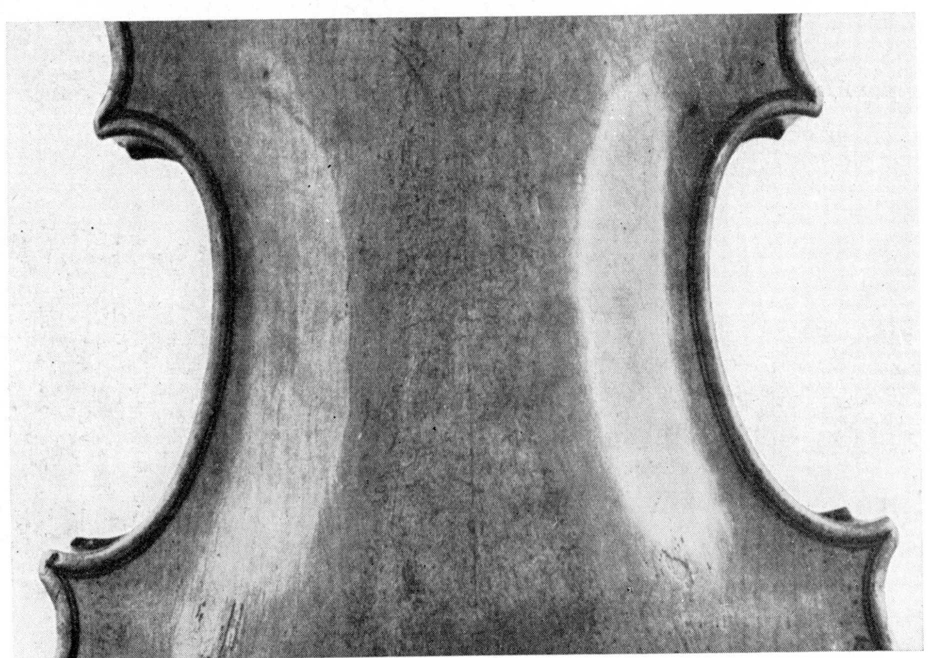

63. Camilli Camillus, Mantova

64. Camilli Camillus, Mantova

65. Cappa Jofredus, Saluzzio 1692

66. Carcassi Tomasso, Firenze 1771

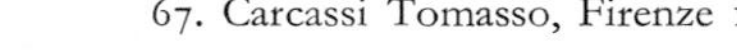

67. Carcassi Tomasso, Firenze 1754

68. Carletti Natale, Pive di Cento
(VIOLA D'AMORE)

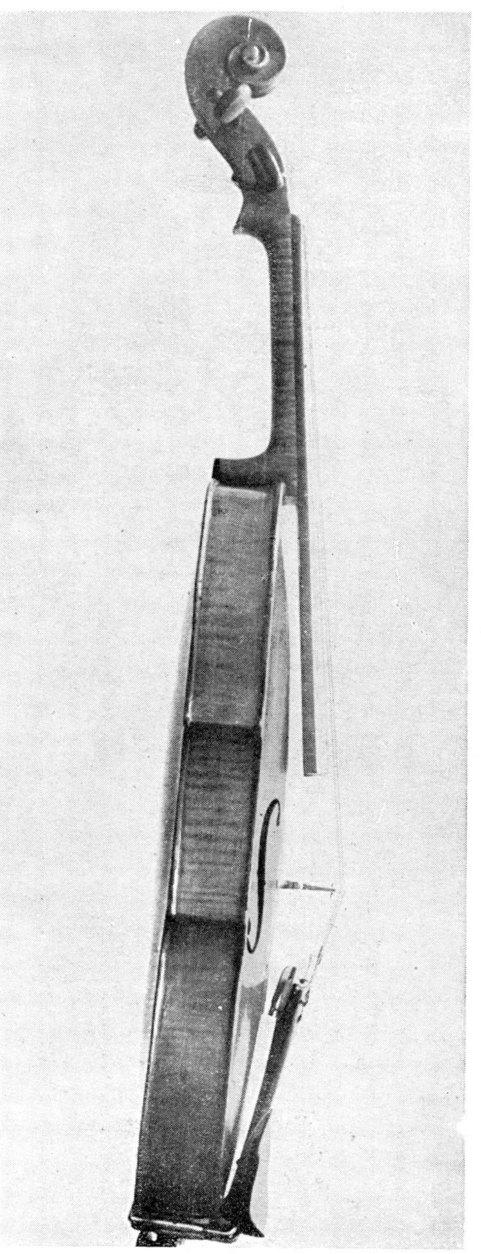

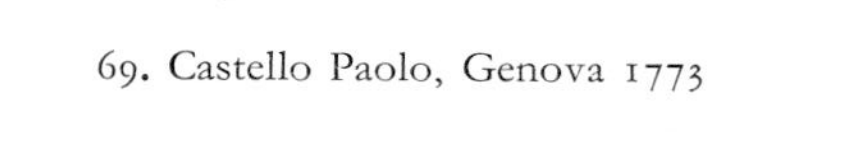

69. Castello Paolo, Genova 1773

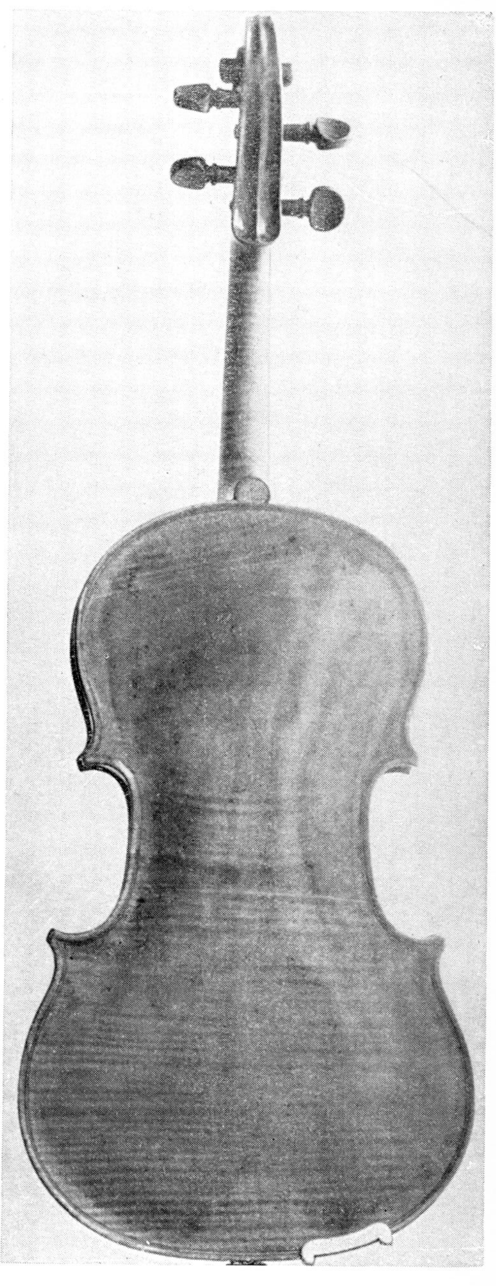

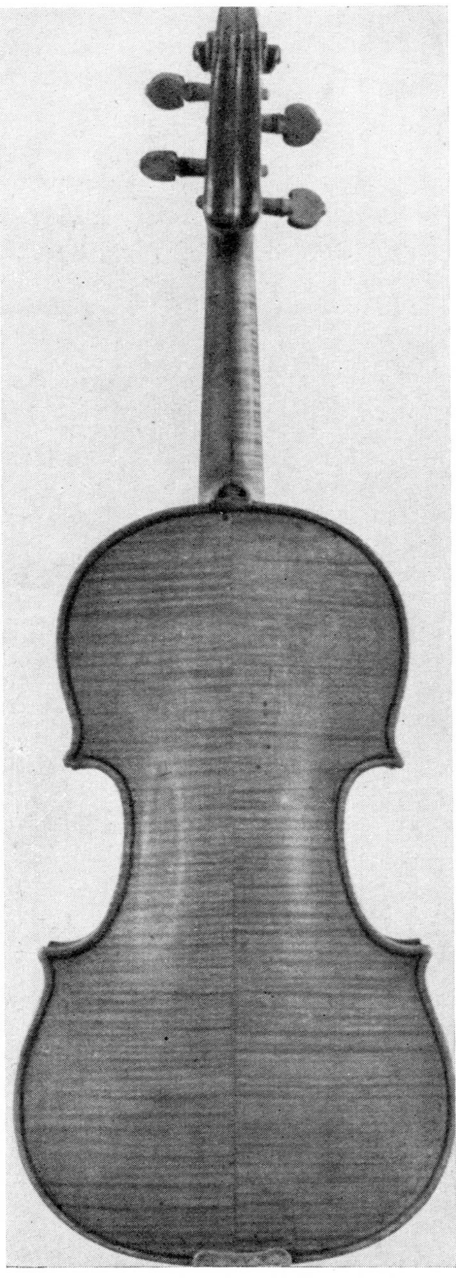

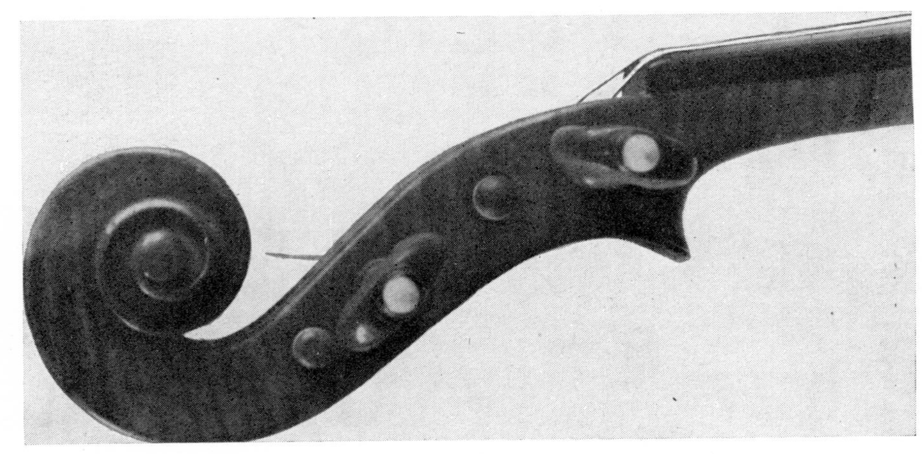

70. Celoniatus Joan Francesco, Torino 1735

71. Celoniatus Joan Francesco, Torino 1729
Photo Hamma & Co

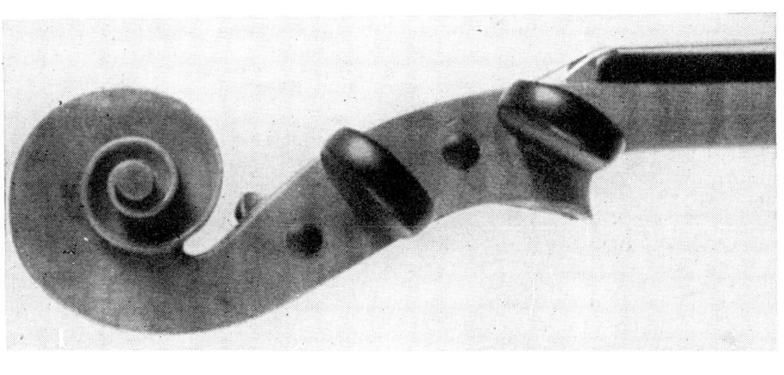

72. Ceruti Enrico, Cremona 1852

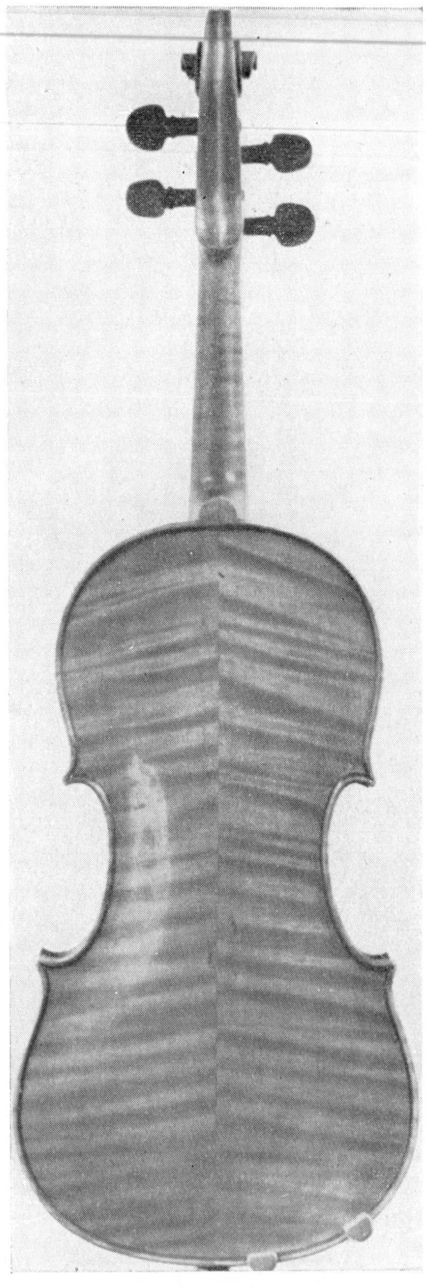

73. Ceruti Enrico, Cremona 1852

Cavalli Savino, Cremona. Born 1830 in Cremona. Was already dead in 1861. Organist, violinist and violin-maker. The finish and the tone of his instruments are good.

Cavallini Luigi. Born 1831. Died 1903, Arezzo and his son Oreste (1868—1938) specialized in double-basses and made improvements to them. They lived at Arezzo.

Cavallini Luigi & Figlio, Arezzo. 20th century producers of various musical instruments.

Cavalorio. Genoa. 1725.

Cavallini Giovanni, Arezzo. B. Aug. 13, 1851, d. June 21, 1936. Skilful violin maker.

Cavanni Giovanni, Spilamberto (Modena). B. Aug. 13, 1851, d. June 21, 1936. Successful violin maker who preferred the model of Guarneri del Gesù; was aided by his son (after 1950) and signed then Giovanni Cavanni & Figlio.

Cavanni Vincenzo, Spilamberto (Modena), son and pupil of Giovanni Cavanni, b. Nov. 8, 1889, exhibited a violin and a 'cello at Cremona in 1937. He imitated the forms and colours of Pietro Guarneri I.

Cavani Vincenzo
da Spilamberto Modena
Fece Anno 19..

Cavani Vincenzo a. del. p. Giovanni
Fece in Spilamberto A. 19..

Cavazza Sandro (Alessandro), Ravena. Born 1903. Amateur violin-maker who used red varnish.

Cecco Christoforo, Venice. 1654. Lute-maker. Tyrolese school, yellow-brown varnish.

Celani Emilio, surnamed "il Turco", Ascoli, Piceno. B. July 4, 1866, d. July 18, 1898. Skilled craftsman who made good repairs.

Emilio Celani
detto il Turco
Fece in Ascoli Piceno
1889.

Restaurato da Emilio
Celani

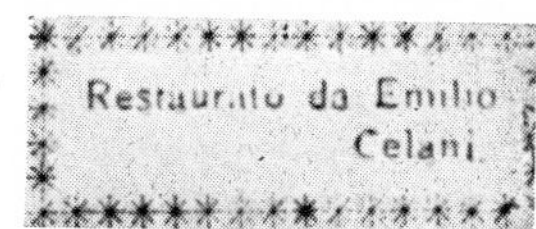

Celani Constantino, Ascoli. B. Apr. 15, 1869. Brother of Emilio Celani, productive and successful master, also teacher at a school of violin making.

Constantinus Celanius
Emidii frater vulgo il Turco
Asculi in Piceno fecit An 19..

Celani Costantino
fece in Ascoli Piceno 1900

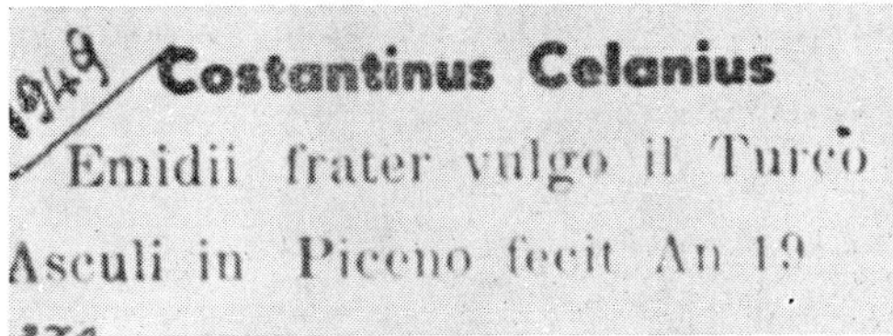

Celani Luigi, Ascoli Piceno. 1890—1896.

Celentano Michael, Naples. Mandolin maker.

Cellini Giovanni, Florence. Born 1460, died 1527 or 1528 in Budapest. Built violas, lutes and harps.

Celoniatus Gian Francesco, Turin (1725—1742, date of birth unknown). Pupil of Goffredo Cappa from whom he took over the Amati-like outline. His archings are, however, lower, the edges flat. Good workmanship. He was at the same time influenced by Carlo Bergonzi, e. g., in his gracefully cut sound-holes. The scrolls are carved with much taste and remind us of Stradivari. Praised for his lustrous, transparent varnish of fine quality, golden-yellow or golden-brown. Outstanding both for beauty and tone are his 'cellos (one of them was sold as early as 1905 for 4000 K of old Austro-Hungarian currency). Hamma does not praise the tone of his violins; the typical specimen on our picture has, however, a sweet and carrying, though not a very powerful tone. Price 32—50.000 Kč.

Joannes Franciscus Celionatus fecit
Taurini anno Domini 1737.

Joannes Franciſcus Celoniatus
ſecit Taurini Anno 1734

Ioannes Franciscus Celoniatus
fecit Taurini Anno 1735

Centurio Giuseppe, Padova. 1750—1784. Worked on Amati's pattern.

Jos. Centurio Tirburtinus f. in
Padua 1780.

Cerin Marco, Venice. 1610. Lute maker who also made mandolins.

Marco Cerin fece in Venezia 1610.

Cerini Marco Antonio, Venice. 1780—1824. Pupil of Anselmo Bellosio; worked on Stradivari's model, often also on the grand pattern of N. Amati. Careful workmanship. He applied a beautiful light-yellow or reddish varnish. Some of his instruments bear Deconetti's or Bellosio's labels. Price 30—40.000 Kč.

Marcus, Antonius, Cerin, Alumnus
Anselmii, Belosii, Fecit Venetiæ An. 1794

Ceruti Carlo, Turin. 1886. Son and pupil of Giuseppe Ceruti. He worked after the Cremonese school and used yellow-brown varnish.

Ceruti Enrico, Cremona. Born 1808, d. Oct. 20, 1883. Son of Giuseppe Ceruti. He seems to have been a pupil of Giambattista Ceruti, for he worked on the latter's pattern. During his life-time he built 400 violins, all of good workmanship. He applied amber-yellow varnish; his instruments have characteristic full edges. Price 25.000 Kč. at least. (The first violin maker of the family Ceruti was Sebastian who worked as early as 1617. But after him there is a break of almost 150 years. There may have been men during this period whose works have not come down to us under their own names. Giovanni Battista Ceruti, who lived already in Cremona (1755—1817), was the father of Giuseppe (1787—1860) and grandfather of Enrico (1808—1883) who also stayed at Cremona.)

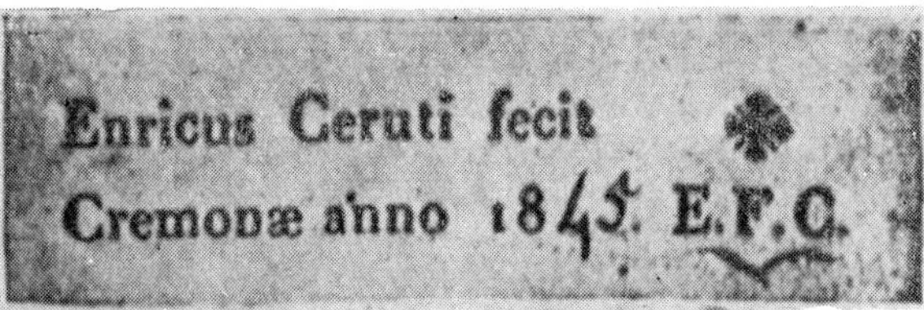
Enricus Ceruti fecit
Cremonæ anno 1845 E. F. C.

Enricus Ceruti fecit
Cremonæ anno 1870 E. F. C.

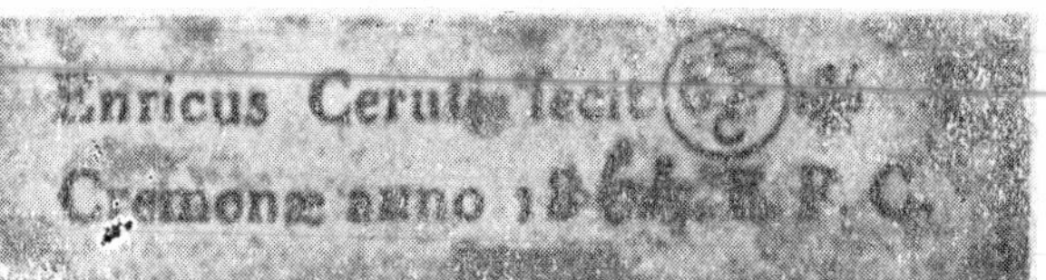
Enricus Ceruti fecit
Cremonæ anno 1864 E. F. C.

Ceruti Giovanni Battista, Cremona. Born 1755, dead after 1817. Pupil of Lorenzo Storioni and after 1790 his successor. Worked on the patterns of Stradivari, Guarneri del Gesù and Nic. Amati (large model), but also on a pattern of his own. His instruments are carefully built of well selected wood, usually coated with varnish varying from light agatine yellow to dark red. Very good tone. It is his peculiarity that the belly is sometimes darker than the back. The best instruments of his making are his cellos. Price 30—40.000 Kč, 'cello more.

Jo: Baptista Ceruti Cremonensis
fecit Cremonæ An. 1804 GB C

Ceruti Giuseppe, Cremona. Born about 1787, died 1860. Son, perhaps also pupil and successor, of Giovanni Battista Cerutti. His work is very similar to that of his father, differing in one respect: Giuseppe made somewhat broader edges and purflings. The scrolls and sound-holes are gracefully cut. His best instruments bear besides a label the brand G. C. They are highly valued. He was renowned for the splendid way he repaired instruments by old masters.

Josephus Cerutti filius Joanis Baptista
Cremonensis fecit anno 1830.

Joseph Ceruti filius Joannis Baptistae
Cremonensis fecit anno 1844 G. C.

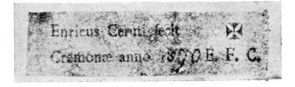

Joseph Ceruti filius Joannis Baptistæ
Cremonensis fecit anno 1844 GC

Ceruti Sebastiano, Piedmont. 1615—1630. Lute maker. Place and works unknown.

Cervo Giovanni, S. Angelo. 1489. Ancient lute maker.

Cesarano Ernesto e figlio. Rome. ? Mainly mandolins; violins and violoncellos are rarer.

Chatelin Adrien-Benoist, Valence. 1757—1759. Made beautiful violas.

Fait par Adrien Benoit
Chatelin a Valenciene
1758 (written)

Chely Francesco, Venice. 1742—1753. Worked after Stradivari and used golden-yellow and golden-red varnish.

Chelz Stephan, Rome. Ca 1602. Lute-maker.

Chericoni Carlo, Pisa Lodi, Massa. 1935. Bank clerk who made violins using golden-yellow varnish.

Cheron David. ? 19th century.

Chiaraffa Guglielmo, Rome. 1900.

Chiarelli Andrea, Messina. Born at Messina about 1675, died 1699. Lute maker and virtuoso on the archilute. He was also a composer. Worked in the style of G. P. Maggini. His violins have a double purfling like those by Maggini. He applied a deep red varnish. Price 15.000 Kč.

Chiarellino Francesco, Genoa. 1855—1890. Flat model, golden-yellow varnish.

Chiareschi Paolino del, Bagno. Ca 1827, built good instruments.

Chiari Francesco, Villa Minozza (Modena). 1880, 1883. A violin maker who also did very good repairing work.

Chiavellati Domenico, Lonigo. Ca 1780—1796. Built good violins and violas. Price 12.000 Kč.

Dom^co^ Chiavellati
Fece
L'anno 1796
In Lonigo.

Chiericato Luigi, Venice. 1912. He made violins, violas, double-basses.

Chiocchi Antonio, Venice. 1770—1790. He used brown varnish.

Chiocchi Gaetano, Padua. Born Jan. 13, 1814 at Moselici near Padua, died after 1880. He applied himself more to repairs, which he executed in a masterly way, than to the building of new instruments. During his lifetime he made only about fifty violins.

Chiocchi Gaetano fece in Padova 1866.

Chiochini Pietro, Pisa. 1740—1760. Second-class instruments, although he used fine wood.

Chiodi Giambattista, Florence. 19th century. Worked on the model and in the style of Lorenzo Carcassi.

Chisole Antonio (di), Roveredo. 1775—1786. Built mostly double-basses in the style of the Tyrolese school. Red-brown varnish.

Antonius de Cchisolis
fecit 1784.

Antonius de Cchisolis
facebat Boboreti.. Opus II.

Christophorio Pietro. 1780—1800. Used red varnish.

Cianchi Sebestiano di Rocco, Florence. 1662. Violin and lute maker, son of a Rocco Cianchi.

Cianibri Gaetano, Ascoli. After 1818 built good 'cellos and contrabasses of small size, using yellow and orange varnish.

Gajetanus Cianibri
Asculanus fecit anno Domini 1818.

Ciarma Domenico, Ascoli. B. 1836. D. Feb. 17, 1889. A self-taught maker, followed Stradivari, but made also guitars and mandolins; reputed for his 3/4 contrabasses.

Ciarma Francesco, called "Nicchito", Ascoli. 19th century.

Ciarma Nazzareno, Ascoli. B. Apr. 26, 1879. D. 1915. Was son and pupil of Domenico, and made the same kind of instruments.

Ciarma Nazzareno fece in Ascoli nel 1906.

Cicognani Umberto, Lucca. 1945. He studied violin at the Milan Conservatoire. Amateur violin-maker.

Cigarini Artemio, Cavriago. Born 1923. He established himself in 1945. Pupil of Fernando Soncini.

Cimapane Simone, Rome. 1690—1700. He made mainly violoncellos which were very good.

Cinino Angelo, Vittoria (Ragusa). 1900.

Cinquegrandi Luigi, Rome. 19th cent.

Cinquegrani Ercole, Rome. 1882. Mandolin maker.

Cinti Giuseppe, Bologna. 1856. Very good repairer of instruments.

Ciochi Antonio, Venice 1790.

Antonio Ciochi di Venezia
anno 1790.

Ciocchi Gaetano. 1836.

Cioni Emilio, Mont' Orso (Frignano). 1884—1894. Assiduous disciple of R. Fiorini.

Ciotti Leone, Siena. 1889.

Circapa Tommaso, Naples. 1730—1735. Worked on the pattern of Alessandro Gagliano. Instruments of his hand are good; he applied orange-yellow varnish. Price 20.000 Kč.

Circapa Tomaso fecit Neap. 1733.

Cirilli Giovanni, Tolentino (Macerata). 1925—1945.

Citared Francesco Urbinas, Cisterna. 16th century. Quoted, but unknown.

Clementi Pietro, Cremona. 1678. Instruments of small pattern, yellow varnish.

Cliricato Luigi, Venice. 1899. Pupil of E. Degani.

Cocks Christoforo, Venice. 1654. Good lute maker.

Christofer Cocks All' insegna
Dell' Aquila d'Oro
Venetiae 1654.

Colombo Camillo, Milan, Viale Col di Lana 13. Exhibited two violins at Cremona in 1937.

Colonardi Marco, Cremona. 17th century. Mere name.

Comel Stefano, Gorizia, Via Scuola Agraria 7. Born 1890. Exhibited two violins, made after Stradivari, at Cremona in 1937.

Compare Vittorio, Livorno (Leghorn). 1898. Mandolin maker.

Compostano Antonio, Milan. 1699—1710. Worked carefully. His instruments, resembling those by Giovanni Bapt. Grancino, have often been sold as genuine Grancinos.

The gracefully carved scrolls are rather large, the sound-holes of beautiful shape and well cut. He selected fine wood, only the maple seems not to have been well seasoned, for it shows signs of warping. The tone of his instruments is rich. He built violins, violas and contrabasses and labelled them with written or printed labels. Price 25—35.000 Kč. Möckel quotes only half the price.

Antonio Compostano fece in Milano in
contrada Larga 17..
Antonio Compostano Fece in Contrada-Larga
Milano 1799.

Comuni Antonio, Piacenza. 1820—1823. Worked on the pattern of J. B. Guadagnini II.

ANTONIUS COMUNI
fecit Placentiae Anno 1820

Consili Giovanni, Terni. 1825—1835. Probably an experimenting amateur.

Giovanni Consigli a Terni inventò
la nuova forma del Violino
per eseguirvi con maggior faci-
lità e sicurezza la difficoltà
nelle portamenti acuti op. quart.
A. 1829.

Joannes Consili
fecit Interamnae
Anno D^ni 1828.

Contavalli Luigi, Imola. Born at Imola Oct. 24, 1862 D. Nov. 6, 1954. Built instruments of his own model, resembling those of Stradivari. Applied a clear golden-yellow or yellow varnish. His instruments are of careful workmanship and have a mellow, yet sometimes nasal tone. For his finish, pleasing to the eye, he was awarded several prizes of distinction.

Contavalli Primo di Luigi, Imola, Via Valsalva 13. Born at Imola on July 26, 1899. Son and pupil of Luigi Contavalli. Worked on the model of Stradivari, but made the sound-holes in the style of Guarneri. Contavalli junior's instruments are free from the nasal and metal timbre of the instruments built by his father. By his experiments he also improved the quality of varnish. He exhibited two violins, two violas and a 'cello at Cremona in 1937.

Conte Giacomo, Turin. 1906—1915.

Contegiacomo Giovanni, Turin, beginning of the 20th century. Manufacturer of musical instruments.

Conti Luigi, Florence. B. Feb. 17, 1891. Died June 10, 1957. Was a piano tuner, later also violin maker and indulged in naïve experiments.

Contino Alfredo, Naples. Born Feb. 2, 1890. The only pupil and successor of Vincenzo Postiglione who, like his teacher, imitated old masters in an excellent way and with particularly delicate taste. He applied golden-yellow or red oil varnish. Many prizes of distinction and diplomas were conferred upon him for his careful workmanship.

ALFREDO CONTINO
allievo di V. Postiglione
Napoli, anno 1914

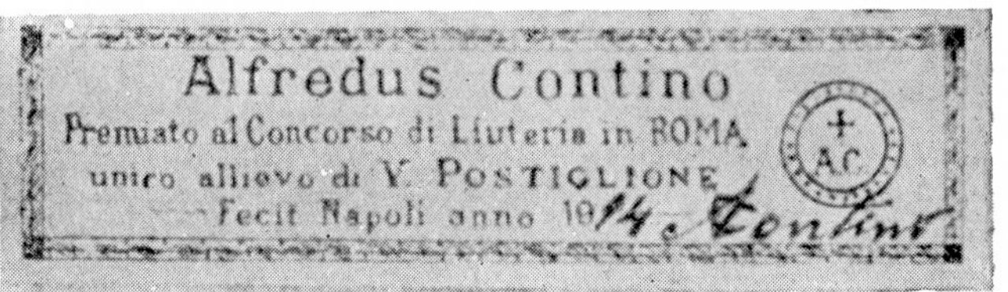

Coppi Sante de, Mantova. 1800—1817. He worked after Alessandro Zanti and his violins have good tone.

Sanctus de Coppi fecit
Mantoae Anno 1815.

Coppo Armando, Naples. 1608. Good lute maker.

Coppo Raffaele, Naples, 1909. Was disciple of Antonio II Gagliano.

Corani Vincenzo, Terst. 1815—1850.

Corara Giacomo, Venice. 1775. Violin maker who built instruments of medium quality.

Giacome Corara
fecit in Aug^o 1775
Venezia No 3

Corbucci Domenico, Venice. 1775.

Cordano Giacomo Filippo, Genoa. 1750—1780. Worked on the grand pattern of Amati, made rather high archings according to Francesco Ruggeri and short sound-holes in the style of Stainer. All his instruments possess gracefully finished purflings, narrow edges and large scrolls of delicate cut. He applied good orange, or brown-red varnish. Instruments built on the Amati model are better in tone. Price 20.000 Kč at least.

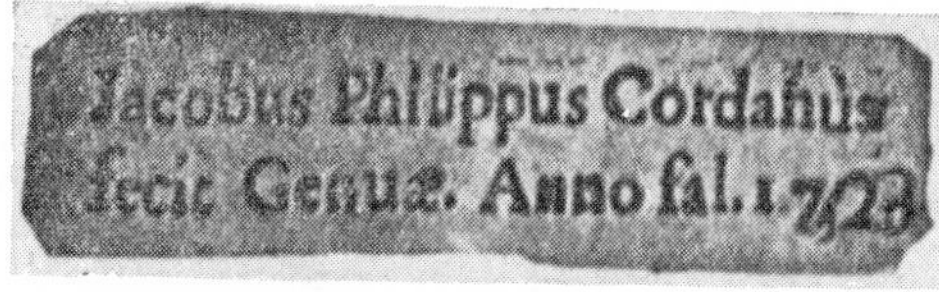

Iacobus Philippus Cordanus
fecit Genuæ. Anno sal. 1774

Cordano Pietro, Venice. 1913.

Corna Giovanni Giacomo dalla . . . — See Dalla Corna.

Cornelli Carlo, Cremona. 1702. Price 15.000 Kč. Little known.

Carolus Cornelli fecit
Cremonae anno 1702.

Cornelli Giorgio, Venice. 1797. Skilled violin maker who built instruments of low arching. Applied a wonderful red varnish. Price according to the merits of the specimen.

Cornia Giuseppe, Iddiano (Modena). 1884—1894. Built good contrabasses.

Cornino, Spilamberto (Modena). 1800—1820.

Corradotti Luigi, Rome. 19th century. Violin maker who also devoted himself to mandolin making.

Corsi Giuseppe, Rome. Born 1876, died 1931. He studied double-bass at the Rome Conservatoire and later was a member of various orchestras. He modelled his work on Januarius Gagliano. His violoncellos and double-basses have personal traits.

Giuseppe Corsi fece in Roma
Anno 1900 No. .

Corsini Giorgio, Rome. Born July 21, 1913 in Tivoli. He studied violin at the Santa Cecilia Conservatoire in Rome. He devoted himself to violin-making at the instigation of Rodolfo Fredi of Rome. He worked after Stradivari and used golden-red or crimson varnish, both alcohol and oil. He also won distinction at the International Exhibition in Cremona in 1937 and is known for his excellent repairs.

GIORGIO CORSINI
ROMA 1949

Corsini Pietro, Arcidosso (Toscana) Made harps (1652); hardly a violin maker.

Arcidosso
L'ANNO 1652
Pietro Corsini
Fece.

Cortaro Antonio, Rome. 1614.

Cortese Andrea, Genoa. Born 1889. A skilful master, admirer of Pressenda's style and tone, followed this master's example. Used red and golden-yellow varnish.

Andrea Cortese all insegna dei
tre conti in Genova 19. .

Cortesi Carlo, Pesare. 1612. Built violins of full arching in the style of Gasparo da Salò, Mariani and Maggini. Price 15.000 Kč, tolerably preserved specimens even more.

Carlo Cortesi.

Cosetto Giuseppe, Venice. 1760—1790. Large pattern instruments of carefully selected wood, worked with exemplary craftsmanship; particularly remarkable for their beautiful cut are the scrolls and sound-holes. Length of violin 364 mm. The belly and back of his instruments are rather thick throughout, which makes them heavy. Price c. 20.000 Kč, at least.

Giuseppe Cosetto Fecit
anno 1786 Venezia.

Costa di, Agostino, Verona. 1600—1622. Lute maker who had come from Brescia.

Costa di Agostino di Brescia 1600.

Costa Antonio. B. Aug. 23, 1891 in Bertinoro (Forli). Worked for the most part in Forlimpopoli Capocolle. Stradivari and Guarneri patterns, yellow or golden-red varnish.

Costa Felice Mori, Parma. 1802—1812. Worked in the

style of C. F. Landolfi, but took higher archings. The distance between the upper parts of the sound-holes is smaller than that designed by Landolfi. Price 15.000 Kč., some red varnished instruments reached a price of 50.000 Kč.

Mori Costa Felice di Parma 1802.

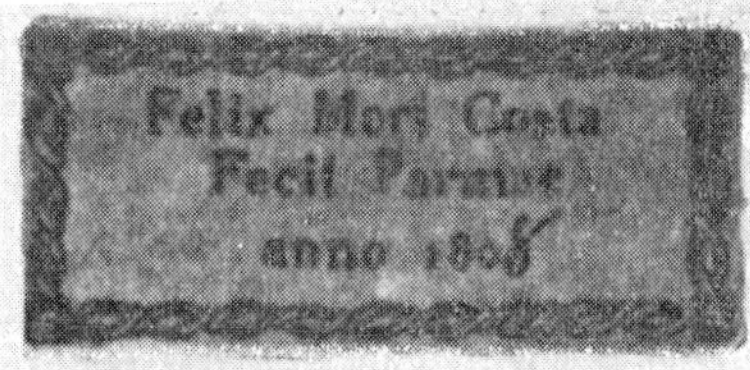

Costa Giovanni Baptista, Venice. 1765—1778. Worked in the style of Santo Seraphin (he was perhaps the latter's pupil) and on the pattern of Stainer. Instruments of his making are of a rather high and full arching, careful finish and good smooth tone. Price of violin 25—80.000 Kč.

Costa Lodovico, Urbino. 1786. Little known.

Coste Alfonso della, Naples. 1876. Built excellent 'cellos.

Coti David, Florence. 19th cent.

Cotugno Giovanni, Ancona, Via Duomo 3. Born 1894 in Pizzo Calabro. Exhibited a violin, a viola, a violoncello and a stringed quartet at Cremona in 1937.

Covi Francesco, Cavareno (Trento). Born May 10, 1870 in Ceio (Trento), died Sept. 20, 1957.

Cozzi Battista, Venice 19th century. Devoted himself mostly to repairs.

Craile (also Grail) Magno, Rome. B. ca 1572, d. Feb. 22, 1642. Was famous for his lutes which are now cherished relics. Probably a native of Augsburg.

Craile Pietro (Peter), Rome. Born 1617. D. Apr. 14, 1649. Son and helper of Magno Craile.

Cricca Alfonso, Ferrara. 1591. Organ-builder who constructed also lutes.

Cricca Giulio, Ferrara, 1594. Brother of Alfonso.

Cristofaro E. de, Naples, Paris. Born Feb. 11, 1870. Built excellent mandolins.

Fabbricazione Artista
di Mandolini e Mandole Napoletani con nuovo
sistema triplicando la sonorità. E. de Cristofaro
199 bis Via Mergellina Napoli. Vendita e deposito
a Paris.

Cristofori Bartolomeo, Florence. Born about 1667 in Padua, died in Florence after 1731. From his thirteenth year he was a pupil of Nic. Amati. In Florence there was a beautiful contrabass of his making, and in Munich a 'cello dated 1716. Rare—the collector's price is high.

Bartolomeo Cristofori Firenze 1715.

Cristoni Eusebio, Modena. 1847—1883. He worked after the Cremonese school.

Cruciani Vincenzo, Monte Vidon Combatte. 1848. Amateur violin-maker.

Crugrossi Vincenzo, Florence. 1767.

Curatoli Alfredo, Naples since 1885. Producer of guitars and mandolins.

Curatoli Antonio, Naples. Ca 1900. Son and partner of Alfredo Curatoli, manufactured guitars and mandolins.

Curletto Anselmo, Turin. B. 1888 in the same city. Probably pupil of Enrico Marchetti in Turin, copied Pressenda, applying red varnish.

CURLETTO ANSELMO
PREMIATO IN ESPOSIZIONE E CONCORSI C. A.
FECE IN TORINO ANNO 1947 T

Cutugno Giovanni, Ancona and San Benedetto (Ascoli). B. June 2, 1894 in Calabria, followed Stradivari and Guarneri del Gesù; varnish (oil almost always) yellow or red.

D

Dagli Instrumenti Marco (i. e. Marco, the instrument maker, or M. in charge of instruments). Ca. 1541. Was in the service of Alfonso d'Este in Ferrara.

Dal Canto Giusto. Castelfranco di Sotto (Pisa). Born 1902. He was born in France. He made violins, violoncellos and guitars.

Dal Chitarrino Biagio, Ferrara. 1464—1467. Known as a good lute player in 1445—1446, later as a lute maker. Works lost.

Dalla Corna Giovan Giacomo, Brescia. Born about 1484, died after 1548. Son of Giovan Maria dalla Corna.

Dalla Corte Alfonso, Naples. 1828—1882. Built instruments in the style of Nicolo Gagliano, with lower archings, wide edges and scrolls, which are not always well carved. He applied a varnish of various shades, mostly lemon-coloured. Price c. 25.000 Kč.

Dalla Costa Marco, Treviso. 1640—1680. He worked after the Amati Brothers and used orange varnish. Only a three-string pochette made by him survives.

Dalla Costa Pietro Antonio, Treviso, Mantua, Venice. 1700—1768. Worked on the models of Stradivari and Nic. Amati. Valuable instruments, made of beautiful wood, good workmanship. Golden-yellow, red-brown or dark-red varnish. Price 60—80.000 Kč.

Cremonenses Filii Andrae Tarvisii Anno 1757
Petrus Antonius a Costa fecit
Tarvisii, anno 1740.

Petrus Antonius a Costa fecit ad
Similitudinem illorum quos fecerant Antonius
& Hieronymus Fraters Amati.
Petrus Antonius a Costa
fecit Tarvisii, anno 17..

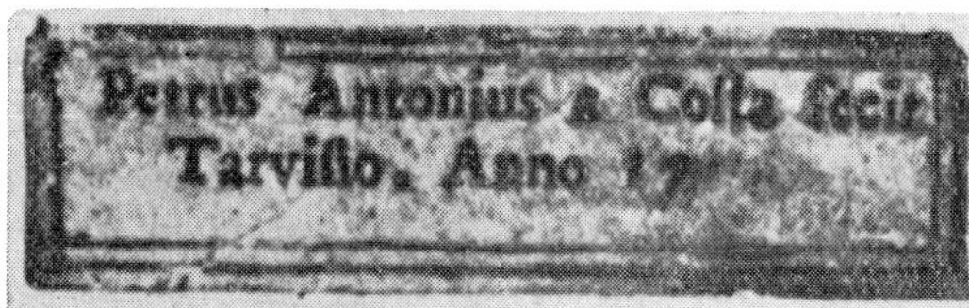
Petrus Antonius a Costa fecit
Tarvisio, Anno 17..

Pietro Antonio dalla Costa
fece in Treviso Anno 1741

Pietro Antonio dalla Costa
fece in Treviso Anno 1760
Ad exemplar Antonii & Hieronymi
Amati Cremonensis

Dall Aglio Giuseppe I, Manova. 1723—1775. Probably father of Joseph Dall Aglio II. He used brown varnish.

Giuseppe dall' Aglio
Fecit Mantue 1723

Dall Aglio Giuseppe II., Mantua. 1795—1840. Violin maker who worked in the style of Camilli and Pietro Guarneri. His activity belongs to the end of the 18th and the early part of the 19th century. He made instruments with a higher arching, worked conscientiously and applied a wonderful yellow varnish. His cellos are excellent. Value 16—24.000 Kč.

Joseph dall' Aglio fecit
Mantua, anno 17..

JOSEPH DALL' AGLIO FECIT
Mantuæ anno 1814

JOSEPH DALL' AGLIO FECIT
Mantuæ anno 1800.

JOSEPH DALAGLIO
FECIT IN MANTUÆ
Anno 1823

JOSEPH DALAGLIO
FECIT IN MANTUÆ
Anno 1826

Dalla Porta Marc Antonio, Venice. 1601. Good lute maker.

Marc Antoniuo dalla Porta
in Venecia MDCI.

Dalle Molle Gregorio, Genoa, Rome. Born 1876 in Venice. He worked as an artistic cabinet-maker in ebony and was only an amateur violin-maker.

Dall' Hocha Casparo, Ferrara. 1568.

Dall' Oglio Domenico, Padua. Born 1700, died 1765 in the town of Narva. Good violin and lute maker. Used handsome wood, his varnish, however, was not of desirable quality. He died on his way back from Russia to Padua.

Dall' Ongaro Ignazio, Venice. 1747—1783. Indifferent violin maker. Price 10.000 Kč.

Dall' Osso Umberto, Bologna. B. 1888. Opened his shop at Bologna in 1920 and specialized in guitars.

D'Ambrosio Antonio, Naples. 1817. Made guitars and mandolins.

Antonio d'Ambrosio in Napoli Anno 1817.

D'Amelio Teresa, Rome, Piazza Prati Strozzi 26. Exhibited three violins at Cremona in 1937.

Daniele, Verona. 18th century. Violin and lute maker.

Danieli Giovanni, Padua. 1745—1785. In his later years he worked jointly with Pietro Bagatella. Orange varnish. Price ca 10.000 Kč.

Danieli et Bagatella
fecerunt Patavii Anno 17..

Joannes Danieli fece Patavii
1745.

Danota Giovanni Battista, Cremona. 1710—1735. He worked after Alessandro Gagliano and used golden-yellow varnish.

Dardelli Fra Pietro, Mantua. 1497—1500. A Franciscan friar who worked with fine craftsmanship. Instruments made by him are excellent. Violins are not reported.

Padre Dardelli 1497.

Dario de Vectoriis, Firenzuolo (Florence). Born 1903 Pupil of Primo Contavalli. He worked after Stradivari and Guarneri.

Darrini Antonio, Cremona. 1746—1757. He worked after Nicolo Amati's small model and used red-brown varnish.

D'Avenia Carlo, Naples. 1788. Pupil of Alessandro Gagliano. Skilful mandolin maker. Professor Dr A. Bensande of Lisbon had a 'cello by him bearing a written label.

D'Avenia L., Naples. 1888.

Davini Giusto, Lucca. 1870—1896. Little known violin maker.

De Barbieri Paolo, Genoa, Corso Buenos Aires. Exhibited two violins, a viola and a 'cello at Cremona in 1937.

De Blosij Nicolaus, Naples. 1795.

Nicolaus De Blosij
fecit Neapoli in Rua
Carolana al nummero 13. A. D. 1795.

De Bonis Alfonso, Bisignano (Cosenza). B. 1862, d. 1892. Son of Umile I.

De Bonis Antonio I, Bisignano. B. ca 1809, d. 1863. Son of Vincenzo I, guitar producer.

De Bonis Antonio II, Bisignano. Born 1874, died Sept. 8, 1950. Son and pupil of De Bonis Giacinto II.

De Bonis Domenico, Bisignano. D. 1843. Son of Giovanni Battista, worked along the same special line.

De Bonis Espedito, Bisignano. B. 1909. Brother and pupil of Nicola II, ditto.

De Bonis Francesco (I), Bisignano. B. 1850, D. 1927. Son and pupil of Antonio I, also guitar maker, fine work.

De Bonis Francesco (II), Bisignano. B. 1888. Son and pupil of Alfonso.

De Bonis Francesco (III), Bisignano. B. 1894. Son of Vincenzo II.

De Bonis Francesco (IV), Bisignano. D. 1895, son of Giacinto I, continued his father's craft.

De Bonis Giacinto (I), Bisignano. B. 1783, d. 1832. Son and pupil of Michele I, guitar and mandolin maker.

De Bonis Giacinto (II), Bisignano. B. 1836, d. 1867. Son of Antonio I, ditto.

De Bonis Giacinto III, Bisignano. B. 1882. Second son of Niccolo, continued the family tradition of guitar making.

De Bonis Giacinto IV, Bisignano. D. 1896. Son of Francesco II.

De Bonis Giovanni Battista, Bisignano. B. 1813, d. towards the end of the 19th century. Son of Giacinto I.

De Bonis Luigi, Bisignano. B. 1933. Son of Giacinto II.

De Bonis Michele (I), Bisignano. Died there at the end of the 18th century. He was a brother of Vincenzo I de Bonis.

De Bonis Michele (II), Bisignano. Son of Vincenzo I, 1825—1881, also guitar and mandolin producer.

De Bonis Michele (III), Bisignano. B. 1891. Fell in the First World War, son and pupil of Alfonso; worked for some time in the USA.

De Bonis Nicolo, Bisignano. B. 1842, d. 1895. Son and pupil of Antonio I, guitars, very careful workmanship.

De Bonis Nicola II, Bisignano. B. 1896. Fell in the war 1917, ditto.

De Bonis Nicola III, Bisignano. B. March 1, 1918. Added violins to guitar and mandolin building. Careful work.

NICOLA DE BONIS
Costruttore di Strumenti Musicali a Corde
(COSENZA) BISIGNANO

Medaglia d'oro e d'argento
da Enti dello Stato

De Bonis Pasquale (I), Bisignano. B. 1818, d. 1852. Son of Vincenzo I, also guitar producer.

De Bonis Pasquale (II), Bisignano. B. 1858, d. 1922.

De Bonis Rosario, Bisignano. B. 1876, son and pupil of Niccolò, guitar maker.

De Bonis Umile, Bisignano. B. 1828, d. 1906. Further son of Vincenzo I, also guitar and mandolin producer.

De Bonis Umile (II), Bisignano. B. 1883, d. Oct. 23, 1949. Son of Vincenzo II.

De Bonis Vincenzo (I), Bisignano. B. 1780 in Bisignano, d. 1850. Manufacturer of guitars.

De Bonis Vincenzo (II), Bisignano. B. 1855, d. 1924. Son and pupil of Michele I.

De Bonis Vincenzo (III), Bisignano. B. 1929, son of Giacinto, pupil of Nicola III de Bonis.

Decaniis Nunzio, Florence. 1789.

Deconetti Giov. Battista, Venice. 1720—1762. Worked on the pattern of Nic. Amati. Instruments with high archings.

Gio Bapt. Deconet fecit Venezia 17..

Deconetti Michele, Venice, Padua. 1752—1795. Good violin maker, perhaps a pupil of Domenico Montagnana. His examples were Stradivari and Guarneri. From 1790 on he dated his works from Padua. He built his instruments on a broad, flat and wide-edged model, using beautiful wood; particularly the wood of the belly is of excellent quality. He applied yellow-brown, red-brown and brown varnish with wonderful lustre. Price 40.000 Kč at least, outstanding specimens according to beauty.

Michiel Deconet
Fecit Venetij Anno
1786.

Michael Deconet fecit
Venetiae an. Dom. 17..

Michael Deconet fecit Venetiae
an Dom. 17..

Michele Deconet
fecit Venezia 1775.

Michiel Deconet
Fecit Padua, L'anno 1790.

Michele deconet, fecit Venezia 1775.

Michael Deconet, Fecit Anno Venetij 1786.

Michael Deconet, Fecit Venetiis 1752.

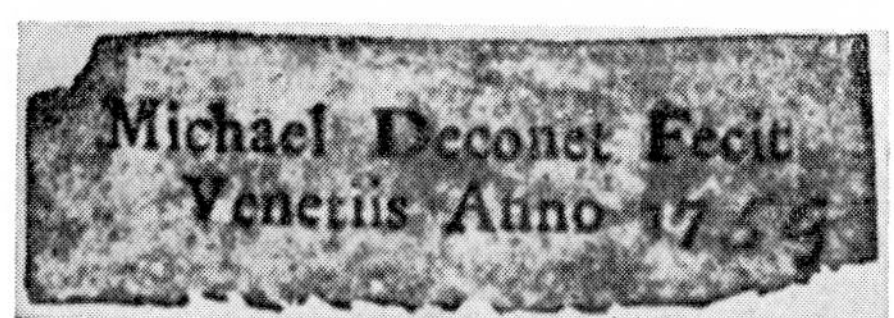
Michael Deconet Fecit
Venetiis Anno 1755

Michiel Deconet Fecit Pa
dova l'anno 1795

Michele deconet.
Venetijs Anno
1754

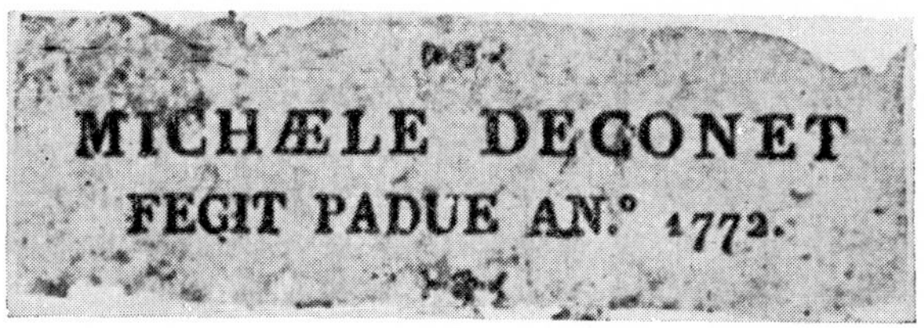
MICHÆLE DEÇONET
FEÇIT PADUE AN.° 1772.

MICAEL DECONET
Fecit Venetiis 1752

MICAEL DECONET
Fecit Venetiis 1754

Degani Domenico, Montagnana. Born about 1820, died 1887. Simple, cheap, good violins.

Degan Domenico
fecit in Maggio 18..
Montagnana.

Degani Eugenio, Venice. Born May 20, 1840 at Montagnana (Padua), died 1915. From his tenth year, he was pupil of his father, Domenico Degani. He imitated old masters in an excellent way, inserted sometimes purflings consisting of 5 and even more strips, carved good scrolls and applied a wonderful varnish. In 1898 he founded the firm of Eugenio Degani & Figlio.

EUGENIO DEGANI
Piu volte premiato
Medaglie d'ORO 18..
VENEZIA

EUGENIO DEGANI
Più volte premiato
Medaglie d'Oro 18
VENEZIA

DEGANI EUGENIO
FECE
VENEZIA - ANNO 189

Degani Giulio, Venice. Born in 1875 at Montagnana. Son of Eugenio Degani, worked on the latter's model.

DEGANI GIULIO di EUGENIO
premiato con gran diploma d'onore in Milano
e medaglia d'oro in Torino
Anno 190.
FECE IN VENEZIA

DEGANI GIULIO DI EUGENIO
premiato con gran diploma d'onore in Milano
e medaglia d'oro in Torino
Anno 190
FECE IN VENEZIA

De Giorgi Remo, Castione di Strada (Udine), Via Roma 64. B. Dec. 24, 1894. Exhibited a violin, a viola and a quartet at Cremona in 1937.

Remo De Giorgio
fecit
Castione di Strada
Anno 1947

De Esposito Lorenzo, Rome. 1920.

Del Coradel, Pesaro. 1860—1870. He used brown or red-brown varnish.

Del Fiume Fausto, Rome. 1920.

Della Nella Rafaele. See Nella.

Del Senna A., Pisa. Born 1845, died 1930. Publisher and editor of the magazine, *Il Violino*, who is also an amateur violin-maker following the Italian school.

Del Lungo Alfredo, Florence. Born 1909. Son and pupil of Giuseppe Del Lungo. Beautiful model after Cremonese school. He used orange alcohol varnish.

Del Lungo Giuseppe, Florence. Born 1883, died 1926. Pupil of Valentino de Zorzi. Best of his bowed instruments are the violas.

De Luca Antonio di Matteo, Rotello (Campobasso), Via A.

Diaz 22. Exhibited ten violins, three violas and a 'cello at the Exhibition of Cremona in 1937.

De Luccia Gennaro, Mercato Cilenico. B. Nov. 5, 1901. Violin maker: red spirit varnish.

GENNARO DE LUCCIA
FECE IN CASIGLIANO CILENTO
ITALIA AN. 1945 (SALERNO)

GENNARO DE LUCCIA
figlio di Michele
fece in MERCATO CILENTO
Anno 192.

De Luccia Matteo, Naples, Venice. B. 1819, d. 1877. Guitar maker and repairer.

De Luccia Michele (I), Naples. B. at Cassigliano 1848, d. 1924. Son and pupil of Matteo de Luccia, guitar maker.

De Luccia Michele (II), Salerno. B. Nov. 25, 1912. Son of Annibale de Luccia from Sessa Cilento, guitar maker.

Michele de Luccia
Fecit ann 1949
Italia (Salerno)

De March Carlo, Venice, Treviso. Born 1904. He established himself in Treviso, and came to Venice in 1940. He followed Eugenio Degani.

Denati (Donati) Enrico, Florence? 1705—1715. He worked after the Cremonese school and used red-brown varnish.

De Peccati Umberto, Milan, Soncino (Cremona). Born in Soncino 1878. Died 1944. Used golden-yellow varnish and exhibited a violin at Cremona in 1937.

Depine G. Modena. 1770—1780.

De Santis Giovanni, Rome. 1884—1916. He made stringed instruments and mandolins.

Desiato Giuseppe, Naples. 1890—1906. Violin maker, Stradivari and Guarneri models. Golden-yellow varnish.

Desiato Luigi. Naples. 1885. Probably father of Giuseppe Desiato.

Desiato Vincenzo, Naples 1855. Perhaps a brother of Luigi Desiato.

Desideri Antonio, Ascoli. Violins of medium quality.

Desideri Pietro Paolo, Ripa. 1793—1837. Built on the patterns of Guarneri and Guadagnini, well-shaped instruments of good tone with beautifully cut sound-holes. He applied orange or yellow-brown varnish.

Pietro Paolo Desideri
fecit Ripe 1837.

P. Paulus Desideri
Fecit Ripae 1794

Desiderio Raffaele, Ripa (Ascoli). Born 1797, d. June 16, 1871. Built good sounding violins and 'cellos besides nicely finished guitars and mandolins. Yellow varnish. Presumably son of Pietro Paolo Desideri, pupil of his father and of Eugenio Galeazzi. Price c. 10.000 Kč.

Raffaele Desideri fece a Ripae 1827.
Desideri Raffaele fece in Ascoli nel 1855.

Desideti Pietro, Riva. Little known violin maker, descending, perhaps, from the family of Raffaele Desiderio: this could be explained by a wrong reading of his name: "t" mistaken for "r".

Despine G., Modena. 1774. It has not been possible to ascertain whether there existed a violin maker of this name. Instruments labelled "Depines" seem to be fakes (see d'Espines).

G. Despine à Modène 1774.

D'Espines Alexandre, Turin. 1828—1842. Pupil of Gianfrancesco Pressenda. Worked on the pattern of Jos. Guarneri del Gesù. The instruments made by him are wide-edged and have long, rather open sound-holes. Beautiful wood and careful workmanship as well as a rich fine tone render his works increasingly popular, also as concert instruments. Varnish varies from orange to chestnut brown and is of good quality. Price 15——25.000 Kč, rising.

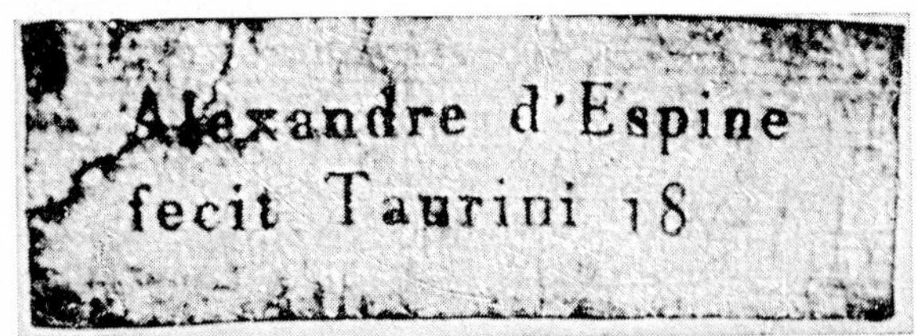
Alexandre d'Espine
fecit Taurini 18

Alessandrus d'Espine Fecit.
Taurini anno Domini 1828.

De Vitor Pietro Paolo, Brescia. 1738—1751. He worked on the pattern of Maggini, built full arched violins with narrow edges, small sound-holes, small, neatly carved scrolls and applied a wonderful red varnish. The wide-grained wood endows the high-arched violins with a deep tone. Price 20.000 Kč. and more. Rare instruments.

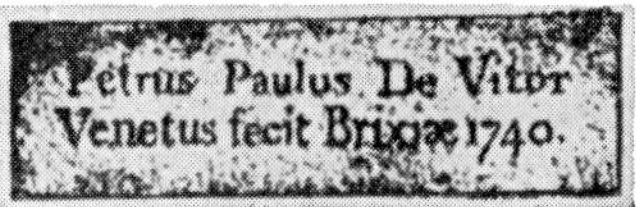
Petrus Paulus De Vitor
Venetus fecit Brixiae 1740.

De Zorzi Valentino, Florence. Born at Vittorio near Venice in 1837, died in 1916. Worked at Pistoia from 1880 till 1885, when he moved to Florence. He worked on the patterns of Stradivari and Stainer and was very diligent.

Valentius de Zorzi
Genetensi Venetum fecit
Florentiae A 1908 No 7
Credo questo sia perfezionato.

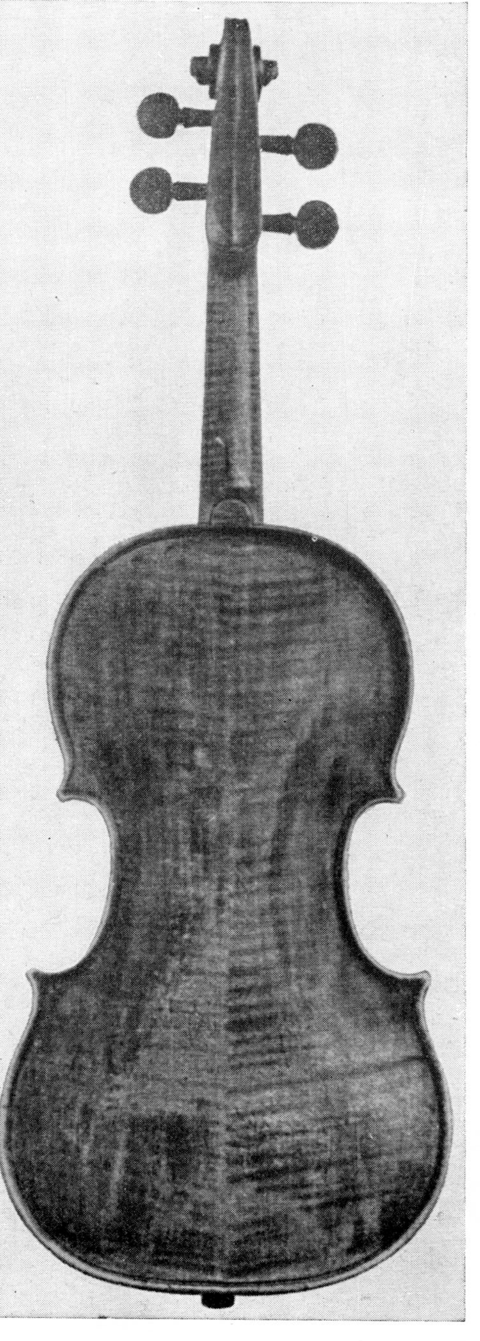

82. Dalla Costa Pietro Antonio, Treviso 1740

83. Dalla Costa Pietro Antonio, Treviso

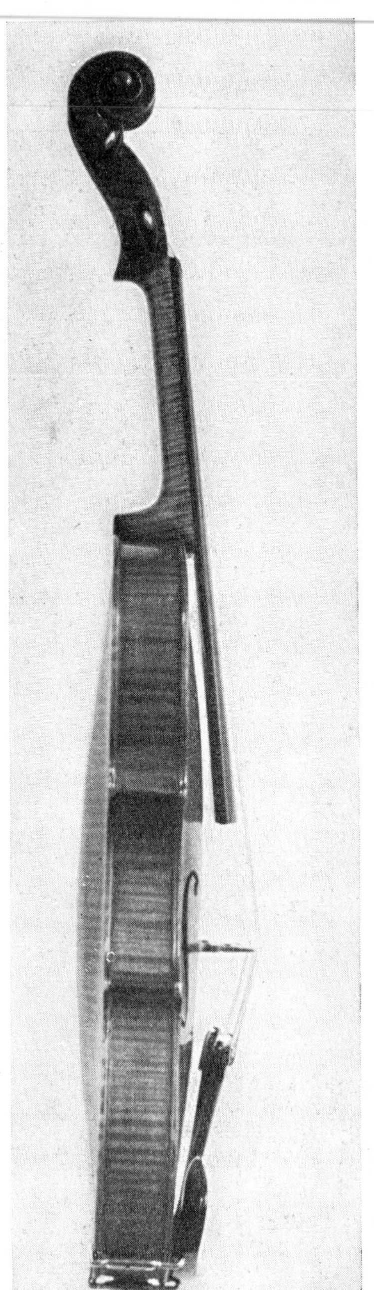
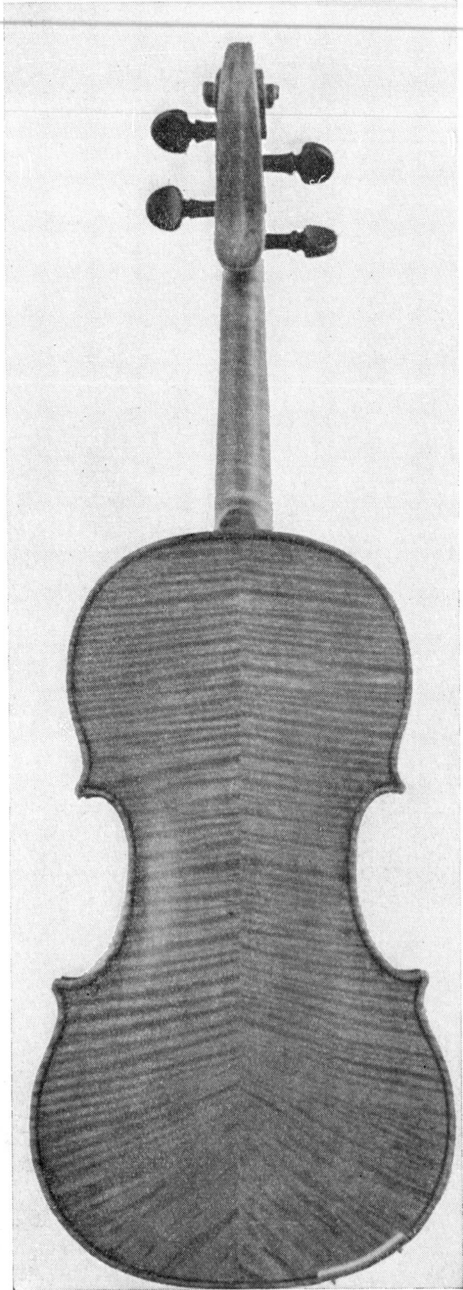

84. Deconet Michael, Venezia 1754

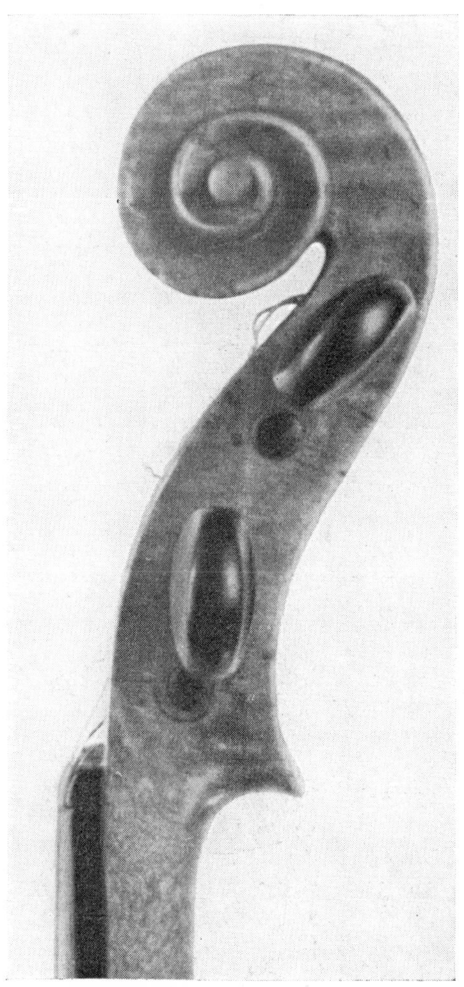

85. Deconet Michael, Venezia 1754

86. Deconet Michael, Venezia
Photo Hamma & Co

87. Deconet Michael, Venezia
Photo Hamma & Co

88. De Emiliani Francesco, Roma 1734

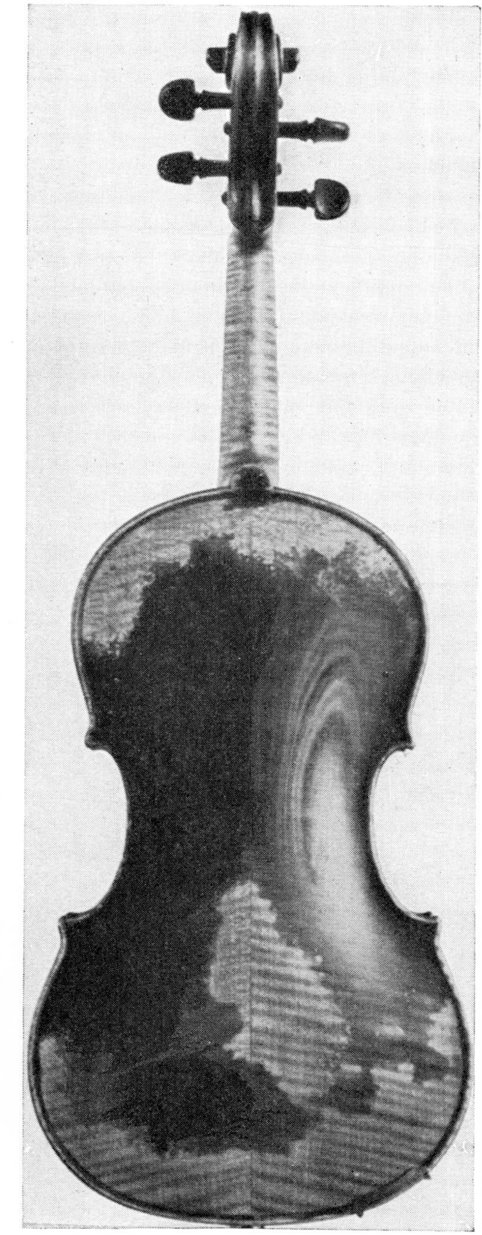

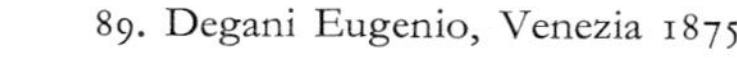

89. Degani Eugenio, Venezia 1875

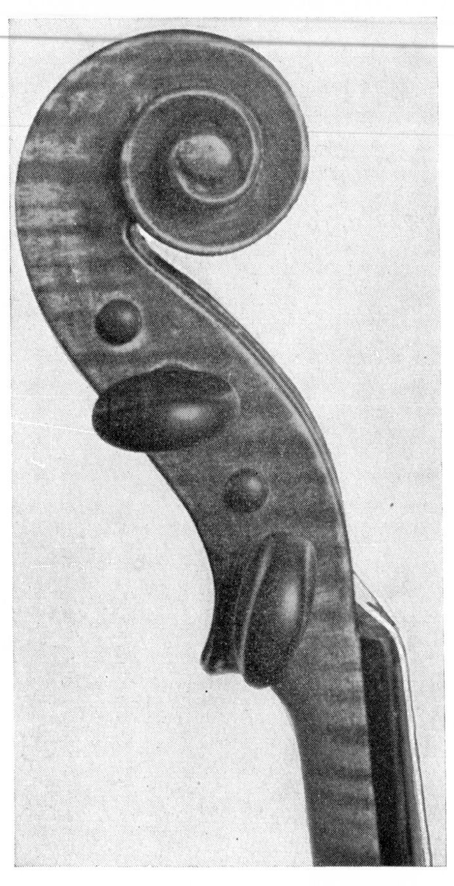

90. Degani Eugenio, Venezia 1875

91. Desiato Giuseppe, Napoli
Photo Hamma & Co

92. D'Espines Alessandro, Torino 1840

93. D'Espines Alessandro, Torino 1830

94. Fagnola Anibale, Torino 1890

95. Fracassi Arturo, Rimini 1957

96. Gabrielli Giov. Bapt., Firenze 1750
Photo Hamma & Co

97. Gabrielli Giov. Bapt., Firenze 1770 (VIOLA)

98. Gagliano Alessandro, Napoli 1700

99. Gagliano Alessandro, Napoli 1710

100. Gagliano Alessandro, Napoli 1724 (CELLO)
Photo Hamma & Co

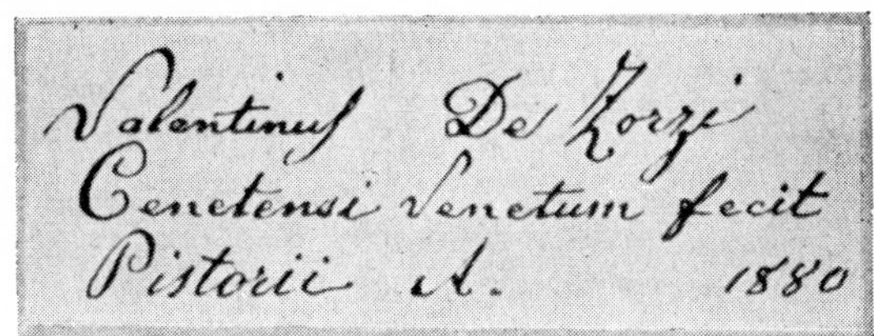

Digiuni Luigi, Cremona. Born Apr. 14, 1878. Died Sept. 8, 1937. He made violins and experimented with an instrument called *Violetto*, which was intended to supersede the violin. Golden-yellow varnish.

DIGIUNI LUIGI
Fece in Cremona
Anno .... N ....

Diguini Sebastiano, Cremona. 20th century. Perhaps son and pupil of Luigi D., exhibited two violins at Cremona in 1937.

Di Lelio Armando, Rome. B. Nov. 16, 1925. Pupil of Rod. Paralupi in Rome, self-dependent since 1945.

Armando di Lelio
Fece in Roma Anno 1949

Di Leo Camillo, Palermo, Sicily. 20th century. Guitar and mandolin maker.

Di Leo Domenico, Palermo. Born Dec. 13, 1878 in Palermo. Brother of Camillo di Leo and pupil of Antonio Sgarbi. He made mainly guitars and mandolins, but also violins and violoncellos. (Di Leo Domenico fu Francesco Paolo, Palermo. This firm was represented at the Exhibition in Cremona in 1937 by two violins, a viola and a 'cello.)

Dinacci Antonio, Naples. 19th century. Guitar and mandolin maker.

Dinelli Carlo, Fanano. 1887. A few 'cellos of his making are known.

Dini Giovanni Battista, Lucignano. 1700—1707. Highly skilled master. A singular 14-string-viola d'amour was built by him in 1700, a preserved contrabass bears the date 1707.

Gio Ba Dini Fece 1700
in Lucignano.

Dinumerabo Giovanni, Padua. 1661. Reported as good lute maker.

Dionelli Gaetano, Mantua. 1855—1869. His violoncellos are excellent. Red-brown varnish.

Dionigi Alessandro, Siracusa. 1760—1780.

Alessandro Diogini di Syracusa
17..

Diotallevi Michelangelo, Rimini. 1820.

Dodi Giovanni, Modena. Second half of the 19th century. Skilled and assiduous master whose violas and contrabasses are appreciated.

Dodi Fratelli (brothers), Modena. 19th century.

Dolcini Renato di Quinte, Marina di Ravenna. Born 1903 in Forli. He worked mainly after an original model using golden-red varnish.

Domenico ... Pesaro, Venice. 1522—1548. Philip II of Spain had five of his violas.

Domenicus Joannes, Rome. 1570—1610. Probably a priest. He worked after Andrea Amati. His instruments are characterized by long sound-holes and brown varnish.

Dominicelli of Brescia, Ferrara. 1695—1715. A double-bass and a violoncello built on the small pattern of Amati, are adduced. He worked with G. B. Ruggeri in Brescia. Golden-yellow varnish.

Imbero Dominicelli
in Ferrara

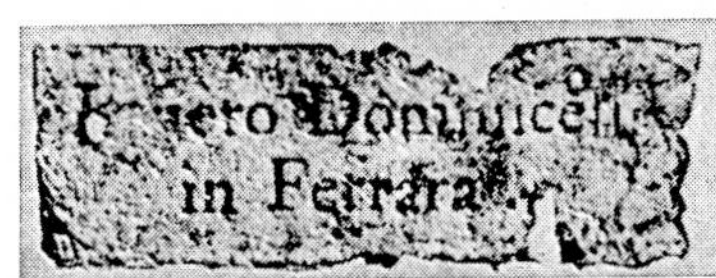

Dominichini Antonio Eduardo, Bologna. 1708—1766. Made mostly mandolins.

Domichino Giuseppe, Verona. 1700—1709. Pupil and imitator of Amati. Price ca 25.000 Kč.

Giuseppe Domichino
Veronensis faciebat anno 17..
Domenicus Pisaurensis
fecit MDXXIII.

Domenicus Joannes, Rome. 1570. A Franciscan friar who made instruments on the pattern of Andrea Amati, particularly the archings and sound-holes which are long and open. He chose good wood and applied a beautiful brown varnish. Instruments of good tone, rare.

Joanes Domenicus
ord. frum
Minorum
Romae 1570.

Joannes Cesar Domenicus
Roma minorum 1570.

Donati Frederico, Parma. 1765—1775.

Donato Serafius, Venice. 1411. Otherwise unknown, lute maker.

Doneda Gian Battista, Brescia. Born 1525, died Jan. 19, 1610 in Brescia. Lute maker, son of a Paolo Doneda.

Donelli Aldo, Campeigne (Emilia). Died 1942. Violin-maker who worked after J. B. Gagliano. Yellow varnish.

Doni Giambattista, Florence. 1635—1663.

Doni Roco, Florence. 1600—1660. A priest who devoted himself to the building of good lutes and violins.

Donozetto Pietro, Naples. 1760—1790. A good imitator of Nicolo Gagliano.

Dorelli Giovanni, Brescia. 1780. He worked after Gasparo da Salò, using brown varnish with a high gloss.

Dosi Pietro, Bologna. 1880—1885. Born in Leghorn. He was a self-taught craftsman of no particular merit.

Pietro Dosi di Livorno
fece per diletto.

D'Ovidio Antonio, Trivento (Campobasso). Born 1910. He established himself in 1931 and exhibited two violins at the Cremona Exhibition in 1937.

Drinda Giacomo, Pienza. 18th century.

Dulfenn Alexander, Livorno (Leghorn), 1689—1700. An immigrant. Good workmanship, brown varnish. Price 10—12.000 Kč.

Alexander Dulfenn
in Livorno 17..

E

Eberle Tommaso, Naples. 1760—1792. Worked on the pattern of his teacher Nicola Gagliano still more carefully than his master. He made narrow-edged instruments with deep purflings, which often pass for works of Nicola or Joseph Gagliano, although his instruments differ from them by their smaller sound-holes, more elegant scrolls and general appearance. Eberle used carefully selected wood. Every part of his instruments is worked with solicitous care. He applied yellow-brown or brown-red varnish. Price at least 40.000 Kč.

Tomaso Eberle Fecit
Nap. 1776.
Thomas Heberl
Fecit Neap. 1780.

Eberspacher Bartolomeo, Florence. 1660. Lutemaker. He came from Tyrol. His theorbas are tastefully ornamented.

Bartolomeo Eberspacher
In Florenza.

Ebert Enrico, Venice. 1655 — Skilful lute maker.

Enrico Ebar fecit
anno Domini 1655.

Heinrich Ebert in Venetia.

Ecchio Giovanni, Rome. 1610, d. July 10, 1622.

Eisele Michele, Brescia. 1614—1664. Lute and violin maker; instruments made by him have not been preserved.

Embergher Luigi, Rome. 1898—1900. Produced excellent mandolins.

Emiliani, Francesco (d'), Rome. 1704—1736. Built instruments on two patterns: high-arched, on the pattern of Stainer, and low-arched ones in the style of David Tecchler. For the small model he always used low arching. The sound-holes resemble those of Nic. Amati's instruments. He applied varnish of various colours in strong coats. Instruments are known coloured amber-yellow, yellow-brown, brown, brown-red and red. The varnish is always of good quality, the wood beautiful. Very carefully carved scrolls, good tone, yet of little carrying power. His instruments have often been sold as creations of more famous masters. Price 25.000 Kč, some instruments as much as 50.000 Kč. according to Hamma.

Franciscus Emilianus Roma.
Franciscus de Emilianis fecit.

Enrico Giovanni di, Naples, Rome. 1590—1608. Called "Maestro Giovanni", was an excellent lute maker, but is reported to have been a still better drinker.

Erba Carlo fu Paolo, Mariano Comense (Como), Via E. Adda 10. Born Dec. 26, 1907. Son of Paolo Erba. He exhibited a violin and a viola at Cremona in 1937.

Erba Paolo, Mariano Comense (Como). Born 1874. Died 1927. Probably father and teacher of Carlo Erba.

Erhard Paul, Genoa. 1690. Was a German. A good violin of his making used to be in Dresden.

Paul Erhard
Geigenmacher
Genua 1690.

Erthel Leopold, Venice, 1710. It has not been safely ascertained whether a violin maker of this name existed at all.

Esposito Giosue, Naples. 1890—1900. Mandolin maker.

Raffaele Esposito
in Napoli Anno 1888

Estudiantina, see Vito Moro.

F

Fabiani Antonio, Tolignano, Ascoli Piano. Born 1898. Pupil of Léandro Bísiach. He established himself in 1920 in Piceno.

Fabricatore Gennaro I, Naples. 1773—1832. Son and pupil of Giovanni Battista Fabricatore. Built very good lutes, violoncellos, mandolins and guitars, but no violins of his making are reported. There is known a 'cello dated 1826 which is of neat workmanship and good tone.

Gennaro fabricatore
Anno 1820 Napoli
Strada S. Giacomo No 42.
Genaro fabricatore
Napoli A 1805.

Fabricatore Gennaro II, Naples. 1820—1843. Perhaps son of Gennaro Fabricatore I. Maker of violins and guitars. He worked after Gagliano.

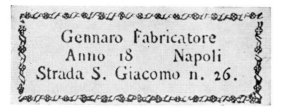

Gennaro Fabricatore
Anno 18 Napoli
Strada S. Giacomo n. 26.

Fabricatore Giovanni Battista, Naples. 1761—1811. Skilful violin and lute-maker. Devoted himself more to the building of guitars and mandolins than to violin-making. Dark-amber-coloured varnish.

Gio: Battista Fabricatore fecit
An. 1793 in S. M. dell'Ajute No 32
Napoli.

Fabricatore Pietro, Naples. 1780—1799.

Pietro Fabricatore Fece
Napoli Anno 1790

Fabricatore Vincenzo, Naples. 1770. Perhaps father of Giov. Battista, Gennaro and Pietro F.; produced lutes and mandolins of mediocre quality.

Fabris Luigi, Venice. 1838, d. 1873. He built excellent instruments, mostly violins and violoncellos and applied a beautiful red, orange or brown varnish. He modelled his work on Stradivari and Guarneri. Skilful repairs of instruments. Price 20.000 Kč.

Luigi Fabris fecit
Venetia l'anno 1860.

LUIGI FABRIS, fecit.
VENEZIA, Anno 1872.
Premiato con Medaglia d'argento
all'Esposizione di Treviso 1872

Facini Fra Augustinus, Bologna. 1732—1742. A friar of the order of St John. He worked very well on the pattern of Stradivari and Amati. Instruments built by him are characterized by careful workmanship and grace; the sound-holes are designed exactly on the pattern of Stradivari; yellow, yellow-red or red-brown, beautifully applied varnish. Rich, soft and powerful tone. Price 20.000 Kč and more. Rare.

Fr. Augustinus
Fecemi
Ords. S. Joanis
de Deo
Fecit Bononiae
1733.

Fagnola Annibale, Turin. B. 1890, d. 1939. Able master who followed Stradivari and Pressenda; red varnish.

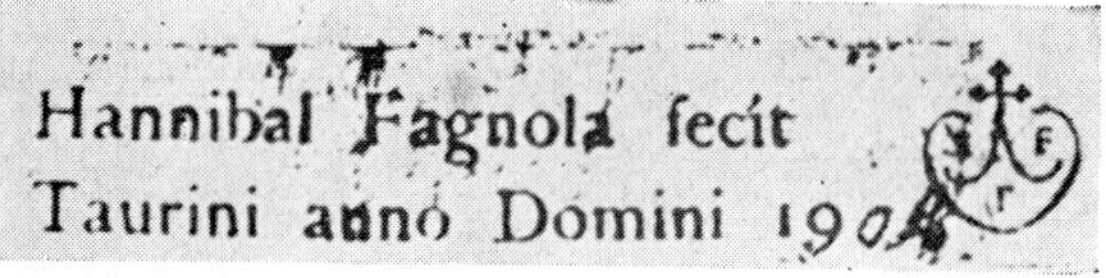

Falciani Paolo. Apignano del Tronto. Born 1924. Pupil of C. Celani.

Falco Andrea, Cremona. 1738. Pupil of Giuseppe Guarneri filius Andreae.

Falco Paolo, Cremona. 1750—1760. Pupil and imitator of C. Bergonzi. Instruments of good quality. Price 20——25.000 Kč.

Fantozzi Pietro, Rome. Born Aug. 25, 1876, died March 8, 1961. Pupil of Giuseppe Sgarbi. Producer, almost a manufacturer of guitars, mandolins, violins, etc.

Premiata Fabbrica di Strumenti a Corda
Pietro Fantozzi
ROMA
Via DEL BOSCHETTO N. 123
Telefono 44564

PREMIATA FABBRICA
D'ISTRUMENTI MUSICALI A CORDA
PIETRO FANTOZZI
Via Boschetto, 123 - Roma

Farinato Paolo, Venice. 1695—1725. Good and careful craftsman who worked in the style of Santo Serafino. His instruments are of a characteristic shape and sound well. He applied yellow-red varnish. Especially his violas are said to be of outstanding quality. Price 25.000 Kč.

Paolo Farinato
Fecit Venetiis 1700.

Farotti Celeste, Milan. B. July 7, 1864, d. 1928. Skilful violin maker; he spelled his name both Farotti and Farotto.

Farotti Celeste
Fece in Milano nell'anno 1901
da San Germano di Casale.
C. Farotti.

Celeste Farotto
da San Germano di Casale
fece in Milano l'anno 19..

FAROTTI CELESTE
da San Germano di Casale
FECE in Milano nell'anno 1928

FAROTTI CELESTE
DI S. GERMANO DI CASALE
Fece
in Milano il 190

Farotto (*-i*) Celestino, Milan. B. Nov. 10, 1905. Pupil of his uncle Celestino (Celeste) Farotti whose shop he took over. Inspired by Stradivari and Pressenda. Exhibited a violin at Cremona in 1937.

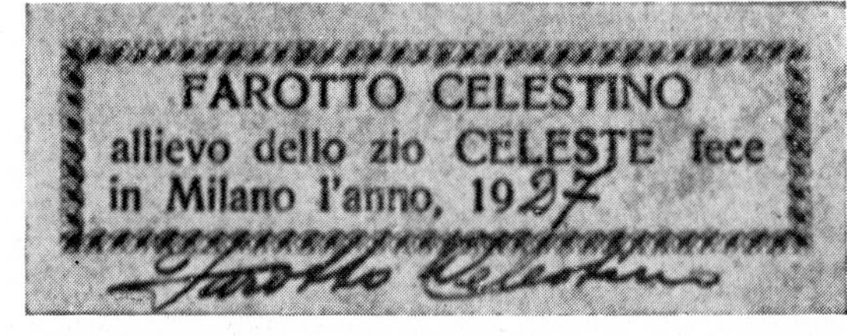

FAROTTO CELESTINO
allievo dello zio CELESTE fece
in Milano l'anno, 1927

Farotti Cœlestes a Sancto Germano
Casalense Mediolani fecit anno 1920

Farotto Salvatore, Milan. Born 1875 at Granzzano (Monferrato). Brother and pupil of Celestino Farotto. He worked after Stradivari, Rocca and Pressenda. He used handwritten labels.

Ferraris Oreste, Vicegnano (Pavia). 1930.

Faruzi Francesco, Venice. 1842—1860. Repaired excellently instruments by old masters: few works of his are known.

Fasani Giovanni, Brescia. Born about 1785 in Cremona. Died about 1850.

Jo. Fasani Cremonensis
restauravit Brixiae an 1832

Fasciolo Angelo, Turin. Born in Turin in 1887. Died 1942. A violoncellist who also made instruments, following Annibale Fagnola.

Fattorini Francesco, Finale Emilia (Modena). 1854. Self-taught instrument-maker, who built fairly good contrabasses. A violin of 1831 is designed on the model of Stradivari.

Faustino Lucca, Modena. 17th cent. Violin and lute maker.

Faversani Carlo Fernando, Treviso. Born 1886 in Cremona. He worked with Antoniazzi and had two of his violins exhibited at the Cremona Exhibition in 1937.

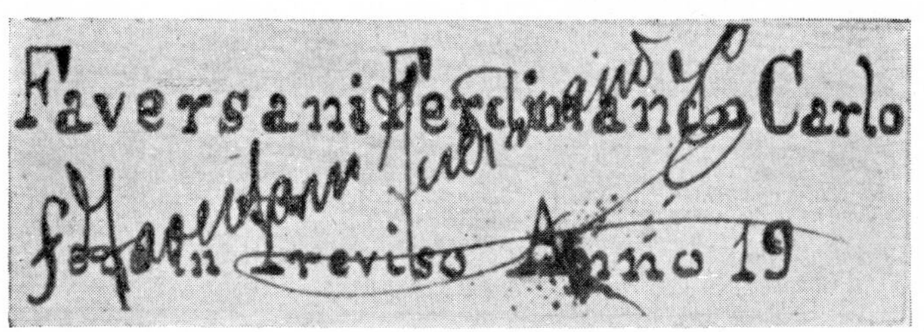

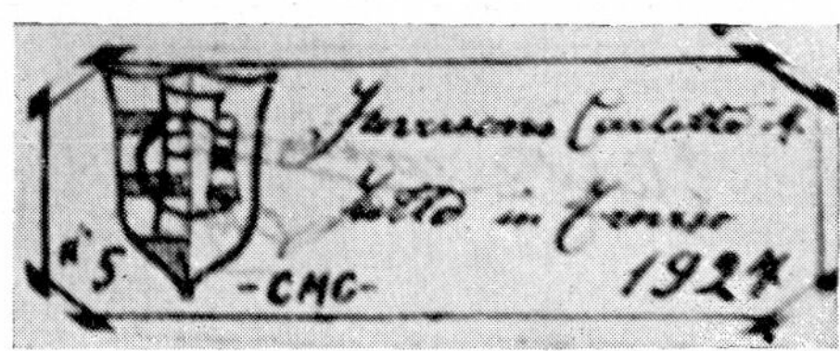

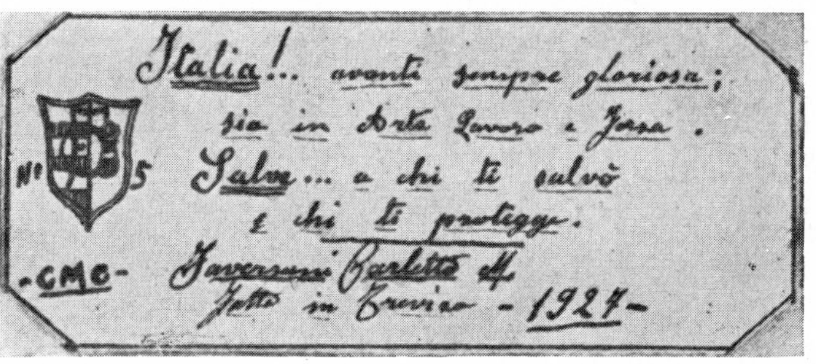

Faversani Cervino, Treviso. B. 1904 in Bergamo. Son of Carlo F. Faversani.

Fedeli Giuseppe, Foligno. 1860—1894.

Felipuci Pier Lodovico, Pesaro. 1660.

Fenga Luigi, Catania (Sicily). Born at Catino, Sept. 29, 1866. He established himself in 1890. Violin-maker who made also guitars and mandolins. His instruments are made of carefully selected wood; they are noted for their good varnish and fairly good tone.

Aluisius Pahenga Catanensis fecit 1900
Luigi Fenga — Catania (Italia)

Ferrati Pietro, Siena. 1754—1764. Instruments built by him are distinguished by faultless workmanship, good old wood, good dark-brown varnish and a sufficiently powerful, rich tone. He worked after Stradivari and varnished his instruments brown. Price 10.000 Kč.

Pietro Ferati
Fecit Siena 1760

Ferrara Fratelli and Sapienza, Catania (Sicily). A firm which produced mostly guitars and mandolins.

Ferrari Agostino, Budrio. 1720. Amati model.

Ferrari Alfonso. Carpi (Modena). 1712—1740. Double-basses are the best instruments he made, whereas his violins are of inferior quality.

Ferrari Carlo, Siena. 1740. Although he was not a master, some of his instruments are good: they are estimated at 8—15.000 Kč.

Ferrari Francesco, Bisignano. B. 1797, died in the second half of the 19th century. Brother of Giovanni Battista Ferrari, was trained in the workshop of Vincenzo I de Bonis, guitar and mandolin maker.

Ferrari Gasparo, Rome. 1731—1776. Skilful maker of lutes and mandolins, which are characterized by handsome workmanship and bright yellow varnish.

Gasparus Ferrari Romanus
fecit anno 1751.

Gasparo Ferraro Romano
fecit in Roma nel mese di Maggio
del Anno 1744.

Gasparo Ferraro Romano
Roma A° 1751.

Gaspar Ferrari Romany
fecit = anno = 1776

Ferrari Gian Battista, Bisignano. B. 1795, died after 1855. Same as Francesco F.

Ferrari Giovanni. 18th century. Indifferent; only cases by him survive.

Ferraris Oreste, Vicegnano (Pavia). 1930.

Ferraresi Vincenzo, San Felice (Modena). Born c. 1793, died 1869. Made good violins, 'cellos and contrabasses.

Ferrarotti Dionigi, Turin. B. in Turin Nov. 18, 1903. Son of Luigi Ferrarotti, guitar maker.

Ferrarotti Luigi, Turin. B. Oct. 30, 1878, d. 1920. Guitar and mandolin maker.

Ferrarotti e Figlio, Turin. 20th century. Guitars and mandolins.

Ferrer Antonius, Naples, ca 1481. A monk who devoted himself to instrument-making. It was written about him:

Frate Ant° Ferrer, quale fa
certi stromenti da sonar per la
S. R. graziosamente
adi 4 dicembre. 1*

Ferri Primo, Mirandola. 1848—1860. A dealer; his own instruments of medium quality.

Ferroni Fernando. Florence. Born July 14, 1868 in Florence, died Dec. 9, 1949. Pupil of Zorzi. He followed Stradivari not only in his patterns, but imitated the tints and shades of this master's varnish. Exhibited at Cremona in 1937 five violins, a viola and a whole quartet.

F. Ferroni
Firenze 1942

Fifo del Pagliano, Rolo (Modena). 1810—1840. Worked assiduously in a professional, but not a masterly fashion. He left many violins and contrabasses.

Filano Antonio, Naples. 1787. Mandolin maker.

Filano Donato, Naples. 1763—1783. He does not belong to the great violin makers, although he took great pains in adorning his instruments with mother-of-pearl, ivory, tortoise shell and ebony. He applied a brown varnish of medium quality. Price 10.000 Kč and more, according to the merits of the specimen.

Donato Filano fecit alla via
di s. Chiara A. D. 1782, Napoli.
Donatus Filano Fecit
Anno Dni 1773
Av. Rue de la Sainte Claire.
Donatus Filano fecit anno D 1770
Neap. alla Rua de Tafettanari.

Filano Giuseppe, Naples. 1785—1797. Son and pupil of Donato Filano. He made also guitars and mandolins. His instruments do not come up in quality to those built by his father. Price 4—7.000 Kč.

Joseph Filano, Filius Donati fecit Neap.
Alla Rua di S. Chiara
Anno 1787.

Filano Luigi, Naples. 1820—1859. He worked after Gagliano, making also guitars and mandolins. Yellow varnish.

* Brother Antonio Ferrer who is making gratuitously certain musical instruments for His Reverence, the 4th of December.

Fillippi Filipo, Rome. 1857—1890, built violins in the traditions of the Brescian school using, however, spirit varnish.

Philippus de Filippis
fecit Romae anno 1876
et DD Regiae Acade-
miae S. Caeciliae.

Finocchio, Bibbiano (i.e. in Bibbiano, Reggio Emilia). 17th century maker, known by his guitars.

Finolli Giuseppe Antonio, Milan. 1750—1762. Good neat craftsmanship. Few labelled instruments survive. His works form a connecting link between those of Landolfi and Camilli. He used good wood with wide grain. The tone of his instruments is excellent. Orange-yellow varnish of subdued lustre.

Joseph Antoni Finolli in
Milano. 1755

Fiorani Vincenzo, Pergola. 1853—1875. He modelled his instruments, built in a professional manner on Guarneri and G. B. Ceruti, but applied alcohol varnish.

Fioravanti Andrea, Macerata near Ancona. 1741—1747. Good contrabasses of large pattern.

Andrea Firovanti
fecit Macerata a. 1747.

Fiorentini Astore, Bologna. B. Jan. 2, 1887 in Bologna. Guitar maker.

Fiori Amilcare, Casinalbo. 1815. Good, but little known violin maker.

Fiori Andrea, Modena. Born 1796, died 1870. Skilful violin maker who worked with his brother Gaetano. They used spirit varnish.

Fiori Gaetano, Modena. Born 1798, died 1873. Brother and partner of Andrea. Yellow-red varnish.

Fiorillo Giovanni, Ferrara, 1760—1780. His instruments are a combination of the Italian and Tyrolese schools. The sound-holes are short in the fashion of Jac. Stainer. 'Cellos built by him are excellent. Some flatter German violins have been provided with labels spelled Florillo. Price 20.000 Kč, 'cello more.

Fiorini Alessandro and Antonio, Bologna. 1671—1720. Little known violin makers. They are often being mistaken for Floreno. Price 20.000 Kč.

Antonius Fiorini Bononiae
fecit Anno 1720.

Fiorini Giuseppe, Munich, Zurich. Born 1861 at Bazzano, d. 1934. Came with his parents to Bologna in 1867. He was a pupil of his father Raffaele. As early as 1881 he worked already as independent craftsman on repairs and built good 'cellos. He also made violins and dealt in instruments of old masters. From Italy he went to Germany, where he married the daughter of Andr. Rieger and in 1899 founded the firm of Rieger & Fiorini. At the beginning of World War I, he moved to Zurich as an Italian citizen, although he was offered German citizenship as well as an excellent position at the professional school for violin makers. He left for Zurich in May 1915 and after the war returned to Italy, where he attracted notice when he bought the property left by Ant. Stradivari. — See Stradivari.

Fiorini Raffaele, Bologna. Born at Pianoro 1828, died at Bologna in 1898. He came to Bologna about 1867. Excellent, assiduous violin maker, who left a great many violins, 60 'cellos and other instruments; repaired, with much skill, instruments by old masters. His successor was Armando Monterumici, not his own son Giuseppe.

Fiorini Tivoli. — See Tivoli.

Fiscer Carlo Vincenzo, Milan. After 1770. Brother of Giuseppe Fiscer. With him he worked jointly till about 1764, afterwards as independant craftsman.

Carlo Vincenzo Fiscer
Fabricator d'Istrumenti
Alla Balla in Milano anno 1770.

Fiscer Giuseppe, Milan. 1760—1764. Good instruments, particularly excellent are his 'cellos. He applied good red or red-yellow varnish on yellow grounding. Worked jointly with his brother Carlo. Nothing is known of Giuseppe's work after 1764; it seems probable that he died about 1764. Price 12.000 Kč.

Giuseppe Carlo Fratelli Fiscer
Fabricatori di strumenti in Milano
Violino alla balla 1764.

Giuseppe e Carlo fratelli Ficher
fabricatori di strumenti in Milano
vicino alla Balla 17..

Giuseppe Fratelli Fiscer
Fabbricatori d'instrumenti in Milano
Vicino alla Balla 17..

Fiscier Tobia, Siena. B. 1680, d. 1721. Lute and theorbo maker, probably father of Giuseppe and Carlo Fiscer. The name is German (Fischer).

Tobbia Fiscier Siena 1710.

Flarotti Celeste, Milan. 20th century.

Floreno Fiorenzo, Bologna. 18th century. Imitated with much skill Nic. Amati's instruments. Careful workmanship, yellow or orange varnish. — Price 30.000 Kč.

Florentus Florinus
fecit Bononiae an 17..

Floreno Giovanni Guidante, Bologna. 1685—1730. Known under the name of "Guidantus". His instruments are beautifully finished and of high arching. They resemble in shape violins of the Amatis, as to arching those of the Stainer model. Narrow, yet rather high edges, indelicately cut sound-holes. Yellow and agate-coloured varnish of high lustre, the agate-coloured being superior to the yellow varnish. Violins of full tone. Price 32—50.000 Kč.

Floreno Guidante, Bologna. 1710—1740. Son and perhaps also pupil of Giovanni Floreno. He worked skilfully, taking the outline of N. Amati's grand pattern, yet with lower archings and a red-brown varnish on yellow ground. The tone is good. Price 40.000 Kč.

Giudante Florenus
fecit Bononiae 17..

Florinus Guidantus Fecit
Bononiae Anno 1710.

Floreno Joannes Quidantus, Bologna. 1710—1740. We are quoting the name, as it is spelled on a handwritten label, found in a middle sized 'cello. The instrument is certainly the work of a master, sounds well and is provided with good old-Italian varnish, dark red on yellow ground. Should the label be genuine (in spite of the spelling *Quidantus* for *Guidantus*, which is improbable even in a Latinized name), the man might have been a descendant of Giovanni Floreno Guidante (1685—1730) and of Floreno Guidante, who worked in the same city 1710—1740. His name does not occur in parish registers. Having carefully studied the 'cello, we can say the following: the varnish makes the impression of old Brescian and the instrument seems to be older than indicated. The sound-holes are wide, upright, with upper and lower curves of the same diameter, not well executed. The scroll has two and a half turns; the back is of almost plain maplewood, the belly of wide-grained pine with the soft wood between the annual lines sunk in. Thet one is not powerful, but of fine quality. Length 750 mm., upper width 331.5, middle 220, lower 426; sides: upper 110, middle 113, lower 118 mm.; sound-holes: height 136, total length 145, distance between their upper ends 75.5 mm.

Joannes Florenus Quidantus
fecit Bononia 1772. (written)
Joannes Florenus Guidantus Fecit
Bononiae Anno 1731

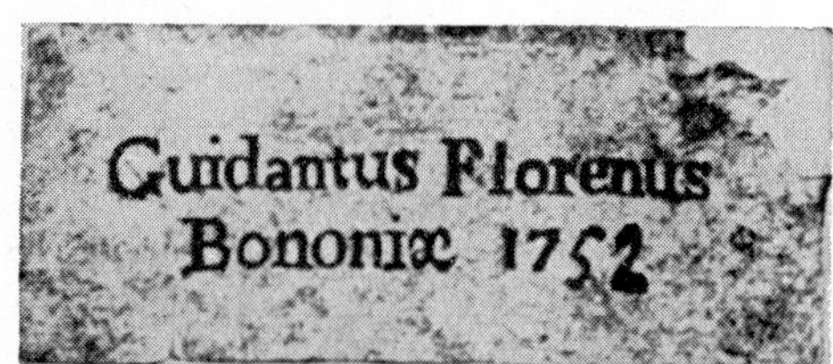
Guidantus Florentus
Bononiæ 1752

Florentin N. Place allegedly Cremona, no dates. The man, who worked at the end of the 18th and beginning of the 19th century, was probably French. Lüttgendorff mentions several specimens, the description of which fully answers the one we have seen in Brno. Varnish golden-yellow, spread in thick coats, tone very good, with excellent carrying power. The instruments are of a large, broad Stradivari pattern.

A la ville de Cremone N. Florentin.

Floriani Benedicti, Florence. 1558—1571. Probably not a violin maker; he is known to have made spinets.

Benedictus Floriani 1559.

Floriani Pietro, Riva. Born June 3, 1787 at Alboa near Riva on Lake Garda, died Jan. 17, 1870. Son of Francesco Ant. F., a cabinet maker. Instruments of his making (four violins, two violas and two 'cellos) are not masterworks.

Pietro Floriani fecce a
Riva di Trento 1858.
PIETRO FLORIANI
1858
RIVA BENEACENSE

Fodera Ercole, Catania. Born 1895. He was working in the style of H. Sgarbi, applying brown-red and golden-yellow oil varnish.

Hercules Foderà filius Philippi - Panormitanus
fecit Catanae sub titulo Clementinae anno 19

Follis Carlo, Naples. 1790—1810. He made double-basses of smaller size. Brown varnish.

Fontana Giovanni, Ferrara. 1568.

Fontana Nicolo, Venice. Born in Brescia c. 1499, died at Venice ca 1557. Mere name. Works lost.

Fontanelli Giovanni Giuseppe, Bologna. 1733—1773. Excellent lute maker who inlaid his lutes with ivory and ebony.

Giovanni Giuseppe Fontanelli
Bolognese f. an. 1772.

Giov. Giuseppe Fontanelli
fece in Bologna, l'anno 1733—3 × bre.

Fontanini Andrea Pietro, Cremona (Brescia), Salò. Born Nov. 30, 1871, d. Dec. 26, 1923 at Salò, active till 1906 in Cremona, then till 1911 in Brescia, finally at Salò. Son of Giuseppe F., apprenticed by Aristide Cavalli, he had worked also with Luigi Digiuni and Carlo Bodi. Instruments of the violin family, also guitars and mandolins.

Fece il Cremonesi
Andrea Pietro Fontanini
in Cremona anno 1890.

Fece il Cremonese
Andrea Pietro Fontanini
in Brescia anno 1908.

Fece il Cremonese
Andrea Pietro Fontanini
in Salò anno 1912.

Fontanini Aristide, Salo, Rome. Born Sept. 21, 1894 in Cremona. Son and pupil of Andrea Pietro Fontanini. He established himself in Rome in 1921 and in 1946 he was teacher at the Salò school.

Scuola Sup. di Liuteria "GASPARO DA SALO"
Direz. e Brevetti Aristide Fontanini
Strumento N. 100 coustruito da ....
SALO

Foradori Giovanni, Verona, Bologna. 1845—1880. Adroit joiner, but a bad violin maker.

Fornarone il, Bologna. Quoted, but unknown.

Forni Stefano, Pesaro, 1666. Delicate workmanship, fine wood, excellent varnish. The tone of his instruments is faultless.

Stefano Forni Fece
In Pesaro, L'anno 1666.

Forno Christoforo del, Rome. 1608. Lute maker.

Fracassi Arturo, Gesena (Forli), via L. Sostegni. B. May 25, 1899 in Santo Antonio di Gatteo (Forli). Learned in the workshop of Carlo Biondi. Successful master, various patterns after old originals, transparent yellow or light brown oil varnish. Had a violin and a viola at the 1937 Cremona Exhibition.

Fracei Pietro, Pescia. 1816. Good workmanship on the model of Guarneri del Gesù. He applied a wonderful golden-orange varnish.

Franco Stefano, Florence. 1686—1692. Lute maker.

Stefano Franco
Fece l'an 1699
restaurato
Z. Torre Boldone

Fraiser Giorgio, Cremona. 1648—1666. Worked on the model of Amati, whose employee he was in 1666.

Franchi Celso, Ravenna. Born 1905. He followed the Cremonese school, using yellow-orange or brown varnish.

Franchi Galliano, Gorizia, Via Ascoli 10. Exhibited a violin in Cremona in 1937.

Franchi Ernesto, Legnano (Milan). 1940.

Franciolini Leopoldo, Florence. 1760—1780.

Fredi Fabio (Cte, i.e., conte, count), Todi, Rome. Born at Todi in 1845, died in Rome 1894. Good violin maker and musician, who worked with Toldi at Perugia 1875—1878 and in Rome about 1879. He applied spirit and oil varnishes.

Fredi Cte Rodolfo, Rome. Born June 18, 1861 at Todi (Perugia). Rome, Via Vincenza 24. Feb. 22, 1950. Son of Fabio Fredi. Worked carefully on Stradivari's model. He established himself in Rome on Jan. 1, 1885 and built instruments on ten different models. Cheaper violins he coated with spirit varnish, good instruments with oil varnish. Exhibited two violins at Cremona in 1937.

Rodolfo Fredi
fece in Roma anno 1901.

Rodolfo Fredi fece
in Roma l'anno 19.........

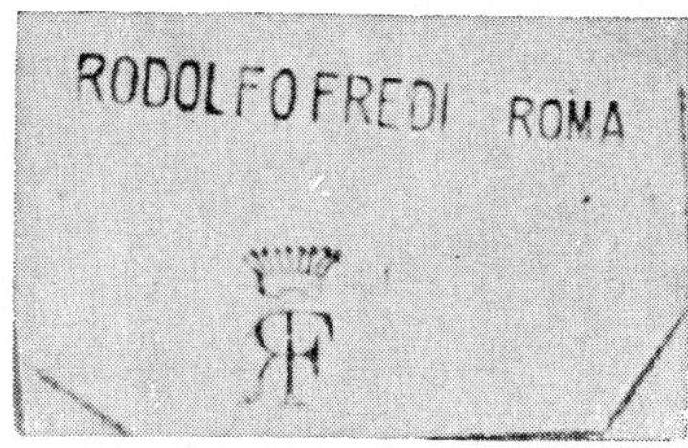

Fredimaur Joannes Baptista, Florence. 1740—1750. Good workmanship. His instruments are of high arching, have large sound-holes, wide purfling and are coated with golden-yellow varnish. The small flat scrolls are beautifully carved.

Joannes Baptista Fredimaur eximius
ligneus faber, Florentie anno 1645.

Frezza Bartolomeo, Brescia. 1624. Lute maker.

G

Gabrielli Antonio, Florence. 1750—1760. Good workmanship, golden-yellow varnish, small pattern, good tone. Price 16—20.000 Kč.

Antonio Gabrielli
Fece in Firenze 17..

Antonio Gabrielli fece
in Firenze 1760.

Gabrielli Bartolomeo, Florence 1730. Probably a brother of Cristoforo Gabrielli. Worked in the style of Pietro Lorenzo Vangelisti, i.e. with high arching.

Bartolomeo Gabrielli
fece anno 1734 in Firenze.

Gabrielli Giovanni Battista, Florence. 1739—1770. The best violin maker of his time in Florence. Worked with great care on a model similar to that of Jacob Stainer. Used good wood. His sound-holes are short, neatly cut in the fashion of Stainer. He applied, in thin coats, a yellow transparent varnish of high lustre. Instruments of wonderful tone. Particularly good are his 'cellos. (Not many violins extant.) Besides labels, he also used the trade mark I. B. G. Price 50.000 Kč, a 'cello far more.

Gio Battista

Gabrieli Firenze
Anno 1762.

Joannes Baptista Gabrielli
florentinus fecit 17..

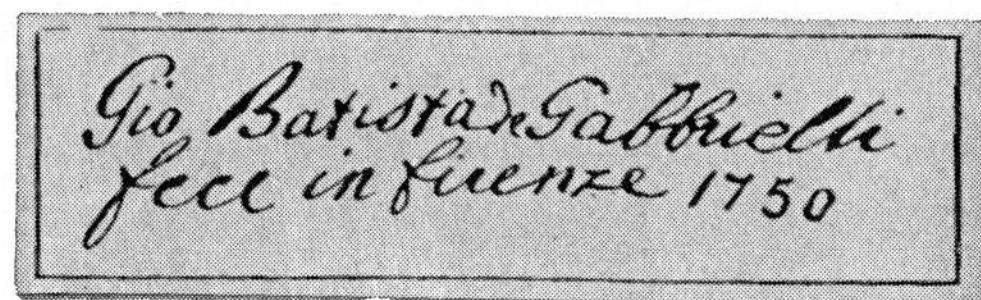

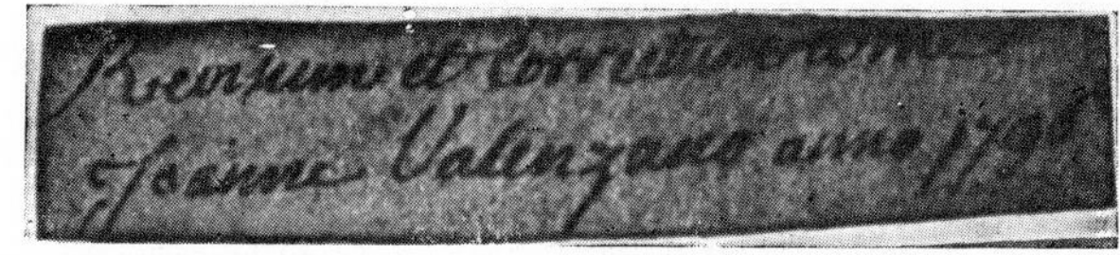

Gabrielli Cristoforo I, Florence. 1730—1745. Little known.

Gabrielli Cristoforo II, Florence. 1937. Exhibited a violin and a viola at Cremona in 1937.

Gadda Gaetano, Mantua. Via dell'Accademia 45. Born Apr. 13, 1900, died March 1, 1956.

GAETANO GADDA di MANTOVA
premiato con Medaglia d'Oro
Allievo di Stefano Scarampella
Fece in Mantova anno 19..

GAETANO GADDA di MANTOVA
premiato con Medaglia d' Oro
Allievo di STEFANO SCARAMPELLA
Fece in Mantova anno 19

Gada Mario, Mantua. Born March 13, 1931. Son and since 1949 also pupil of Gaetano Gada. Precise craftsmanship, more careful than that of his father, whose best instruments always inspired the son.

Family Gagliano

Alessandro Gagliano 1660—1725 | Gio. Battista 1728 | Carlo 1732

Nicola 1695—1758 | Gennaro 1700—1770

Fernando 1724—1785 | Giuseppe 1725—1793 | Antonio 1728—1795 | Giovanni (Joannes) 1740—1806

Gaetano 1770—1824 | Nicola 1772—1826 | Raffaele 1790—1857 | Antonio 1794—1860 | Giovanni 1800—1867

Vincenzo 1870—1886 | Alberto 1877

Gagliano Alberto, Naples. Ca 1877. Son of Raffaele Gagliano, perhaps his pupil, too, as Alberto's work resembles very much that of Raffaele G.

Gagliano Alessandro, Naples. Born in Naples in 1660, died in 1725. Pupil of Stradivari, with whom he worked till 1690. The first work of his own is of the year 1695. He worked carefully, using fine pine wood with wide grain and maple wood with beautiful curl. His model has outlines anticipating those of Guarneri del Gesù. It is large and rather flat. Large, delicately cut sound-holes. His small scrolls not always well carved. The back is often made of one piece. The varnish is mostly red, sometimes dark red, but also yellow or orange-coloured, transparent and of excellent quality, almost matching the varnish applied by the Cremonese masters. His last works resemble the style of Carlo Bergonzi. Very good tone. Alessandro had two sons, Nicolò (Nicola) and Gennaro. His parents are not known. Price up to 120.000 Kč.

Alessandro Gagliano Alumnus
Stradivarius fecit Neapoli anno 17..

Alexander Gagliano Alumnus Antonius
Stradivarius fecit anno 17..

Alesandro Gagliano Alumnus
Stradivarius fecit Neapoli anno 1700

Alexander Gaglianus
me fecit Neapoli 172.

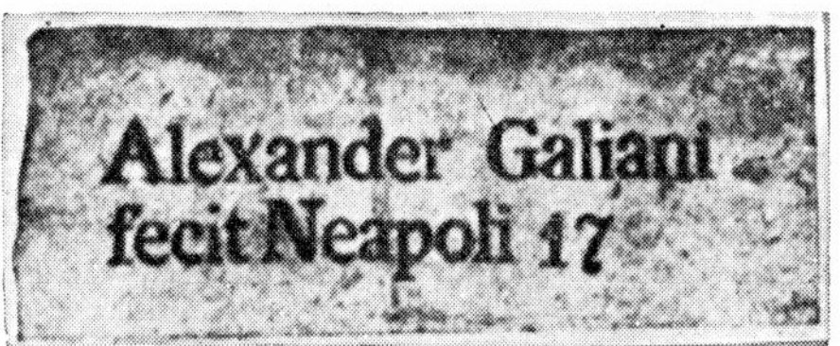
Alexander Galiani
fecit Neapoli 17

Alexander Gaglianus Fecit Neap.
1712

Gagliano Antonio I, Naples. Born Ca. 1728, died in 1795. Third son of Nicolo Gagliano. Worked on different models. Low arching, ruby-coloured varnish, somewhat less careful workmanship. He was less skilled than his brother Giuseppe, who worked jointly with him; nevertheless, the two brothers' works are so similar that they can hardly be told apart. Their style reminds of that of their father. The back of the violins is mostly made of one piece.

Joseph et Antonivs
Gagliani Filii Nico-
laj et Nepotes Ja-
nuari F. Neap. 1771.
Joseph & Antonius Gagliano
fec. anno 1787
In Platea dicta Cerriglio.

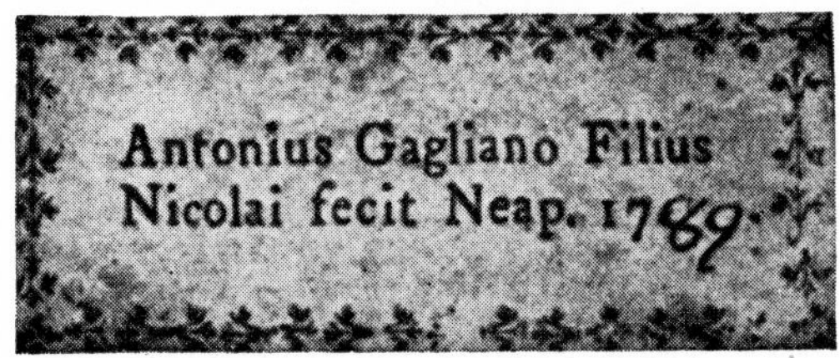
Antonius Gagliano Filius
Nicolai fecit Neap. 1789

Gagliano Antonio II, Naples. Born 1778, died May 27, 1860. Son of Giovanni and grandson of Nicolo. Worked in the style of his brother Raffaele, who shared his workshop. Antonio was his brother's superior in the cutting of sound-holes, but his scrolls are less nicely made. The bodies of his instruments weigh little, though they are solidly built, which is due to light wood. He applied amber-coloured varnish. His instruments excel in tone, particularly his 'cellos. Price 25—50.000 Kč, 'cello far more.

Antonius Gagliano
Via Ciriglio No 75 Neap.
fecit Anno 1835.

Antonio Gagliano
Via Ciriglio No... Neap
fecit Anno 1845

Gagliano Carlo, Belluno 1732. Little known member of the family. Perhaps a brother of Alessandro and of Giambattista. Only one genuine specimen is known.

Carlo Gagliano
me fecit
Belluno anno 1732.

Gagliano Fernando, Naples. Born in Naples 1724, died 1785. Eldest son of Nicola Gagliano. Worked on the pattern of his grandfather Alessandro, then in the style of Stradivari's later stage. His model is broader, his workmanship less finished than that of his father Nicola. The scrolls are beautifully carved after the fashion of Amati. The sides of his instruments are higher than those by his father, the arching, however, is lower, almost flat. Good varnish of the Neapolitan type, i. e. drier than the Cremonese, though transparent; it is yellow, yellow-brown or red-brown. Excellent is the tone of his instruments, although the wood he used was not always of best quality. Short, open sound-holes. Price 50—80.000 Kč.

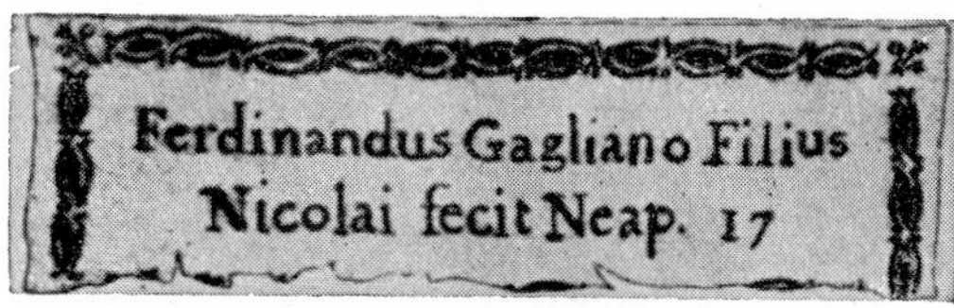

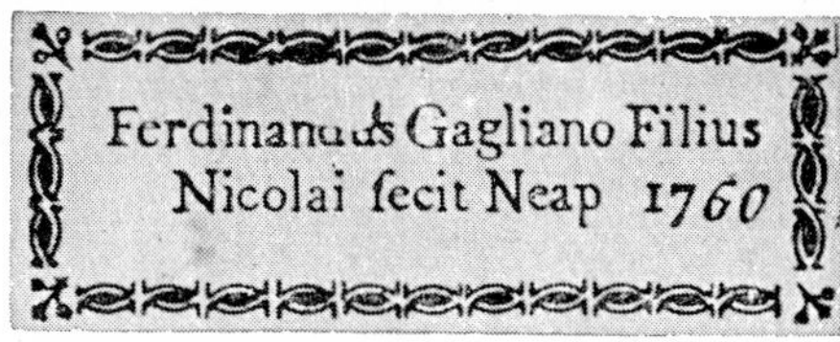

Gagliano Gaetano, Naples. Born about 1770, died 1824. Eldest son of Giovanni Gagliano. Worked on the pattern of his father, but made the arching higher and broader. Few of his instruments show careful workmanship, the quality of wood, however, is always excellent so that most instruments of his making have a powerful tone. He also made guitars and mandolins.

Gaetanus Gagliano filius
Joannes Neapolis 1820.

Gagliano Gennaro, Naples. 1700, died about 1770. Second son and pupil of Alessandro Gagliano. Worked on various patterns, mostly on Stradivari's model, but built his violins with a somewhat higher arching. All his works have beautiful outlines, pleasant to the eye. He chose hard wood which he worked in a masterly way so as to endow his instruments with a tone of beautiful colour and outstanding carrying power. Connoisseurs admire the fine cherry-red varnish he used. The sound-holes, shorter than those of Stradivari, are neatly cut and well placed. The nicely finished purfling is rather close to the edge. The sides of violins are for the most part of the same height at the top as at the bottom (29 mm.). The prime of his creative activity is the period from 1730 to 1750. His works are in great favour as concert instruments and their price is steadily rising. Price 80.000 Kč. and more.

Measures of his violins in mm:

	1748	17..	1753	17..	1759	1760
Length of back	359	354	355	355	351	354
Width of top	167	166	163	163	161	166
Width of centre	110	111.5	111	113	108	112
Width of bottom	208	207	207	201	201	208

Januarius Gagliano Filius
Nicolai fecit Neap. 1760

Januarius Gaglianus
fecit Neapoli 1767.
Genaro Gagliano fecit Neap. 17..

Gagliano Giovanni I, Naples. Born 1740, died 1806. Perhaps son of Nicolo Gagliano II and probably pupil of Genaro Gagliano. He worked after Stradivari using brown varnish. In 1761 he was in Venice. Also known are his guitars.

Gagliano Giovanni Baptista, Cremona. 1728. Brother of Alessandro G. Few specimens extant.

B Gagliano alomnus Stradivarius
Fecit Cremone anno 1728

Gagliano Giovanni II, Naples. 1800—1867. Brother of Raffaele, able follower of his ancestors, son of Giovanni Gagliano I. Price 25—40.000 Kč.

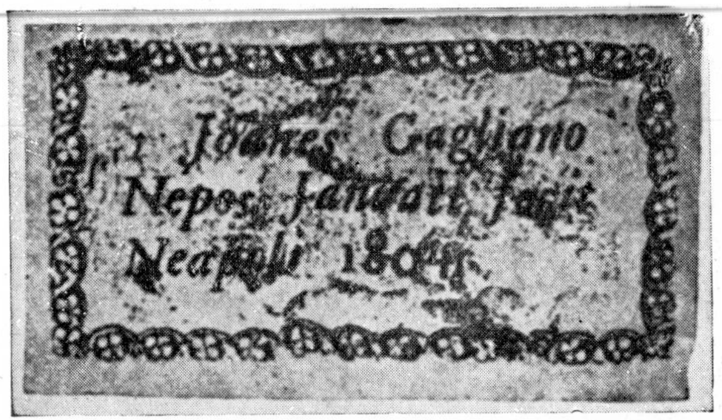

Gagliano Giuseppe, Naples. B. 1725, d. 1793. Second son of Nicola. Worked on his father's model, yet lacked to a certain degree the latter's accurate workmanship. His varnish of a brownish-red shade is good, but the yellow-brown varnish of some instruments labelled "Joseph and Antonius Gagliano" is considered as his distinctive feature and such instruments are generally assigned to him. There are some specimens of quite an outstanding value. Otherwise he worked jointly with his brother Antonio. (The two brothers' works are very similar to those created by their father.) He chose wood of rather different quality. The small scrolls of his instruments are carved with less taste. His 'cellos are of great merit, length of table, 745 mm. Price according to quality 25—80.000 Kč. and more.

Giuseppe Gaglianus Filius Nicolini
fecit Neap. 17..

Joseph & Antonius Gaglianus
Fec. Ann 1793.

Joseph Gagliano filius
Nicoli et nepos ja-
nuarius fecit Nea-
poli 1793.

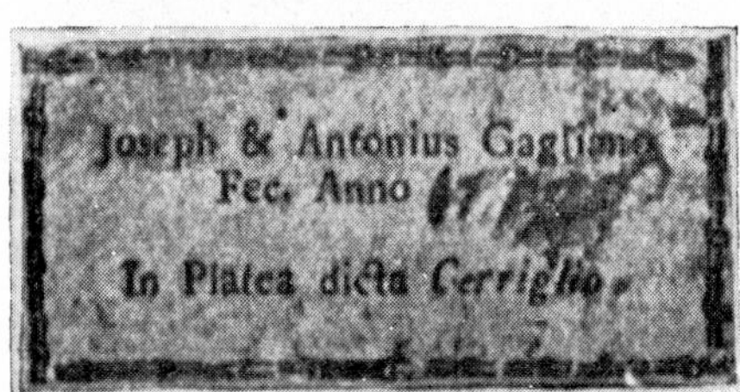

JOSEPH ET ANTONIVS
GAGLIANI FILII NICO-
LAJ ET NEPOTES JA-
NUARJ F. NEAP. 1771

Fabbrica di Violini, ed altri
strumenti armonici dei Fratelli
Giuseppe, ed An-
tonio Gagliano Napoli 1815
Strada Cerriglio num. 37.

Gagliano Joannes (Giovanni I), Naples. Born about 1740, died 1806. Fourth son of Nicola, pupil of Gennaro Gagliano. Worked on the pattern of his uncle and master Gennaro. His large, rather low arched instruments have broad, flat edges; the wood is not always of good quality, the scrolls not particularly well carved, but the tone is outstanding. Rich yellow, sometimes brownish varnish. Price 15—25.000 Kč, some specimens much more.

Joannes Gagliano fecit sub disciplina
Januaris Gagliano.

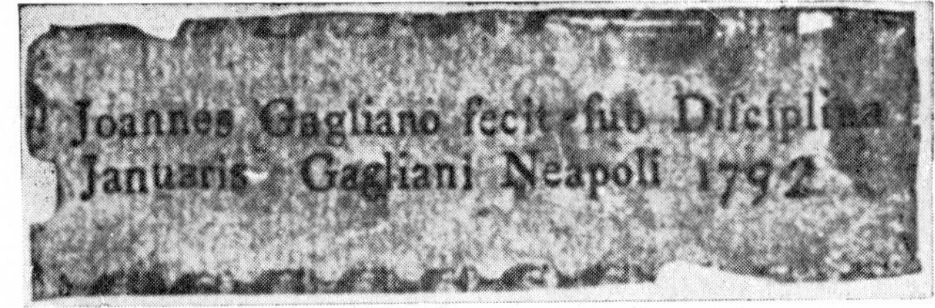

Gagliano Nicola I, Naples. Born 1670 (according to Lüttgendorff 1695), died about 1758. Eldest son of Alessandro Gagliano, endowed with excellent talent, he worked carefully on the flat model of Stradivari. The belly is for the most part more arched than the back. Beautifully finished purfling, yet its black lines look nowadays faded, little or badly stained. Beautifully carved scrolls. The wood of the belly is, however, inferior to that of Cremonese instruments, because Cremonese pine-wood was probably not available. Belly and back are rather thick and the thinning toward the edges more outspoken. Golden-yellow, yellow-brown, sometimes also red or red-brown, transparent and rather hard varnish. The tone of his instruments is mellow, yet not always powerful. Price 80.000 Kč. and more, particularly for inlaid instruments.

Sizes of violins of the years 1736 and 1739:

Length of back	356 mm.	357 mm.
Width of top	166.5 mm.	167.5 mm.

Width of centre	114 mm.	111 mm.
Width of bottom	209 mm.	205 mm.

Nicolai Gagliano
fecit in Neapoli 17..

Nicolaus Gagliano Filius
Alexandri fecitNeap. 1735

Gagliano Nicola (II), Naples. 1772—1826. Second son and pupil of Giovanni. Handsome, model not too flat, with rather strong and broad edges, coated mostly with a lemon-yellow varnish.

Nicolaus Gagliano
Filius Joannis
Neapoli 1793.

Nicolaus Gagliano
Filius Joannis Neapoli 1800.

Gagliano Nicolo III, Naples. 1780—1795. Son and pupil of Nicola Gagliano I who worked after the Stradivari model (324 mm.). Orange varnish.

Gagliano Raffaele, Naples. Born 1790, died Dec. 9, 1857. Third son of Giovanni. Worked in the style of his brother Antonio II. His violins have a flat arching, long and wide sound-holes, the scrolls are not satisfactory. He applied a dark-red, brown or red-brown varnish. His instruments sound well. Price from 15.000 Kč. upwards.

RAFFAELE ED ANTONIO GAGLIANO
Quodam Giovanni Napoli 1859

RAFFAELE, ED ANTONIO GAGLIANO
Fabbricanti e Negozianti
Di Violini, Viole, Violoncelli, Controbassi,
e Corde armoniche
Strada Sedile di S. Guiseppe n. 17 primo piano

RAFFAELE ED ANTONIO GAGLIANO
Quondam Giovanni Napoli 1857

I FRATELLI
RAFFAELE, ED ANTONIO GAGLIANO
Fabbricanti e Negozianti
Di Violini, Viole, Violoncelli, Co[illegible]si,
e Corde armoniche
Strada Sedile di S. Giuseppe n.° 17. Pr[illegible]

Gagliano Vincenzo, Naples. B. 1870, d. 1886. Son of Raffaele Gagliano. Worked in an industrial manner under the firm Vincenzo Gagliano & Figlio in Naples. With Vincenzo the Gagliano family died out; he was unmarried and there were no other descendants.

VINCENZO GAGLIANO E FIGLI

Gaibisso Giovanni Battista, Alassio. Born June 24, 1876. Diligent modern maker. Mostly Stradivari, Guarneri and Rocca models. Orange-red varnish.

RIPARATO DA
GAIBISSO G. BATTISTA
ALASSIO ANNO 1949
MEDAGLIA d'ORO ESPOSIZIONE INT. TORINO 1911

Gaibisso Giovanni Battista — G
FECE Alassio ANNO 1949 — G B
Medaglia d'oro Esp. Int. Torino 1911

Galassi Giacchino, Gattea (Forli). Exhibited one violin at Cremona in 1937.

Galbani Pietro, Florence. 1610—1640. His instruments are, despite their great age, only of mediocre value. Price 10.000 Kč. and more, for collectors.

Galbicellis Giambattista, Florence. 1750.

Galbusera Carlo Antonio, Milan. 1813—1833. His instruments sound well. He also made violins in the shape of the guitar.

Galeazzi Adelino, Ascoli. B. Jan. 1, 1828, d. Feb. 22, 1910. Excellent violinist and amateur violin maker. Handwritten labels: Adelino Galeazzi in Ascoli nel 1863—this label has an addition "dono a suo nipote Giuseppe" (presented to his nephew Joseph).

Galeazzi Eugenio, Ascoli. B. 1790, d. Dec. 22, 1862. Son of a professor of mathematics, violinist and amateur violin maker. Applied yellow-brown varnish and made also mandolins and guitars.

Galeazzi Eugenio II, Ascoli. 1849. Son of Francesco Galeazzi. Worked in the violin-craft only in winter, otherwise he was busy with farming.

Galerzena . . . Piedmont. 1790. He is reported to have been a skilful violin maker who worked in the province of Piedmont.

Galiani Alexander, Naples. Suspicious.

Galieri Filippo, Naples. 1720—1763. Worked on the model

of Nicola Gagliano, whose pupil he may have been. Otherwise little known.

Galieri Giuseppe, Padua, Piacenza. Ca 1753. He calls himself pupil (i. e. follower) of Nic. Amati. The sound-holes of his instruments are cut slantwise. He applied good yellow varnish. Few violins of no particular merit.

Giuseppe Galieri, Paduensis
placentinus Alumnus di Nicola Amati
Faciebat 1753.

Galileo Arcellaschi, Como. Born 1910 in Como. Pupil of Carlo Giuseppe Oddone in Turin. He made violins, violas, violoncellos, lutes and violas d'amore. Golden-yellow varnish.

Galimberti Luigi, Milan. Born Oct. 21, 1888, died Oct. 21, 1957. An assiduous worker; golden-yellow oil (or alcohol) varnish. Pupil of Antoniazzi.

LUIGI GALIMBERTI
fece a Seveso l'anno 1924

Riparato da L. Galimberti - Milano
Via Dolomiti N 17

LUIGI GALIMBERTI
fece a' Milano l'anno 1933

Gallesi Gioacchino, Rome. B. there Jan. 10, 1876, d. March 24, 1956. Paris, later Rome, was owner of a large atelier producing for the most part guitars and mandolins.

G. GALLESI
Fabbricante
di
Strumenti Musicali
CORDE — ACCESSORI
RIPARAZIONI
VIA MARGUTTA N. 17
ROMA
Anno 1949
N............

Galli Domenico, Parma. 1687—1691. Violoncellist and musical composer of the 17th century, amateur violin maker, made a few good instruments.

Domenicus Gallus Parmensis
fecit Parmae anno salutis 1691.

Gallingani, Mancasale, prov. Reggio. B. July 4, 1885. Good workmanship. Stradivari and Guarneri models.

Gallinoti Pietro. Salera (Alessandria). Born July 4, 1885 at Salerno (Piedmont). According to R. Vannes maker of repute both for his own instruments and for repairs. He worked after Stradivari and Guarneri.

Galtani Rocco, Florence. 1640—1670. Violin maker of good repute, yet it is impossible to verify this assertion.

Galvani Giuseppe, 1815—1840. Only one (good) instrument is known.

Gamberini Claudio, Pieve di Cento and Bologna. B. July 5, 1895 at Pieve di Cento. Diligent master, by 1948 producer of 325 instruments.

LIUTERIA CENTES
GAMBERINI CLAUDIO & COMP.
CENTO (Ferrara)

liutaio
Gamberini Claudio
via de Poeti N° 4
Bologna

GAMBERINI CLAUDIO
CENTO (ITALIA)

Gambini Sebastiano, Genoa. Contemporary violin maker.

Gamboni, Naples. Born 1724, died 1814. Built instruments of medium quality. Used very fine wood which had come from the property left by Ant. Amati.

Gandolfi Giuseppe, Cremona. 1925. He used beautiful Cremonese models and golden-yellow varnish.

Ganzerle Luigi, San Felice (Modena). Born about 1794, died 1861. Made good instruments.

Garani Michel Angelo, Bologna. 1685—1720. Worked well on the pattern of Stradivari and applied yellow varnish. Best are his violas. Price 12.000 Kč. and more.

Michel Angelo Garani
in Bologna 1687.

A. Michael
Garanus
F. Bonon. 1724.

A.
MICHAEL
GARANUS
F. BONON:

Garani Nicola, Naples. Ca 1700. Worked on the pattern of Alessandro Gagliano, lacking sometimes in careful workmanship, although he always used the best wood. Brown transparent varnish. Price 14.000 Kč.

Gardelli Federico, Naples. 1880—1900.

Garenghi Giuseppe, Brescia. 1833—1857. He worked after Maggini using orange varnish.

Gargnono — a mere name, otherwise unknown.

Heredes q. Gaſparo
Cargnono de Salodio

Gargo Giovanni, Forli. 1760—1785. Lute- and violin-maker of minor importance who made also guitars.

Garimberti Ferdinando, Milan. Born. Jan. 6, 1894 in Mammiano near Travesatelo in Parma. Violin maker and excellent 'cellist. Conscientious work patterned on the classical Italian school which he imitates both in form and tone. First-class repairs of masterpieces, many first prizes at international exhibitions in Italy and Switzerland.

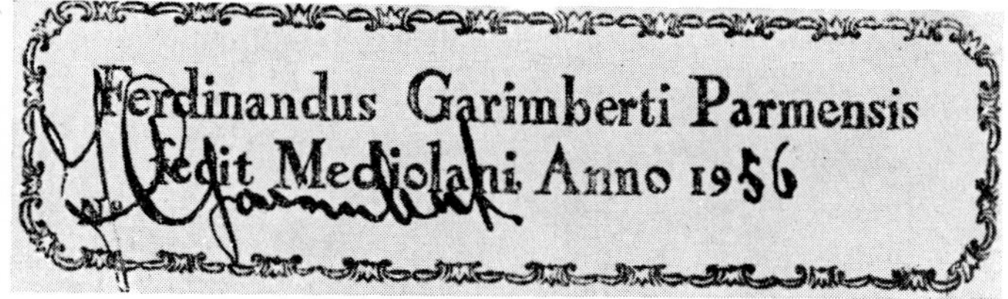
Ferdinandus Garimberti Parmensis
fecit Mediolani Anno 1956

Garini Michelangelo. 19th century.

Garsi Antonio, Parma. 1875—1914. He worked after Cremonese school using brown varnish.

Garzano Giuseppe, Catania. (Sicily). In literature his name occurs without any date: we quote it for the sake of completeness.

Gasta Gaetano, Cremona. 1703.

Gastano Antonio, Messina, Sicily c. 1880—96.

Gatti Angello, Milan. 20th century.

Gatti Ernesto, Turin. C. 1886. Good instruments.

Gatti Giorgio, Turin. 1899—1910. His violins are modelled after Stradivari, and his guitars on G. B. Guadagnini.

Giorgio Gatti
fece in Torino l'anno 1899

Gatto Andrea, Turin. 1665, 1679.

Gavani Giovanni, Spilamberto (Modena). 1860—1908. Apart from bowed instruments he made also guitars and mandolins.

Gavelli Giacomo, Perugia. 1730—1797. Practically unknown.

Gavoni Antonio, Modena. Ca 1760—1777. Built violoncellos and double-basses of medium quality.

Gaynkar Augustin, Cremona. 1746. He worked after Nicolo Amati.

Gazzeri Domenico, Florence. 1682. Lute maker.

Gazzola Prosdocimo, Crespano. Born 1822, died 1884. Built excellent contrabasses and repaired instruments with much skill.

Gelmini Geminiano, Ferrara. 1508.

Gelmini Giovanni, Brescia. Born 1804, died 1864.

Joannes Gelmini
Brescianus Inventor
Anno 1863 No 26. (written labels).

Genova Giovanni Battista, Turin. 1765—1780. Pupil of G. B. Guadagnini who modelled his instruments on Amati. Yellow varnish.

Fecit Taurini Joannes
Baptista Genova 1765.

Genovese Riccardo, Lecco, Montiglio. Born 1883. Pupil of Annibale Fagnola. He worked after Stradivari and Guarneri.

Gentile Michele, Lucca. 1883.

Gerani Turin, 1740—1763. A few medium quality instruments. Orange varnish. Price 10—12.000 Kč.

Gerani N., Naples. 1790—1830. Good instruments coated with yellow varnish.

Gerani Paolo, Cremona. 1614—1630. Little known lute and violin maker.

Gerardi Marco, Milan, Terst, Novara. 1920—1950. He established himself in Milan, in Terst he worked in 1930 and in Novara in 1949.

Geroni Domenico, Ostia near Brescia. 1800—1820. Good imitator of old masters. Applied red varnish. Price c. 8.000 Kč.

Domenico Geroni Ostiano
fecit Anno 1817.

Gerosa Giovanni, Montegno (Sondrio). B. June 19, 1895. Good work, choice wood, alcohol varnish variously coloured, brown, golden-yellow or red.

Gerosa Giovanni
fece in Montegno
l'anno 1947

Gherardi Giacomo, Bologna. 1653, 1677. Only one fine carefully built contrabass of his making is known.

Ghidini Carlo, Parma. 1746—1773.

Ghirardi Giovanni Baptista, Venice. 1785, 1791. Little known violin maker.

Joannes Bapta: Ghirardi
fecit anno 1791
Venetijs.

Joannes Bapta: Ghirardi
fecit anno 1791 Venetijs

Giacchetti Giuseppe, Rome. B. March 26, 1890. A pupil of Rodolfo Freddi, applies oil varnish of orange or golden-red colour.

Giacco Antonio, Osimo (Ancona). Contemporary (since 1928) violin and guitar maker.

Giacco Antonio Liutaio
Osime Marche 1928.

Giacinti Celeste, Milan. 20th century specialist in guitar making.

Giacometti Giambattista, called "Del Violino" Rome 1586. He is reported to have made harps. It cannot be ascertained whether he built also violins, but his epithet "Del

Violino" supports the supposition that he was also a violin maker.

Giacomo in Chioggia. Ca 1346. Mediaeval lute maker whose works have not come down to us.

Giacomo .... Chioggia, another lute maker about the middle of the 16th century, probably descendant of the former.

Giamberini Alessandro, Florence. 1771. Good violin of that date; golden-yellow varnish.

Giamberini Claudio — perhaps a faked name, known from just one specimen.

Giamberini Giovanni Lodovico, Florence. 17th century. Lute maker, perhaps ancestor of Alessandro Giamberini.

Giamberini Simeone, Florence. 18th century. Amati and Stradivari models, arched or flat; golden-red varnish.

Giammarini Egidio, Ascoli. B. July 1, 1865, d. June 1, 1915. Worked mostly for agents; violins, etc., he varnished himself are brown or reddish-brown.

Gianmarini Egidio
Ascoli, Piceno 1898.

Gianni Alessio, Modena. 1770, 1793. His violins are reported to have a very good tone.

Giannini Fabrizio, Viareggio. Born in Arezzo 1912. Distinct model of his own, also inlaid specimens and good guitars.

Gianoli Domenico, Milan. 1710—1731. Good follower of the Cremonese masters who modelled his instruments on Stradivari and used golden-yellow varnish. One of the "submerged" violin-makers who was worthy of a better fate. Price 15.000 Kč.

Gianotti Achille, Sarazano. Ca 1870, dealer and repairer.

Giaroni Elviro di Venerio, Reggio Emilia. Had one violin at the 1937 Exhibition in Cremona.

Gibertini Antonio, Parma, Genoa, 1797—1866. Excellent imitator of Stradivari and Guarneri (he modelled his imitations on Paganini's Guarneri violin). The few surviving instruments corroborate the supposition that he applied himself more to repairing work than to the creation of new instruments. His violins have a good, strong tone. Deep red varnish applied in thick coats. From 1833 he worked in Genoa. Price 12—16.000 Kč.

Restaurò e corresse nell anno 1839 in Genova
Antonio Gibertini di Parma.

Premiato più volte in Milano con Medaglia etc.
Antonio Gibertini
Parma 18.

Gibertini Antonio fece in Parma anno 1840.

Gibertini Giuseppe, called "Paninino" (i.e. "Baker"). Modena. 1800. Price 6—8.000 Kč.

Gigli Giulio Cesare, Rome. 1721—1762. Worked sometimes on the pattern of Amati, but more often in the style of David Tecchler. Some of his rather broad-edged works are good: their arching is higher than that of the instruments built by Tecchler. He applied a red-yellow or red varnish. The best of his 'cellos and violins are the red ones. Price 60—80.000 Kč, 'cello more.

Julius Cæſar Gigli Romanus
Fecit Romæ Anno 1761

Julius Cæſar Gigli Romanus
Fecit Romæ Anno 17..

Gioffreda B., Turin. 1860.

Giorgetti Giovanni Antonio, Barga (Toscana). B. 1847.

Giombini Egidio, Jesi (Ancona). B. Oct. 25, 1907. Orange varnish with a reddish tint.

Giombini Egio
Jesi 1949

Giordano Alberto, Cremona. 1725—1740. Worked on the pattern of Stradivari, but not with much success. The wood is not well selected. Broad edges, roughly finished purfling. His 'cellos, however, have a beautiful tone. Yellow-brown or red-brown varnish. Price 25.000 Kč, 'cello far more.

Al... to Giordano fecit
Cremonae 17..

Giordani Enrico, Genoa. Exhibited two violins at Cremona in 1937.

Giorgi Nicola, Turin 1717—1760. Pupil of G. Cappa, but at the same time follower of Stradivari. Best are his violas and violas d'amore. Price 15—18.000 Kč.

Nicolaus Giorgi faciebat
Famini anno 17..

NICOLAUS GIORGIS
fecit Taurini a.nno 1750

Giovannetti Leonardo, Lucca. Born 1816 at Lucca, died Nov. 30, 1884. He was a lawyer, a good musician and good amateur violin maker.

Leonardo Giovannetti
fece in Lucca Anno 18..

107. Gagliano Fernando, Napoli 17..

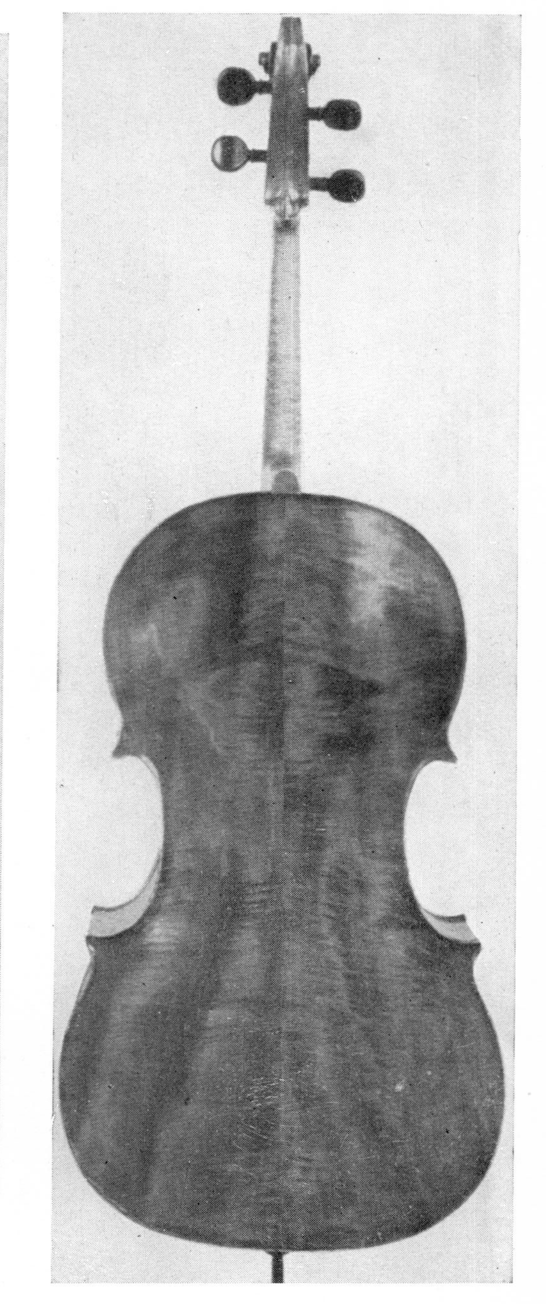

108. Gagliano Fernando, Napoli (CELLO)

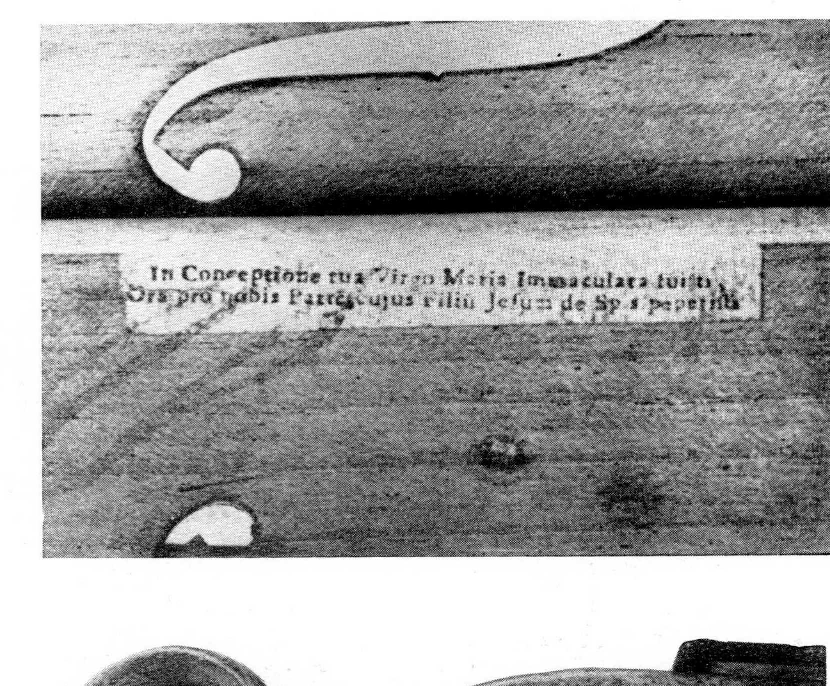

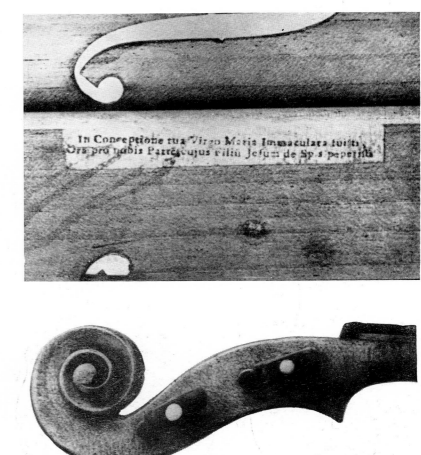

109. Gagliano Januarius, Napoli 1743
Photo Hamma & Co

110. Gagliano Januarius, Napoli 1750
Photo Hamma & Co

111. Gagliano Januarius, Napoli 1748
Photo Hamma & Co

112. Gagliano Januarius, Napoli 1755
Photo Hamma & Co

113. Gagliano Januarius, Napoli 1759
Photo Hamma & Co

114. Gagliano Januarius, Napoli 1775
Photo Hamma & Co

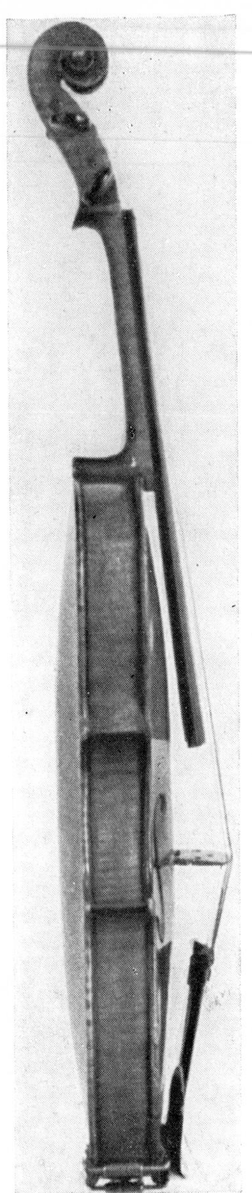
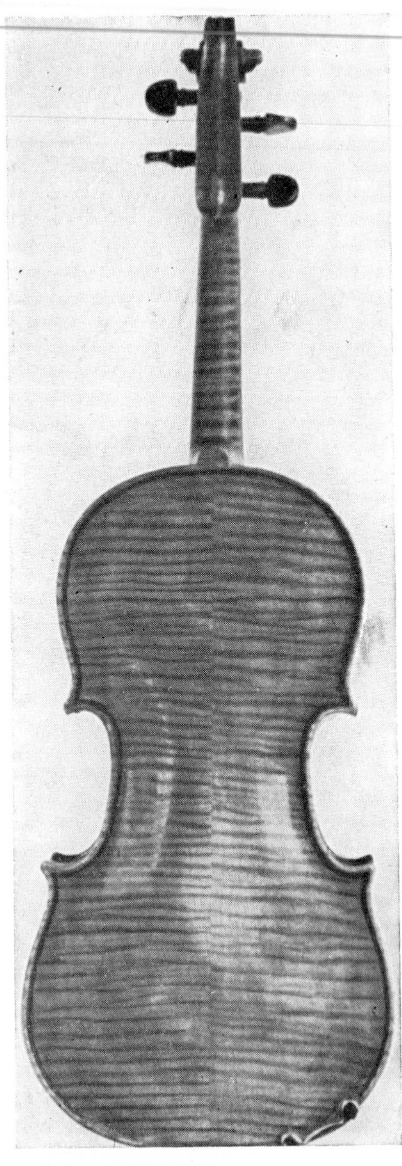
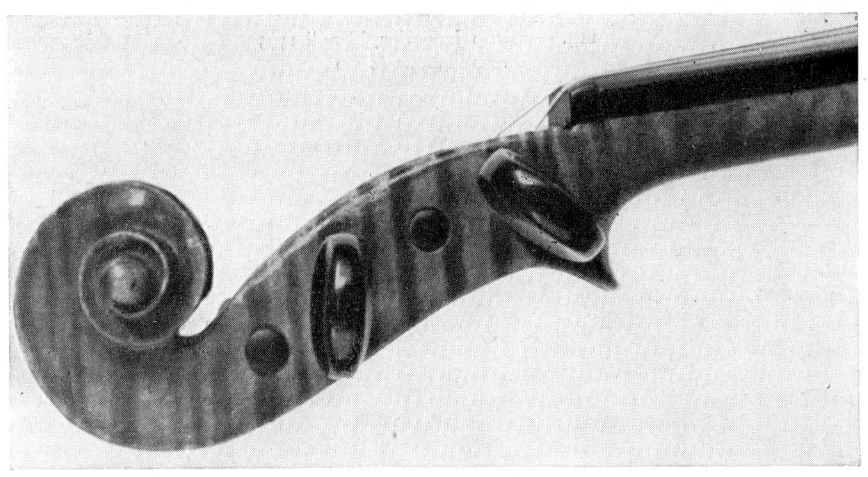

115. Gagliano Joannes, Napoli 1804

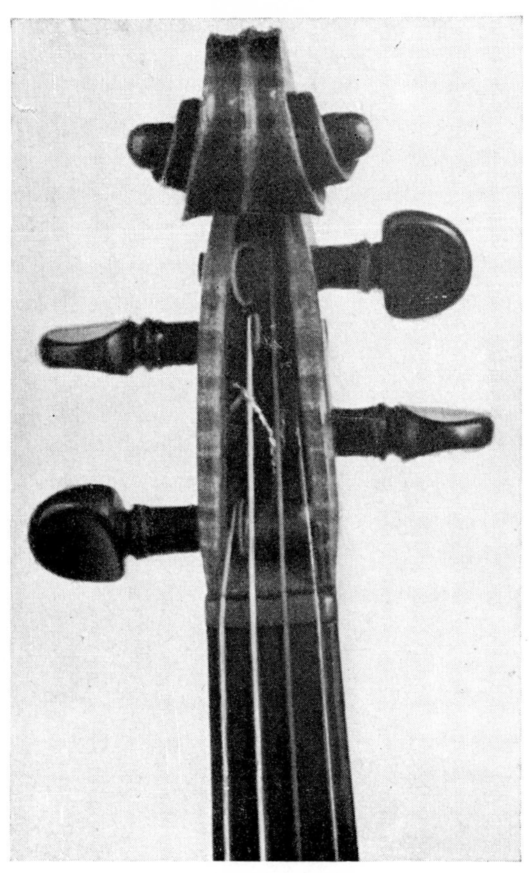

116. Gagliano Joannes, Napoli 1804

117. Gagliano Joannes, Napoli 1860
Photo Hamma & Co

118. Gagliano Joseph, Napoli
Photo Hamma & Co

119. Gagliano Joseph, Napoli 1793
Photo Hamma & Co

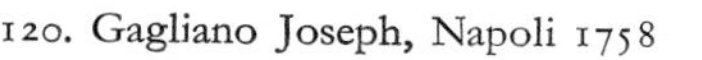

120. Gagliano Joseph, Napoli 1758

121. Gagliano Joseph, Napoli 1740

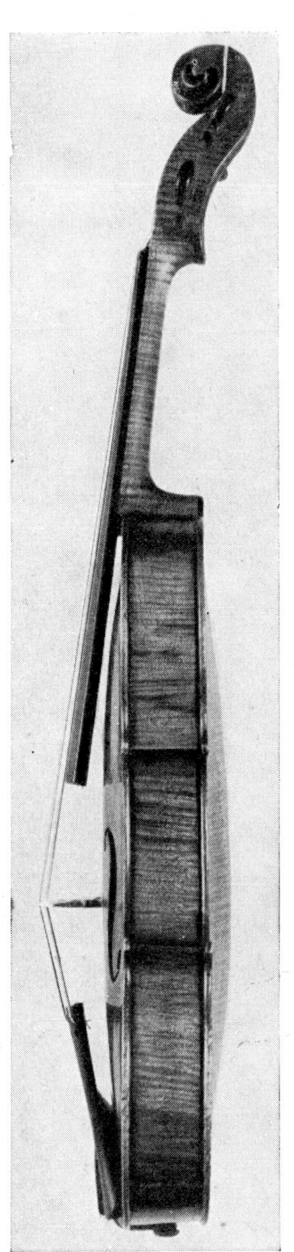
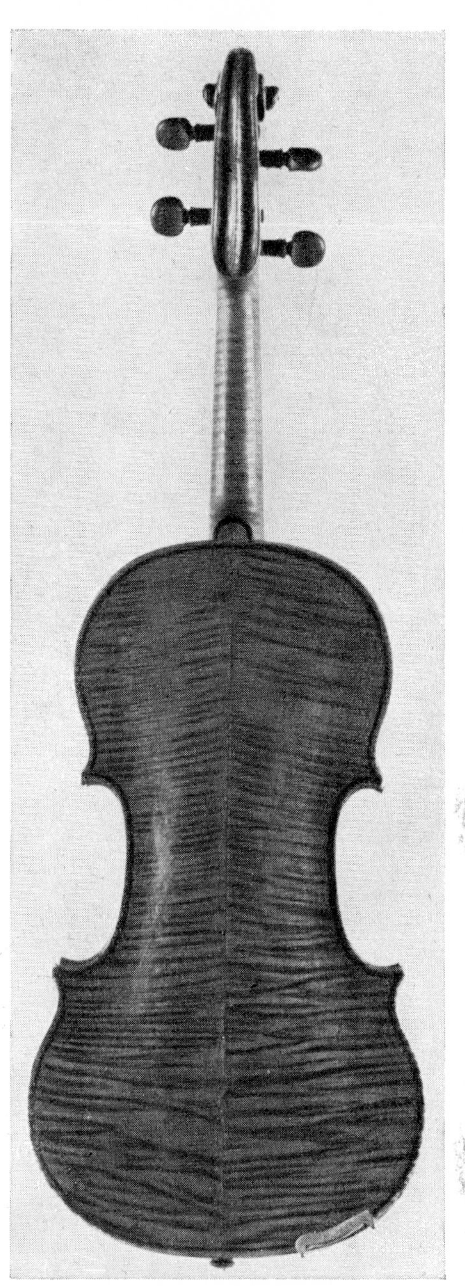

122. Gagliano Joseph, Napoli (VIOLA)

123. Gagliano Alessandro, Napoli 1760
Photo Hamma & Co

124. Gagliano Joseph, Napoli 1784
Photo Hamma & Co

125. Gagliano Joseph & Antonio, Napoli (CELLO)
Photo Hamma & Co

126. Gagliano Nicolo, Napoli 17..
Photo Hamma & Co

127. Gagliano Nicolo, Napoli 1725
Photo Hamma & Co

128. Gagliano Nicolo, Napoli 1735
Photo Hamma & Co

129. Gagliano Nicolo, Napoli 1740
Photo Hamma & Co

130. Gagliano Nicolo, Napoli 1732

131. Gagliano Nicolo, Napoli 1732

132. Gagliano Nicolo, Napoli 17.. (CELLO)

133. Gagliano Nicolo, Napoli 1739

134. Gagliano Nicolo, Napoli 1751
Photo Hamma & Co

135. Gagliano Nicolo, Napoli 1740

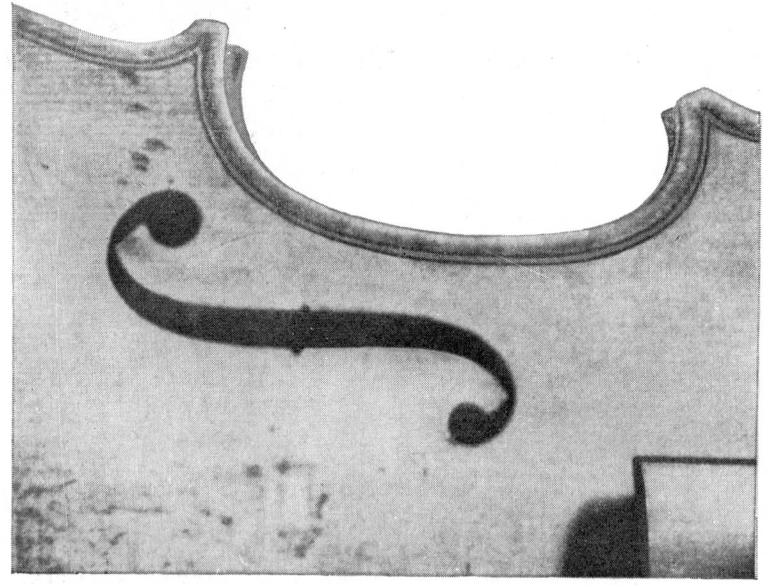

142. Gobetti Francesco, Venezia
Photo Hamma & Co

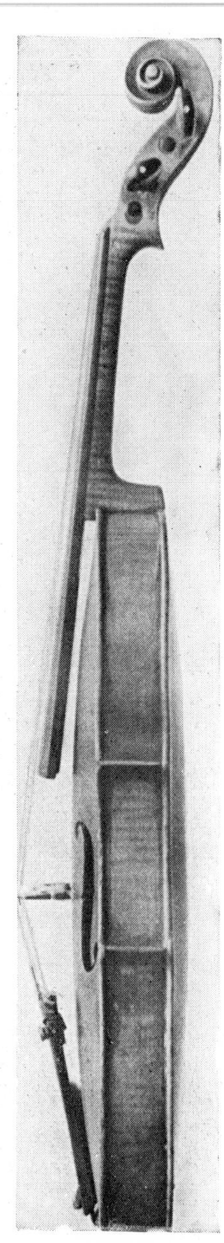
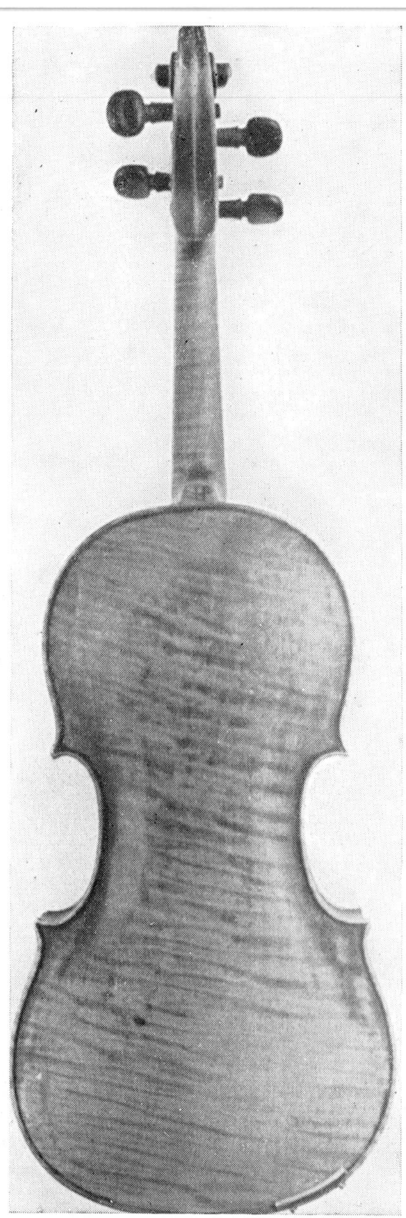

143. Gobetti Francesco, Venezia 1730

144. Goffriller Mateo, Venezia
Photo Hamma & Co

145. Goffriller Mateo, Venezia
Photo Hamma & Co

146. Goffriller Mateo, Venezia
Photo Hamma & Co

147. Goffriller Mateo, Venezia 1691
Photo Hamma & Co

148. Goffriller Mateo, Venezia 1707
Photo Hamma & Co

149. Goffriller Mateo, Venezia 1700

150. Goffriller Mateo, Venezia 1730
Photo Hamma & Co

151. Goffriller Mateo, Venezia 1724

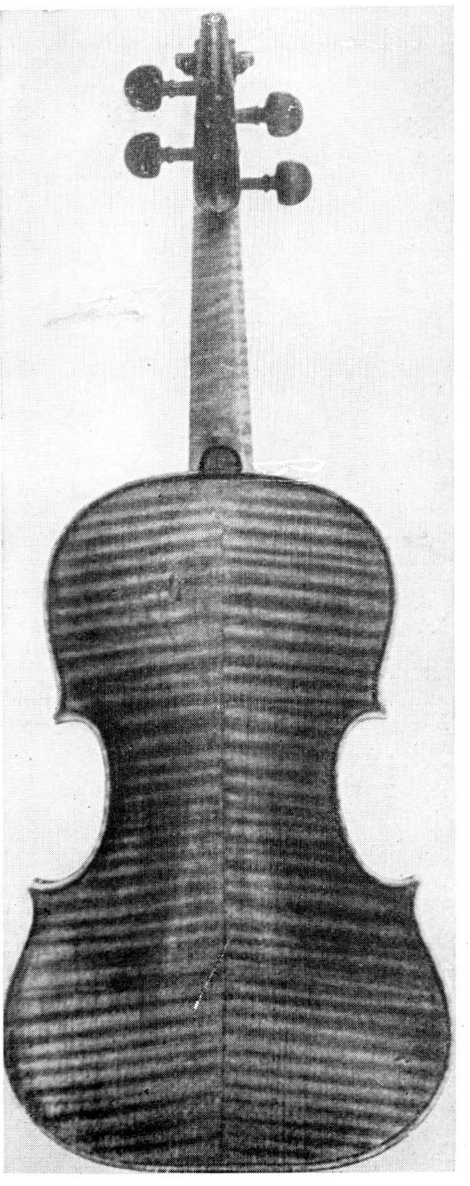

152. Goffriller Mateo, Venezia 1728

153. Goffriller Mateo, Venezia 1725
Photo Hamma & Co

154. Goffriller Mateo, Venezia 1724
Photo Hamma & Co

155. Goffriller Mateo, Venezia 1737
Photo Hamma & Co

161. Grancino Giovanni Battista, Milano 1704

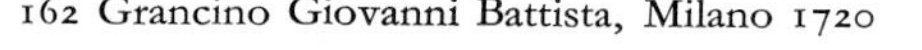

162 Grancino Giovanni Battista, Milano 1720

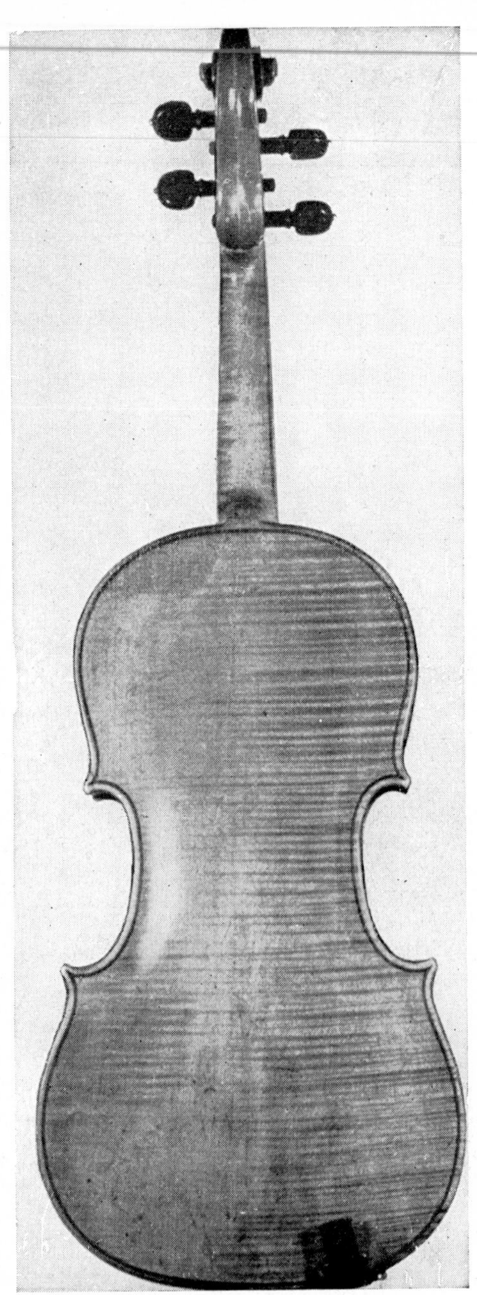

163. Grancino Giovanni Battista, Milano 1707

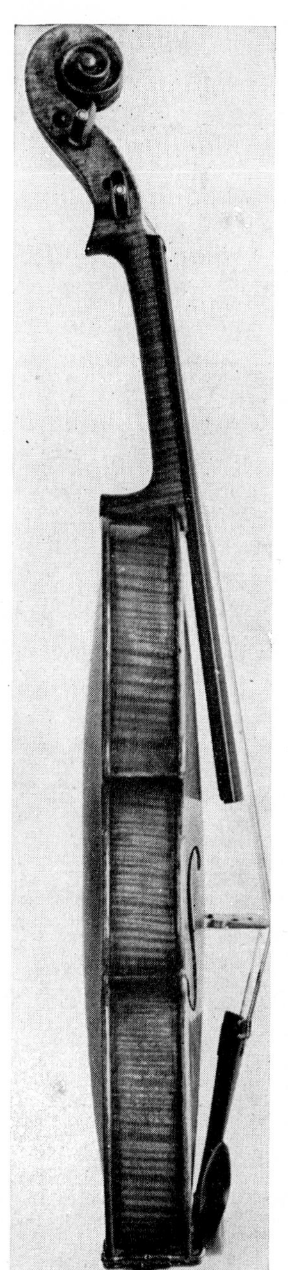

164. Grulli Pietro, Cremona

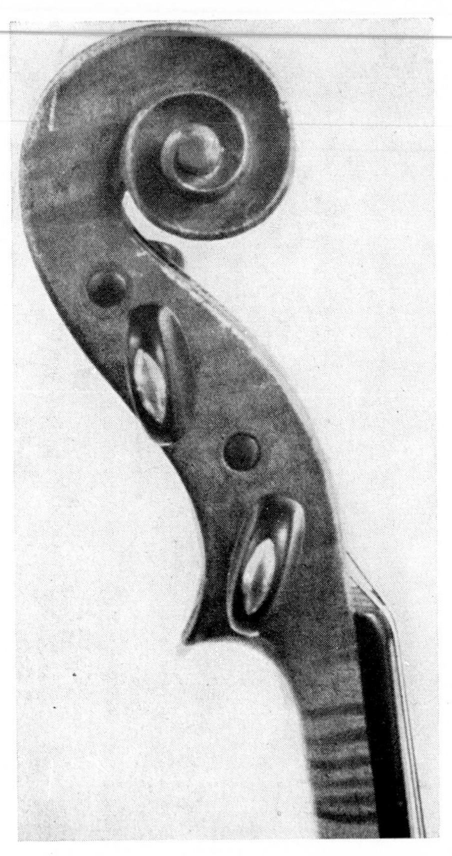

165. Grulli Pietro, Cremona

166. Guadagnini Carlo, Torino 1829

167. Guadagnini Carlo, Torino

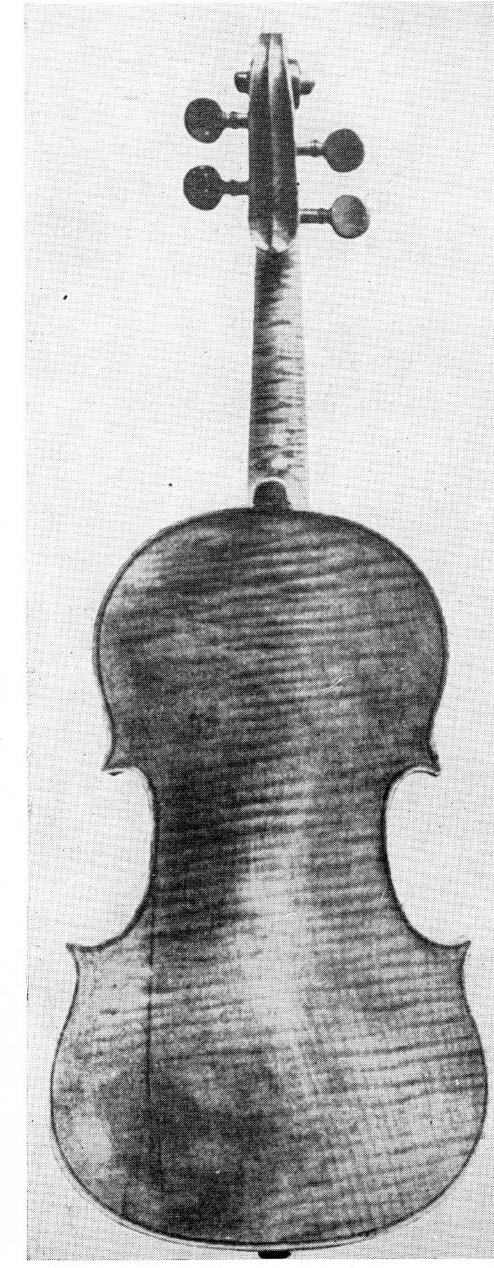

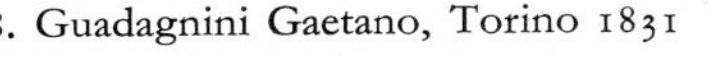

168. Guadagnini Gaetano, Torino 1831

169. Guadagnini Gaetano, Torino 1831

170. Guadagnini J. B., Torino 17..
Photo Hamma & Co

171. Guadagnini J. B., Torino 17..
Photo Hamma & Co

172. Guadagnini J. B., Piacenza 1740
Photo Hamma & Co

173. Guadagnini J. B., Piacenza 1741
Photo Hamma & Co

174. Guadagnini J. B., Piacenza 1745
Photo Hamma & Co

175. Guadagnini J. B., Piacenza 1749 ('CELLO)
Photo Hamma & Co

176. Guadagnini J. B., Milano 17..
Photo Hamma & Co

177. Guadagnini J. B., Milano 1753

178. Guadagnini J. B., Milano 1754
Photo Hamma & Co

179. Guadagnini J. B., Milano 1754
Photo Hamma & Co

180. Guadagnini J. B., Parma 1760
Photo Hamma & Co

181. Guadagnini J. B., Parma 1761
Photo Hamma & Co

182. Guadagnini J. B., Parma 1764
Photo Hamma & Co

183. Guadagnini J. B., Parma 1765
Photo Hamma & Co

184. Guadagnino J. B., Torino 17..
Photo Hamma & Co

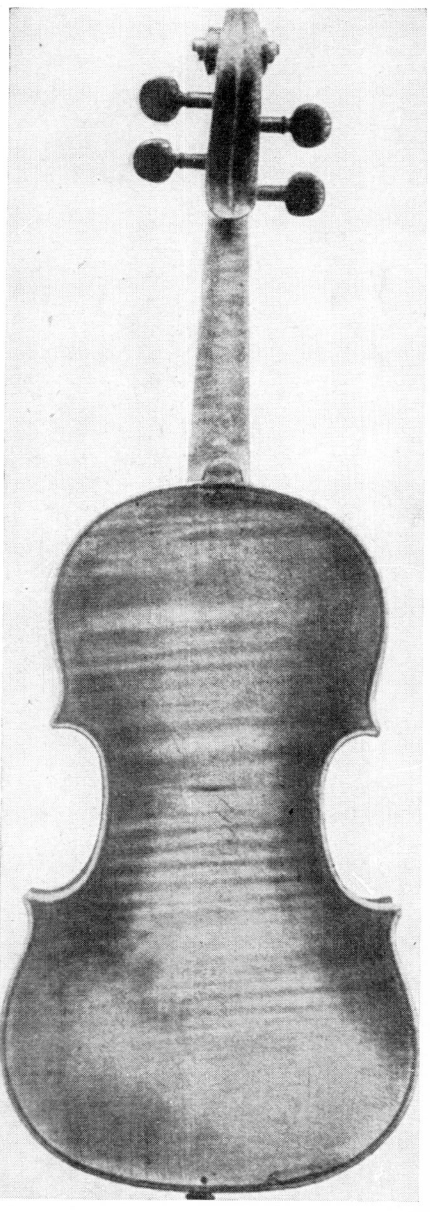

185. Guadagnini J. B., Torino 1770
Photo Hamma & Co

186. Guadagnini J. B., Torino 1770
Photo Hamma & Co

187. Guadagnini J. B., Torino 1772

193. Guadagnini J. B., Torino 1780
Photo Hamma & Co

194. Guadagnini J. B., Torino 1799
Photo Hamma & Co

195. Guadagnini Joseph, Parma 1770

196. Guadagnini Joseph, Parma 1784
Photo Hamma & Co

197. Guadagnini Joseph, Parma 1798
Photo Hamma & Co

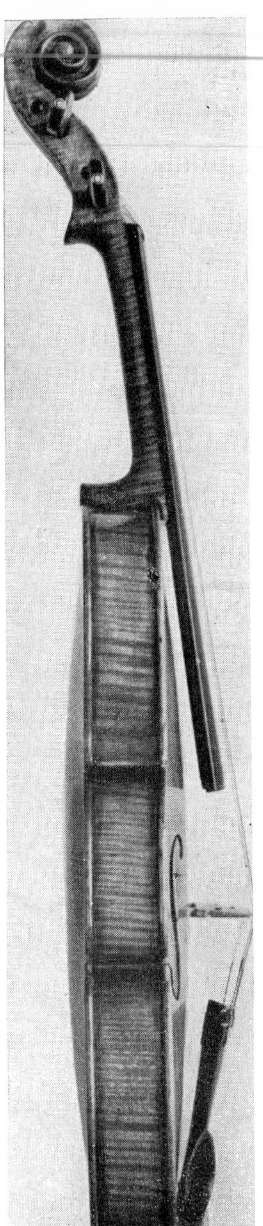
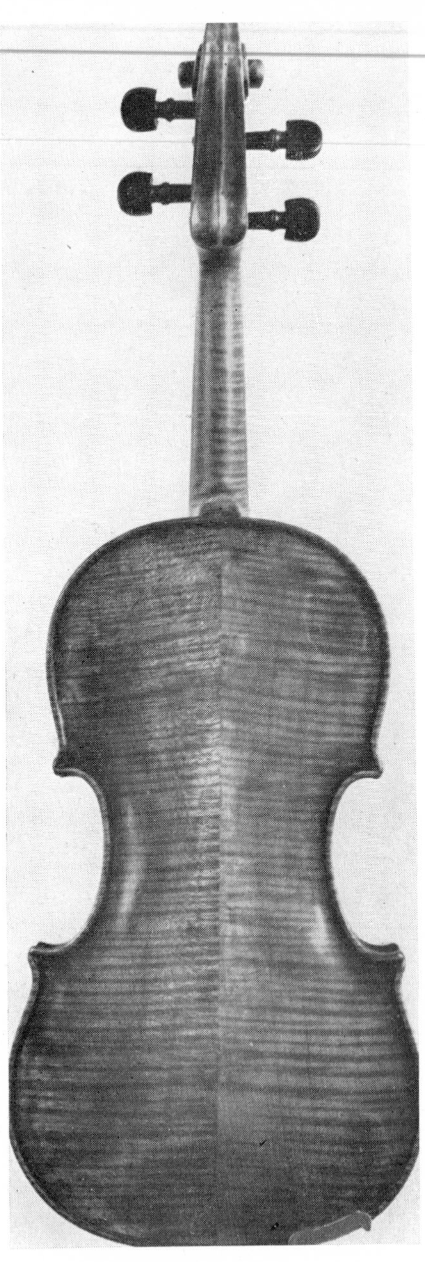
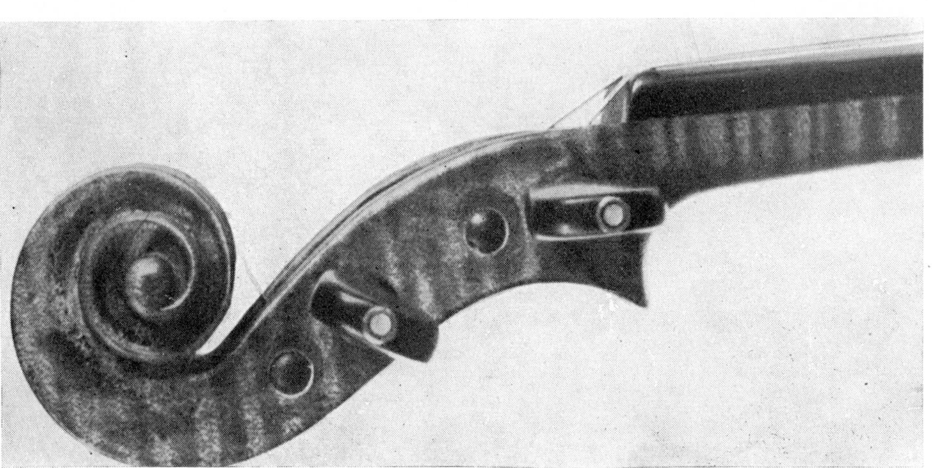

198. Guadagnini Lorenzo, Cremona

199. Guadagnini Lorenzo, Cremona

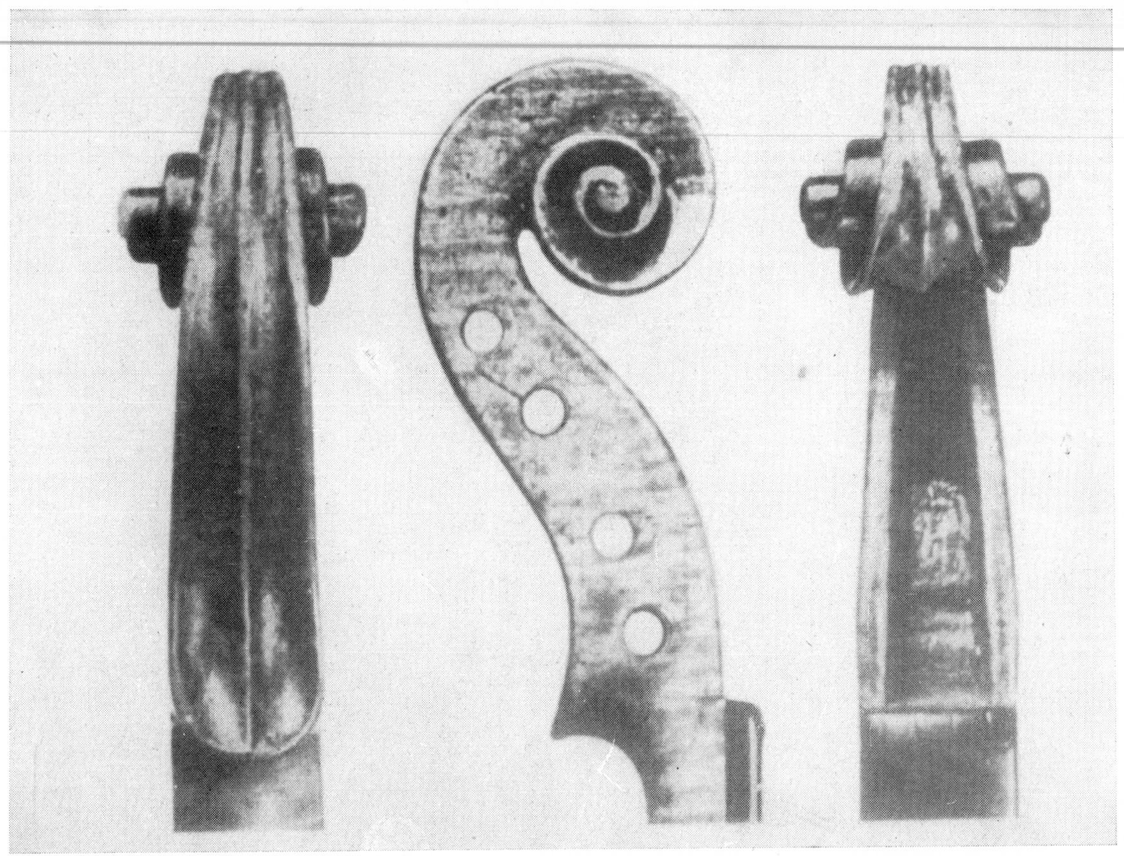

200. Guarneri Andrea, Cremona 1650—1660

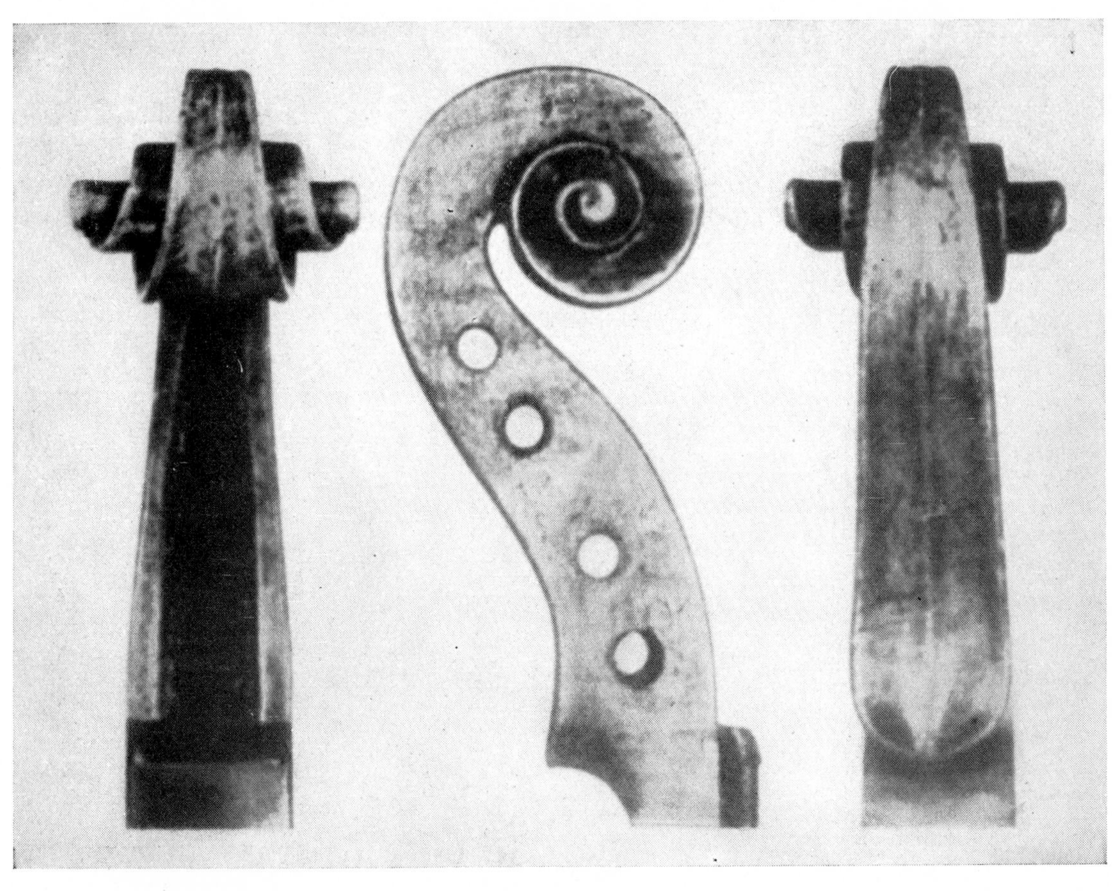

201. Guarneri Andrea, Cremona 1660—1670

202. Guarneri Andrea, Cremona 1680—1685

203. Guarneri Andrea, Cremona 1690—1695

204. Guarneri Pietro I., Mantua 1700—1705

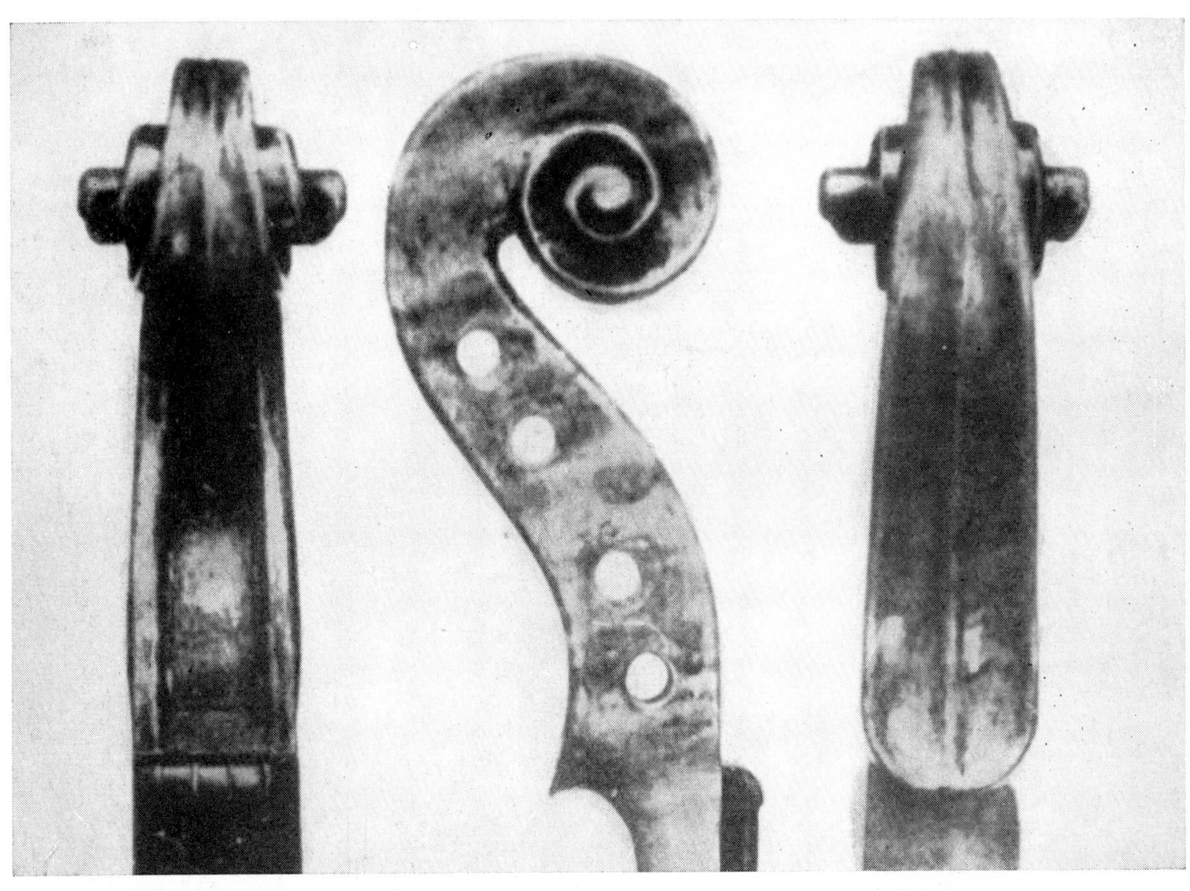

205. Guarneri Josepf, Cremona 1710—1715

206. Guarneri Joseph fil. Andreae, Cremona 1720—1725

207. Guarneri Joseph fil. Andreae, Cremona 1725

208. Guarneri Pietro II., Venezia 1721

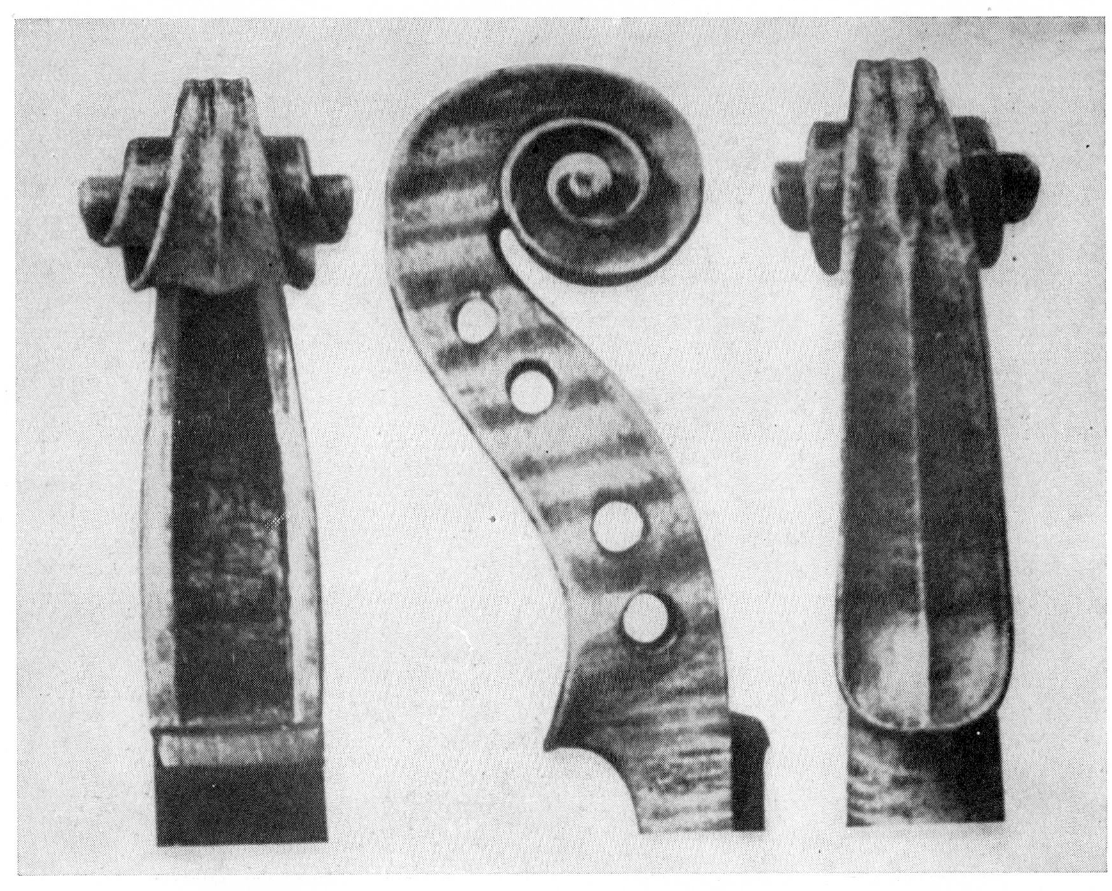

209. Guarneri Pietro II., Venezia 1725—1730

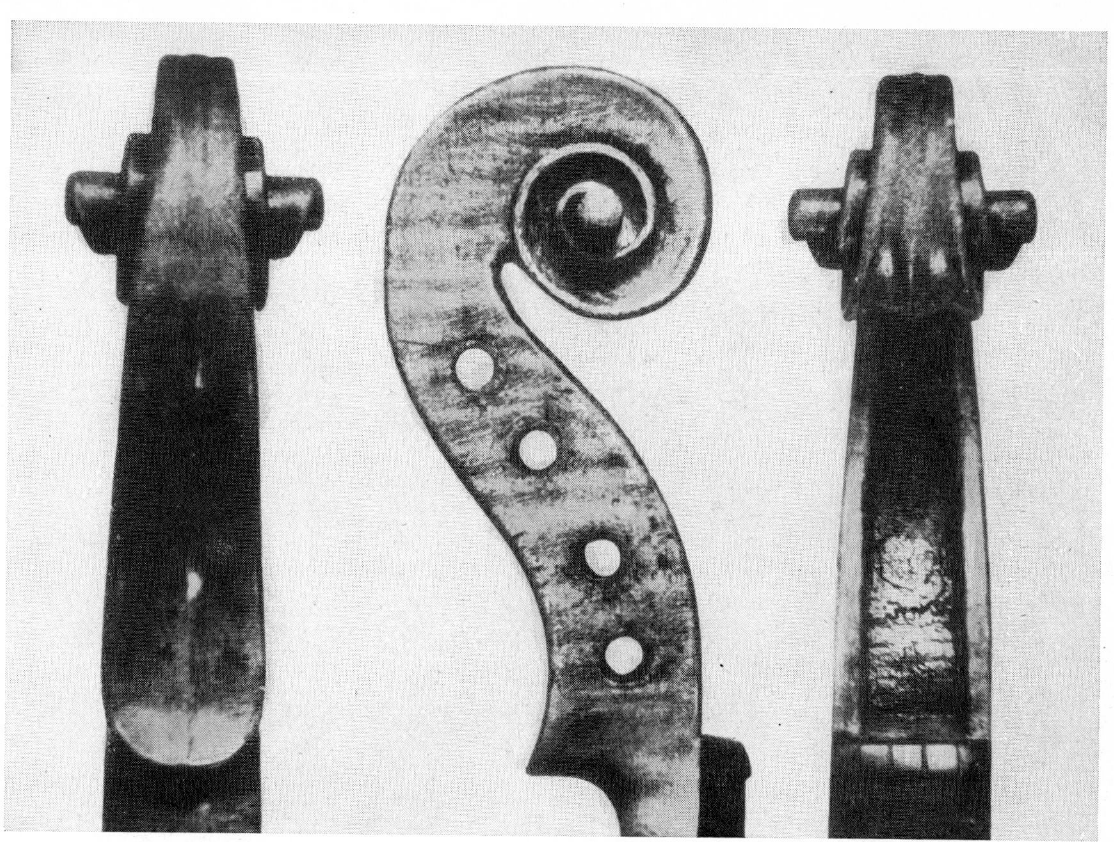

210. Guarneri Joseph del Gesù, Cremona 1725—1730

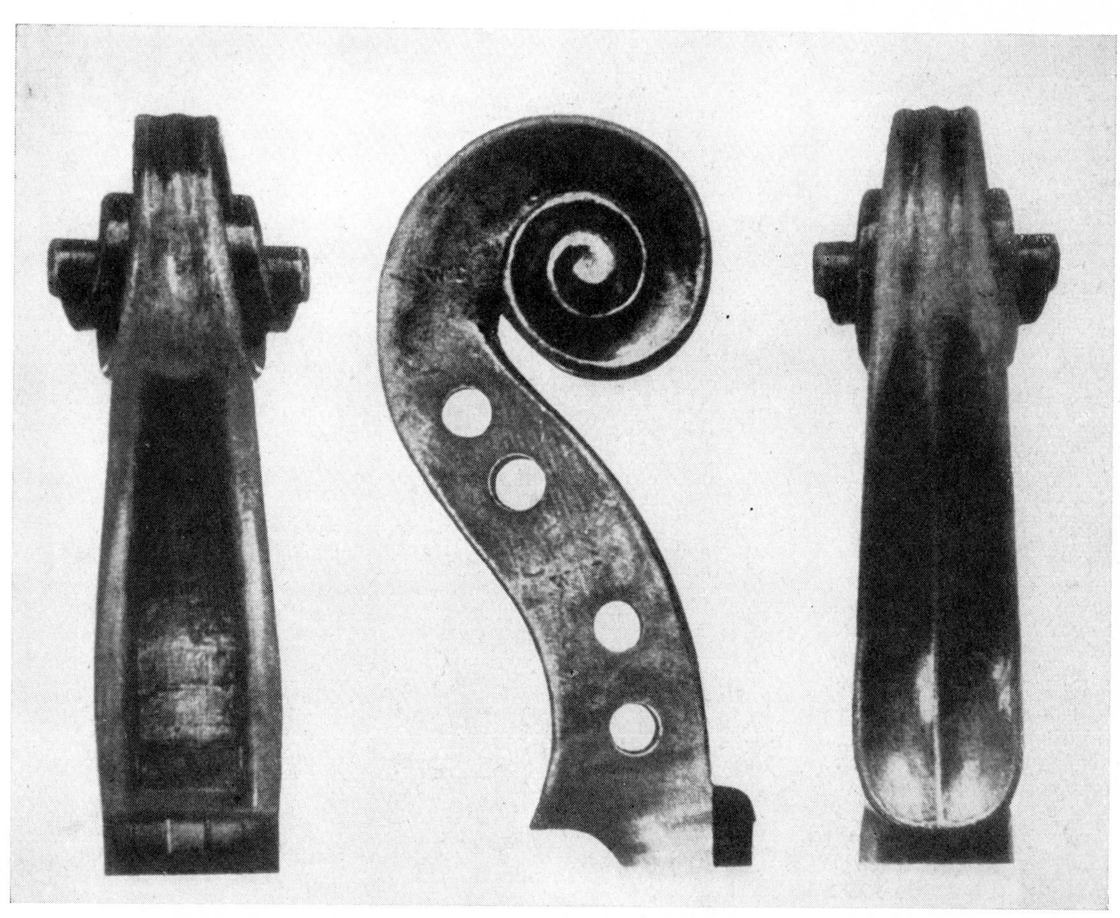

211. Guarneri Joseph del Gesù, Cremona 1730—1733

212. Guarneri Joseph del Gesù, Cremona 1730—1733

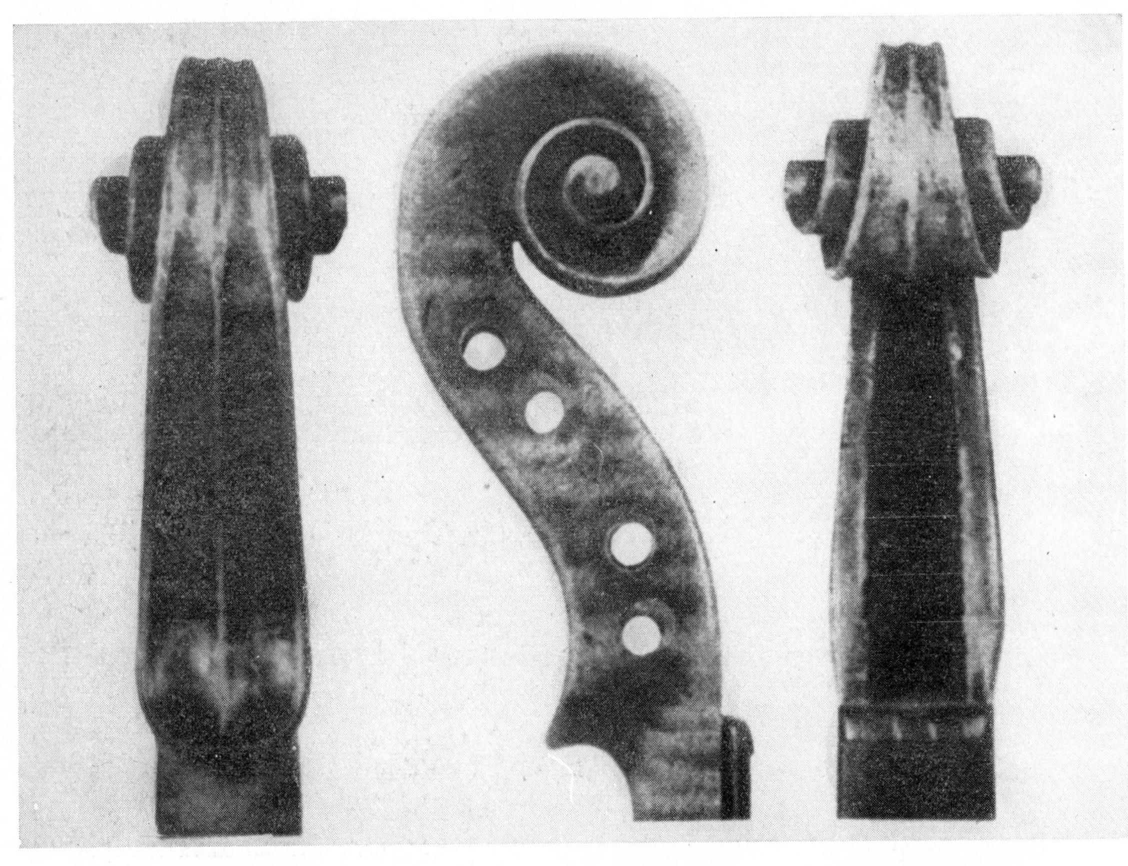

213. Guarneri Pietro II., Venezia 1730—1735

214. Guarneri Joseph del Gesù, Cremona 1740—1741

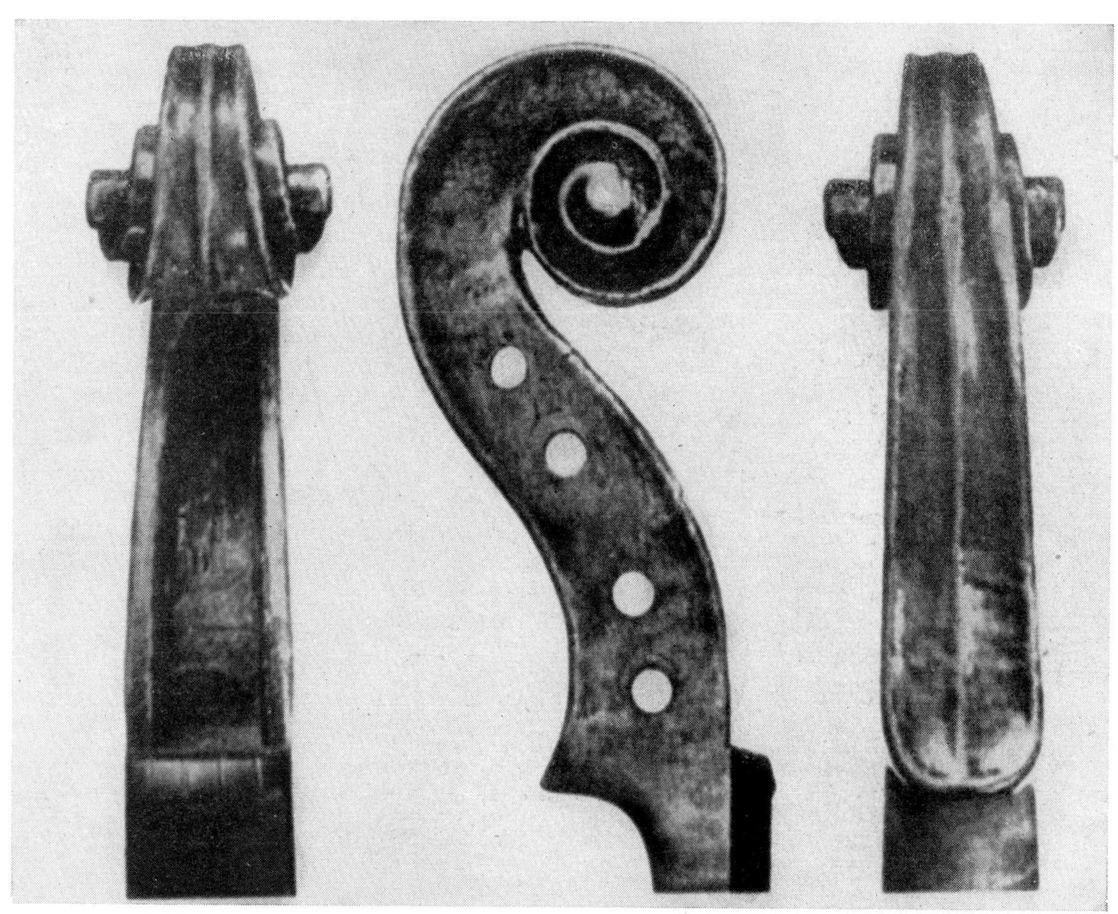

215. Guarneri Joseph del Gesù, Cremona 1735

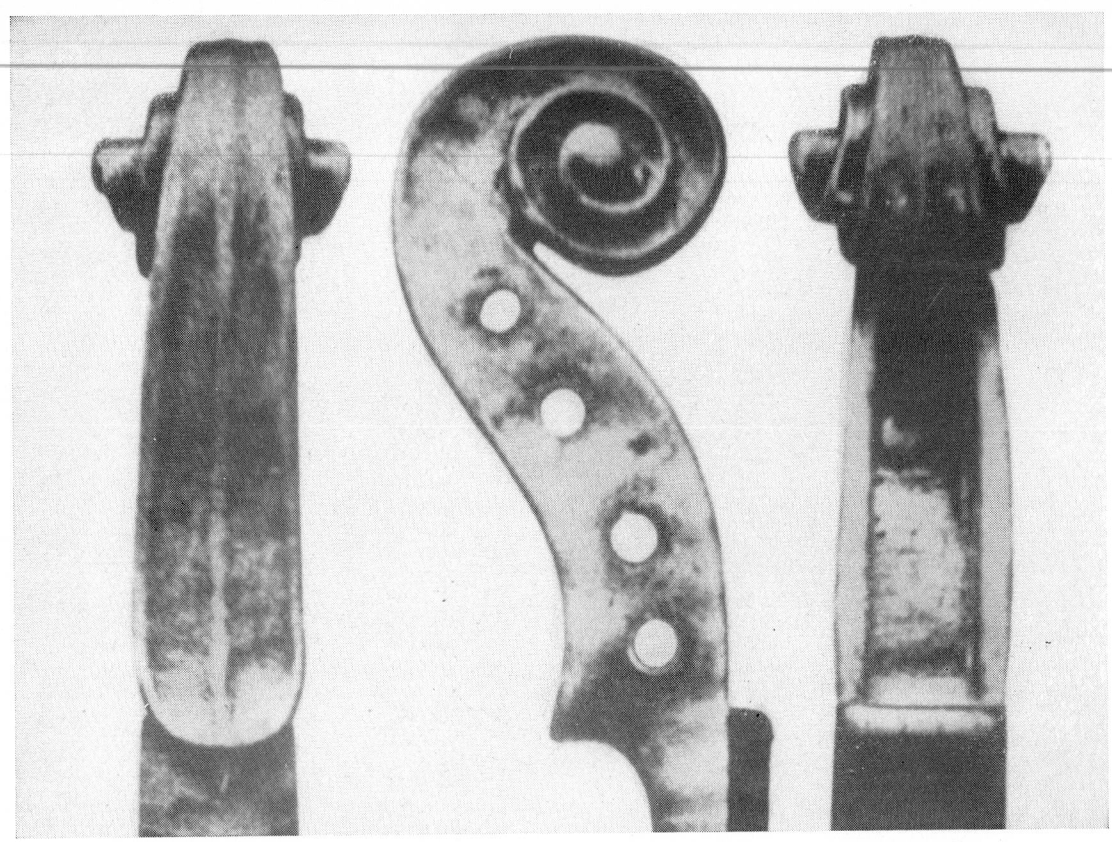

216. Guarneri Joseph del Gesù, Cremona 1740—1742

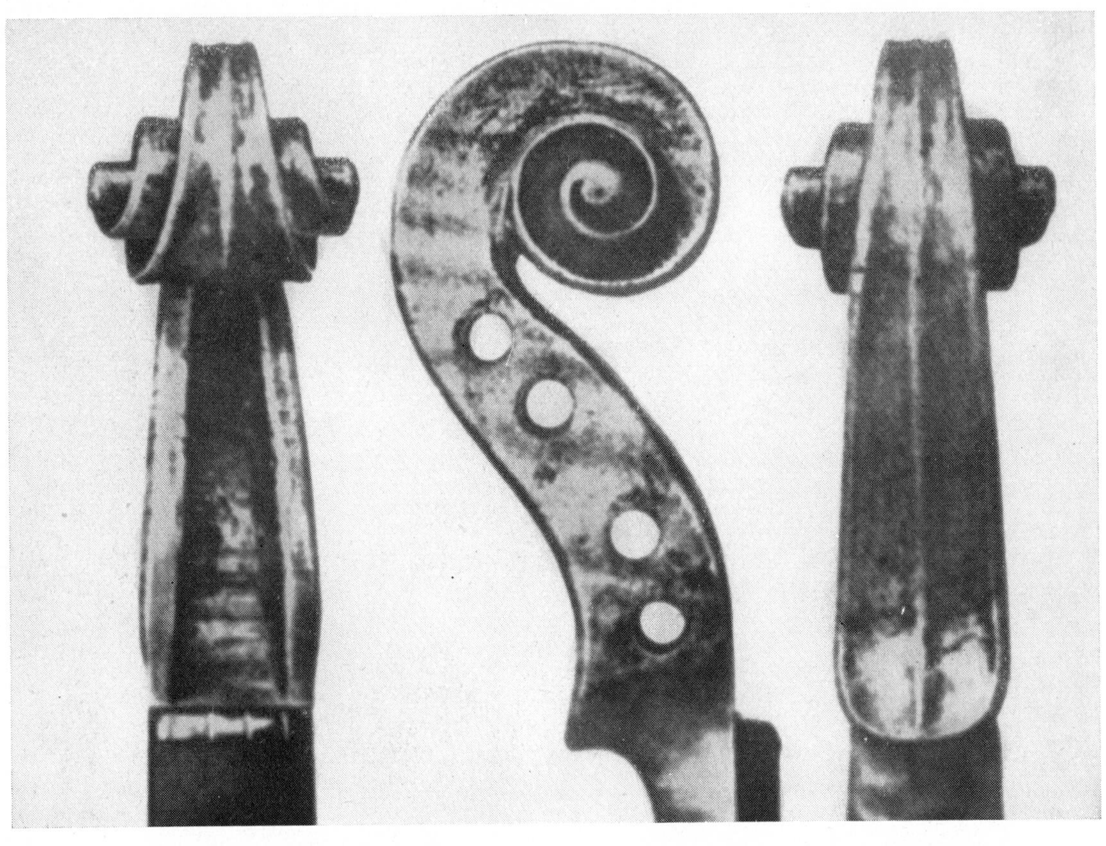

217. Guarneri Pietro II., Venezia 1740—1745

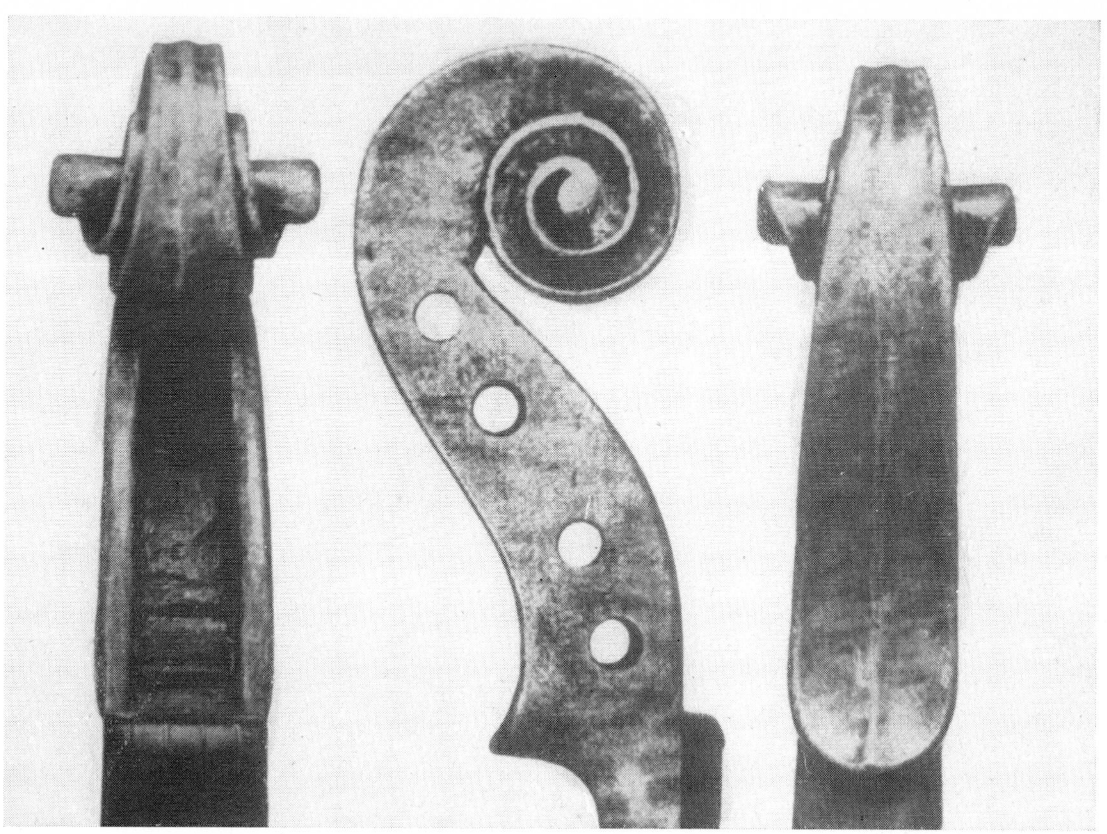

218. Guarneri Joseph del Gesù, Cremona 1742

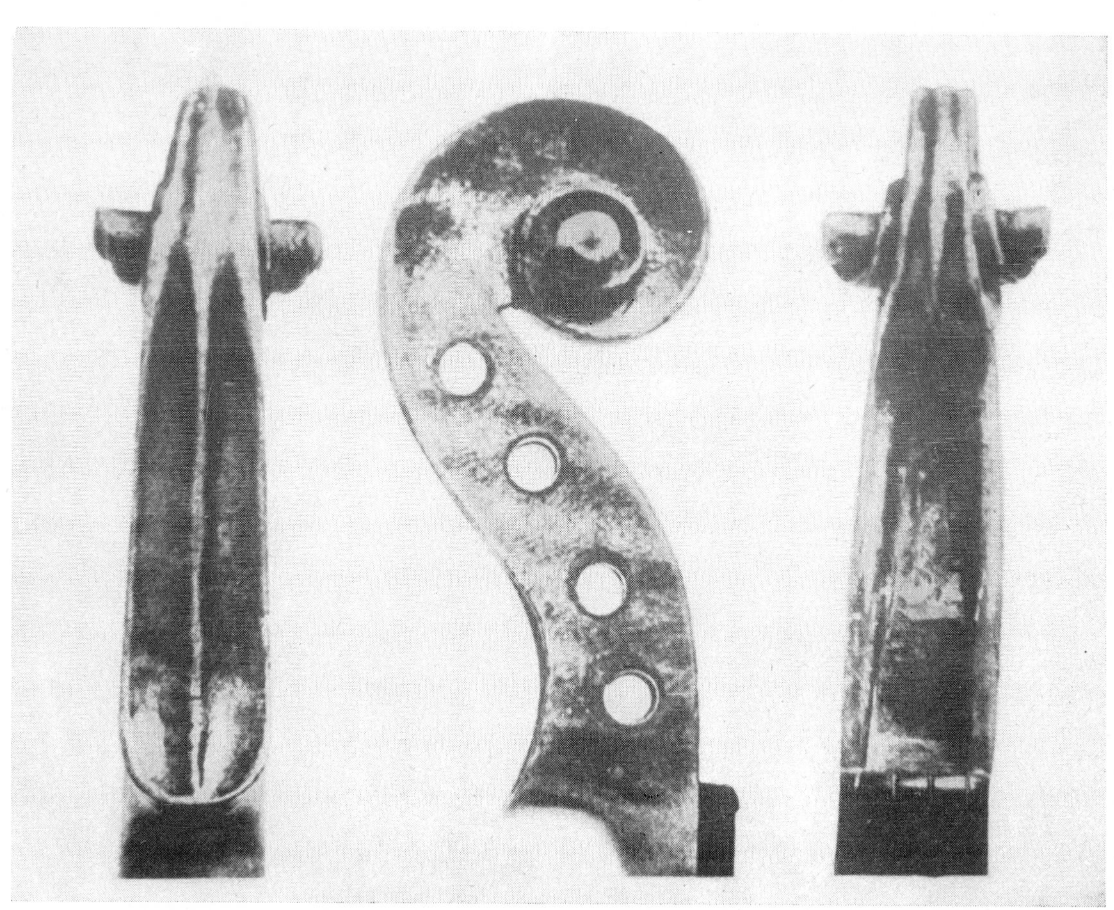

219. Guarneri Joseph del Gesù, Cremona 1743—1744

220. Guarneri Andrea, Cremona

221. Guarneri Andrea, Cremona 1687

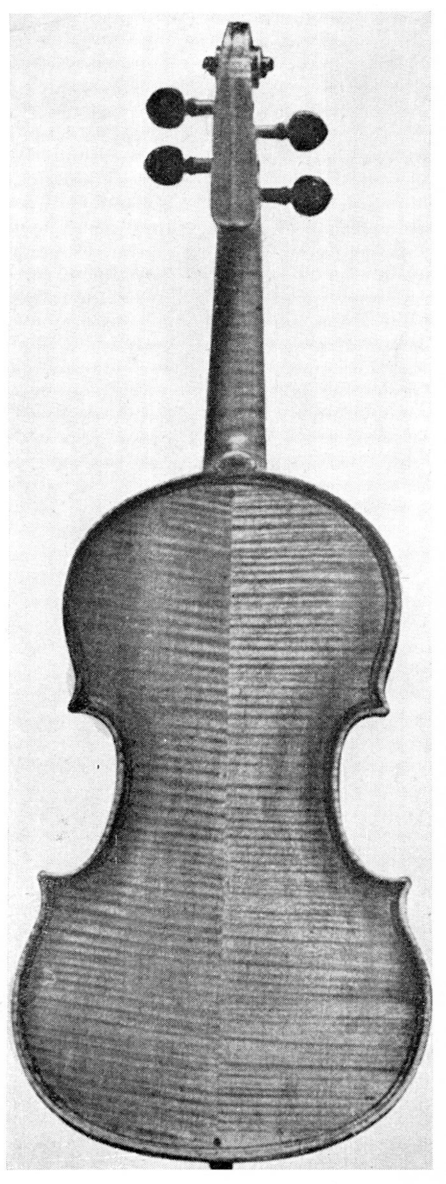
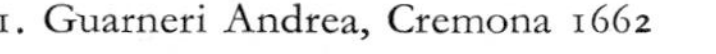

221. Guarneri Andrea, Cremona 1662

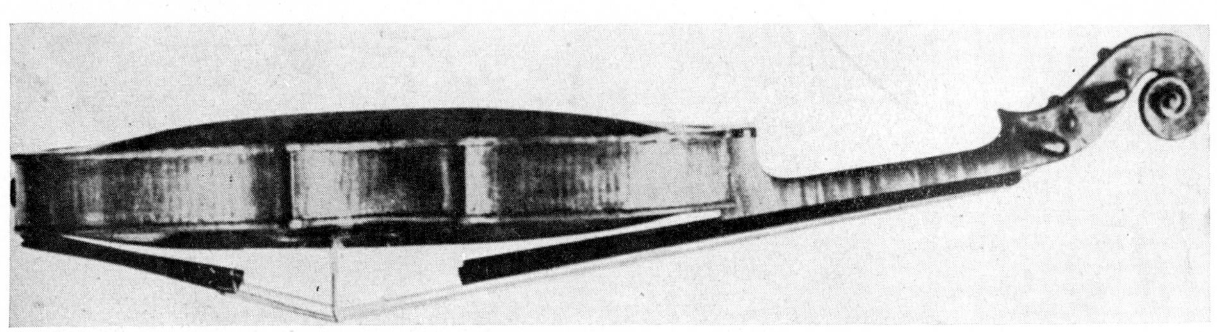

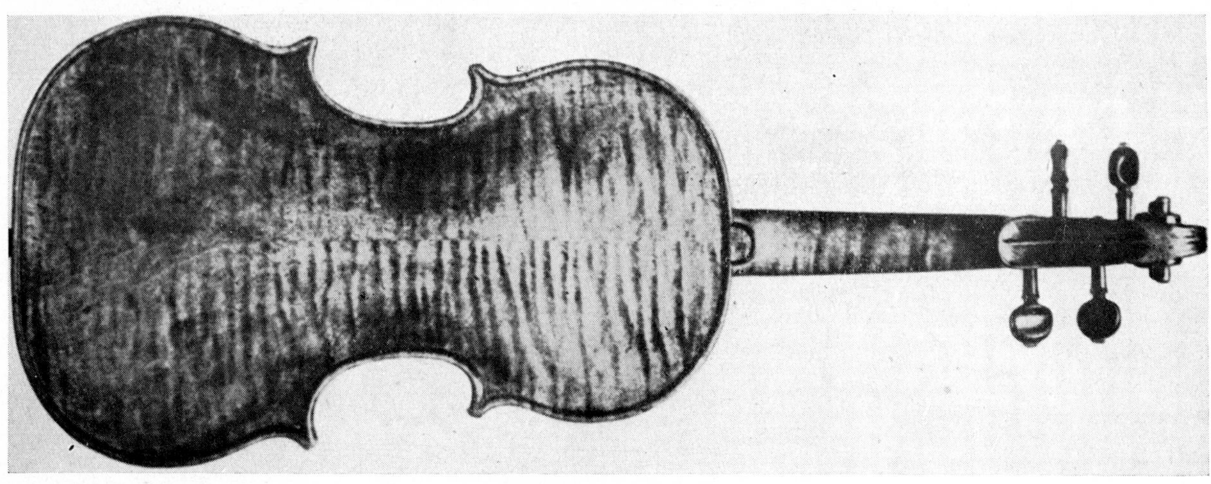

222. Guarneri Andrea, Cremona 1645

223. Guarneri Joseph fil. Andreae, Cremona 1697
Photo Hamma & Co

224. Guarneri Joseph fil. Andreae, Cremona

225. Guarneri Joseph fil. Andreae, Cremona 1707
Photo Hamma & Co

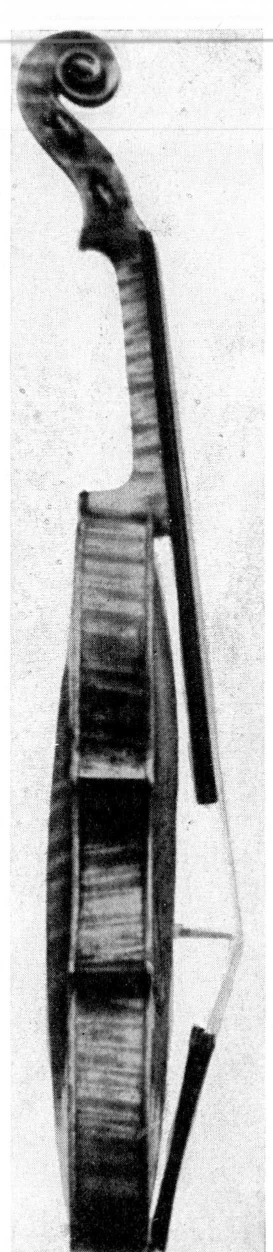
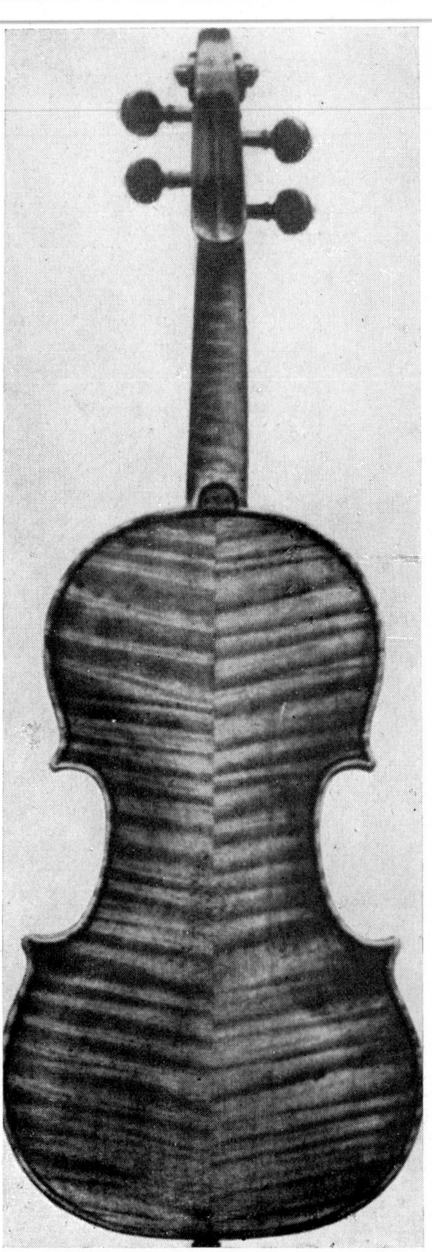

226. Guarneri Joseph fil. Andreae, Cremona 1720

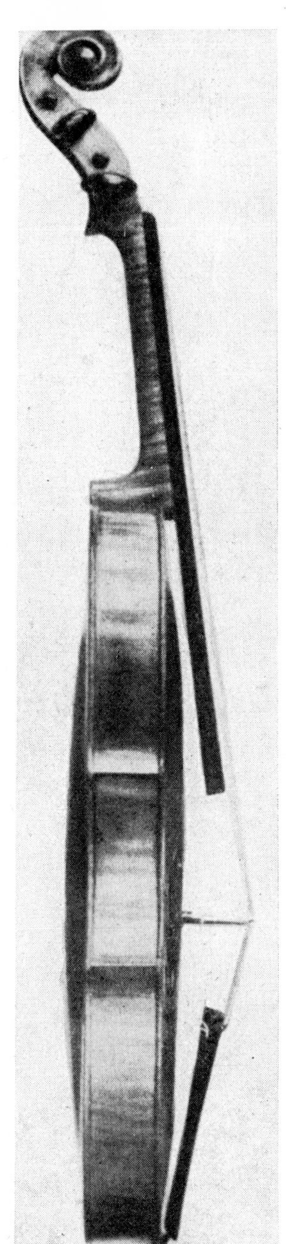
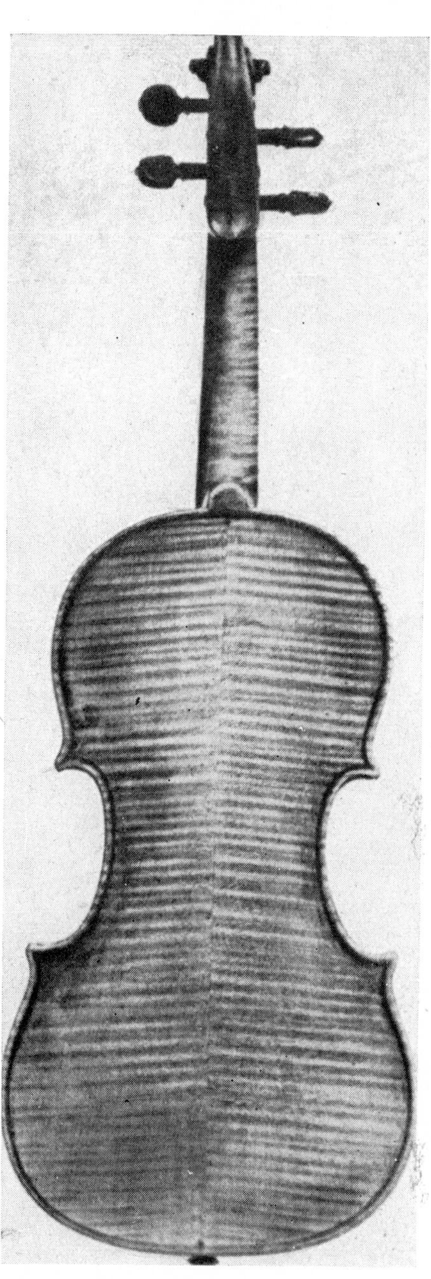

227. Guarneri Giuseppe del Gesù, Cremona 1726

228. Guarneri Giuseppe del Gesù, Cremona 1730 (EX RODE)
Photo Hamma & Co

229. Guarneri Giuseppe del Gesù, Cremona 1733
Photo Hamma & Co

230. Guarneri Giuseppe del Gesù, Cremona 1734 (EX KREISLER)
Photo Hamma & Co

231. Guarneri Giuseppe del Gesù, Cremona 1736 (EX WIENIAWSKY)
Photo Hamma & Co

232. Guarneri Giuseppe del Gesù, Cremona 1738

233. Guarneri Giuseppe del Gesù, Cremona 1740
(CASADESUS)
Photo Hamma & Co

234. Guarneri Giuseppe del Gesù, Cremona 1741
Photo Hamma & Co

235. Guarneri Giuseppe del Gesù, Cremona 1741
(EX VIEUXTEMPS)
Photo Hamma & Co

236. Guarneri Giuseppe del Gesù, Cremona 1742
Photo Hamma & Co

237. Guarneri Giuseppe del Gesù, Cremona 1743
Photo Hamma & Co

238. Guarneri Pietro, Mantova 1683
Photo Hamma & Co

239. Guarneri Pietro, Mantova 1686
Photo Hamma & Co

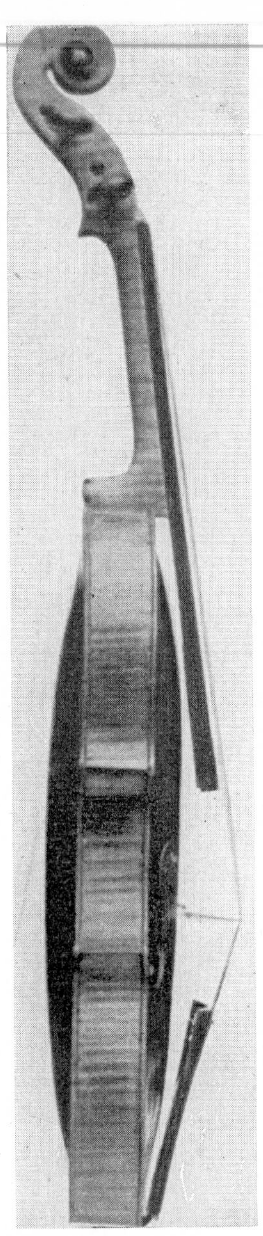
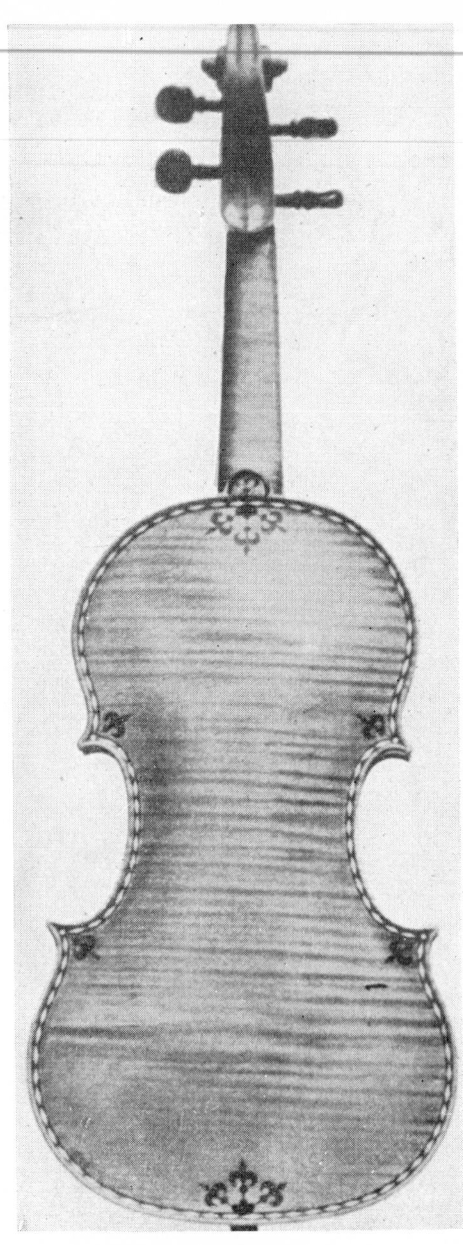

240. Guarneri Pietro, Mantova 1686

241. Guarneri Pietro Mantova 1705
Photo Hamma & Co

242. Guarneri Pietro, Mantova 1706
Photo Hamma & Co

243. Guarneri Pietro II., Venezia 1735
Photo Hamma & Co

244. Guarneri Pietro II., Venezia 1736
Photo Hamma & Co

245. Guarneri Pietro III., Mantova 1727

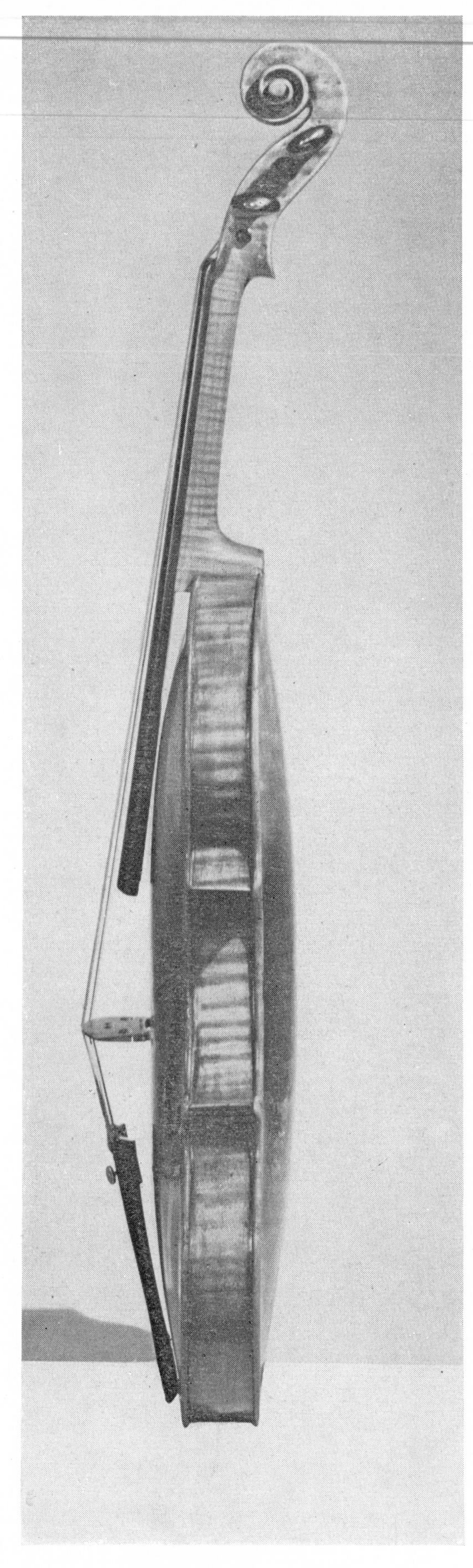

246 Guarneri Pietro III., Mantova 1727

247. Guarneri Pietro III., Mantova 1727

248. Guarneri Pietro III., Mantova 1727

249. Guarneri Pietro III., Mantova 1727

250. Guarneri Ubaldo, Cremona 1721

251. Guidantus Joan Floreno, Bologna 1745

252. Landolfi Carlo Fernando, Milano 17.. (CELLO)

253. Landolfi Carlo Fernando, Milano 1751
Photo Hamma & Co

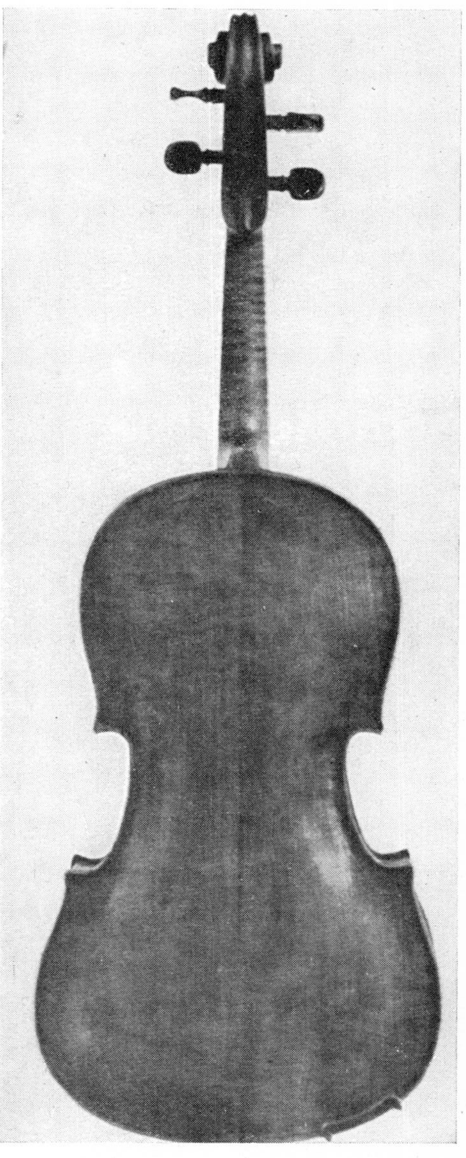

254. Landolfi Carlo Fernando, Milano 1741
Photo Hamma & Co

255. Landolfi Carlo Fernando, Milano 1758

256. Landolfi Carlo Fernando, Milano 17..

Giovannetti Lodovico (a dr. med., surgeon). B. Sept. 13, 1893 in Montefiore dell 'Asso, amateur violin maker: individual work, varnish yellow or golden brown.

Giovannetti Luigi, Lucca. Ca 1840. Good violin maker. Price 8—10.000 Kč.

Giovanni Antonio, Padua, 1725—1744. Known only from a viola d'amore of 1744.

Giovanni Antonio Da
Padova Fecit Anno 1744.

Giovanni, Leghorn. See Enrico Giovanni.

Giovannini Giorgio, Rome 1611. It is only known that he was a lute maker.

Girardi Mario, Trieste, exhibited a violin at Cremona in 1937.

Girardi . . . . . Vicenza. 1810—1820. He worked after Stradivari, using red-yellow varnish.

Giraniani . . . . Leghorn. 1827. Corrupted name, a fake. See Gragnani Gennaro. Yellow varnish.

Gisalberti Andreas. Cremona. Rimini, Parma, Rome, Bozzolo. 1716, 1721. He was a pupil either of Mariani at Pesaro or of P. S. Maggini at Brescia. Built very good instruments in the style of Gasparo da Salò. His thinly coated orange-red varnish resembles that of the Cremonese.

Andreas Gisalberti
Cremonensis
fecit Bozsolo 1716. (written).

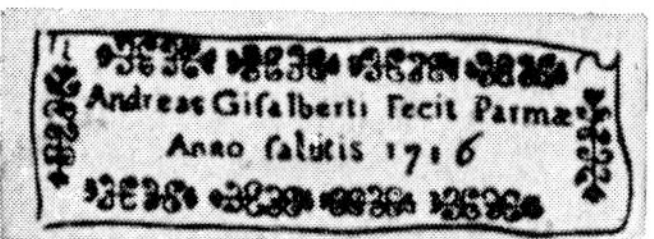

Gisalberti Giulio Cesare, Bologna, 1588. Lute maker.

Gitarino dal (Chitarino). See Petrobono.

Giudici Antonio (I), Varese. B. Feb. 16, 1860 in Masnago, d. March 27, 1931 in Varese. Son and pupil of Giovanni Guidici.

Giudici Carlo, called Mezet, Varese. B. in Masnago Aug. 21, 1894. Son of Antonio I Giudici.

Carolus Giudici
cui cognomen Mezet
Varissii fecit anno 19. .

Giudici Giovanni, called Mezet. B. Aug. 8, 1824 in Masnago (Varese), d. in Varese, Nov. 26, 1903. Is appreciated chiefly for his yellow contrabasses.

Giulani Alessandro, Cremona, Saluzzo. 1650—1667. Pupil of Nic. Amati. Good violas and excellent contrabasses.

Giulani Alessandro, Milan. Born in Rome Dec. 22, 1873, d. Apr. 1, 1933 in Milan. Guitar maker.

Giulietti Armando, Milan. B. Sept. 29, 1903 in Rome. Son and pupil of Tullio Giulietti. Instruments covered with alcohol varnish of red colour.

Fece in Milano A
Armando Giulietti G

L'ANNO 1939
ARMANDO GIULIETTI
FECE IN MILANO L'ANNO 1948
AG

Giulietti Tullio, Milan. B. in Rome Dec. 22, 1873, d. Apr. 1, 1933 in Milan. Guitar and mandolin maker.

TULLIO GIULIETTI
FECE IN MILANO L'ANNO 1930

Giusgnani Raffaele, Arezzo and Terni. Born ca 1870.

Giusti Giovanni Baptista, Lucca. 1682—1693. Lute maker of very careful workmanship.

Joannes Baptista Giusti
Lucensis faciebat anno 1693.

JOANNES BATISTA GIUSTI LUCENSIS FACIEBAT 1681.
(written).

Gobetti Francesco, Venice. 1690—1732. He is reported to have been a pupil of Stradivari, but worked, very skilfully, also on the pattern of Amati. He built his instruments with a moderate arching and in a rather short, broad, characteristic shape. Very fine wood, delicately and neatly carved scrolls, sound-holes cut in the style of F. Ruggeri. Applied a wonderful varnish, as a rule pale red, but also deep red or amber-coloured. His violins are coveted concert instruments. Price 100—160.000 Kč.

Franciscus Gobettus
Venetijs Fecit Anno 17. .

Gofriller Antonio, Venice. 1730. His instruments are inferior to those of his namesakes.

Antonio Gofriller
fece in Venezia 1730.

Goffriller Francesco, Venice, Udine. 1660—1740. Brother of Matteo Goffriller, with whom he jointly worked. He built very valuable instruments, with yellow-brown varnish. Price 100—120.000 Kč.

Goffriller Matteo, Venice. 1690—1742. His first works were in the style of the Tyrolese school, otherwise he worked on the patterns of Stradivari and Carlo Bergonzi. He made the purfling and edges broader, the sound-holes elegant and cut in a vertical position; large, beautifully carved scrolls, exemplary workmanship; faultless fine-grained wood. The back is mostly made of one piece. Beautiful and of powerful tone are his 'cellos, for the back of which he used beautiful curled maple, rarely poplar wood. These 'cellos are first-class concert instruments and equal those of Carlo Bergonzi. Excellent varnish, red-brown, sometimes darkened to a certain degree, sometimes colour of old gold, yellow-brown and red. Price 120—240.000 Kč., 'cello more.

Dimensions of his instruments in mm:

Year	17	1725	1711 (viola)	1737 (viola)
length	356	355	402	408
upper width	167	154	186	195
middle width	105	104	123	127
lower width	204	201	229	235

Mattio Goffriler Fece in
Venezia Anno 1709

Mattio Gofrilleri in Venetia
Al' Infegna di Cremona 169?

Mattio Gofrilleri in Venetia
Al' Infegna di Cremona 1695

Mattio Gofrilleri in Venetia
Al' Infegna di Cremona 169?

Mattio Goffriller
Fece in Venetia Anno 17??

Matteo Goffriller fecit
Venetijs anno 1724

Gondolo Giorgio, Turin 1884.

Gonzales Aurelio. Rome. Born March 17, 1908 in Cittaducale.

AURELIO GONZALES
PREMIATO CON MEDAGLIA d'ARGENTO
e diploma d'onore al Concorso al Nazionale Liutai
fece in Roma l'anno 1930

Gori Pietro, Rimini (Forli). 1810—1850. Second-rate instruments.

Gorrieri (Corieri) Antonio, Padua. 1802.

Gottardi Antonio, Treviso. 1878.

Gotti Anselmo, Ferrara. Born Nov. 2, 1902 in Pivo di Cento. Pupil of Ettore. Soffriti, is working on the patterns of Stradivari and Guarneri and applies a red oil varnish.

Gotti Emiliano, Ancona. Ca. 1770. Worked on the pattern of Jacob Stainer, at a later state in the style of the Italian school. He built his instruments with a high arching and applied yellow-brown varnish. Beautiful, carefully carved scrolls, small sound-holes, cut in the fashion of Stainer. He used carefully selected wood, especially for the back of his instruments. Rare.

AEMILIAN Gotti, Ancona
1770.

Gotti Orsolo, Pieve di Cento (Ferrara). Born Sept. 1, 1867 at Pieve di Cento, d. Aug. 2, 1922. Pupil of Carlo Carletti; chestnut-brown spirit varnish. Some of his instruments, imitations of Gagliano, Stradivari, Cerutti. Montagnana, etc., are said to be much in demand.

Gotti Orsolo
Pieve di Cento 1920
(Ferrara)

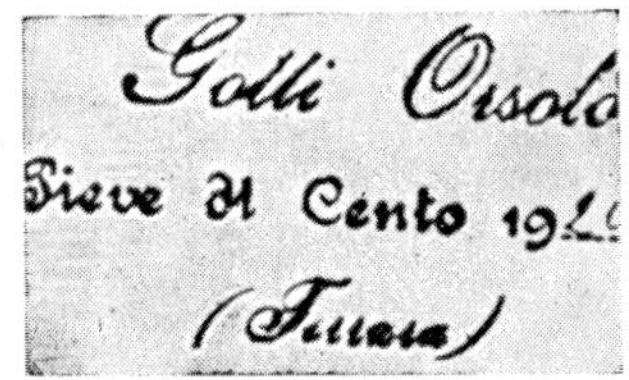
Gotti Orsolo
Pieve di Cento 192?
(Ferrara)

Gouvernari Antonio, Cremona. 1600—1633. The larger model of his violins has a medium arching and is coated with olive-yellow varnish. Beautiful scrolls, sound-holes after the fashion of Nic. Amati, but longer. Valuable, if preserved.

Antonius Gouvernari
Cremonensis Faciebat Anno 16..

Govoni Guglielmo, Pieve di Cento. B. Dec. 25, 1911. Orig. cabinet maker, then imitator of Stradivari and Guarneri del Gesù in all details of shape and colouring.

Grado Gaetano da Naples. Guitar maker.

Gragnani Antonio, Leghorn. 1741—1800. Worked on the pattern of Nic. Amati; his model is large, arching full, sides higher than usual, edge narrow, purfling neatly finished, scrolls tastefully cut and sound-holes longer than those of Nicolo Amati. He used a very good golden-yellow, deep-yellow, light-brown or red-yellow varnish. The best of his instruments are coated with red-yellow varnish. They are outstanding for their beautiful, mellow tone of good carrying power. The wood is not always of the best quality. Price 30—50.000 Kč.

Antonius Gragnani fecit
Liburni anno 17..

Antonius Gragnani fecit
Liburni Anno 1751

Gragnani Gennaro, Livorno (Leghorn). Ca 1730. Brother of Antonio Gragnani. Good workmanship, resembling that of Antonio. Beautiful yellow varnish; the labels are often handwritten. Price 30.000 Kč.

Januarus Gragnani fece
Lib. Anno 17..

Gragnani Jacopo, Livorno. 1743.

Gragnani Onorato. Livorno. 1785—1799. Son of Antonio Gragnani. His workmanship is not of masterly finish. Model Amati, golden-yellow varnish. Price 10—15.000 Kč.

Onorato Gragnani
Figlio d'Antonio
Fatto in Livorno il 1799.

Graile Magno, Rome. 1572, died 1642.

Gramino Giovanni, Milan. 1722—1724. Known only from two violins kept formerly at Wiesbaden. Suspicious. — See Lüttgendorff.

Giovanni Gramino
Milano 1724.

Gran Geno, Cremona. 1711. He used brown varnish.

Grancino Andrea, Milan. C. 1646. He worked after the style of the Milanese school and built very good instruments.

Andrea Grancino in Contrada
Larga in Milano al Segno
della Corona 16..

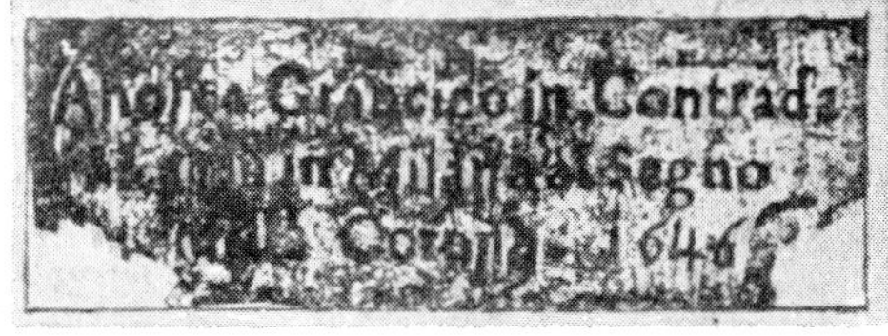

Grancino Francesco, Milan. Ca 1690—1746. Younger son of Giovanni. Worked on his father's pattern and in the style of Amati. Good instruments; best are his violas and 'cellos. Fine wood, yellow or dark-red varnish of good quality. His instruments have a mellow, clear tone. Cheaper specimens also sound very well; their purfling is not inlaid, but engraved.

Gio Battista & Francesco fra Grancini
In contrada larga di Milano 17..
Francesco Grancino Figlio
Giovanni fecit Mediolani 17..

Grancino Giovanni I, Cremona. Ca 1645—1682. Perhaps a brother of Andrea. Learned the craft at Cremona. Worked freely on the pattern of Amati, but followed also old Tyrolese masters.

Giovan Grancino
in Cremona 1682.

Grancino Giovanni II, Milan. Ca 1675—1737. Second son and pupil of Paolo Grancino. His style resembles that of his brother and companion Gio. Battista. He worked on the smaller pattern of Amati and used fine wood. The arching of his instruments is higher and broader than that adopted by his father. The varnish is yellow or, more often, yellow-brown, rather dry. So far as the tone is concerned, his instruments are fit for concert halls, especially his 'cellos are excellent. Price 30—50.000 Kč. 'cello more.

Fratelli Grancini in Contrada
larga di Milano al Segno della
Corona 16..

Gio Grancino al Segno della Corona
in contrada larga di Milano fece 1699.

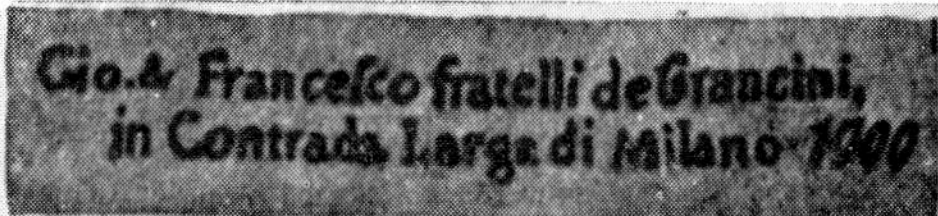
Gio. & Francesco fratelli de Grancini,
in Contrada Larga di Milano 1700

Gia. Bapt. Grancino in Contrada
Largha di Milano anno 1695

Ioannes Grancino fecit
Mediolani an. 1697

Dimensions of some of his instruments in mm:

Year	1697	1707
length	357	357
upper width	162	169
centre width	113	114
lower width	206	210
sides	—	29
sound-holes	—	76

Grancino Giov. Battista I, Milan, Ferrara. Ca 1669—1710. First-born son of Paolo. Worked better than his father and was perhaps a pupil of Joseph Guarneri, Fil. Andreae of Cremona; may have worked also for this master. His beautiful instruments, with low arching, are built on a larger pattern. Delicately finished purfling, fine resonant wood, golden-yellow or orange-coloured, often reddish varnish, mellow and powerful tone. According to Hamma & Co.'s statement some instruments, recognized as his particularly good creations, are labelled as Joseph Guarnerius. fil. Andreae, which proves that he really worked with Guarneri. Hamma values these instruments at 15—20.000 marks, which would amount to 120—160.000 pre-Munich crowns. Otherwise, the price of his violins is 50—65.000 Kč.

Giov. Bapt. Grancino, Filius
Paoli, fecit in Ferrara 16..

Giouanni Grancino in Contrada
Largha di Milano al segno
della Corona 1705

Grancino Giov. Battista II, Milan. Ca 1697—1735. Eldest son of Giovanni Battista I (1669—1710), worked jointly with his brother Francesco in the workshop bequeathed to them by their father. Good workmanship. Varnish for the most part deep red.

Grancino Giovanni Battista III, Mantua. (1727?) Perhaps a son of Gio Battista Grancino II (1697—1735). Rather high-arched model, chestnut-coloured varnish. Broad, yet beautifully finished purfling; the sound-holes are usually not well cut, whereas the flat scrolls are neatly carved.

Grancino Gramino, Milan. Ca 1722. His instruments possess a medium arching, gracefully carved scrolls. The belly is coated with yellow-brown, the back with yellow varnish. Beautiful smooth tone of good carrying power.

Gramino Grancino
in contrada Larga di Milano
1722.

(written)

Grancino Paolo, Milan. Ca 1655—1692. Pupil of Nic. Amati, whom he imitated freely and in a rather good way, though he failed to equal the quality of his master's instruments. His model has a flatter arching, broader edges, shorter corners, long, broad, plain-looking sound-holes. The wood is not always faultless. The back and sides of his larger instruments, especially the 'cellos, are often of poplar wood. Good yellow or red-yellow varnish. His instruments sound very well; particularly excellent are his violas. Price 40—60.000 Kč.

—

Giovanni Grancino (1645—1682) is the oldest known violin maker of the Grancino family. We do not know whether Andrea (c. 1646) was his brother or son. Which of the two was father of Paolo Grancino, is also uncertain. Giovanni Grancino continued to live in Cremona even after Paolo had taken over the shop left by Andrea in Milan. Paolo's sons Giambattista (Giovanni Battista I, 1669—1710), and Giovanni III (1675—1737) worked in Milan, as did also Francesco and Giambattista II, sons of Giambattista I. It has not been fully proved that Gramino (c. 1722) was a son of Giovanni Battista II, but it seems probable. Giambattista II (c. 1727) moved to Mantua at the time when three others, viz. Giambattista II, Francesco and Gramino were all active in Milan; he may have been superfluous. Another possible conjec-

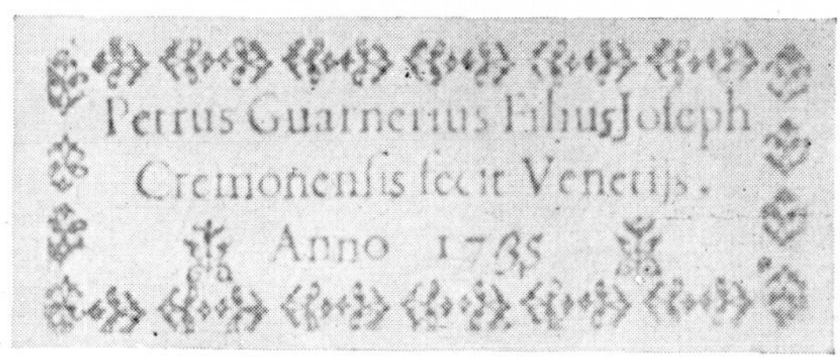
Petrus Guarnerius Filius Joseph
Cremonensis fecit Venetijs.
Anno 1735

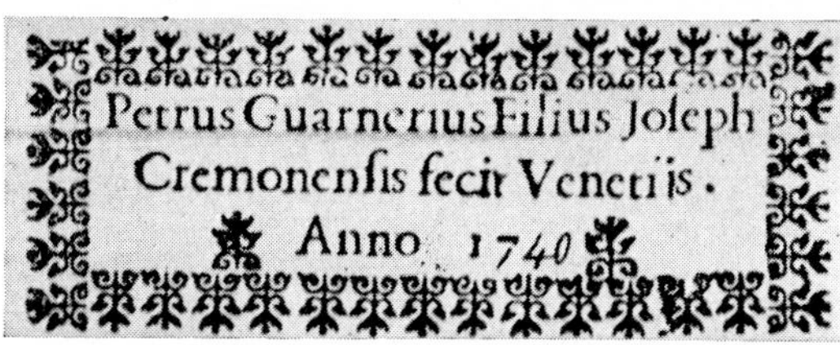
Petrus Guarnerius Filius Joseph
Cremonensis fecit Venetiis.
Anno 1740

Petrus Guarnerius Filius Joseph
Fecit Cremonae sub Titulo Sanctae Teresiae
17.. — 17[illegible]

Guarneri Pietro III, Mantua. Born ca 1700, was still alive after 1750. Son and pupil of Pietro Guarneri I who worked with his father until the latter's death. We know of two of his violins: one from 1735, the other from 1727. The 1727 instrument is an original Guarneri work. This instrument was once in Prague where it was repaired by Antonín Sitt, and later it was sold to the U.S.A. The violin from 1735 is still in Czechoslovakia and is too narrow. Length 354 mm, upper width 154 mm, middle width 103,8 mm, lower width 192 mm, distance between the upper "eyes" of the sound-holes 48,2 mm, their height 71 mm, their length 76,8 mm, height of sides 30,29 and 29.6 mm. Measure 198 mm.

Petrus Guarnerius Cremonensis fecit
Mantua sub tit. Sancta [illegible] 1735

Guarneri Ubaldo, Cremona. 1683—1721. Perhaps son of Andrea Guarneri. An excellent master who delighted in experiments. Judging by an instrument from 1721 he was a virtuoso violin-maker. Beautifully carved heads are not so powerful as those carved by his contemporaries, they are somewhat more slender. Magnificent sound-holes remind us of Gothic shapes. The violin is small and flat:

length of back: 352
width of top: 168
width of centre: 106.5
width of bottom: 206
sides at top: 28.8
sides at centre: 30.3
sides at bottom: 32.5
measure: 192
bouts: 87.6/87.6 — 88.5/88.5
height of sound-holes: 76
length of sound-holes: 80.5
distance between the upper eyes of sound-holes: 42.4

The violin measure under the bridge is only 47.7 thick, so that the arching of both belly and back does not exceed 17.3 mm. The back is slightly more arched than the belly; the ratio is approx. 8.3 : 9. The tone of the instrument is unique.

Ubaldus Guarnerius
Cremonensis Fecit 1721

Guarneri Caterina, Cremona. Died in 1658. Perhaps a sister and pupil of Giuseppe and Pietro Guarneri or the wife of one of the Guarneris, who ran a violin workshop after her husband's death. It is not quite sure whether she really made any violins herself. In 1912, the Prague violin maker B. Lantner owned a viola bearing Caterina Guarneri's label: it was sold at the price of K. 1.000, old Austro-Hungarian currency.

Guastalla Alfredo, Reggiolo. A pupil of Stefano Scarampella. B. Nov. 11, 1898. His instruments, when signed, are of the same character as those of his brother Dante. For the most part the brothers worked together.

ALFREDO GUASTALLA
LIUTAIO
in REGGIOLO—Emilia ITALIA 1949

Guastalla Dante, Reggiolo (Reggio d'Emilia). B. Oct. 11, 1893 in Reggiolo. Pupil of Stefano Scarampella of Mantua, worked on the models of Stradivari, Guarneri and Balestrieri: instruments of his own design are golden red. Careful work. Was aided by his brother Alfredo.

Dante e Alfredo Guastalla
Anno 1949
REGGIOLO (EMILIA)
GUASTALLA DANTE
LIUTAIO
Alievo di STEFANO SCARAMPELLA
Fabbricatore e Riparatore istrumenti ad arco
in Reggiolo—Em. ITALIA 1949

Gudi Hieronymus, Cremona. 1726—1727. Masterly craftsmanship, wonderful wood, golden-yellow varnish, beautiful noble tone. Price 24.000 Kč. and more.

Hieronimo Gudi da Cremona 1727.

Guerra Alberto, S. Donnino Nizzola (Modena). B. 1908. Instruments with yellow alcohol varnish.

ALBERTO GUERRA
Anno 1945
S. DONNINO NIZZOLA
(Modena)

Guerra Evasio, Turin. B. 1880. D. Feb. 2, 1956. Pupil of Carlo Oddone, worked on various patterns and used an oil varnish of golden-red or red colour.

Guerra Giacomo, Modena. 1804—1822. Average work, brown varnish.

Guerrini Giuseppe, Siena. Ca 1813. Good workmanship.

Guglielmi Giovanni Battista, Cremona. 1747. Good master; he worked on the pattern of Amati. Price 12.000 Kč.

Guidante Bernardo, Genoa. Ca 1750. Followed N. Amati.

Guidante Floreno, same as Florenus Guidantus, see Floreno.

Guillani Sanctus, Rome. Ca 1710. Violin maker, little known.

Sanctus Guillani
fecit Rom 1710.

Gulino Salvatore. B. in Cataldo (Caltanisetta) Nov. 2, 1910. Cataldo, Girgenti (Sicily), Palermo (Sicily) and Pinerolo. Stradivari and Guarneri models, but he was also cabinet-maker and repairer.

Gusetto Nicolo, Cremona. 1785—1828. Built high-arched instruments. The sides of his violins (both top and bottom sides) measure 32 mm. Short sound-holes. The purfling is not evenly finished. He applied a yellow or brown varnish. The wood is not of the best quality.

Nicolaus Gusetto Fiorentinus
Musicus Instrumentalis
a Cremona. Ao 1785.

Nicol. Gusetto Firentino
Fabrricante di violini, Cremonae (written)

Gusnasco Lorenzo, Pavia, Venice. Ca 1500. Renowned lute maker.

Guzzi Luigi, Brescia. Known is one viola da gamba, dated 1540.

Guzzi Luigi S. Savino, Fecit Bresciae
Anno 1540.

H

Harford Patrick, Rome. Ca 1742. A foreigner who worked in Rome in the style of the Italian school. His beautifully shaped instruments are coated with bright brown varnish.

Harton Michael, Padua. Ca 1602—1624. Lute maker.

Padove Michielle ....on
M ÷ H

in Padova
Michielle Harton 160.

Hec (Hek) Giovanni, Rome. Ca 1606. Probably a German (Italianized his name into Ecchio). He seems to have worked as a lute maker in Rome as early as 1590.

Heel Martino, Genoa. Ca 1697—1708. Built high arched instruments and applied a brown-red varnish of splendid lustre.

Mardino Heel in
Genova 1697.

Heisele Jacob, Modena. Ca 1614—1629. Violin and lute maker, probably a German from Tirol.

Hesin Giacomo, Venice. Ca 1566. Lute maker.

Hetel G., Rome. Ca 1763. Lute and guitar maker.

Hieber Giovanni, Venice. Ca 1560—1590. Known from a lute bearing the following label:

Giuane Hieber
e Martino Facebit [sic]
in Venezia Ao 1581.

Hoch Christian, Venice. 17th—18th century. Probably a German settled in Venice. His workmanship is more after the German school than in the style of the Italians.

Hocha Gasparo dall', Ferrara. See Dall'Hocha.

Horil Jacob, Vienna, Rome. Ca 1720—1759. A Czech from Vienna, who moved to Rome in 1740, where he soon adapted himself to the Italian ways of violin making and built good instruments. He applied a fine yellow varnish.

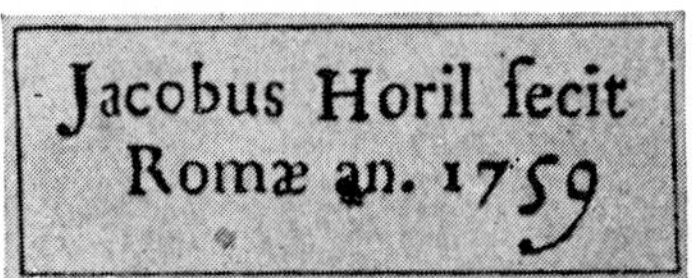
Jacobus Horil fecit
Romæ an. 1759

Jacobus Horil restaura

Huetter Martin, Rome. 19th century. Perhaps a German resident in Rome.

I

Imperii Annibale, Pisa. Ca 1750—1756. A violin-maker who followed Amati and varnished his instruments yellow-red.

Annibalij Imperij
opus. 15. (written)
Annibal Imperii
S. Angeli Pisauri fecit
1750

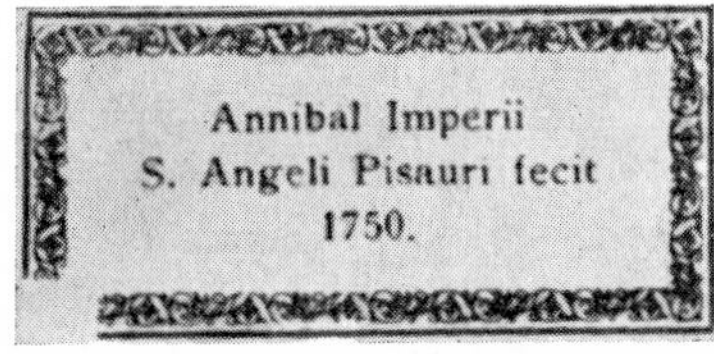
Annibal Imperii
S. Angeli Pisauri fecit
1750.

Indelanch Stephan, Rome. Ca 1640—1643. Lute maker.

Indelicato Salvatore, Catania (Sicily). Ca 1889. Industrial manufacture of mandolins.

Indri Antonio, Venice. Born about 1781, died in Venice on Dec. 25, 1864. Son of Giuseppe Indri. He also owned a business, trading in various musical instruments, which he managed far better than his workshop.

Antonius Indri
fecit Venetiis Anno 1807 (written)

Ionata Luigi, Messina. Born May 25, 1883 in Messina. An amateur, red or golden-yellow alcohol varnish.

Prof. Luigi Jonato fecit
Messina 1949

Isep Carlo Giuseppe, Milan. Ca 1800. Violin maker of medium skill.

Ivrontini Wongelli, Turin. 1834.

J

Jacomini Girolamo, Carbognana (Rome). 1925.

James Mario, Triest, Polcenigo (Udine). 1809—1939. He established himself in Triest and later worked after the Cremonese school in Polcenigo.

Jansen Andrea, Padua. Ca 1629. Probably a Northerner, otherwise unknown, who lived in Italy only temporarily.

Januarius Giacomo Genaro, Cremona. 1641—1654. Pupil of Nicolo Amati who used golden-brown varnish.

Jori Enzea. Born Aug. 4, 1891 in Modena. He established himself in 1925 and was a copying of old masters who used varnish of various colours and compositions to suit the case.

Jori Enea
fece in Modena
1949

Jori Leandro, Sesso (Reggio Emilia). 1819—1880. He applied himself more to repairing work than to the making of new instruments. The tone of the few instruments left by him is good. He worked on the flat pattern of Stradivari. The wood, particularly the pine of the belly, is good; the sound-holes are not delicately cut: the purfling, finished in a clean and neat manner, is inserted farther from the edge. The varnish is applied in thick coats. Price 8—10.000 Kč.

Jori Orlando, Modena. B. 1915. Son and follower of Ensa Jori whom he assisted in his workshop.

Jori Orlando
Fece in Modena
1950

Jorio Giorgio fu Luigi, Molise (Campobasso), exhibited a violin at Cremona in 1937.

Jorio Vincenzo, Naples. Ca 1780—1849. Worked, on the one hand, on the large flat model of Stradivari, on the other according to the high pattern of Stainer. The wood of both belly and back is good, but mostly rather thick: the broad scrolls are not delicately carved. It is true that these instruments are of objectionable workmanship, but if they are rebuilt they become (according to Hamma) excellent concert instruments. He applied a varnish shading from lemon-yellow to brown-yellow and reddish-yellow. Price 16.000 Kč. and more.

Vincenzo Jorio Fabricanti
di Strumenti Armonici
Neapoli 1833.

Vincenzo Jorio
Fabricante
di Strumenti Armonici
Neapoli 1849. (written)

Jornini Antonio, Secondigliano near Naples, later Milan. 20th cent. Is working together with his son Enrico under the firm of Jornini & Son.

Juliano Francesco, Rome. Ca 1690—1725. Violin maker of no particular renown. Price 12.000 Kč.

Francesco Juliano in Roma
1725.

K

Kasermann Giovanni, Naples, Via Carbonara 112. Exhibited a violin at Cremona in 1937.

Kasperger Joh. Hieronymus, Rome. 17th century. A German; made lutes and theorbi.

Kaysser Georgius, Venice. Ca 1595. Lute maker who was a pupil of Vend. Dieffenbrugger.

Georgius Kaysser fabricatto
da Vendelino Dieffenbruger
1595.

Kaysser Martino, Venice. Ca 1609—1632. He was also pupil of Vend. Dieffenbrugger or Giovanni Hieber in Venice. Price 12.000 Kč.

Kelle Sebastian, Cremona. 1690—1720.

Kerlino Giovanni, Brescia. Ca 1449—1495. He was a native of Brittany in France. Some authors have doubted his existence. He seems to have been a self-taught lute and viol maker. His viols are handsome, of old type; one of them has a flat back.

Io. Kerlino an 1449.

Krebar Andrea, Padua, 16th—17th century. Lute maker. Worked in company with Giovanni Krebar at Padua.

Krebar Giovanni, Padua. Ca 1629. The only work still extant is a theorbo, now in London.

L

Lafranchini Giacomo de, Brescia. Born Apr. 8, 1604. Could not have been a pupil of Gasparo da Saló who died in 1609. In 1614 Lafranchini became apprenticed to G. P. Maggini. Small violas modelled on Bertolotti and G. P. Maggini.

Lamagni Rosolino, Gussola (Cremona). Contemporary violin-maker. Born Feb. 8. 1925, established since 1946.

Lamo Antonio, Rome. Ca 1608—1610. Instruments by him are not known.

Lanari Giambattista, Fiesole. 20th century. He used yellow-brown varnish.

Lanaro Luigi, Padua. Born Dec. 4, 1920 in Vicenza. Orange varnish.

Lancelotti Bernardino. Barigato. 1865—1887. He devoted himself mainly to the making of double-basses.

Lancilotto Jacopino, Modena. Born about 1507, died about 1551. Poet, painter, notary, astrologer, musician and violin maker. A prodigy; at the youthful age of 13 years he is said to have had a thorough knowledge of Latin and Greek. He built lutes, violas, violas da gamba and harps.

Landi Nazareno, Fiume. Ca 1889. Amateur who developed a model of his own.

Nazareno Landi.
Parroco di S. Maria
di Fiume fabbrico
l'anno 1889.

Landi Pietro, Siena. Ca 1774. Little-known violin-maker, who worked after Stradivari and whose instruments may have been rechristened. Price 8—12.000 Kč.

Landius Francesco, called "Il Cieco", Florence. 1325—1397. Ancient lute maker and organ-builder.

Landolfi Carlo Fernando, Milan. B. 1714, d. ca 1787. Worked in the style of Pietro Guarneri II, whose pupil he probably was, but his creations are rather varied. He built instruments both on large and small pattern, both of low and high arching; the belly is, as a rule, more arched than the back. There exist instruments executed faultlessly, and others worked with little care, which, ascribed to such a good violin maker, may be suspected of being faked. All the genuine instruments are made of flawless, fine wood, with edges finished in a plastic manner, with faultlessly executed purflings, reaching to the very points of the corners; the sound-holes are cut in a rather up.ight position, but with a very graceful bend; neatly carved scrolls; careful workmanship; exquisite yellow, yellow-red or brown-red varnish. The tone of his high-arched instruments is excellent, whereas those with a low arching are inferior. His 'cellos (of small model and with high arching) sound magnificently. In England his 'cellos and violas of smaller pattern are highly valued. Price 80.000 Kč and more.

Dimensions of his violins in mm.:

	1763	17..	1750	1751
Length of back	358	353	353	356
Upper width	166	166	161	160
Middle	109	109,5	100,4	107
Lower width	203	204	199	204
Height of body with sides, belly and back	64,5	—	—	—
Distance between corners (belly)	78	—	—	—
Distance between corners (back)	79	—	—	—

Carolus Ferdinandus Landolphus
fecit Mediolani in Via S. Mar
garitæ anno 1735

Carlo Ferdinando Landolfi
nella Contrada di Santa Margarita
al Segno della Sirena. Milano 1758

Revifto da Carlo Ferdinando
Landolfi l'Anno 1741

257. Landolfi Carlo Fernando, Milano 1761
Photo Hamma & Co

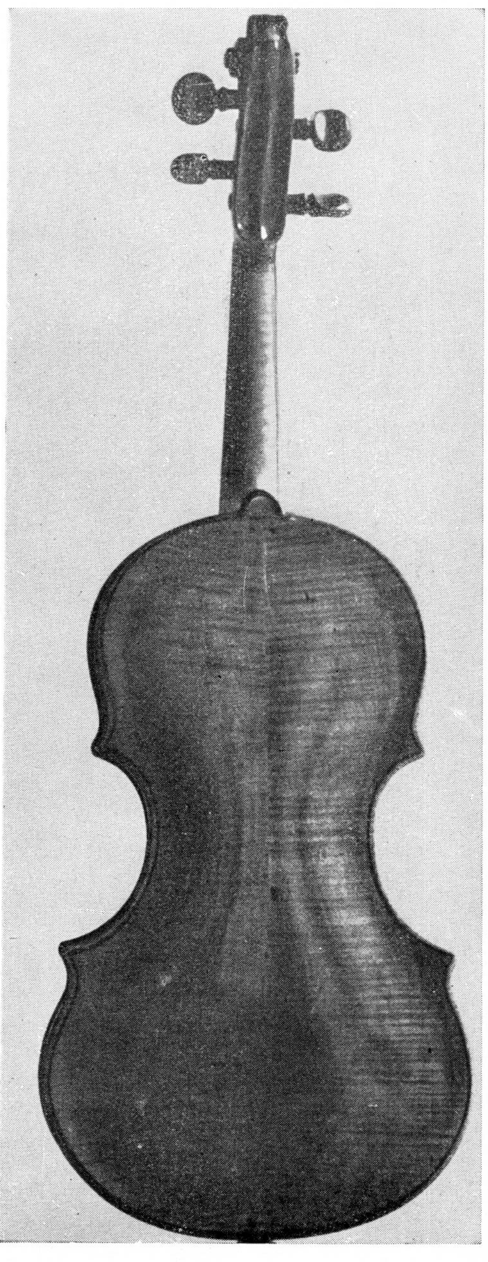

258. Lanza Antonio Maria, Brescia 1706
Photo Hamma & Co

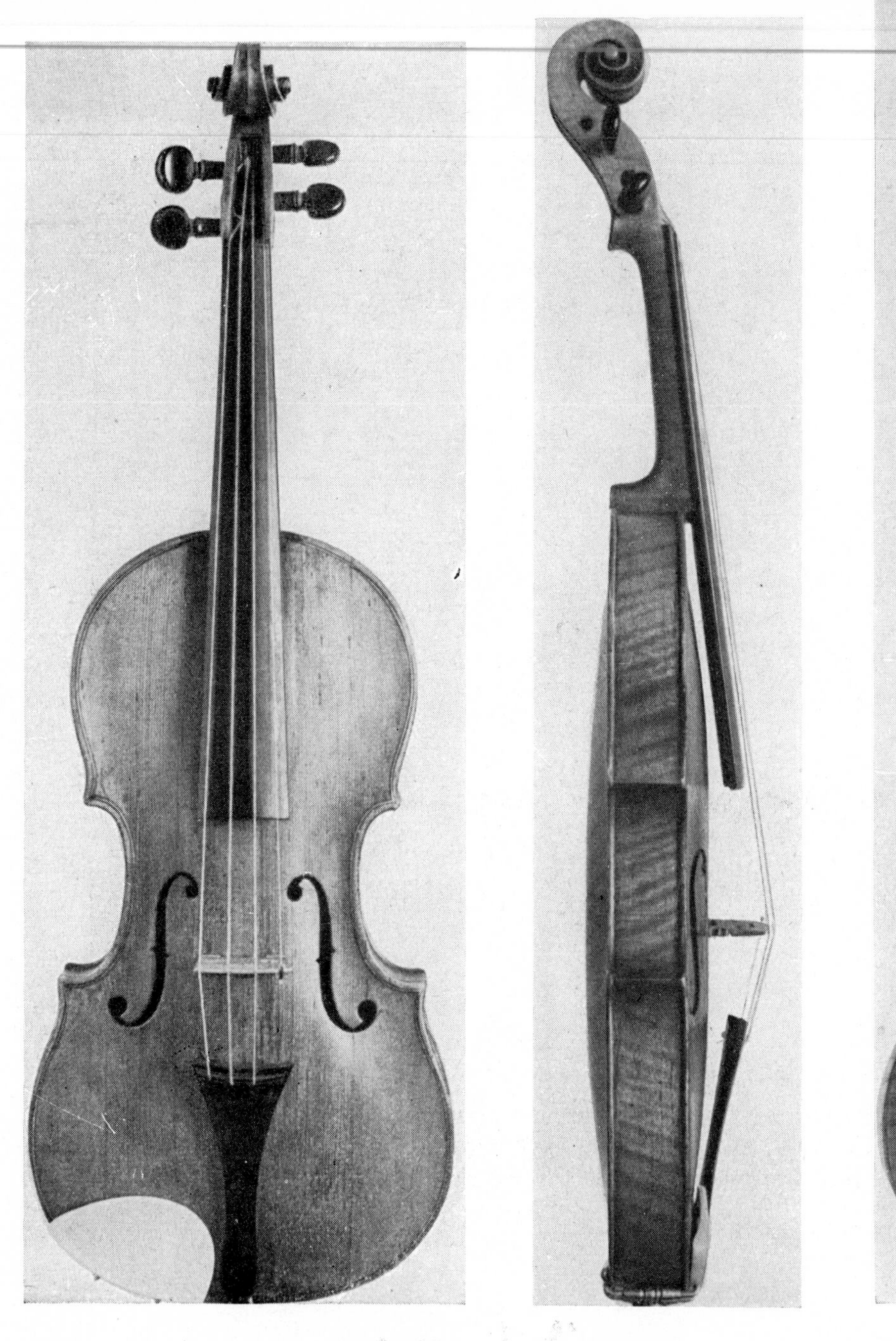
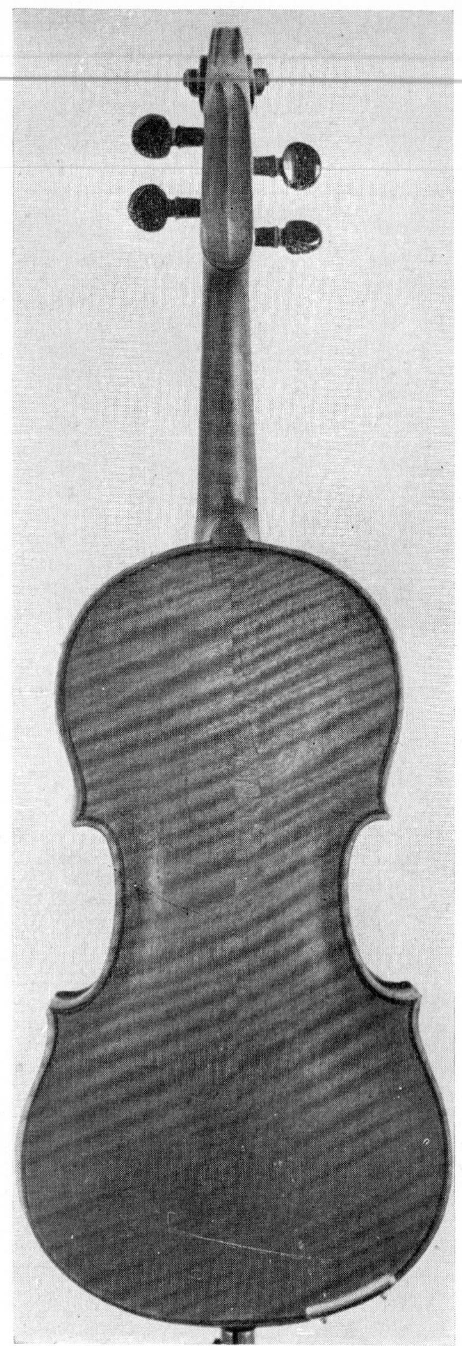
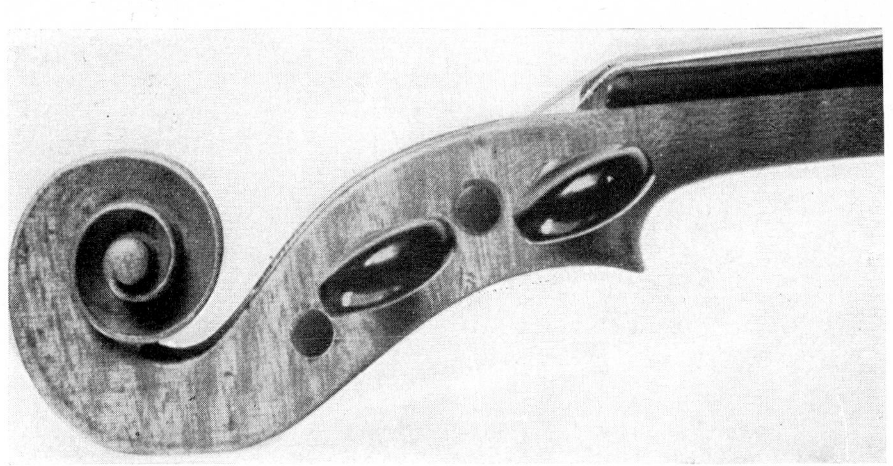

259. Lavazza Santino, Milano 1634

266. Maggini Giovanni Paolo, Brescia (VIOLA)

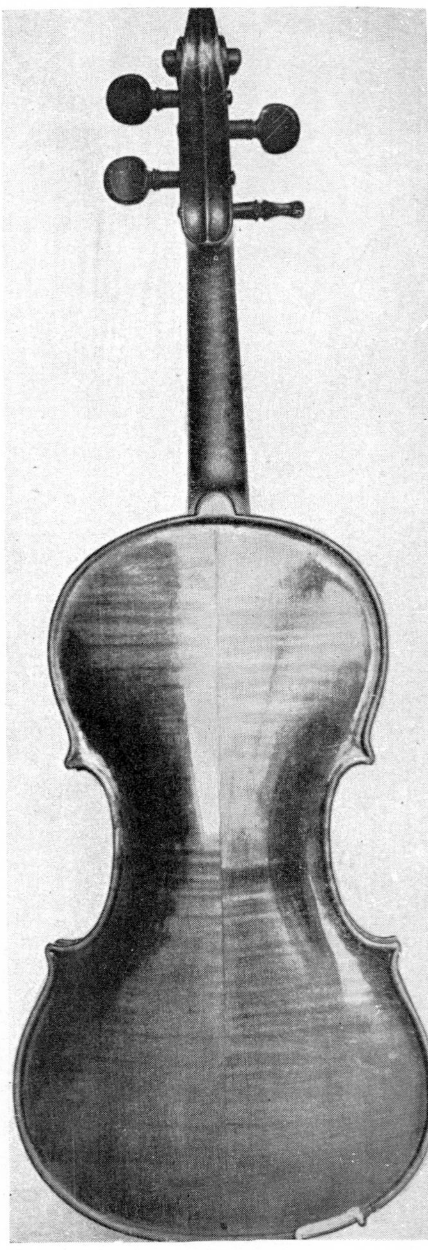

267. Mandotti Giuseppe, Piacenza 1755

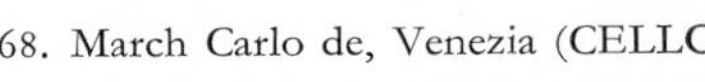

268. March Carlo de, Venezia (CELLO)

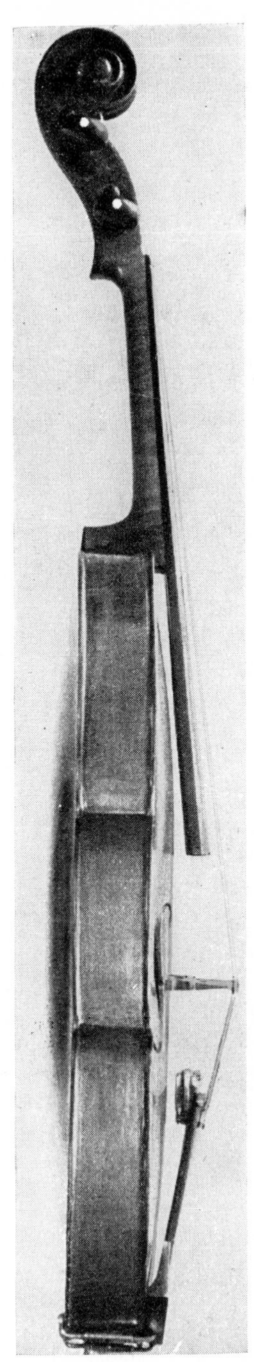
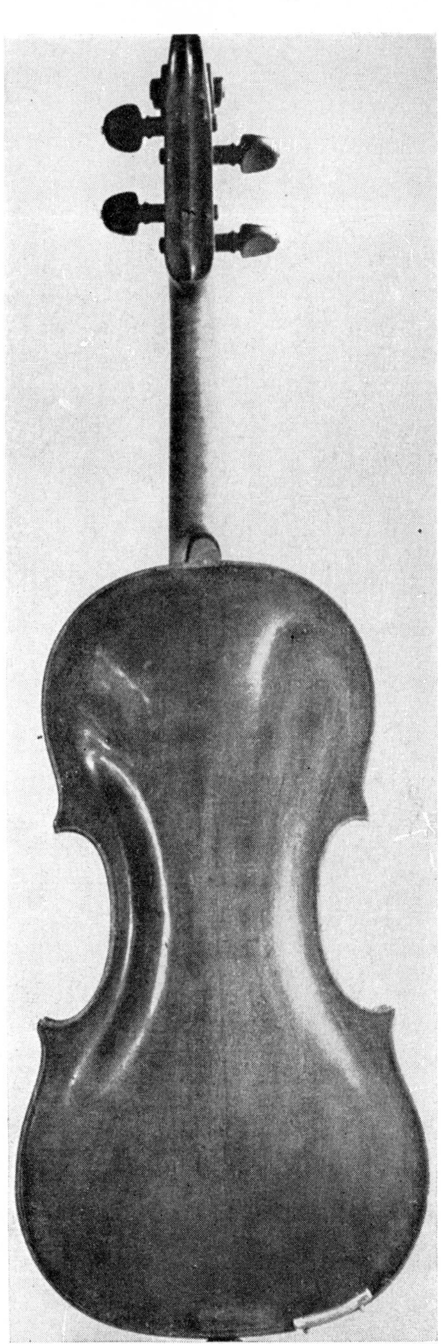

269. Montade Gregorio, Cremona 1620

270. Montagnana Domenicus, Venezia 1726
Photo Hamma & Co

271. Montagnana Domenicus, Venezia 1737
Photo Hamma & Co

272. Montagnana Domenicus, Venezia 1729
Photo Hamma & Co

273. Montagnana Domenicus, Venezia 1733
Photo Hamma & Co

274. Montagnana Domenicus, Venezia 1742
Photo Hamma & Co

275. Montagnana Domenicus, Venezia 1735 (CELLO)

276. Obici (Obizzi) Bartolomeo, Verona 1753

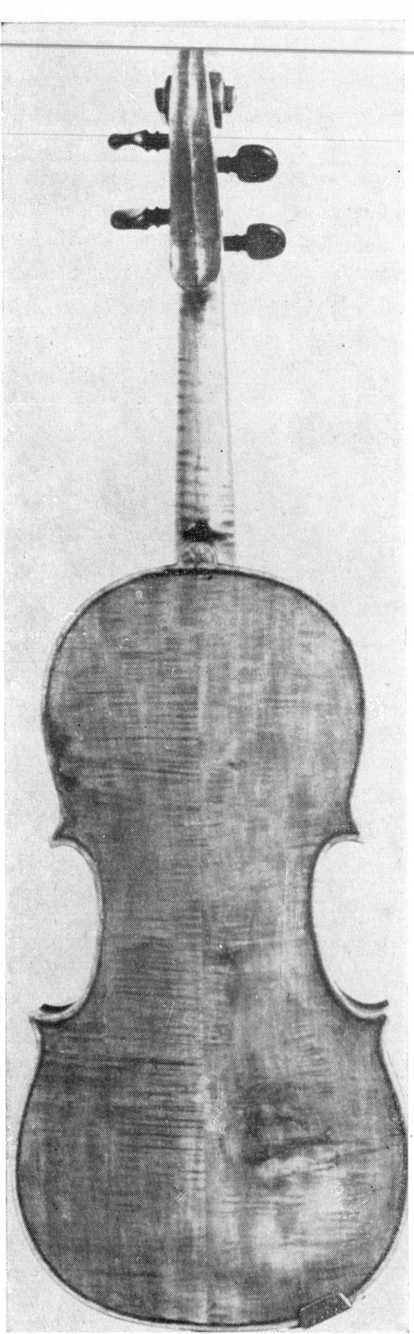

277. Odoardi Joseph, Piceno

Landolfi Pietro Antonio, Milan. 1750—1800. Son and pupil of Carlo Ferd. Landolfi. He lacked his father's skill. His instruments are of slender shape and high arching, but there are also broad and flat specimens. The scrolls and sound-holes are well cut, the tone fine. Price 30—40.000 Kč.

Pietro Antonio figlio di
Carlo Ferdinando Landolfi
in Milano al Segno della
Seren a l'Anno 1780

Pietro Antonio figlio di
Carlo Ferdinando Landolfi
in Milano al Segno della
Seren a l'Anno 1779

Lantini Loris, Pontedera. Born 1908 in Marti (Pisa).

Lanza Antonio Maria, Brescia. 1650—1715. Worked in the style of Giov. Paolo Maggini. Small model, well finished purfling placed at some distance from the edges, the sound-holes cut in an upright position. The rather large scrolls lack grace. Red-brown varnish. Price 20—28.000 Kč.

La Rosa Giuseppe, Catania (Sicily). Manufacturer of guitars and mandolins.

Lassi Enzo, Faenza. Born Jan. 26, 1927. Son and probably also pupil of Francesco Lassi. He worked after Stradivari and Guarneri.

ENZO LASSI
FAENZA 1949

Lassi Francesco, Faenza (Ravenna), Via Domizia 84. Born Nov. 16, 1874. He worked after Stradivari and Guarneri and varnished his instruments yellow-orange. One of his violins was exhibited at Cremona in 1937.

Francesco Lassi
fece in Faenza 1918
Francesco Lassi fece
Faenza — An. 1949

Laurenti Alfredo, Terni. Born 1882. He made guitars and mandolins.

Lauro Antonio, Rome. 1608—1610. A Flemish lute maker in Rome.

Lavazza Antonio Maria, Milan. 1703—1722. Worked in the style of J. B. Guadagnini I, but took a lower arching and even the outline according to Stradivari. He was a skilful and careful master, but used mostly wood of inferior quality; applied dark red-brown varnish in thick coats. Price 20—30.000 Kč.

Antonio Maria Lavazza fece in
Milano, habita in contrada
Largha 1703.

Lavazza Matteo, Guastala. 1918. He used red varnish.

Lavazza Santino, Milan. 1634.

Lavazza Santino, Milan. 1718—1780. Son of Antonio Maria Lavazza. A violin he made in 1734 is in St. Vitus' Cathedral of Prague, another in St. Vojtěch's church in Prague. Price 15—20.000 Kč.

Sãntino Lauazza
fece in Milano in
Contrada Larga

Santino Lauazza fece in
Milano in Contrada
Larga 1718

Lavezzani Antonio, Bergamo. Ca 1860. Repaired instruments.

Antonio Lavezzani
reparò nell anno ... Bergamo via XX settembre 29—33.
(written)

Laviguetta Antonio, Milan. Ca 1900. Few instruments in the style of the Neapolitan masters, mainly Gagliano.

Antonio Laviguetta
fece in Milano An 1900.

Lazzaretti Francesco, Vicenza. 1852—1900.

Lazzaro Giovanni, called Rosario, Messina (Sicily). Born in Messina Nov. 22, 1913. Stradivari model, yellow or yellow-brown spirit varnish.

Giovanni Lazzaro
Messina anno 1949

Leb Mathias, Piacenza. Ca 1775. He came probably from Bratislava or Vienna, where the Lebs were numerous. Careful workmanship, fine wood: the back is made of one piece of beautiful curled maple. Delicately cut scroll and sound-holes. He worked on the large model of Amati applying good brown-red varnish. The measurements of a violin of 1775 are: length of back 356 mm, upper width 161 mm, middle 110 mm, lower width 206 mm. The top and bottom sides are of the same height, i.e., 30 mm. Price 25—30.000 Kč.

Lecchi Antonio, Cremona. 1900—1930. Large flat model, red-brown varnish.

Lecchi Enrico, Modena. 1885.

Lecchi Giuseppe Bernardo, Genoa. Born Aug. 20, 1895 in Felizzano. Pupil of Cesare Gandi. He imitated the Amatis, Stradivari and Guarneri del Gesù using orange varnish tinted with red. Exhibited two violins, a viola and a 'cello at Cremona in 1937.

Legnamaro Pietro, Mantua. D. Feb. 12, 1569. Lute and zither maker.

Legnani, Ravenna. B. Nov. 17, 1790, d. Aug. 5, 1877. Guitar maker.

Legnani Luigi, Naples. 1760—1770. Pupil of Zosino Bergonzi, whose works he imitated with much skill. In most instances he made the back of one piece. He used a red-brown varnish.

LUIGI LEGNANI alumnus
Zosimo Bergonzi fecit Neap. 1766

Legnani Rinaldo Luigi, Ferrara. Born Nov. 7, 1790 in Ferrara, d. Aug. 5, 1877 in Ravenna. Was a virtuoso on the guitar and built a number of guitars, tenor violas and violins.

Lelli Dino, Cesena. B. at the same place May 9, 1919. Instruments covered with chestnut-brown or orange varnish.

Lelli Dino
Fece in Cesena 1949

Leni Francesco, Florence. A 17th century lute maker, little known.

Leonardi Eleuterio, Spoleto. Born 1847. Pupil of Francesco Fabri who made violins and violoncellos.

Leoni Carlo, Treviglio, Treviso. 1851—1861. Violin maker who manufactured and traded in guitars and zithers.

Leoni Ferdinando, Parma. 1816. Worked on the pattern of Amati. Instruments by him are in no way remarkable.

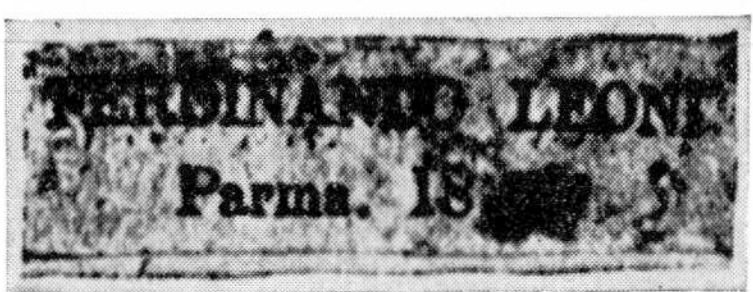

Leoni Giovanni, Naples, Padua. Father and son. 1829—1870. They worked together, making good instruments after Stradivari and using red-brown varnish.

Giovanni Leoni
Napoli 1829

Giovanni Leoni
1870

Leoni Guido, San Benedetto del Tronto (Ascoli Piceno). B. May 15, 1902. Orange or bright brown varnish.

Leoni Matteo. Florence. 1895—1925. Stradivari model.

Leoni Nicolo, Rome. Born in Rome in 1903. A violoncellist who made violoncellos and double-basses, varnishing them brown.

Leonori Paolo, Rome. Born in Rome Apr. 7, 1903. Instruments of golden-yellow colour.

PAOLO LEONORI
Roma 1949

Leoriporri Giovan Francesco, Milan. 1755—1760. Worked in the style of Amati and Stainer whose arching he imitated with particular skill. In Stainer's fashion he cut short sound-holes with circular ends. Yellow-brown varnish according to the Milanese school.

Fatto da Giovan Francesco
Leoriporri Milanese nel aquila 1758.

Leper Domenico, Rome. 19th century. Made instruments, but was hardly a violin maker.

Lepore Luigi, Rome, 1850—1880. Followed the example of David Tecchler and applied a brownish-yellow varnish. His 'cellos are very good.

Lepri Giuseppe, S. Arcangelo di Romagna, Via Cavour 26. Born Nov. 18, 1896. Pupil of Pollastri. Model Stradivari, golden-yellow varnish.

Giuseppe Lepri
fece anno 1947 GL
Santarcangelo Romagna

Lepri Luigi, Gubbio (Perugia). Ca 1880. Violin maker (bad workmanship).

Leutis Gerolamo de, Rome. 1638. Lute maker. George Kinský stated in the catalogue of the Cologne Museum of the History of Music that the name had been read incorrectly, his true name being Girolamo Zentis.

Liainer Alberto, Rome. 1665—1680.

Alberto Lianer
In Roma 1674.

Libera Agostino. Ca 1600. A violin maker who had come from Paris. The Paris Conservatoire owns a mandora of his making.

Agostino Libera fecit Anno Domini 1600.

Lignoli Andrea, Florence. 1681. Known only by name.

Linaro Luigi, Padua. Born Dec. 4, 1920 in Venice. He worked after Stradivari using orange varnish.

Linarolo Francesco. Venice. 1516—1540. A lute-maker who had come from Bergamo and made violas da gamba and tenor violas.

Franciscus Linarolus Bergamensis
Venetiis faciebat.

Linarolo Giovanni, Venice. 1590—1622. Son of Ventura Linarolo and perhaps his pupil, too. A violin survives, provided with a label written in Indian ink.

Giovanni di Ventura Linarol
In Venetia 1622. (written)

Giovanni di Ventura
in Venezia 1622.

Linarolo Ventura, Venice, Padua. 1577—1591. Son of Francesco Linarolo. Worked in Venice up to 1584, at Padua in 1585, and again in Venice in 1590. Maker of old-type instruments: violas da gamba (also lira da gamba, lira da braccio), violas d'amore, etc.

Ventura di Francesco
Linarolo In Venetia 1577.

1585
Ventura de Franco
Linarol in Padova (written)

Lione Francesco, Turin. Ca 1790. Mandolin and guitar maker.

Francesco Lione
Fabbricatore di Strumenti
Torino sotto li Portici
di Piazza s. Carlon 1790.

Liorni Augusto, Rome. Ca 1900. Died 1923. Little-known.

Augusto Liorni
Via del Gonfalone Num. 8
FECE IN ROMA 1900

Liotta Domenico, Catania (Sicily). 1911. Mandolin maker.

Liverani Ettore, Palermo, Via A. Veneziani 63. Exhibited two violins and one viola at Cremona in 1937.

Livorno Vincenzo da, Leghorn. 1862. There were two men of this name, father and son. The father was indisputably a good violin maker.

Locicero Luciano, Naples. 1830. Produced for the most part guitars.

Lodovico, Genoa. 1795—1830. Lodovico is this violin maker's Christian name. His family name is unknown.

Revisto da me Lodovico
Piazza porta vecchio Genova 17.. (written)

LODOVICO
da ME RISTORATO

Lolij Jacopo, Naples. 1727—1735. Worked on the model of Grancino. Instruments of medium quality. Inferior wood, yellow varnish. Price nevertheless 15—20.000 Kč.

Lolio Giovanni Battista, Valtezze (Bergamo). 1740—1750. Worked on the pattern of Grancino. The wood is not of the best quality. He applied yellow varnish. Price 15—20.000 Kč.

Jo Batta. Lolio di Valtezze
F. Anno 17.

Lombardi Colombo, Rome. 1930.

Lombardi Giulio, Rimini. 1789—1793. Golden-yellow varnish.

Julius Lombardi
Fecit a Rimini 1789.

Longo Mango, Padua. 1599. The only instrument known, a lute, bears besides a label the inscription "M. L. 1599" engraved on the neck plate.

Mangno [sic] Longo
in Padua 1599. (written)

Lorenzi Antonio. San Raffaele. 1925. He used red varnish.

Lorenzi Giovanni Battista, Piacenta, Pieve San Stefano, Venice. 1848—1878.

Lorenzini Gasparo, Piacenza. 1743—1804. Pupil of G. G. Guadagnini. Brown varnish. The initials G. L. P. are engraved on the back below the finger-board.

Gaspare Lorenzini
Fecit Placentiae 1750
GLP.

Lorenzo Laurentius, called "Papiensis", Pavia. 1497—1510. Built lutes, violas and organs. Beautiful workmanship.

Loveri Carlo and son, Naples. 1881—1898. Violin and mandolin makers.

Loveri Diego, Naples. Born 1888 in Naples. Followed Stradivari and applied a chestnut-brown varnish.

Diego Loveri

Loveri Giuseppe, Naples. 20th century. Little known.

Lubino ..... Lugano. 1740—1755. He is said to have worked in the style of the Cremonese school. Golden-yellow varnish.

Lucarini Vincenzo, Faenza. 1803—1830. Produced lutes and mandolins. Violins were only repaired by him.

Lucca Antonio. Verona. 1905—1923. Large model, red-brown varnish. He made especially large violoncellos.

Lucci Giuseppe, Modena. B. Sept. 17, 1910 at Bagnacavallo (Ravenna). Followed Stradivari and Guarneri; his varnish is reddish brown.

LUCCI GIUSEPPE
LIUTAIO
BAGNACAVALLO 1947
RAVENA ITALIA

Luigi C., Venice. 1840.

Ludici Girolamo, Pietro di. Conegliano. 1698—1709. Inferior workmanship, golden-yellow varnish.

Hieronymus Petrus de Ludice
animi causa faciebat Conegliani
A. D. 1709.

Hieronimus [sic] Petrus de Ludice
animi causa faciebat Conegliani
A. D. 1709 (written)

Luglioni (Lugloni) Giuseppe, Venice. 1777.

Luchano Matthias. Brescia. 1631. He worked in the style of the Tyrolese school combined with elements from the Brescian school. Light-brown varnish.

Lupp Franc. Antonio. See Luppo.

Luppi Giovanni, Mantua. 1896.

Luppo Francesco Antonio, Milan. 1716.

Luzzati Jacopo, Corvetto. Born 1886. Amateur without importance.

Luzzini Angelo, Bologna. 1840—1848. He worked after Stradivari, using red varnish.

Lybeert Alessandro, Florence. 1899. He worked in company with his son. Their craft was mandolin making.

M

Maccaferri Mario, Cento (Ferrara). Born 1900 in Cento. Guitar-virtuoso. He also made mainly guitars: his violoncellos have smallish shape. In 1948 he left for New York.

Maccari Antonio, Modena. 1885—1890. He worked after Giuseppe Rocco.

Maffei Lorenzo. Lucca. 1767—1787. Instruments of no particular merit. He worked in the style of the Florentine school. Golden-yellow varnish. Price at most 10.000 Kč.

Lorenzo Maffei, Lucca
fecit 1767.

Laurentius Maffei
restauratur [sic] Anno
1787 (written)

Magatelli A. Cremona. 1790—1800. Orange varnish.

Maggiali Cesare, Carrara (Fossola). B. Aug. 12, 1886. Followed Stradivari, applying golden-yellow varnish. Exhibited four violins and 'cello at Cremona in 1937.

CESARE MAGGIALI
FECE IN CARRARA
19..

CAESAR MAGGIALI MONETENSIS
FECIT ANNO 19..
CARARIAE

Maggini Giovanni Paolo, Brescia. Born 1580, died 1632. Son of Giovanni Maggini (born 1518). While still a little boy, reputedly seven years old, he became apprentice with Gasparo da Salò, in whose workshop he was till his twenty-first year. At the age of thirty-four he married a girl of nineteen. During the first years he worked exactly in the fashion of his master. Later on he also made instruments on the pattern of Girolamo Amati. For the backs of his instruments he used besides maple-wood also nut-tree, pear, platane-tree and poplar wood. His model is for the most part large and broad, only some violas are of slender shape, but long. Sometimes he inlaid his violin with mother-of-pearl, ivory and ebony. The arching he preferred less high, but full. Instruments by him are always of beautiful workmanship and wonderful wood. He used to provide his violins with a double purfling and with ornaments on the back. Neatly cut, slender sound-holes in upright position; both plates rather thick; low sides, rather small scrolls which have half a turn less than those which became established later on; varnish applied in thin coats of various shades of brown, mostly light brown. The sound-holes of the 'cellos, cut in a higher position, are of particular beauty. G. P. Maggini created excellent concert instruments with a powerful, yet mellow tone. His pupils were, besides Pietro Santo Maggini, A. Lanza, G. G. Pazzini of Florence and A. Mariani of Pesaro (according to Lüttgendorff). The price is 240—320.000 Kč. Labels, if genuine, are not dated.

Sizes of some works by G. P. Maggini in mm.:

	Violins				Violas		Violoncello
Length of back	369	369	369	366	432	386	754
Upper width	173.5	173.5	168	178	208	182	360
Middle width	115	115	110.5	123	140	120	250
Lower width	214.5	214	208	218	248	220	465
From the upper edge to the centre of the sound-holes	—	—	—	197	234	210	391
From the lower edge to the centre of the sound-holes	—	—	—	169	198	176	363
Length of sound-holes	—	—	—	79	89	80	163

Gio: Paolo Maggini in Brescia.

Paolo Maggini in Brescia

Maggini Pietro Santo, Brescia. 1630—1680. Good violins and 'cellos; still better are his contrabasses. His instruments are of fine wood, have neatly cut sound-holes and scrolls, bright yellow varnish, moderate arching, double purfling. There was also a certain Pietro Zanetto who was sometimes — quite erroneously — identified with him. Price from 8.000 Kč. upwards.

Pietro San Maggini.
Bresciae 1641.

Maghelli Severo, Rome. 1790—1800.

Maglia Stelis, Cremona. B. May 25, 1925 at Cingia di Botti near Cremona. Imitated G. P. Maggini, Stradivari and Guarneri del Gesù.

STELIO MAGLIA
Diplomato della Scuola Int. Liuteria
fece in Cremona l'anno 1949

Magnoni Carlo Antonio, Sienna. Ca 1514. A native of Bologna, a monk of the order of St. Augustin.

F. Carolurus Antonius Magnoni
de Bononia ordinis minorum Conventualium
Fecit Senis
Anno 1514.

Malagoli Eleuterio, Modena. Died 1827. Guitar maker.

Malagoli Folgenzio, Modena. 1856—1863. Repaired instruments with much skill.

Malagutti Arminio, Milan. B. May 23, 1914 at Palidano di Gonzaga (Mantua). Pupil of Stefano Scarampella of Mantua.

Malaguti Erminio — M
Milano — E
Fece nell'anno 1947 — (written)

Maldura Giovanni Battista, Rome. Ca 1900. Guitar and mandolin maker.

Maler Laux (Lucas), Bologna. 1500—1528. Lute and viola maker. Two lutes by him were in the Roudnice (Lobkowicz) collection, now in the National Museum in Prague.

Laux Maler

Maler Sigismondo, Bologna, Venice. 1460—1526. Skilful lute maker.

Malta Simone, Venice. Ca 1499. A mere name (was sometimes erroneously identified with Sigismondo Maler).

Malvolti Pietro Antonio, Florence. 1700—1733. Built good instruments on the pattern of Stainer, the longer sound-holes, however, are in the style of Nicolo Amati. He applied light brown, orange or yellow varnish. The scrolls are beautifully carved, the edges narrow, rather high, like those made by Giov. Bat. Gabrielli, who may have been a pupil of Malvolti. Price 16.000 Kč.

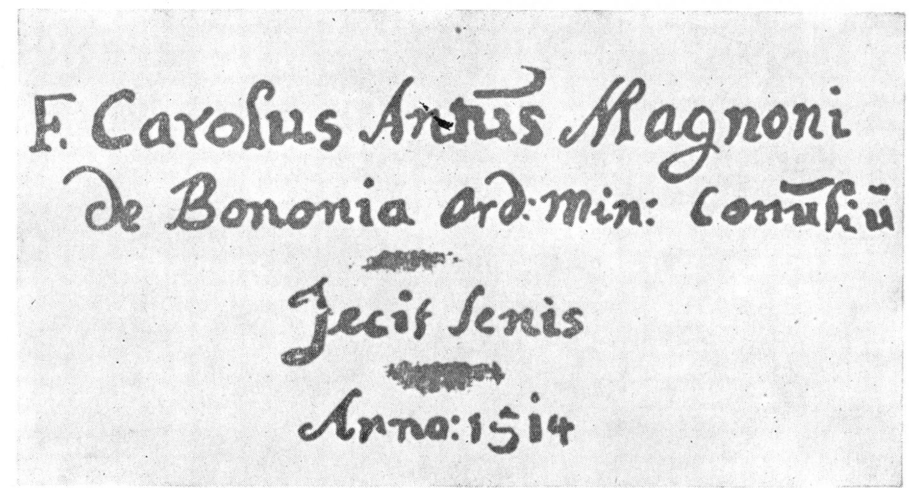
F. Carolus Antus Magnoni
de Bononia Ord: min: Conuētu
Fecit Senis
Anno: 1514

Magnus Antonio, Naples. 1780—1802. Worked in the style of the Neapolitan masters.

Magri Francesco, called "Bischeri", Leghorn. 1766—1784. Good workmanship. Golden-yellow varnish.

Magrini Enrico, Trieste. 1865—1880. He worked after G. B. Guadagnini using red-brown varnish.

Mainelli Luigi, Cremona. Ca 1823. Good instruments of low arching, coated with a beautiful red varnish.
Trade-mark: L. M. C.

Petrus Antonius Malvolti
Florent. fecit Anno 170

Mambelli Guido, Forli. Born in Fiume (Forli) on May 16, 1904, independent since 1925. He is working on the models of various old Italian masters.

Guido Mambelli
Forli 1947

Man Hans, Naples. 1710—1750. Worked on the patterns of Stradivari and Guarneri. Lutes by him are known for their quality.

Hans Man
fecit Neapoli A° 1736.

Mancini Giuseppe, Cortona (Prov. Tosca). 1839.

Mancini Ventura, Padua. 1678. Good lute maker.

Mandelli Camillo, Calco (Como). Born 1873. Pupil of Riccardo Antoniazzi. He went to Buenos Aires in 1899, returned in 1920. He worked conscientiously on various patterns of old masters, applied good brown-red oil-varnish as well as spirit varnish. Instruments by him are highly valued.

CAMILLO de CALCO
Fecit Anno 1922

Mandina Francesco, Castelvetrano (Trapani). Born Jan. 13, 1874, died Jan. 29, 1941. He had one violin at the Cremona Exhibition of 1937. Stradivari pattern, brown and yellow varnish.

Mandotti Giuseppe, Piacenza. 1755. He made narrow instruments with long middle bouts. The lower "eyes" of the sound-holes are placed near the edges opposite the corners.

Manfredi Francesco, Modena. B. 1902 at Colombaro di Formigine near Modena. Followed Stradivari, later developed his own model; handwritten labels and branded initials.

Manfredi Giambattista, Airuno near Como. 19th century maker of guitars and mandolins.

Manfredini Eros, Milan. 1940. Soon vanished from sight as violin maker.

Manfrini Luigi, Rome. Ca 1810—1820. Devoted most of his time to repairs; his own instruments are built on the Stradivari model.

Luigi Manfrini restaurò in Roma 1810.

Mango-Longo, Naples. 1749. Built guitars and mandolins inlaid with mother-of-pearl and ivory.

Mani Paolo, Modena. 1809—1811. Besides violins he made guitars.

In Modena Paolo Mani
fece anno 1809.

Manni Pietro, Modena. 1827. Son of Paolo Mani. He produced only guitars and mandolins.

Manosi Matteo, Cremona. 19th century. Good workmanship on the model of Amati. Price 15.000 Kč. and more.

Mantegazza Carlo, Milan. 1760. Perhaps son of Pietro Giov. Mantegazza. A good master.

Mantegazza Francesco, Milan. 1747—1790. Good workmanship in the style of Amati. He was a brother of Pietro G. Mantegazza. Price 30.000 Kč.

Francesco Mantegazza nella Contrada
di Santa Margarita in Milano
l' anno 1787

Mantegazza Giovanni, Milan. 1760, d. 1790. Perhaps son or the youngest brother of Pietro Mantegazza.

Mantegazza Pietro Giovanni, Milan. 1750—1790. The best master of the family. Built instruments on the large model of Nic. Amati; worked at first in company with his brothers, later alone. Beautiful work, lower, but broader arching. Fine wood; the somewhat large scrolls are delicately carved and tastefully shaped. Best are his violas. He applied a red, sometimes also dark orange or chestnut-coloured varnish of inferior quality. Instruments by him are of good tone and their price fluctuates between 25—40.000 Kč.

Petrus Joes fratresq. Mantegatia
Mediolani in Via S. Margaritae anno 17..

Pietro Giov. e fratelli Mantegazza nella
Contrada di Santa Margarita in Milano
al Segno dell'Angelo 1770.

Petrus Joannes Mantegatia
fecit Mediolani in Via S. Margaritae.

Petrus Joannes Mantegatia fecit Me.
diolani in Via S. Margaritæ 1783

Petrus Io: Fratresq
Mantegatia Mediolani
in Via S. Margarite anno
1750

Mantelli (Christian name unknown), Modena 1750—1780. Good contrabasses.

Mantovani, Parma, 18th century. Little known violin maker.

Mantovani Alessandro, Parma. 1853—1880. Little-known violin-maker, pupil of Rocca. He worked on the model of Stradivari and Guarneri. Fine, original scrolls, tastefully cut sound-holes, red oil-varnish of good quality. Good finish; fine mellow tone.

Alessandro Mantovani
fece in Parma Anno 1853.

Manzini Lodovico, Modena. Born 1804, died 1878 at Reggio Emilia. Guitar and mandolin maker.

Manzone Giovanni, Milan. 1624. Lute maker.

Maprochini Giuseppe. Ca 1801. Unpretentious violins of good tone.

Marafi Ambrosio, Milan. 18th century. Made good lutes and mandolins.

Ambrogio Marafi
Milano vicino a St.
Giovanni alle case rotte (written)

Maratea Domenico, Naples. 1887—1900. Mandolin maker. Worked with his brother Michele and his sons under the firm: Maratea Michele e Domenico e figli. He built but few violins, on the pattern of Vinaccia.

Maratea Michele, Naples. 19th century. Worked in company with his brother in the style of Vinaccia.

Maratti Giambattista, Verona. 1690—1700. Built middle-sized instruments of medium quality.

Marcelli Giovanni Antonio, Cremona. 1696—1697. Good workmanship; particularly the 'cellos are excellent. He applied yellow or red-yellow varnish and made purflings of splendid finish. Price 24.000 Kč, 'cello more.

Joanes Marcelli
fecit Cremonae
MDCXCVI (written on parchment)

Marchetti Abbondio, Milan. 1815—1840.
He built few violins, but they are carefully finished. Selected wood; beautiful brown-red varnish; noble powerful tone.

Marchetti — Abbondio
Fece in Milano l'anno 1816.

Marchetti Edoardo. Turin. 1890—1910. Son and certainly also pupil of Enrico Marchetti. He worked after Cremonese and Neapolitan schools.

Marchetti Enrico, Turin. Born 1855, died 1930. Good master.

Marchetti Severino, Rome. Ca 1797. Instruments by him are noted for their fine wood.

Marchetti Vittorio, Turin. 1894. Son and successor of Enrico Marchetti.

Marchi Gian Antonio, Bologna. 1660—1726. He adopted the outlines of Alessandro Gagliano, but took rather high archings. His instruments are of very good wood; fine scrolls and sound-holes well-cut after the fashion of Stainer. The tone of his violins and particularly that of the 'cellos, is powerful and full. Price 25.000 Kč, 'cello more.

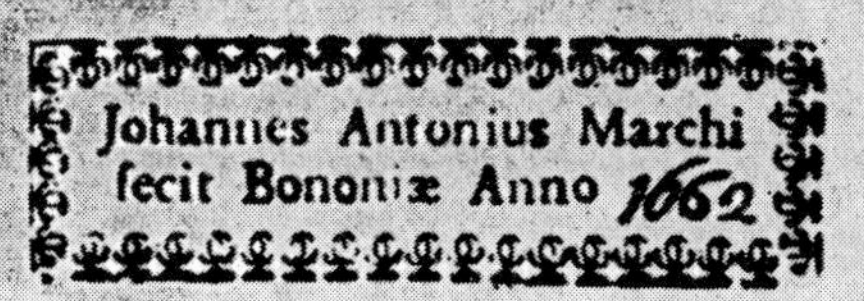
Johannes Antonius Marchi
fecit Bononiæ Anno 1662

Joannes Antonius Marchi
Fecit Bononiæ Anno 1726

Marco Antonio, Venice. 1700.

Marconcini Gaetano, Ferrara. 1830. Son of Luigi Marconcini. Instruments of medium quality.

Marconcini Giuseppe, Ferarra. Born about 1774, died Jan. 17, 1841. Son of Luigi Marconcini. Worked on the pattern of his master Lorenzo Storioni. Instruments by him are of good wood, have rather high edges, medium arching, small, well-carved scrolls, long sound-holes. He applied a good golden-yellow or red, but somewhat hard, varnish. Worked conscientiously. He was also a good violinist and personal friend of Paganini. Price 20—25.000 Kč.

Marconcini Luigi, Bologna, Ferrara. 1760—1791. Reportedly a pupil of Omobono Stradivari. Since the Hill Bros. declared they had never seen any instrument by Omobono they could acknowledge as genuine, the conjecture is certainly only an attempt to bring Marconcini in connection with the magic name. He does not need it, for he was a good master in his own right. Especially his violas and contrabasses are of excellent quality. He applied a good, delicately red varnish. Price from 30.000 Kč upwards.

Luigi Marconcini
F. Bologna.
Luigi Marconcini
in Ferrara.
Luigi Marconcini
Ferrariensis Fecit Ferrare.

Marconcini Aloisio (but also called Luigi), worked in Bologna and Ferrara betw. 1760—1778. According to René Vannes disciple of Omobono Stradivari — a doubtful conjecture. Red varnish.

Aloysius Marconcini
Ferrariensis de Ferrara anno 1770.

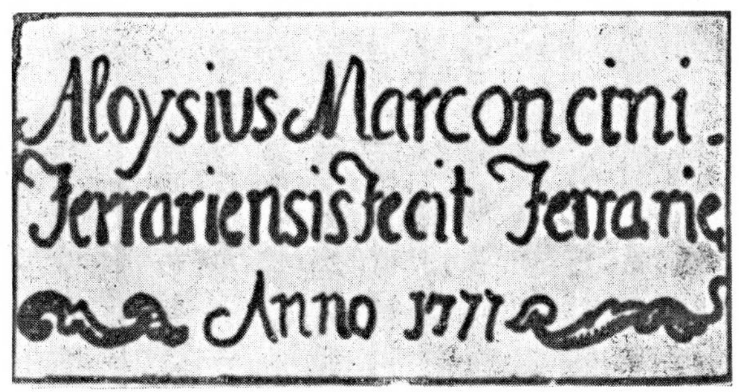
Aloysius Marconcini
Ferrariensis Fecit Ferrarie
Anno 1771

Marconi Antonio. Coneglio. 1878.

Marconi Lorenzo, Cremona, Via Giordano. B. 1881 in Codogno near Milan. Exhibited four violins at Cremona in 1937. Oil and alcohol varnish of various colouring.

Marconi Luigi, Ferrara. 1768. Doubtlessly Luigi Marconcini, judging from the excellent contrabasses provided with Marconi labels, the like of which occur, in the same quality and coated with the same varnish, under the name of Marconcini. Certainly a misprint. Besides these contrabasses no other instruments by Luigi Marconi are known.

Marcucci Custode, Santa Agata. Born Aug. 20, 1864. Applied himself mostly to the larger instruments of the violin family; maker of repute.

Marengo, Rinaldi Romano, Turin. Born June 20, 1866 at Alba (Piedmont). Pupil of Enrico Marchetti. Worked before joining G. F. Rinaldi (whose successor he became in 1888), in Paris and London. He was an expert on instruments by old masters. Good workmanship; golden-yellow varnish.

Marengo · Romanus - Rinaldi,
Albensis, fecit Taurini Anno 189 ...

Margini Antonio, Cremona. Ca 1693. Good instruments coated with dark red varnish. For rather mysterious reasons little is known of him.

Antonius Margini
in Cremona. 1693.

Maria Giuseppe da, Naples. Instruments of the years 1770—1779. Violins by him are not of good quality, but they are provided with a beautiful orange-yellow varnish.

Joseph di Maria di Nap.
in strada S. Pietro a Maiella
fece in Napoli Anno Dni 1778.

Joseph de Maria fecit
Napoli 1771.

Joseph di Maria di Napoli in strada
S. Pietro a Majella f. in Napoli
A. D. 1779.

Maria Joannes, Bologna (?). 1515—1540. Old-type violas by him survive. Marked his labels, before his name, with; Casparo Duiffeprugger Bononiensis anno 1518.

Maria Joannes (Giovanni) del Bussetto. See *Bussetto* Giovanni Maria.

Mariani Antonio, Pesaro. 1636—1680. Worked on the patterns of Maggini and Gasparo da Salò. Rugged workmanship; large, unsightly, badly cut sound-holes; tastelessly carved scrolls. Particularly the instruments of his younger years fall short in quality of the violins he built at a later stage, which are good, at least so far as the tone is concerned. He chose good wood. Applied a fine brown varnish. Best are his 'cellos. Price 16.000 Kč, 'cellos even more.

Antonio Mariani
Fece in Pesaro
Anno 1680.

Antonio de Marianis
fecit Pesaro
anno 1680.

Antonius de Marianis
fecit Pisauri anno 1638.

Antonio Mariani fecit anno 1694.

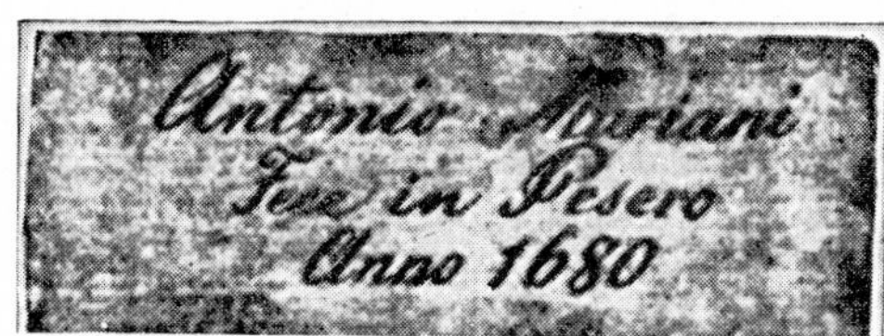

Antonio Mariani
· Pesaro 1669

Mariano Davide Chirone, Como. Early part of the 20th century. Skilful violin maker.

Mariani Fabio, Pesaro. 1679. Perhaps son of Antonio Mariani.

Mariani Lodovico, Pesaro. 1692—1702. Son of Antonio Mariani, Brescian school.

Mariatti Giambattista, Veron. 1700.
Built violins of medium quality on a small model. Price 10—15.000 Kč.

Marinelli Antonio, Ancona. 1830. Golden-yellow varnish.

Marino Bernardo, Rome. 1770—1805. A good imitator of David Tecchler's works. He applied red-brown varnish. The tone of his instruments is good. Price 8—10.000 Kč.

Maris ......, Firenzuola. Known only by name.

Marsigliese Biagio Caruano, Rome. B. Nov. 28, 1885 near Agrigento. Chiefly noted for repairs. For his own instruments he used a yellow, orange varnish.

B. CARUANA MARSIGLIESE
PREMIATO STUDIO DI LIUTERIA ARTISTICA
ROMA — Via Crescenzio, 103

Biagio Caruana Marsigliese
fece in Roma anno 1948
per l'amico
prof. Camillo Luzzi Conti

BIAGIO MARSIGLIESE — Siciliano
Fece anno 194. ROMA

Biagio Caruana Marsigliese
fece in Roma anno 1948

Martani Antonio, Reggio Emilia. Born 1804, died 1866. Violin maker, noted for excellent repairs.

Martinenghi Marcello, Milan. Via Giuseppe 81. Exhibited two violins and one 'cello at Cremona in 1937.

Martinelli, nicknamed "il Gobbo", Modena. 17th century. Built chiefly contrabasses.

Martini Odoardo (Edoardo), Florence. B. at Firenzuola near Florence 1880, d. 1930. Latin labels. Unimportant, aided by others.

Martini Giovanni Simone, Todi. 1608. Lute maker.

Martini Luigi, Florence, 1635. Perhaps son of Giov. Simone Martini. Only lutes survive. Violins by him are not known.

Luigi Martini
Fece in Firenze
l'anno 1635.

Martini Oreste, Mantua, Via Vittoria. B. at the same place Sept. 2, 1893, d. May 3, 1957. Exhibited a violin, viola, 'cello and two contrabasses at Cremona in 1937. Varnish orange or dark red.

MARTINI ORESTE
MANTOVA
FECE ANNO 19..

Martini Oreste
Instrumenti ad Arco
Premiato con Gran Premio e Medaglia d'Oro

Martini Oreste — Mantova
Premiato con Medaglia d'Oro
fece anno 19..

Martino "Presbyter", Padua. Ca 1572. Was a priest who is reported to have built valuable instruments. Very good are his guitars, rare relics.

Martino Presbyter
faciebat in Padova anno Domini 1572.

Marverti A., Modena. 1834. Violins of average quality. Considering their usually moderate prices, they are fairly good.

Mascioli Philippo, Fabriano. 1779.

Mascotti Giuseppe, Rovere. 1637. He made violins, violas and guitars.

Giuseppe Mascotti
da Rovere fecit anno 1637.

Masetti Carlo. Florence. 1915—1920.

Massai Giuseppe, locality unknown. End of the 18th and first part of the 19th century. Violins from him are not known.

Giuseppe Massai
fece l'anno 1800.

Massenzio Ernesta, Rome. B. Oct. 6, 1900. Modern violin maker.

Massrelli Giuseppe, Turin. 1847—1855.

Mastracci Amedeo, Rome. Born March 31, 1895. Applied a dark brown oil and spirit varnish.

Mastracci Amedeo
fecit Violino 20. 6.
1950 Via dei Latini
N 26 B Roma.

Maurizi Carlo, Bologna. 1900. He worked after the large Stradivari model (s. c. *Amatise*) using orange-red varnish.

Maurizi Francesco I. Appignano del Tronto. 1786—1840. Working in the style of Maggini he created a very sightly model. He carved large scrolls. On the whole his work is good. He applied a brown-yellow and, less frequently dark-brown, good varnish. Instruments by him are of good tone. Price 10—20,000 Kč.

Fecit
Franciscus Maurizi
Appineani.

Franciscus Maurizi
Appineanensis fecit.

Maurizi Francesco (II). Appignano del Tronto. Born 1816, died Jan. 24, 1903. Probably son and pupil of Francesco Maurizi I. He was a farmer, but may have had a part in the firm Fratelli Maurizi.

Francesco Maurizi
fece in Appignano
nel 1856.

Maurizi Giovanni, Appignano del Tronto, 1850—Sept. 24, 1922. Worked along the lines of the Amatis and of the old Brescian masters. Was probably a son and pupil of Francesco I.

Anno 1902
fecit Maurizi Giovanni
fu Francesco
Appignano del Tronto.

Maurizi Brothers, nicknamed "Pulghina", Appignano. 19th century makers. Probably sons of Francesco and farmers who occupied themselves with violin making only in winter.

Maurizi Fratelli, Florence. 19th century. Mandolin producers. They were farmers at Appignano and sold their produce in Florence.

Mauro Raffaele, Catanzaro. Ca 1865. Produced good guitars.

Maviglia Francesco, Chietti (Abruzzi). Modern maker, b. Feb. 9. 1902; he applies an orange, brown-red or brown varnish.

Mazzochi A., Milan. Ca 1901. Mandolin maker.

Mazzotti Jacopo, Florence. 1699. Son of Santo Mazzotti. Skilful lute maker.

Mazzuoli Felice, Rome. Ca 1783. Is renowned for his contrabasses.

Felix Mazzuoli Fecit Anno Domini
MDCCLXXXIII Romae
ad usum Canonici Francesci Orlandi.

Medard Henri, Turin. Born at Nancy Feb. 10, 1629. Frenchman, son and pupil of Henri Médard of Nancy. Reportedly very good workmanship.

Henri Médard a Turin
164.

Megazzi Enrico, Palermo (Sicily). Ca 1830. Instruments with brown varnish.

Mei Giovanni Ranieri, Viareggio (Lucca), via S. Martino 163. B. 1863. Exhibited a violin at Cremona in 1937.

Meiberi Francesco. Leghorn. Ca 1750—1763.

Melagari Enrico Clodoveo, Turin. Instruments are dated 1860—1888. About 1872 he worked with his brother Pietro. Built good violins, violas and 'cellos, applied red and yellowish varnish.

Melagari Pietro, Turin. Ca 1850. Worked well in company with his brother Enrico Cl. Melagari.

Melatti Luigi, Ferrara. 1820—1850. Probably a pupil of Luigi Marconcini. He worked after the latter's model and was no particular master.

Meleandri Adolfo. Pisa, Viareggio. 1940—1945. Little productive, imitator of Cremona masters.

Mellini Giovanni, Guastalla. 1768. Mediocre workmanship.

Meloni Antonio, Milan. Instruments of the years 1690—1694. He came perhaps from Bologna. Worked on the model of Amati and was the best violin maker of his time in Milan. Gracefully cut sound-holes and scrolls; yellow varnish of excellent quality. Violins of very good tone.

Price 16—20.000 Kč.

Antonius Meloni Mediolani
fecit A. D. 1690.

Meneghesso Pietro, Padua. D. ca 1939. Mediocre workmanship.

Meneguzzi Carlo, Padua. 1884. Instruments of medium quality.

Menichetti Luigi, Faenza. 1851.

Menighetti Martino, Turin. D. after 1940. Indifferent.

Menticasia in Milan. 1813. Probably a fictitious name, although it has been asserted that it stood for Pietro Giovanni Mantegazza or some other member of that family.

Da me Menticasiae Restauravit
in Mediolani 18..

Merffeotto or *Marfeotto* Giuseppe, Rovigo, or Rovere. Both spelling of the name and the locality uncertain. He was even identified with Giuseppe Mascotto in Rovere who lived ca 1637. Specimens and labels are so rare that the uncertainty cannot be dispelled.

Isepo Merfeotto di Rovigo.

Mercati Domenico, Tortona (near Alessandria), modern violin maker. B. 1894 in the Toscana region. Yellow-red varnish.

Mercolini Pietro, called Venie. 1821. Died June 6, 1891, Arcarano. Active at various other places (Colli del Tronto, Contraguera, Civitella del Tronto). Instruments without finish, but with good tone, brown-red varnish.

Pietro Mercolini
fece in Ancarano Anno 1865.
Pietro Mercolini
Fece in Contraguera nel 1852.

Merighi Ant., Milan. 1800—1830. Perhaps son of Pietro Merighi, guitar maker.

Merighi Pietro, Parma. 1770—1794. He devoted himself more to the production of guitars and mandolins than to violin making.

Pietro Merighi detto de Leoni
Fece in Parma l'anno 1794.

Petrus Merighi
fecit Parmae
anno 1770.

Merloni Pasquale, Ascoli. Ca 1818.

Pasquale Merloni Ascoli 1818.

Merosi Antonio, Rome. 1899.

Merosi Giuseppe. Firenzuola. Ca 1830, 1846. Golden-yellow varnish.

Meschini Paolo Giorgio. Brescia. 1667. Pupil of Antonio Mariani.

Messini Alfio. Catania (Sicily). Born March 15, 1889 in Adderno. Died 1957. Careful violin-maker who worked after Stradivari. He applied a golden-yellow varnish and provided his works with the initials A. M. H. C. sometimes I. M. I. (i. e. Jesus, Maria, Joseph).

Alphius Messina ab Hadrano
Faciebat Catanae A. D. ni 1948

+
A M H
C

Messini Girolamo, called Arcangelo, Florence ca 1687, lute and guitar maker. Violins, if any, are rare.

Messori Pietro. Modena. Born Oct. 18, 1870 at Modena. He had a workshop in Via Emilia 20. Built very good instruments on the patterns of Amati, Stradivari and Guarneri. The specimens he exhibited at Cremona in 1937, six violins, two violas and one 'cello, were splendid. He applied agate-red, red-yellow and amber-yellow varnish.

Mezzabotte Domenico Giov. Battista, Brescia. 1720—1765. Instruments of no particular merit.

Mezzadri Alessandro, Ferrara. 1690—1732. The statement that he was a pupil of Stradivari has not been confirmed. Instruments by him are built after the fashion of Joseph

Guarneri, son of Andrea. The wide-grained wood of the belly is good, the maplewood very handsome. Narrow small sound-holes in the manner of Amati, tastefully cut scrolls. He applied a fiery red, yellow, red-yellow, or brown-red varnish. Careful workmanship; instruments of fine tone. Price 80.000 Kč.

Mezzadri Francesco, Ferrara, Milan. 1700—1758. Worked in the style of his father Alessandro, whose pupil he was, but with less skill and less carefully. Works by him are little known. He applied a red, amber coloured or red-yellow transparent varnish. Price 10—15.000 Kč.

Francesco Mezzadri
fece in Milano 1749. (written)

Mezzano Frederico, Venice. Ca 1695. Good instruments which he liked to embellish with ivory and ebony. He built violins on a small model. The scroll of one violin is adorned with a gracefully carved head of a Moor.

Frederico Mezzano fecit Venezia Anno 1695.

Miani .... Bologna. 19th century. Known only by his family name.

Miani Domenico, Ravenna. 18th century guitar maker.

Miari Noe, Crespino (Rovigo). Contemporary violin maker, independent since 1930.

Micheli Giuseppe, Gajato (Modena) 1884—1894. Little known violin maker.

Michelis Peregrino di Zanetto, Brescia. Born about 1520, still alive in 1603. Son of Zanetto de Michelis. A very skilful instrument maker: built violas, lutes and 'cellos. He had three sons: Giovanni, born 1565; Battistino, born about 1571, and Franceschino, born June 18, 1579, who died June 8, 1615. The labels of Michelis Peregrino di Zanetto have very often been imitated and put into instruments of other makers (see Peregrino, Pelegrino, Zanetto). Price 25.000 Kč.

Peregrino Zanetto in Brescia
1610.

Michelis Zanetto de, Brescia. Born about 1495 probably at Montechiaro near Brescia. Died 1561. Lute and guitar maker.

Michetti Plinio, Turin. Born 1891. He worked after Guarneri and Pressenda, using brown, yellow or yellow-brown varnish.

Michetti Giovanni Baptista. Gorizia (Trieste). 1764.

Micle Gennaro, Naples. 1823. Guitar maker.

Migliai Antonio, Florence. Works of the years 1682—1703. Son of a Michelangelo Migliai. He was a good lute maker, built also cembalos and harps.

Antonius de Migliais Florentinus Fecit anno
1703.

Miglini Carlo, Turin, Via Cristina 7. Exhibited two violins at Cremona in 1937.

Milandri Galiano, Macerone near Cesena. Pupil of Arturo Fracassi. 20th century.

Milani Francesco, Milan. 1742—1751. Pupil of Lorenzo Guadagnini. Fine workmanship in the style of Stradivari, but unhandsome wood and broad irregular purfling. The few surviving instruments are, however, all of good tone. Price 16—25.000 Kč.

Milani Giuseppe Carlo, Milan. 1769—1780. Good work after the fashion of Nic. Amati.

Milella Giuseppe, Lecce. 1880. Son and successor of Vito Milella. Good instruments.

Milella Vito, Lecce. 1870, 1880. Modern violin maker. Careful workmanship.

Minelli Giovanni, Bologna. 1808, 1812. Modern violin maker.

Minelli Lorenzo, Florence. 1664. Son of a Francesco Minelli, good lute maker.

Mingazzi Luigi, Ravenna. Born Oct. 3, 1859 in Ravenna. Died Jan. 23, 1933. He made mostly mandolins, guitars, also double-basses. Golden-yellow varnish.

Mingo Alberto, Pesaro. 20th century.

Minotti ..... in Carate Brianza near Milan. 19th century. Worked as a rule anonymously for others; otherwise he produced mostly guitars and mandolins.

Minozzi Matteo. Bologna. 1742—1769. He worked after Stradivari and Guarneri applying yellow-brown or red-brown varnish.

Modaudo Giuseppe, Catania (Sicily). Born in Syracuse 1880. Pupil of C. V. Carabba. He modelled his work on the instruments by Cremonese and Brescian masters. In 1905 he was working in New York, later he returned to Italy. He used red or brown varnish. His instruments bear indication of which school they are modelled on, either "Cremonese" or "Brescian".

Modeni Antonio. Modena. 1831.

Moglie Alberto Fernando, Rome. B. Dec, 16, 1890 in Rome. Good violin maker who learned his craft in the workshops of Antonio Sgarbi in Rome and Leandro Bisiach in Milan. He left Milan for the USA, where he was associated with the firm Wurlitzer. His instruments are characterized by a yellow, orange or golden-red varnish.

Alberto Ferdinando Móglie
Fecit Romæ Anno 19
AF M

Mola Francesco, Cremona. Born 1641. Pupil of Nic. Amati, in whose workshop he was employed as early as 1653.

Molia Angelo, Genoa. Instruments are reported dated 1758, 1760. Good work, small model, fine wood.

Angelo Molia
Fece in Genova A. 1758. (written)

Molinari Antonio, Venice. 1672—1703, made mediocre instruments on a large model. Price 12.000 Kč.

Antonius Molinarius
fecit in Venezia Ao 1701. (written)

Molinari Giuseppe, Venice. 1737—1763. Probably son of Antonio Molinari; good instruments modelled on Venetian school. Golden-yellow varnish.

Mombelli Giacomo, Novara. Born in Novara in 1886. He worked in Trieste and in Brussels, in 1926 he was in Buenos Aires. He was a violinist and his favourite model was Stradivari's. He also made violas d'amore.

Monachini Francesco, Naples. 1725, mandolin, lute and guitar maker.

Monfrini Luigi, Rome. 1810.

Mongel A., Turin. 1820, 1830. Worked carefully in the style of some French school.

Monopoli Vito...., guitar maker; time unknown.

Montade Gregorio, Cremona. 1620. Most likely a disciple or assistant of the brothers Antonius and Hieronymus Amati, though he may have been a pupil of Andrea Amati. The style and finish of a specimen which has recently attracted attention, is very much the same as the work of the brothers Amati; the transparent yellow-brown varnish is of excellent quality, the belly of regular, close-grained pine-wood, the back in two pieces of faintly curled maplewood. The purfling is placed at 3.2 mm from the edge, is 1.5 mm broad, very carefully executed and reaches to the very ends of the corners, where the lines meet at a sharp angle, a proof of high skill. The long middle bouts make the instrument appear prolonged; the scroll is elegant, but not deeply cut. The back is somewhat more arched (16.8 mm) than the belly (15.5 mm). The instrument measures: belly 353 mm, upper width 162, middle 101.4, lower width 200, upper sides 29, at the lower end 29.7, length of sound-holes 71 mm, distance of their upper ends 39.7; the middle bouts are not regular (not made on a form); they measure left 87.1/83.4, right 85.3/83.8. The label reads "Gregorio Montade Cremonensis 1620". Evidently one of the "lost masters". In the 17th and 18th centuries there lived in Cremona five Montades: Fernando, Giuseppe, Antonio, Giovanni and Gregorio II. Their mutual relations can no longer be ascertained, e. g., which of them was the father of Gregorio II.

Gregorio Montade
Cremonensis 1620.

Montade Gregorio II, Cremona. Born 1729, died 1806. A great-grandson of Gregorio I. His instruments are as well finished as that of his ancestor, but the intervening time had brought the influence of Antonio Stradivari to the fore. He applied a golden-brown varnish of good quality. The conjecture that he had been pupil of Omobono Stradivari, which we declinei (see Luigi Marconcini), merely reflects the manifest nfluence of Antonio Stradivari.

Montagnana Domenico, Venice. 1690—1750. A very famous master; it is not known whose pupil he was, but it is ascertained that he used to work with Stradivari. Instruments by him, built in the style of the Cremonese school, are of outstanding quality: fine wood, large, beautifully carved scrolls; graceful sound-holes, cut after the fashion of Joseph Guarneri I. Best is his large model which follows the outlines of Stradivari, but is more massive. He applied a gorgeous golden-red varnish. Montagnana did not create many instruments, or, possibly, his creations bear nowadays still more renowned names. His works are known in two sizes, all of exquisite tone and excellent carrying power. Still more admired are his 'cellos and contrabasses. Altogether first-class concert instruments. Price 160—300.000 Kč; violins of large pattern have fetched as much as 400.000 Kč.

Dimensions of violins by Dom. Montagnana in mm.:

	1723	1734	1737
Length of back	348	360	360
Upper width	159	170	170
Middle width	106	109	109
Lower width	199	206.5	206.5

Montana Gregorio, Cremona (1690—1735) (?). Most likely a fraudulently invented name, but a number of fakers must have joined in, for the name appears often and labels are vague.

Montanari Enrico, Modena. 1900. Died 1945. Reputedly he worked very well. Golden-yellow varnish.

Montanari Luigi, Milan. 1880. Died ca 1908. He left a small number of violins and violoncellos modelled on

Stradivari and Guarneri, reported to be in great esteem. Red or light brown varnish.

Montani Costante, Milan. Guitar maker.

Montavoci Fernando, Airuno (Como). D. ca 1938. Indifferent.

Montanari ...., Bergamo. Although contemporary (until ca 1930), very little is reported about him.

Montefiori Erminio, Genoa. 1860. Died 1915. Golden-yellow and yellow varnish.

Montechiaro Giovanni. See Montichiaro Zanetto.

Montelatici Filippo, Florence. 1697. Built good lutes.

Montenari. See Montanari.

Monterumici Armando, Bologna. Born 1875. He was a pupil of Raffaele Fiorini whose successor he became. Died before 1939. Good instruments modelled on Stradivari and Guarneri, especially the violoncellos.

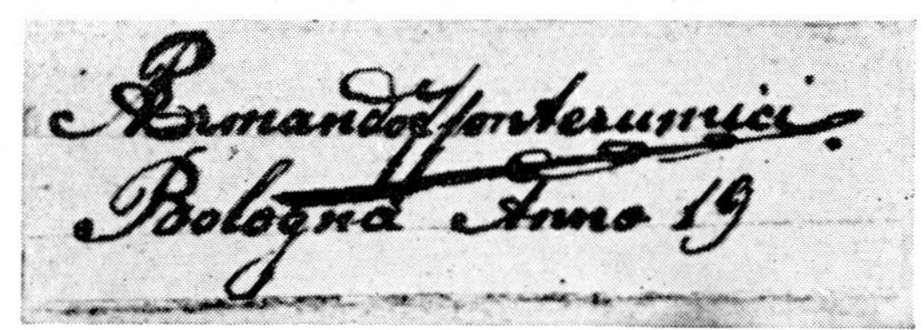
Armando Monterumici
Bologna Anno 19

Montevecchi Luigi, Cesena. B. 1868, d. after 1939. Adopted various models of the old Italian masters.

Montichiaro Zanetto, Brescia. Extant specimens bear dates ca 1530, 1533. Good workmanship. Particularly fine are his lutes and violas.

Monturri Giuseppe, Piumazzo. 1840.

Monzino Antonio I, Milan. B. 1725, d. 1800. Was chiefly mandolin and guitar maker.

Antonio Monzino
Fabricatore d'Istrumenti a corde Armonichi
in Milano nella Contrada della Dogana N 4037
all Insegna della Sirena.

Antonio Monzino
nella contrada dei
pannegiari in Milano
fecit Anno ....

Monzino Antonio II, son of Giacomo Antonio. 1799—1872. Unimportant. At his time the workshop was being run by Gaetano Antoniazzi.

Monzino Antonio III, son of the former. 1847—1930. Was pupil of Gaetano Antoniazzi; it was mainly due to the latter that the family atelier became well known and won distinctions; this Monzino is said to have been a good maker himself.

Monzino Antonio IV, Milan. 1885—1918. Head of the firm (at his time called Monzino-Garlandini) was chiefly a dealer.

Monzino Antonio V, son of Antonio IV. B. in Milan June 17, 1909. Trained abroad, conducted the firm and made good, but few, instruments himself. The house employed a number of outstanding workers whose instruments remain unfortunately anonymous.

Monzino Giacomo Antonio, Milan, son of Antonio I. 1772—1845. Was chiefly a performing artist and pedagogue (also composer) who carried on his father's business, but did not distinguish himself as craftsman.

Antonio Monzino
nella Contrada dei pennachiari in Milano
fecit Anno.

Monzino & *Figli*, Milan. Musical instrument factory.

A. Monzino
Fabbricatore e negoziante
d'istrumenti musicali a corde
e
corde armoniche
Milano
Via Rastrelli 10.

Mora Giacomo, Bagolino. 1701. Mandolin maker.

Giacomo Mora 1701
in Bagolino.

Morano Arnaldo, Turin (with a branch at Rosignano Piedmont). B. in Turin Jan. 8, 1911. Won distinction at Cremona in 1937.

Arnaldo Morano fece
Rosignano anno 194.

Arnaldo Morano fece
Torino — Anno 1942

Morara Paolo, Budrio near Bologna. B. Dec. 17, 1889, d. 1960. Was pupil of Giuseppe Fiorini in Rome and for some time his assistant. Exhibited one violin at Cremona in 1937.

+ Paulus Morara fil. Stanislai
J N P Josephi Fiorini Discipulus
fecit Butrium An. D. 1949

Morella Morglato, Mantua, Venice. 1545—1602. Pupil of Dardelli; lived in Venice after 1550. Good workmanship, red-brown varnish; most likely he did not produce any violins.

Morglato Morella
Mantuae 1545.

Morglato Morella
fece in Venecia 1594

Moreno Arturo, Naples. Mandolin maker.

Moretti Alberto, Rome. Mandolin maker, beginning of the 20th century.

Moretti Antonio, Milan. Ca 1730. Violin maker of no particular merit, who produced chiefly lutes and mandolins.

Moretti Carlo, Rome. B. in Ancona Aug. 21, 1891. Profilic violin maker, golden-red varnish.

Carolus Moretti Anconitanus +
Fecit Anconae — Anno Domini 1927

Moretti Egidio, Udine and Lavagna. Born March 9, 1894 in Udine, d. Nov. 17, 1958. Followed Stradivari, Amati, and Guarneri. Golden-yellow and red-yellow varnish.

COSTRUTTORE
MORETTI EGIDIO
UDINE
anno 1924

Moretti Egidio-Udinese
fece in Lavagna anno 1949

Mori Otello, Florence. B. Jan. 31, 1907. Was a guitar virtuoso who also built these instruments (according to Spanish patterns).

Morilli Mauro, Varese (Prov. Como), Via Walder 36. Exhibited one violin at Cremona in 1937.

Moro Bartolomeo, Padua. 1678. Lute maker.

Moro Vito, Naples. Since 1883 owner of a large atelier for the manufacture of stringed instruments; the products bear labels with the word *estudiantina*.

Morselli Arturo, Quistello, 1862. Built very good contrabasses.

Morutto Carlo, Turin. 19th century. Guitar and mandolin maker.

Morutto Marcelo, Turin. First half of the 20th century. Guitar and mandolin maker.

Mosca-Cavelli C., Rome, Padua, 1726. Lute maker.

Mosca-Cavelli Martino, Rome. 1608. Lute maker.

Martino Mosca
Caveli fece ao 1608
a revisto ..... (written)

Mozzani Luigi, Bologna and Roveretto. B. March 9, 1869, d. Aug. 12, 1943. Specialized in guitars.

Mucchi Antonio, surnamed "Bastia", Modena. 1800, died Apr. 13, 1883. Pupil of Aug. Soliani of Modena. Good workmanship, particularly his 'cellos are valued. He applied yellow oil varnish of good quality. Repaired instruments with much skill.

Antonius Mucchi
fecit Mutinae 1881.

Muncher Romedio, Cremona, native of Cremona. B. July 21, 1874, d. Jan. 9, 1940. Imitator of the Italian classics; his own models have yellow or yellow-red varnish.

Muratori Rocco, Padua. Ca 1704. Good and original contrabasses.

Rochus Muratoribus
Patavinus Delectans
Opus. 1704

Muschietti Renzo, Udine. Son and successor of Umberto M. 1926—1931.

Muschietti Umberto, Udine. B. 1875. Exhibited one violin at Cremona in 1937.

Mussolessi Giuseppe, Milan. Worked previous to 1940; his later fate is unknown.

Mutti Vittorio, Mantua. B. May 30, 1903. Violins of large pattern and red varnish.

Muzzio Francesco di, Chieti, 1830, 1838, Violins of good tone.

M. Francesco di Muzio
ha fatto questo violino
nell anno 1836 in Chieti. (written)

Muzzarelli Demetrio, Modena. Ca 1880. Unimportant.

N

Nadotti Joseph, Piacenza. Worked in the years 1757—1789. Built moderately arched instruments in the style of Amati. He had worked with T. Balestrieri, perhaps also with J. B. Guadagnini, and his work shows the influence of both masters. Sound-holes cut in the manner of Guarneri del Gesù but narrow. He applied good yellow or, more frequently, golden-yellow varnish. All instruments by him have a good tone. Price 25—40.000 Kč.

Nafissi Carlo, Gubbio. 1867.

Naldi Antonio, surnamed "Il Bardella", Florence. 1550. He was a lutanist and lute maker.

Nardelli Michelangelo, Gubio. 1850—1860. Probably a pupil of Carlo Nafissi.

Nastesi Valento, Gubio. Contemporary.

Nella Raffaele della, Brescia. 1659, 1672. Good and conscientious work in the style of G. P. Maggini. Instruments by him are of good wood; rather thick belly and back; the belly is of wood with regular grain, the back made of one piece of beautiful maple wood; the wood of the sides possesses wonderful curl; the arching and the gracefully cut sound-holes are executed in the style of the Amati brothers. The purfling he made, for the most part, twofold after the fashion of Maggini. Yellow-brown varnish. Price quoted 20.000 Kč and more.

Nella Raphael
Brescia A. 167.

Nelli Nicola, surnamed "Tolla", Salò. Born at Salò in 1861. A cabinet maker who also made violins.

Tolla Nicola
Salo
Fabbricatore Strumenti
e Riparatore a Corda..
Premiato con
Medaglia d'oro.

Nigetti Francesco, called Cestinetti, Florence. 1645, d. 1682. Organist of the Cathedral in Florence, built some violins and invented a new kind of theorbo.

Nobili Antonio Francesco, Florence. Ca 1693. Lute maker.

Francesco Nobili in Roma fecit 1693.

Nofri Floriano, Macerata. B. Dec. 16, 1922 at S. Ginesio near Macerata. Standard patterns, golden-yellow oil varnish.

Nona Francesco, della Rome. 1610, 1612. Lute maker.

Nonini Giuseppe, Udine. B. Dec. 16, 1897. An amateur who followed Stradivari and applied a golden-yellow varnish.

Giuseppe
Udine 949 Nonini

Novelli Natale, Milan. B. March 9, 1908. Nephew and pupil of Giuseppe Pedrazzi. Stradivari and Guarneri patterns, golden-yellow or red varnish.

NATALE NOVELLI
ALL'vo E NIPOTE PEDRAZZINI
FECE MILANO 1947

Novello Marco, Venice. 1720. Violin maker. His two sons followed his profession.

Marcus Novello fecit
Venetia 1720.

Novello Marco Antonio, Venice. 1780—1795. Son of Marco Novello, brother of Pietro Valentino Novello, in whose company he worked. Good representative of the Venetian school. Price 25.000 Kč and more.

Novello Pietro Valentino, Venice. 1764—1800. Brother of Marco Antonio. Pupil of Anselmo Bellosi. Good master of the Venetian school, who modelled his instruments on Amati's. Red-brown or yellow varnish.

Noverci Cosimo, Florence. 1662. Lute and violin maker.

O

Obbo Marco, Naples. 1712—1727. His instruments and varnish show streaks, as if they were soiled. Otherwise, however, he worked well on the pattern of Stradivari, using fine wood and applying a transparent orange-yellow varnish. Violins have a tone of good carrying power. Price 15.000 Kč.

Marcus Obb
Napoli 1712. (written)

Obbo Marco, Naples. 1803. He devoted himself to the making of guitars and mandolins. It is not known whether he was a son or a grandson of Marco Obbo.

Marcus Obbo fecit
Strada S. Ferdinando n. 56
Neap. Anno 1803.

Obici Bartolomeo I, Verona. 1665—1685. Instruments by him are built on the patterns of various Brescian masters, in most instances after the fashion of Giov. Paolo Maggini. He worked on a large model, without particular care. The wood is not always good. Yellow or red varnish of brilliant lustre, applied in thick coats. Valuable instruments, much in demand for the quality of their tone. Price 40.000 Kč; a violin sold in 1938 fetched as much as 80.000 Kč.

Bortolomio Obici [sic]
in Verona 1681

Bortolamio'Obici
in Verona 1681

Obici Bartolomeo II, Verona. 1750, 1755. Son of Bartolomeo I, perhaps his pupil, judging from his work. He worked on the patterns of Bartol. Obici and Maggini. His violins, of slender shape, are coated with a dark yellow-brown varnish. He bestowed careful attention on the wood. Instruments of very good tone. Price 20—25.000 Kč (quoted).

Bartolomio Obizi
in Verona 1750

Obici Prospero, Marano sul Parano (Modena). 1880. Good modern instruments.

Obizzi Tommaso Marchese, degli O. Padua. 1769. A nobleman, collector and amateur violin maker who also himself repaired his instruments.

Tommaso Degli Obizzi ristaurai adi 3. Giugno 1769
in Padova.

Odani Giuseppe Morello, Naples. Ca 1738—1760. Good workmanship. He used the large Guarneri model (360 mm.) applying red-brown varnish which in some instances looks nowadays blackened. Price 15.000 Kč.

Giuseppe Morello Odani
in Napoli 1738.

Oddone Carlo Giuseppe, Turin. Born 1866 in Turin. Pupil of Coffredo Rinaldi, in whose workshop he stayed in the years 1889—1899; for two years he was employed with F. W. Chanot; in 1901 he was in England. After returning home from England he established a workshop in Turin. Imitations of Stradivari, Guarneri, and later also G. Rocca. He used a fat varnish, mostly of dark-red colour. One of the best Italian masters of his time.

Odoardi Antonio, called "Il Lanaro", Ascoli. 19th century. Violin maker of mediocre skill.

Odoardi Giuseppe, called "Il Villano", Ascoli. Born Apr. 6, 1746 at Poggio di Bretta, died about 1786. He worked on the flat model of Stradivari as well as after the higher pattern of Stainer. Instruments without finish, the purfling irregular, the black strips thicker than the light ones or vice versa. The small sound-holes are neatly cut. Yellow-brown, dark-brown, or, most often, red-brown varnish applied in thin coats. He also used platan-wood. Instruments by him have, however, a good tone. Price 25.000 Kč.

Joseph Odoardi fecit in Piceno
prope Asculum In. 1785
De ligno Platano.

Joseph Odoardi, filius Antonii
fecit prope Asculum 1784. Opus
No 149.

Joseph Odoardi
1779.

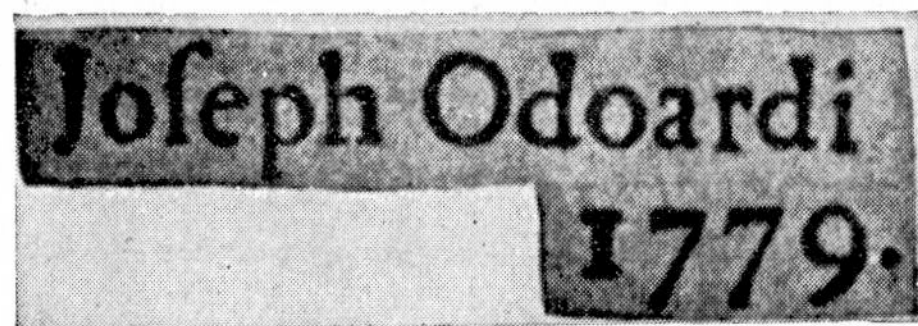

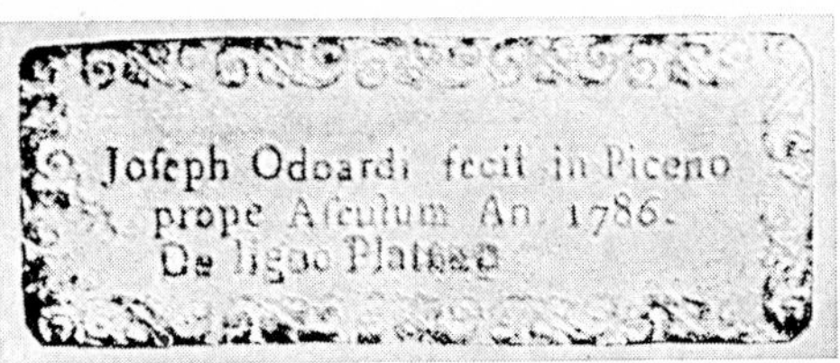

Oglio Domenico dall'. See Dall' Oglio.

Oliveri Felice, Turin. 1870—1904.

Oliveri Francesco, Rome. 17th century.

Oliveri Vincenzo, Turin. 1878—1889.

Olmi Alberto, Siena. 19th century.

Oneda Gio. Battista d', Brescia. See Doneda G. B.

Ongaro Ignazio dall'. See Dall'Ongaro Ignazio, Venice.

Orazio Giovanni Filippo, Rome. Ancient lute maker (1554).

Orelli Joseph, Rome. Ca 1792. Often mistaken for Orselli, was a skilful master who used handsome wood and a good oil varnish.

Orlandelli Paolo, Codogno. 18th century. Violin maker of medium skill.

Orlandi Ernesto, Cremona. B. Oct. 3, 1929. A cabinet maker who made various instruments besides.

MAESTRO LIUTAIO
ERNESTO ORLANDI
Allievo della Scuola Internazionale di Liuteria
di Cremona
....
Fece anno 1949

Orlandi Orlando, Ascoli Piceno. B. Nov. 11, 1875. Violin maker, also manufacturer of mandolins and guitars.

Orlando Orlandi
Fabbricante di mandolini e chitarre
anno 1908 Ascoli Piceno.

Orlandini Archimede, S. Leonardo (Parma). B. Aug. 1, 1909. Exhibited a violin at Cremona in 1937.

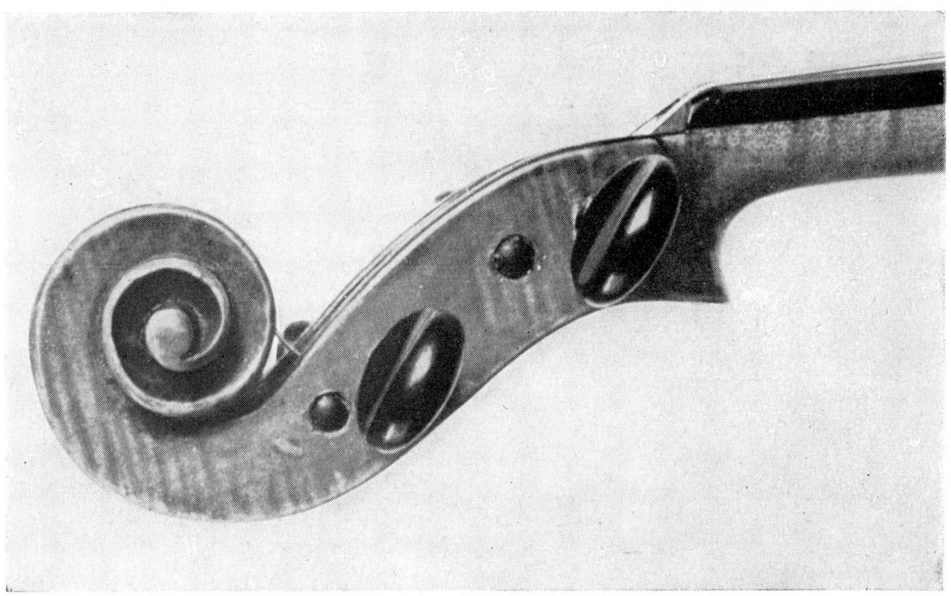

278. Odoardi Joseph, Piceno

279. Pallotta Pietro, Perugia 1787
Photo Hamma & Co

280. Panormo Vincenzo, Palermo

281. Pedrinelli Antonio, Cremona, 1845
Photo Hamma & Co

282. Platner Michael, Roma. 1741
Photo Hamma & Co

283. Postacchini Andrea, Fermo 1842
Photo Hamma & Co

284. Postacchini Andrea, Fermo 1854
Photo Hamma & Co

285. Pressenda Joannes Franciscus, Torino 1823

286. Pressenda Joannes Franciscus, Torino 1826
Photo Hamma & Co

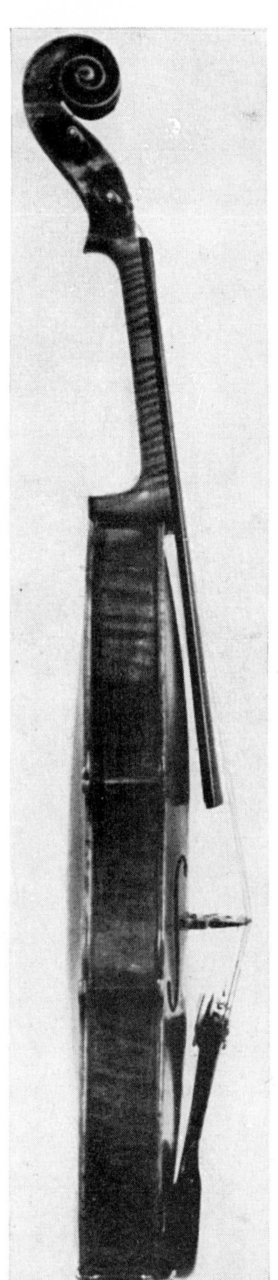

287. Pressenda Joannes Franciscus, Torino

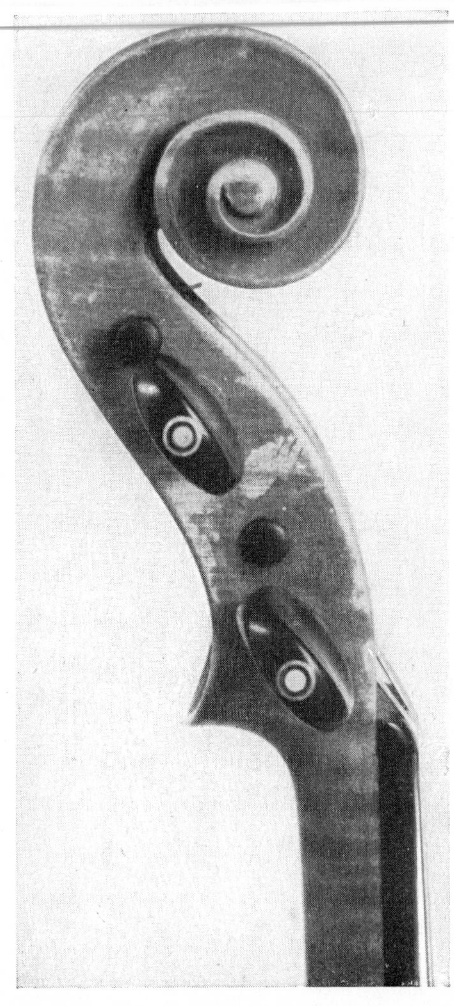

288. Pressenda Joannes Franciscus, Torino

289. Pressenda Joannes Franciscus, Torino 1829
Photo Hamma & Co

290. Pressenda Joannes Franciscus, Torino 1837
Photo Hamma & Co

291. Pressenda Joannes Franciscus, Torino 1840
Photo Hamma & Co

292. Pressenda Joannes Franciscus, Torino 1841
(CELLO)
Photo Hamma & Co

293. Rocca Giuseppe Antonio, Torino 1827
Photo Hamma & Co

294. Rocca Giuseppe Antonio, Torino 1834
Photo Hamma & Co

295. Rocca Giuseppe Antonio, Torino 1842
Photo Hamma & Co

296. Rocca Giuseppe Antonio, Torino 1843 (CELLO)
Photo Hamma & Co

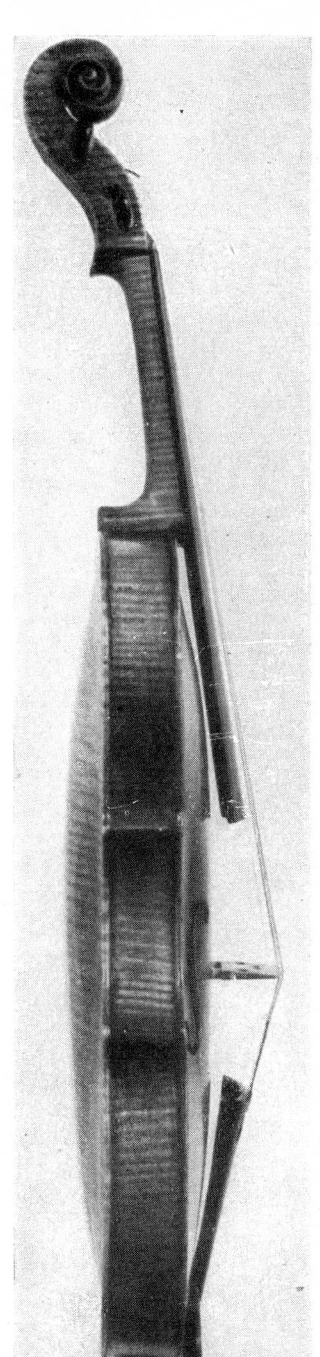
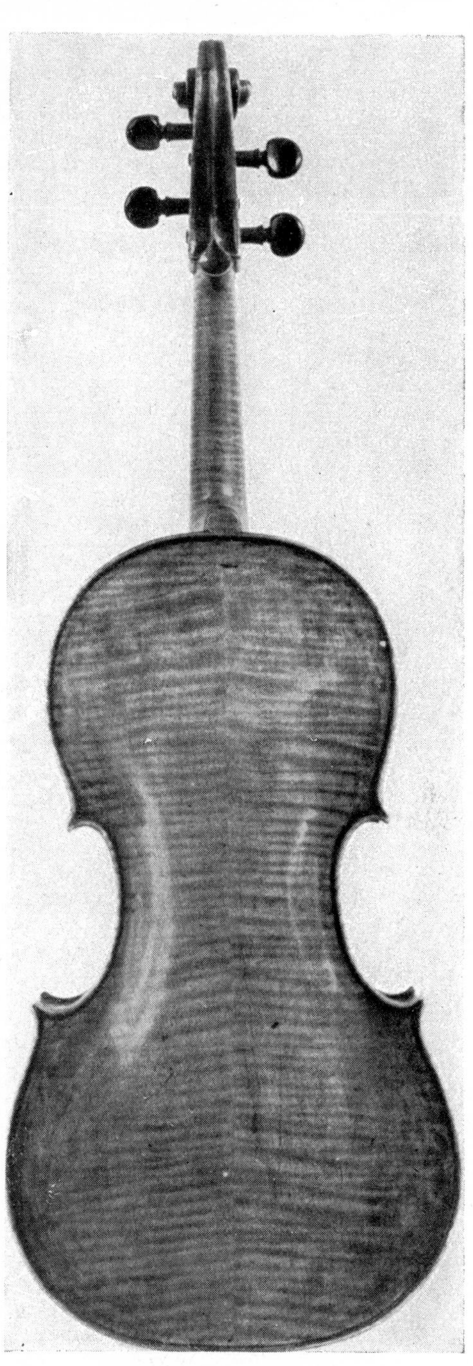

297. Rogeri Giovanni Bapt., Brescia (VIOLA)

298. Rogeri Giovanni Bapt., Brescia
Photo Hamma & Co

299. Rogeri Giovanni Bapt., Brescia 1696
Photo Hamma & Co

300. Rogeri Giovanni Bapt., Brescia 1699
Photo Hamma & Co

301. Rogeri Giovanni Bapt., Brescia 1699
Photo Hamma & Co

302. Rogeri Giovanni Bapt., Brescia 1700
Photo Hamma & Co

Archimede Orlandini
fecit in Parma
Orlandini Archimede

Ornati Giuseppe, Milan, Via Francesco Sforza 44. B. July 3, 1887. Exhibited a violin, a viola and a 'cello at Cremona in 1937.

Orselli Enrico. Pesaro. Born 1891, died 1955. He worked after Stradivari and Guarneri using golden-yellow or red varnish.

Orselli Giuseppe, Rome. 1792—1820. Often mixed up with Orelli. Good workmanship, good tone.

Joseph Orselli Romanus, Fecit Romae
Anno 1792

Joseph Orselli Romanus
Fecit Romae Anno 1792

Orsini Ercole, Teramo. D. 1951. Exhibited a violin and a 'cello at Cremona in 1937.

Orzelli Giuseppe, Rome. Pupil and successor of Crescenzio Ugar. Ca 1800. Various instruments, good work.

Orzero Tommaso. Turin. 1850. Modelled his instruments on G. B. Guadagnini. Golden-yellow varnish.

P

Pacherele Pierre, Paris, Nizza, Genoa, Turin. Born 1803, died Dec. 31, 1871. Fellow-pupil of J. B. Vuillaume with whose father, Claude François Vuillaume, he worked on the pattern of Stradivari. Applied opaque varnish. Repaired instruments with great skill.

Pacherele Vincenzo, Milan. 1885. He worked after Amati using red varnish. His labels are printed on brown paper.

Pafuni Francesco, Forli. Ca 1756. Specialized in repairs; there are but few instruments of his own making.

Restaurato da me Francesco Pafuni
in Forli anno 1756.

Pagani Gian Battista, Cremona. 1735, 1743. He modelled his instruments on Amati and Stradivari. Price ca 15.000 Kč.

Pagani Pietro, San Martino d'Este. Ca 1836. A dilettante, but good violins.

Paganini Alba, daughter of Giuseppe, Forli. 20th century. Worked with her brother Mario. They copied old masters.

Paganini Giuseppe, Florence. B. Jan. 6, 1870, d. June 20, 1913. Son of Luigi Paganini and perhaps his pupil. Exemplary workmanship: flat archings, brown varnish. His daughter, who learned the craft in her father's workshop, remained as violin maker at Forli.

Giuseppe Secondo Paganini de Forli Fece Firenze 1909

Paganini Luigi, Faenza, Forli. Born 1838 at Faenza. Died 1914 at Forli. A maker who produced cheap exercise-violins for pupils. Red varnish.

Paganini Mario, Forli. Born 1896, died April 24, 1921. Son and pupil of Giuseppe Paganini and brother of Giuseppe Paganini. He died early. Cherry-red varnish.

Paganini Nicolò, Florence. Born Oct. 27, 1782 in Genoa, died May 27, 1840 in Nizza. Built instruments of large pattern and applied brown varnish.

Paganoni Antonio, Venice. Ca 1750. Only his name is known.

Palazzoli Giovanni Battista, Verona. 1605. He built fairly good violins which he provided with double purfling, as he worked mostly in the style of Maggini. Instruments by him are now mostly of historic value.

Palla Vincenzo, Perugia. 1790. Violin maker who built also harps. The few stringed instruments by him which are known constitute probably the remainder of his works not rechristened after more famous masters.

Palla Vincenzo
fece in Perugia 1790.

Palladini Giovanni, ... 19th century. Violin and mandolin maker of little consequence.

Palma Orazio, Rome. Born Oct. 30, 1870, died 1922. Mostly mandolin- and guitar-maker. His labels are printed on pink paper.

Palma Paolo, Lucca. 1760—1770. Copied N. Amati without much success. Also a 17th century Palma is mentioned, but nothing is known about him. Perhaps an ancestor of Paolo.

Paulus Palma Lucencis fecit in Luca 17..

Paulus Palma Lucensis
Fecit in Lucca 17.

Palmerio Matteo, Padua. 1743—1759. Some time ago a violin of 1759 emerged at The Hague. Otherwise unknown.

Pallota Pietro, Perugia. 1788—1831. Built large flat violas and 'cellos. His violins have a somewhat higher arching than the violas. Perfunctory workmanship; short, rather wide, uneven sound-holes; large unhandsomely carved scrolls. These shortcomings, however, do not impair the good tone of his instruments.

Pietro Pallota
fece L'anno 1792
Nr. 13 Perugia. (written)

Pietro Pallotta
fece L'anno 1792
N.° 19 Perugia

Pietro Pallotta fece
L'Anno 1790 in
Perugia

Palumbi Bernardino, Pescara. B. Nov. 9, 1921 in Avezzano. His work is reported to be good.

Pandolfi Antonio. Venice. 1710—1740. An assiduous and diligent master. His violins are of large pattern, modelled on Amati, carefully finished with delicate taste; the well designed and neatly cut sound-holes are in a slanting position. He applied yellow-brown or deep-red varnish. The back is usually of one piece. The tone of his instruments is excellent. Price 20.000 Kč and more.

Antonius Pandolfi
Venetiis fecit Anno 1740

Panirillo Pasquale, Naples. 1805.

Panizzi Giovanii Battista, San Remo. Born Nov. 24, 1890, d. March 8, 1956. Yellow-brown or yellow varnish.

Panormo Vincenzo Trusiano, Palermo, Paris, London. Born 1734 at Monreale near Palermo, died 1813 in London. He had two sons: Joseph, born about 1773, who died in 1825, and George Louis, born about 1775, who died about 1842. As a boy he may have been a pupil of Carlo Bergonzi. In 1760 he worked in Paris and after 1772 in London. His life was a continuous travelling. Panormo is said to have bought, on one from his journeys, an old maple-wood board of a billiard-table of which he made the backs of a number of violins. As it is with other masters, whose works have been thoroughly studied (particularly those of Stradivari and Guarneri del Gesù) it is possible to determine the genuineness of these instruments from the identity of the material. Some look exactly alike. Panormo worked conscientiously on the patterns of Stradivari and Bergonzi. Fine wood, tastefully cut sound-holes and scrolls. He applied a wonderful orange-yellow or red-brown varnish. All genuine works are of excellent tone, but not all of the many instruments bearing his labels are genuine. We suppose that he either had several collaborators or some less skilled masters provided their instruments with his labels. The difference is obvious from the workmanship, material and tone: the prices vary accordingly, from 20 to 30.000 Kč (and even more). See also Trusiano.

Vincenzo Panormo
di Palermo fecit
anno 17..

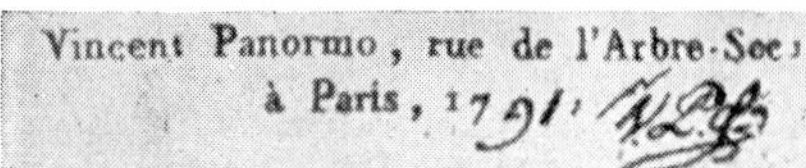

Vincent Panormo, rue de l'Arbre-Sec,
à Paris, 1791

Panza Antonio, Finale Emilia. 1870, 1875. An amateur. Many violins, modelled on Stradivari, are made of good wood and have a fairly good tone. Golden-brown varnish.

Panzani Antonio. Rome. 1735—1785. Instruments of medium quality. Orange-red and golden-yellow varnish.

Paoletti Vezzio Silvio. Florence. Born 1883. Pupil of Valentino de Zorzi. His instruments are mainly varnished brownish-yellow or yellow, but he devoted himself mainly to repairs.

Silvio Vezio Paoletti
fece in Firenze A 1923

Paoli Luigi, Naples and Trieste. B. Dec. 11, 1908. Violin maker.

Paolini Luigi, Todi, Rimini. Born Oct. 29, 1875, d. Aug, 13, 1942. Worked on the models of Amati, Pressenda and Rocca. Sometimes imitations; his individual creations have a golden-yellow or brown-red spirit varnish.

Paolini Luigi fece in Todi.
Paolini Luigi Fece in Rimini.

Paralupi Rodolfo, Rome. B. Jan. 29, 1890. Merchant, then violin dealer, at last maker of guitars, violins, etc.

Rodolfo Paralupi
Fece in Roma Anno 1949

Pardini Bastiano, Florence. 1690—1715. He worked on the model of Gasparo da Salò, but his workmanship is not satisfactory. Instruments chiefly of historical interest. Dark-brown varnish.

Baſtiano Pardini
In Fiorenza.

Bastiano Pardini
in Florenza.

Pardino Francesco, Naples. 1906. Special production of violoncellos. Red-brown varnish.

Pareschi Gaetano, Ferrara. B. Feb. 7, 1900. Worked on the pattern of Stradivari. Golden-yellow or chestnut-brown varnish.

Gaetano Pareschi
fece in FERRARA
.... l'anno 1947

Parmeggiani Romolo, Modena, Via Canalino 1/3. Born 1888. He exhibited two violins modelled on Stradivari in Cremona in 1937.

Romolo Parmeggiani fece in Modena
Anno

Parravicini Pietro, Bovisio (Milan). B. 1889, d. 1957. Pupil of Romeo Antoniazzi, followed Stradivari, Guarneri and Guadagnini with application and success.

PIERO PARRAVICINI
fece in Bovisio (Milano) l'anno 1947

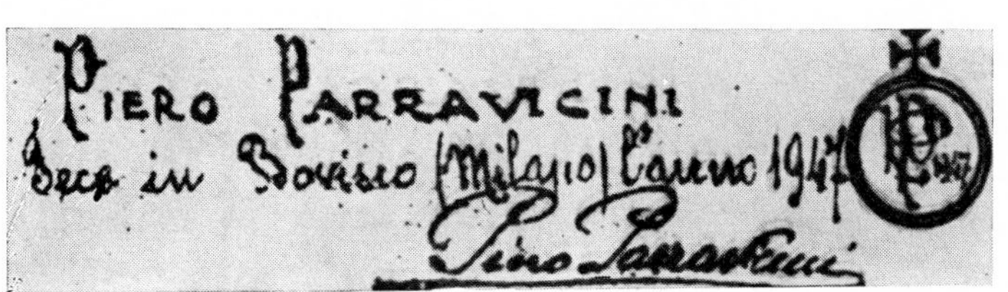

Pasciutti Ferdinando, Bologna. Born 1850 at Bazzano, died after 1885. He was more of an instrument maker in a general sense than a specialist.

Pascuali Giacomo, Ancarano near Ascoli. 18th century. Violin and guitar maker of minor importance.

Pasio Ildebrando, Faenza. 1750. A little known violin maker. Perhaps he devoted more of his time to repairs than to the making of new instruments.

Ildebrandus Pasius Restauravit
Faventiae.

Pasio Lodovico, Modena. 1506. Little known ancient lute maker.

Passaponti Giovanni, Florence. 1750. Highly skilled violin and lute maker who inlaid his violins with complicated purflings. Nothing but this delicately finished purfling is remarkable about his instruments.

Pasqualini Gioacchino, Rome. Born Aug. 3, 1902 in Ascoli Piceno. Studied at the Santa Cecilia Academy in Rome, where he studied violin until 1924. At the same time he also studied the course of physics and mathematics at the Technical High School. In 1935 the Academy awarded him the title "Master of Viola". He taught violin at this academy and three years later he finished his High School studies with the maximum number of points from Experimental Physics. Because he had considerable knowledge of various aspects of art and science, he was able to publish several studies on the resonance of wood and on the qualities of bodies of bowed instruments.

In 1940 he was given a scholarship of the National Council for Research connected with the "Corbino" Institute for Electroacoustics. As an expert he was asked to lecture on musical acoustics at a special course for graduates of the Santa Cecilia. In 1949 he was elected president of the jury of the International Violin Makers Competition in Cremona. In the same year he was entrusted by the government with the reorganizing of the International Violin Makers School in Cremona. He is also the founder and president of the National Union of Italian Bow and Violin Makers, founded on Dec. 12, 1950 under the auspices of the Accademia Nazionale di Santa Cecilia of which he has been President. He is the author of many pamphlets on violin making. He has worked together with Dr Lina Gabrielli of Ascoli Piceno; more detailed biography of Professor Pasqualini can be found in her book, *Gente Piceno.*

Pasta Antonio, Brescia. 1710—1730. Good are his imitations of the models of Gasparo da Salò and Maggini. Instruments of full, yet not too high, arching. The wood is of good quality. He applied, in very thin coats, a good red-brown varnish. The tone of his instruments is very good. Price 20—50.000 Kč.

Pasta Bartolomeo, Milan. 1670—1690. Pupil of Nic. Amati. Worked well on the model of his master and applied a chestnut-coloured varnish.

Bartolomeo Pasta, Alievo di Nicolo
Amati Cremonese, Fece in Milo. 1681

Pasta Domenico, Brescia. 1710—1785. Worked on the grand pattern of Nicolo Amati and Maggini. His workmanship resembles that of Hieronymus Amati and it is quite possible that he was the latter's pupil. His arching is however lower than Amati's or Maggini's. Painstaking craftsmanship, instruments of fine tone. Golden-yellow varnish. Price 25.000 Kč.

Pasta Domenico Bresciano fece anno 1785

Pasta Gaetano, Brescia. 1710—1760. Son of Bartolomeo Pasta. Pupil of Hieronymus Amati. Worked in the style of the Cremonese school, sometimes on the pattern of Gasparo da Salò but his flat instruments are worked on the pattern of G. B. Rogeri. Excellent are his 'cellos; their scroll is replaced by a lion's head. Both varnish and tone are good. Price 25.000 and more.

Gaetano Pasta Milanese allievo
dell Amati di Cremona alla
Pallada in Brescia. A. 1750

Pasta Gaetano II, Brescia. 1788.

Pauli Giovanni, Rome. 1885.

Pazarini Antonio. Genoa. 1720, died 1744. Large pattern, full and high-arched in the style of the Brescian school. He worked in company with Bernando Calcagni. The brown-red oil varnish as well as the tone are of good quality. Price 20—40.000 Kč.

Antonius Pazarinius et Calcanius
Genuae 1740.

Pazzagola Francesco, Ferrara. 1577. A lutanist who also made lutes.

Pazzagola Giovanni, Ferrara. 1580. Little known lute maker. Valdrighi calls him "Pazzavola" (misreading).

Pazzini Giovanni Gaetano, Brescia, Florence. 1630—1666. He was a pupil of Maggini, but went his own way and did not imitate the latter's works. He used always fine wood, made instruments with high arching on the Amati pattern, and applied dark-brown varnish. The tone of his instruments is good. Price 15—20.000 Kč.

Gian Gaetano Pazzini
allievo dell' Maggini di Brixiae.
Fecit Firenze, Anno 16..

Giovanni Gaettano Pazzini
Florentinus Anno 16.

Gian Gaettano Pazzini,
allievo dell Maggini di Brixae
fecit anno 16.

Giovan Gaettano Pazzini. allievo dell
Maggini di Brixiæ.
Fecit Firenze, anno 1660

Peccati Umberto, Soncino (Cremona) and Milan. Born Oct. 22, 1878, d. Oct. 17, 1944. Made mostly guitars, mandolins and also contrabasses.

De Peccati Umberto
Faceva in Soncino (Cremona)
Anno Domini 19.

Peccenini Alessandro called "del Leuto" (i.e. liuto), Bologna, 1581—1595. Lute maker of the duke of Ferrara. Lutes by him were highly valued.

Pecchini Vasco, Suzzara (Mantua). Via Cesare Battisti 15. Born May 4, 1893. Pupil of Ento Arassi. He modelled his instruments on Stradivari. One of his violins was exhibited at Cremona in 1937. There exist but few specimens; they are however of good quality. Yellow-red varnish.

"Viva fui in sylvis-mortua dulce cano"
PECCHINI VASCO
SUZZARA (Mantova) ANNO 19..
Premiato con medaglia d'Oro

PECCHINI VASCO
fece in SUZZARA (Mantova)
ANNO DOMINI 1947
P. V. S.

Pedrazzi Fra Pietro, Bologna. 1784. Friar of the Dominican order who made some violins.

Pedrazii Pietro, Palermo. 1870.

Pedrazzini Giuseppe, Milan. Via Felice Cavalotti 11. Born Jan. 12, 1879, died Oct. 20, 1957. Pupil of Antoniozzi. Originally a cabinet maker who gradually made himself a name as violin-maker. He exhibited two violins, a viola and a violoncello at Cremona in 1937. Red and golden-brown varnish.

Giuseppe Pedrazzini Cremonese
fece in Milano 19..
Giuseppe Pedrazzini
Cremonese
fece in Milano l'Anno 1914

Giuseppe Pedrazzini Cremonese
fece in Milano 1945

Giuseppe Pedrazzini
Cremonese
fece in Milano l'Anno 1914
G.P

Pedrinelli Antonio, Crespano. Born July 21, 1781, died June 1, 1854 at Crespano. He was a cabinet maker, but after a careful study of instruments and numerous experiments he worked his way up to delicately finished copies of the works of Amati, Stradivari and Guarneri. His copies were unfortunately sometimes sold as genuine works of those masters. He also imitated Maggini, but did not succeed in copying violins with double purfling and ornaments on the back. Fine wood; the backs are sometimes even of beech-wood (reportedly taken from old oars); he applied orange-red or golden yellow varnish of good quality. In the corner of his labels he wrote the price of the instruments. Price 15—25.000 Kč for lesser specimens still bearing his name.

Antonio Pedrinelli
ad imitationem Stradivarii
fecit in Crespano Anno 1840. No. 38.

No. 43 Antonio Pedrinelli
fc in Crespano 1844.

Pedroni A., Rome. B. 1867. Little known violin maker.

Pellacani Giuseppe. Gaggio di Piano (Modena). Born Aug. 23, 1900. Pupil of Bianchi and Arassi in Milan. He modelled his instruments on Guarneri del Gesù. Golden-yellow or brown varnish. Most of his instruments have been exported to the United States and France.

Pellacani Giuseppe da
Medolla fece anno 1942
copia A. Straduari

TENORE
IL TOSCANO

Giuseppe Pellacani
da MEDOLLA (Modena)
fece anno 19..

Pellecchio Francesco, Naples. Ca 1891. Mandolin and guitar maker.

Pellegri, Parma. 19th century. Good violin and bow maker. It has not been possible, so far, to ascertain his Christian name.

Pellegrino Giovanni. Lucca. 1689.

Pellegrino Zanetto. See Zanetto Peregrino.

Pellegrino Michele Francesco, Brescia. B. Aug. 18, 1579, d. 1615. Of his works very little is known, all uncertain.

Pellegrino Micheli Zuan (di), Brescia. B. at the same place 1565, d. after 1607 (1615?). Lute maker. Only a few examples of his work are preserved, no violins.

Pellicciari Roberto, San Cesarino near Parano, 1870. Violin maker of medium skill.

Pellizon Antonio I, Gorizia. B. 1759, d. 1850. Follower of Stradivari and Amati, applied a golden-yellow, or orange varnish.

Antonio Pelizon
fece Gorizia 1825

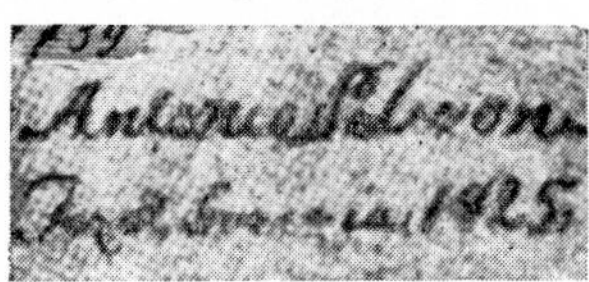

Pellizon Antonio II, Gorizia. B. 1815, d. 1869. Son and pupil of Antonio Pellizon I.

Pellizon Carlo, Gorizia. B. 1811, d. 1891. Son and pupil of Pellizon Antonio I.

Pellizon Filippo, Gorizia. B. 1817, d. 1897. Son and pupil of Antonio I.

Pellizon Giuseppe. Gorizia. Born 1798, died Dec. 15, 1874. Son of Antonio I. Devoted himself mainly to repairs.

Pelluzzi Euro, Milan. Born March 25, 1881, died Apr. 12, 1955. Son and pupil of Giuseppe Peluzzi. Author of several pamphlets on violin making.

Pelluzi Giuseppe, Turin, Cairo Mantenotte. Born 1856 in Cairo Mantenotte, died 1939. He worked after Cappa, Cattenari and G. Rocco.

Penscher Maria, Cremona. 1686. Instruments marked with this name are, as far as we know, products of the poorest class.

Penzenetti Antonio, Bologna. 1801. Violins of large pattern and good wood.

Pera Gerolamo, Pordenone (province Udine). 1846—1847. Good workmanship; particularly excellent are the 'cellos built on the model of Gasparo da Salò. The sizes of one 'cello of his making are as follows; length 720 mm, upper width 325 mm, middle width 240 mm, lower width 410 mm, height of sides 105 mm. Height, measured under the bridge (belly, back and sides) 168 mm. He applied a yellow varnish without lustre.

Hieronymus Pera Portusnaonensis
Fecit anno 1846.

Peregrinio Giovanni, Lucca. 1689. His existence has not been proved. Perhaps a fake.

Ioannes Peregrinius
Lucensis 1689

Peregrino. See Pellegrino.

Peregrino Gianetto. See Michelis Peregrino di Zanetto.

Perni Pietro, Rome. 19th century.

Pietro Perni
Fabbricante d'Istrumenti Armonici
fece in Roma anno 189.

Perollo Luigi, Palermo. 1894. Lute maker and organ builder.

Perugia Ferdinando del, San Cresci, Florence. Born Nov. 16, 1857 at Petriolo near Bruzzi (Florence). Made good guitars and mandolins. After 1899 he worked almost exclusively for dealers.

Pessetti Giovanni Battista, Mantua. 1674. Little known violin maker.

Petrobono Dal Chitarino, Ferrara. 1445—1446. Lute maker; several instruments by him survive as museum relics.

Petroni Antonio, Rome. See Pedroni.

Pettinato Pietro, Messina (Sicily). B. in Messina Nov. 8, 1883. Worked on the pattern of Stradivari.

Pietro Pettinato
Messinese — 17-11-1949

Pevere Ernesto. Ferrara. Born 1891. Pupil of Soffritti. He followed Stradivari and Guarneri. Golden-yellow or golden-brown varnish.

PEVERE ERNESTO
Liutista
Anno 192. FERRARA

Ernesto Pevere
allievo di
ETTORE SOFFRITTI
fecit in Ferrara l'anno 19..

PEVERE ERNESTO
LIUTISTA
Anno 192. FERRARA

Pezzardi, Brescia. 1660—1690. Worked in the style of Pietro S. Maggini, but his elegant sound-holes are designed after the fashion of Amati; he applied a bright yellow varnish. His violins are adorned with a carefully finished twofold purfling, interlaced on the back with exquisite taste.

Pfanzelt Johann, Rome. Died there Oct. 4, 1611. Was a relative, perhaps a brother of Martin and Peter II. Little known.

Pfanzelt (Pfanschel) Martin, called Il Martino, Rome. B. 1597. Perhaps a brother of Peter Pfanschel, lute maker.

Pfanschel, also Pfanzelt Peter I, Rome. Died 1582, lute maker, little known, most likely a native of Füssen.

Pfanzelt Peter II. B. March 3, 1598, d. after 1637. Was apprenticed as lute maker by his father Martin.

Philippi Philippo de, Rome. 1850—1885. Good workmanship in the style of the Cremonese school.

Pianazzi Domenico, Guiglia (Modena). 1760—1780. He worked very well, but instruments still marked with his name are rare. He took the Cremonese masters for his model.

Piarino Marco, Ferrara. 1591. Little known lute maker.

Piatellini Alivisio. Florence. Ca 1790. Son of Luigi Piatellini and pupil of G. B. Gabrielli. He made mainly double-basses though we have but scanty evidence of his work. Allegedly he used a brown varnish.

Piattellini Gasparo, Florence. 1738—1780. Instruments of flat arching, good workmanship, coated with light-brown varnish. Excellent 'cellos. Price from 12.000 Kč. upwards.

Gasparo Piattellini Fece
In Firenze Anno Domini 1738.

Gasparo Piattelini
fece l'Anno 1780
in Firenze. (written)

Casparo
Piattellini
fece l'Anno 1763.

Piattellini Luigi, Florence. B. 1789, d. 1821. Son and pupil of Gasparo Piattellini. Best are his 'cellos, which have a very good tone.

Piazzi Mario, Catania (Sicily). 1925.

Piccagliani Armando, Modena. 1879—1945. Exhibited a violin (Stradivari pattern), a viola and a 'cello at Cremona in 1937.

Piccagliani Armando
fece in Modena
l'Anno 1931

Piccagliani Antonio, Modena. B. July 29, 1914. Followed Guarneri del Gesù. Probably son and pupil of Armando P.

Antonio Piccagliani fu Armando
fece in Modena
l'Anno .... 19..

Picciati Ippolito, S. Giovanni in Persiceto. 1830—1856. Built violins and contrabasses.

Picciotto. Messina. 1930.

Picinetti Giovanni, Florence. 1677—1682. Made lutes and violas and was a skilful master; applied red-yellow varnish.

Gio Picinetti fio
ao 1682. (written)

Picino Carlo, Padua. 1708—1726. Little known.

Picino Giuseppe, Naples. A 19th century manufacturer of guitars and mandolins.

Pieroni Luigi, Gubbio. 1833—1847. He devoted himself more to repairs than to the production of new instruments.

Pierotti Luigi, Perugia. 1787—1833. Perhaps an amateur: indifferent workmanship modelled on Guarneri.

Luigi Pierotti
Fecit in Gubio 1791.

Aloysius Pierotti fecit anno 1787.

Luigi Pierotti fecit in Gubio 1833.

Pini Luigi, Florence. 1800.

Pietri Pietro, Venice 1690. Little known violin and lute maker.

Pilotti Giuseppe, Bologna. Born 1784, died 1838. Master whose works are seldom found. Golden-yellow varnish.

Piotti Lorenzo, Ivrea. 1935.

Pioli Roberto, Cavriago (Reggio Emilia). Born there on Aug. 11, 1892. He was popular for his guitars and double-basses.

PIOLI ROBERTO
CAVRIAGO REGGIO-E.

Piotti, Montebello, Montebello. 19th century violin maker.

Piretti Enrico, Bologna. B. Nov. 19, 1911. A productive maker who considered, however, violin making as a side line; he made mostly mandolins. Varnish orange or mahogany.

Enrico Piretti
LIUTAIO
FECE IN ....
ANNO ....

Pisani, San Angelo. 1756. Violins with high arching, built of fine wood and coated with a yellow-red varnish; scarce.

Pistucci Giovanni, Naples. B. Feb. 18, 1864 in Naples, d. 1954. Was a pupil of Vincenzo Postiglione; good work in the style of old Italian masters.

GIOVANNI PISTUCCI
Napoli 1901

Giovanni PISTUCCI
alunno di Vincenzo Postiglione
fece in NAPOLI anno 19..

RESTAURATO
da GIOVANNI PISTUCCI
Anno 19..

Piva Giovanni, Modena. 1860—1880. A dilettante, who made many violins, but all of inferior quality.

Pizzamiglio Carlo, Sesto ed Unite (Cremona). B. 1914. Said to have been, due to unfavourable circumstances, an indifferent maker. Yellow-red spirit varnish.

CARLO PIZZAMIGLIO
CORTETANO-CREMONA
FECE IN ITALIA — L'ANNO 1949

Pizzurno Antonio, Genoa. 1760. Violin maker of no particular skill.

Pizzurno Davide, Genoa. 1760, 1763. Probably father and teacher of Antonio. He built, very skilfully, instruments of smaller pattern on the outlines of Amati's model. Narrow edges; delicately finished purfling; small sound-holes in the fashion of Stainer. The large, broad, well-finished scrolls, shaped in the style of Gragnani, are rather deeply cut in a peculiar manner, with protruding ends. He applied a golden-brown varnish. Price 20—25.000 Kč.

David Pizzurnus fecit
Genue Ann. 1763

Plani Agostino de, Genoa. 1750—1778. Bad workmanship; unseemly varnish of a brownish hue; tone without power. Price 8—12.000 Kč.

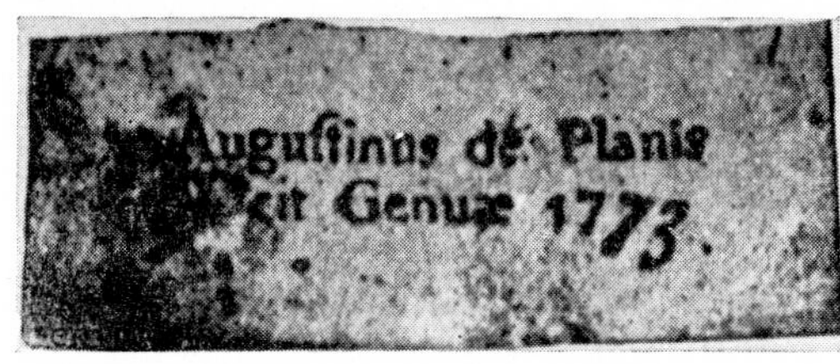

Planta Ulrico, Florence. 1838. Work lacking the assured touch of a master.

Platner Michael, Rome. 1735—1750. Built, on the patterns of Andrea Guarneri and David Tecchler, instruments of fine wood, with high arching, coated with a golden yellow varnish. The sound-holes and scrolls are delicately carved. Price 25—32.000 Kč, 'cellos far more.

Michael Platner fecit
Romae Anno 1741

Plesber Francesco. See Presbler Francesco.

Plesber Giuseppe. See Presbler Giuseppe.

Poggi Ansaldo, Bologna. B. 1893. Perhaps a pupil of Giuseppe Fiorini. Stradivari patterns, yellow-brown, yellow-red or golden-brown varnish. Exhibited at Cremona in 1937 besides an entire quartet, a violin, one viola and one 'cello.

Poggini Milton, Anghiari and Arezzo. B. March. 29, 1911. A sculptor, made violins of his own model with a peculiar scroll. They are cherished abroad. Varnish of various shades of yellow, orange, red and brown. Marked his instruments also with his initials branded inside. Exhibited a violin and a viola at Cremona in 1937.

A. 1946
Liut. Milton Poggini
Arrezzo Anghiari

Poli Giandomenico, Ascoli. 16th century. Very little is known about him.

Poli Giovanni, Milan. 1850—1882. Little known violin maker.

Polis Luca de, Cremona. 1740, 1751. Good craftsmanship on the model of Nicolo Amati and Andrea Guarneri. He applied lustrous and brightly coloured varnishes.

Politi Enrico, Rome, Via Vittorio. Born in Rome June 13, 1885. Son and pupil of Eugenio Politi, profilic master who won high honours at Cremona in 1949. For a time he worked together with Giuseppe Fiorini. Models Guarneri and Stradivari. Golden-yellow varnish.

Politi Eugenio, Cremona and Rome. Born May 8, 1853, he died June 9, 1909. He was a disciple of Enrico

Cerutti, so good that merchants have provided most of his instruments with faked Cerutti labels.

EUGENIO POLITI
ALUMNUS ENRICO CERUTI
Fecit Cremona anno 1886

Politi Fernando, Rome and Turin. B. 1882, d. 1928. Son of Eugenio Politi; used a red or orange varnish.

Politi Raoul. Born Sept. 9, 1913. Son and pupil of Enrico. Model Stradivari. Successful even in other countries.

RAUL POLITI
Figlio di Enrico
Fece Roma — anno 19..

Pollastri Antonio, Modena. 1765—1800. Probably a brother of Giuseppe Pollastri. Good workmanship. Red varnish.

Antonio Pollastri
fecit Mutinae 1765.

Pollastri Augusto. Born 1877, 1910. Highly skilled pupil of Raffaele Fiorini. Worked on the model of Stradivari and applied red varnish.

Pollastri Gaetano, Bologna. B. 1886, d. Oct. 5, 1960. Brother and pupil of Augusto Pollastri.

POLLASTRI GAETANO
fratello ed allievo di Augusto
op. 10 BOLOGNA 1926

Pollastri Giuseppe, Modena. 1764—1873. His violas and guitars have a rich tone.

Polli Francesco, Guastalla. 1616. Little known master.

Pollusca (Paluška) Antonio, Rome. 1750. To judge by his name as well as according to his work, which is characteristic of the Prague school (by the typically jutting-out corner-edges) he was a Czech. By his good workmanship he belongs to the best Roman violin makers of his time. He worked on the whole according to Tecchler (scrolls and broad upper part of violins) and may have been the latter's assistant. He applied a yellow-red varnish. Price 12.000 Kč. and more; rare.

Polverino Rinaldo, Ferrara. 1467. Lute maker.

Pontiggio Vittorio, Como. 1853. Little known.

Ponzetti Arturo, Rome. Born 1864 in Rovigo. Modelled his work on Stradivari.

Ponzi Giulio, Milan. 1850. He worked very well in the style of various old Italian masters.

Popella, Naples. 17th century. Little known master.

Portoghese Francesco, Rome. 1616. Lute maker.

Posta Christofano, Milan. 1666. Worked on the model of Gasparo da Salò, but with less success. Instruments of historic interest.

1666
1. setembre in Milano
da capo di contrada larga
ne la botega di Christofano Posta.

Postacchini Andrea, Fermo. B. Dec. 30, 1786 in Fermo, d. Feb. 3, 1862. Careful workmanship. He imitated with skill J. Guarneri del Gesù and used good wood for the belly and back, which he made rather thick in the middle part. The arching and the edges are somewhat flat, the purfling well finished, the scrolls carved in a delicate manner. He applied mostly a red, sometimes also red-yellow or red-brown varnish. Price 16.000 Kč but it is constantly rising, for his instruments have lately aroused great interest.

Andrea Postacchini Amici filius
fecit Firmi, anno 1810, opus..

Andreas Postacchini Firmanus fecit
sub titulo S. Raphaelis Archang. 1854

Postacchini Andrea II, Fermo. 1810—1857. Andrea's son who worked, however, on the model of Amati. His instruments are distinguished by flatter arching, careful workmanship, orange, yellow-red ('cellos) or brown varnish. Price ca 16.000 Kč.

Postacchini Rafaele, Fermo. B. Apr. 16, 1823, d. Apr. 1, 1892. Son of Andrea and his assistant. Though eclipsed by his father, whose labels he seems to have used for a long time, he should nevertheless pass for a good master.

Andreas Postacchini Firmanus fecit
sub titulo S. Raphaelis Archang. 1854

Postiglione Vincenzo I, Naples. 1790—1840. Perhaps father, or grandfather, of Vincenzo II. But few works are known.

Postiglione Vincenzo II, Naples. B. 1835. Died May 30, 1916. Son or grandson of Vincenzo P. (I). Pupil of Vincenzo Jorio. One of the better Neapolitan masters of the 19th century. His instruments are frequently on the market. Good workmanship on the patterns of Stradivari and Guarneri. Orange-red varnish.

Vincentius Postiglione me Fecit Neapoli Anno.
1875.

Vincentius Postiglione me fecit
Neap. 1875.

Pozzini Gaspare, Brescia. 1691, 1699. Worked well on the model of G. P. Maggini. Price 20.000 Kč.

Praga Eugenio, Genoa. Born Apr. 14, 1847, d. 1901. Pupil of Nicolo Bianchi. Built good instruments in the style of Guarneri and Stradivari. He applied a yellow varnish. Price 12.000 Kč. and more.

Eugenio Praga
fece Genua Anno ....

Pratasini Giovanni, Turin. 1780. Mandolin maker.

Presani Pietro, San Severino. 1755—1780. He made large double-basses.

Presbler Francesco, Milan. 1730—1773. Son of Giuseppe Presbler. He worked together with his son. He made chiefly mandolins.

Francesco Plesber
in Milano
nella contrada della Dogana
al segno del Sole 1773.

Francesco Plesber, e
Giuseppe figlio
in Milano
nella Contrada della Dogana
al Segno del Sole 177.

Presbler Giuseppe, Milan. 1760—1801. Son of Francesco Presbler, his pupil and successor. Built lutes and mandolins. A 14-stringed lute of his making is known.

Giuseppe Presbler
in Milano
nella contrada della dogana
all insegno del sole 1796.

GIUSEPPE PRESBLER
In Milano
nella Contrada della Dogana
all' insegna del Sole: 1796

Pressenda Gian Francesco, Alba, Carmagnola, Turin. Born Jan. 6, 1777, d. Sept. 11, 1854. Humble musician, then, finding he could make his living as violin maker (after trying other professions) he grew to become one of the greatest masters of the century. Son of Raffaele Pressenda and pupil of L. Storioni. Excellent workmanship on Stradivari's model of low arching. The sides of his instruments are somewhat higher. After 1820 he worked in Turin (previously, in 1814, at Alba, then at Carmagnola). He used good and beautiful resonant wood, especially fine maple-wood. The sound-holes and scrolls are cut in exemplary fashion. He applied his exquisite yellow, brown-yellow, brown or deep red varnish on a thin ground coat which was coloured and soaked into the soft pine-wood belly, so that it appears somewhat darker than the back of the instrument. The curl of his maple-wood plates offers a delightful sight. We have not seen enough of his genuine instruments to maintain positively that he was a greater master than his teacher L. Storioni, but one instrument submitted to us in 1949 fully corroborates this opinion.

A much admired and imitated master; even creations of very good violin makers (especially those of G. A. Rocca) were often marked with labels bearing his name. The tone of his instruments is rich, mellowly sensual, carries wonderfully and is sometimes even aggressive. Price above 80.000 Kč, constantly rising.

Dimensions of his instruments:

Year	1837	1841 ('cello)
length of back	355	740
upper width	166	351
centre width	108	243
lower width	207	448

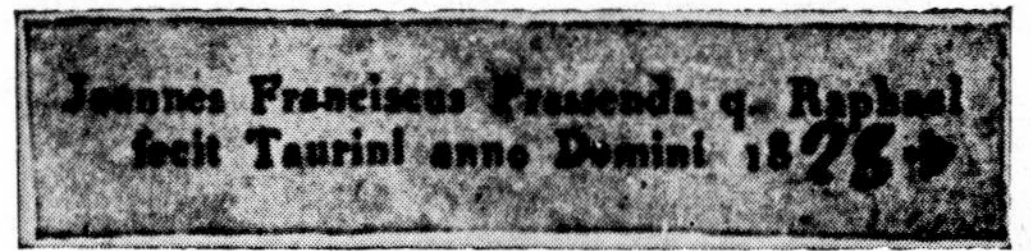

Pressenda Raffaele, Turin. Ca 1790. According to Lüttgendorff, violin maker. René Vannes doubts his existence, at least as maker.

Prochet Enrico. Turin. 1900. Amateur violin-maker.

Pucci Dante, Florence. B. 1876 in Perugia. Guitar and violin maker.

Puccini Eligio, Empoli. B. 1900. Stradivari pattern.

Puppati Francesco, Udine. Born at Udine on Nov. 31, 1838. A violin virtuoso who began to built violins in 1880, on the model of Stradivari. Very good tone.

Puzzini Ben., Rome. 1876. Mandolin maker.

Q

Quadrinelli Pietro, Senigallia (Ancona). 1765—1780. Devoted himself mainly to the production of double-basses.

Querei Vincenzo, Florence. 1630—1643.

R

Rabaglietti Antonio, Verona. 1652. He was violin and lute maker, but none of his instruments survive.

Rabatta Carlo Antonio. 1707. Little known violin maker; it is not even known where he worked.

Raccoris Nicolo, Mantua. 1760. Instruments of average quality, coated with red-brown varnish.

Radrizzani Alessandro, Tour de Peitz (Vevey). Born 1864 in Milan.

Radrizzani Angello, Vevey. Born 1870 in Milan. Pupil of L. Bisiach who established himself in 1898.

Raffo Cipriano, Chivari (Genoa). 1876—1904.

Ragona Pietro. Palermo. 1840. Guitar- and mandolin-maker.

Railich Giovanni, Padua. 1672, 1678. Instruments of the flat Florentine type, coated with yellow or yellow-brown varnish. He was the teacher of Matthias Klotz, whose journeyman's certificate bears the signature *Zuane Railihe.*

Giovanni Railich
Lautaro in Padova

Railich Matteo, Brescia. Born about 1614, died after 1655. Son of Andrea and brother of Pietro Railich. He built lutes.

Railich Pietro, Venice, Padua. 1644—1670. Son of Andrea and brother of Matteo. He worked in Venice till 1655, in Padua from 1655 till 1670. The arching of his instruments is somewhat high, the good brown-red varnish has darkened and appears today black-brown.

Pietro Railich
alla Givia Venetia 1644.
Pietro Railich
Al Santo in Padova 1655.

Raineri Eraclio, Genoa. Born 1912. Pupil of Cesari Candi. He modelled his work on Stradivari.

Ramolo Giovanni, Rome. 1626. Lute maker, who came to Rome from Genoa.

Ramusio Giovanni, Turin. 1779. Lute maker, violin and mandolin maker of minor importance.

Ranaldi Antonio, Naples. 1848. Mandolin maker.

Ranta Pietro, Brescia. 1733. Worked on the model of N. Amati, but his work is not good. He applied a yellow-brown varnish, or, to be more exact, brown varnish on yellow ground. Price 10.000 Kč.

Raphael, Brescia. 19th century. Little known violin maker.

Raphanelli, Brescia. 1652—1700. Worked on the model of G. P. Maggini and coated his instruments with a brown varnish. The instruments are rather thin in wood. The tone is of medium quality and, accordingly, the price is not high.

Rastelli Giovanni, Genoa. 1822—1840. Not an outstanding master. He used red varnish.

Rastelli Lodovico. Genoa. 1800, 1822. Mediocre violin-maker.

Rasura Vincenzo, Lugo. 1785. Very few of his works are on record.

Raula Pietro, Brescia. 1730. He worked after Maggini using golden-brown varnish.

Rauser Sebastian, Verona. 1590—1605. Good lute maker, perhaps of German origin (Rauscher).

sebastian rauser in verona 1605.

Ravanelli, Brescia. See Raphanelli.

Ravena Gio Battista, Lavagna. 1840.

Ravena Luciano, Milan. 1919.

Ravizza Carlo, Milan. Born 1882. Died Apr. 16, 1959. Pupil of Antoniazzi. Instrument-maker and repairer.

Raynaldi Antonio, called "Simonetta", Langres, Rome. 1517. Ancient lute maker.

Razzoli Felice, Villa Minozza (Modena). 1880. He was a good master and violins by him have attained good prices. Applied brown-red varnish.

Realli Cosma Battista, Parma. 1667. Built instruments of medium quality; applied a brown varnish.

Cosmo Battista Realli
in Parma 1667.

Rechardini Giovanni, called "Zuane", Venice. 1605, 1609. Lute and violin maker. The spelling on the labels varies and the instruments are not always beyond doubt.

Zuane Rechardini di Venezia
all'insegno del Basso 1605.

Rechardini Pietro, Venice. 1617. Worked on the pattern of Amati; used good wood; applied a golden-red varnish; took a rather high arching; made good scrolls and sound-holes. The instruments have a good tone.

Rechardini Pietro. 1860. Little known violin maker.

Reggiani Francesco, S. Martino d'Este (Modena). 1836. Little-known violin-maker who modelled his instruments of Stradivari.

Regonini Domenico, Ostiano (Cremona). Born Jan. 29, 1929. Pupil of the Cremonese violin-makers' school.

Reina Giacomo. 1708. Little known.

Remondini Andrea, Bologna. 1720—1723. Good work and good tone. Brown varnish. Price according to beauty and merit of instrument.

Renisto, Cremona (no Christian name). The first word used to be explained as standing for "revisto" (revised); the true label having got lost, it passed for a name. The work being on the pattern of Carlo Bergonzi, "Renisto" was then said to have been Bergonzi's pupil. The first "Renisto" may have been an error, but the further ones were certainly fakes.

Reynaldis Francesco (de), Florence. Ca 1508. Ancient lute maker. One guitarrone is known.

Franciscus de Reynaldis 1508.

Reynaud Andrea. Tarascon. 1750—1766. He made very good 'cellos. Priest and amateur violin-maker.

Ricci Luigi, Naples. 1898. Mandolin maker.

Riccucci Alessandro, San Ginesio. 20th cent.

Riceverti (Ricevuti) Aurelio, Florence. 1650. Good violin maker, according to Valdrighi.

Richardini Pietro. See Rechardini.

Richter, Modena. 1808. Violin and guitar maker.

Ricolazi Davide, Cremona. 1740. Almost unknown.

Ricolazi Lodovico, Cremona. 1729—1760. Little known.

Ricolazi Nicolo, Civitavecchia. 1759—1780. Worked on the pattern of G. C. Gigli. Built high-arched violins with broad purfling. The back is of one piece, the sound-holes beautifully cut. He applied a yellow varnish. Instruments of fairly good tone.

Nicolo Ricolazi Civitavecchia
1759

Ricordi Giovanni, Milan. D. March 15, 1853.

Giovanni Ricordi Milano.

Righi Antonio, Modena. 1817. Self-taught maker who built fairly good contrabasses.

Antonius Righi tinctor
filius Ambrosii, fecit Mutinae, anno 1817.

Rinaldi Celeste, Modena. 1878. Violin maker, mediocre workmanship.

Rinaldi Enrico, Naples. 1895—1905. He worked after Guarneri and the Neapolitan school. Red-brown varnish.

Rinaldi Gofredo Benedeto, Turin. 1850, died 1888. Pupil of Pressenda. Worked well on the model of his teacher, though he finished the edges of his instruments less delicately than his master. His violins are good orchestral instruments; better are his 'cellos. He was a good hand at repairing. Price 12.000 Kč.

Rinaldi Lodovico, Rimini. 1804. Probably son and pupil of Goffredo.

Rinaldi Marengo Romano, Turin. Born 1866. He worked after Pressenda using golden-yellow or mahagony-red varnish.

Ristorini Gianfrancesco, Florence. 1678. Lute maker.

Rittig Cristoforus, Genoa. 1680—1692. Good master, who built 'cellos of excellent quality. Instruments by him are characterized by large sound-holes.

Christopharus Rittig fe
cit Genuae anno 1680.

Riva Giovanni, Piacenza. 1884. Little known violin maker.

Riva Severino, Monzino, Milan. 1917.

Rivolta Giacomo, Milan. 1800—1834. Very good workmanship on the patterns of Stradivari and Nic. Gagliano. He devoted more care to the building of 'cellos. Likewise his contrabasses are of good quality.

Jacobus Rivolta
fece Milano 1828

Premiato di meda-
glia d' argento indi di
quella d'oro per aver fatto
risorgere la scuola del
celebre Stradivari.

Giacomo Rivolta
fecit Mediolani 1821.

Opera di Giacomo Rivolta di
Milano. 1830 Premiato di medaglia d'argento, indi di quella
d'oro per aver fatto risorgere
la scuola del celebre Stradivarj

Rizzotti Nicola, Novellara (Modena). 1880. Good 'cellos and violins.

Rocca ......, Genoa. 1762. Worked on the pattern of Jos. Guarneri del Gesù; built instruments of low arching, with beautifully carved scrolls shaped in a peculiar fashion. He used written labels. His Christian name is unknown. Scarce.

Rocca Enrico, Genoa. B. Apr. 25, 1847 in Turin, d. June 7, 1915. Son and successor of Joseph. Worked on the pattern of Guarneri and applied a golden-yellow varnish. Skilful violin and mandolin maker. Instruments particularly valued in England.

Rocca Giovanni Domenico, Turin. 1800—1809. Worked on the pattern of J. Guarneri del Gesù.

Joh. Domin. Rocca
Taurini 1809. (written)

Rocca Giuseppe, Genoa. 1854. Father of Enrico. Careful work, Guarneri pattern.

Rocca Giuseppe Antonio, Genoa, Turin. B. 1807, d. 1865. Until his twentieth year he worked with his father as baker. Then he became apprenticed to Pressenda. He worked after Stradivari, Guarneri and Maggini, following in this respect his teacher. Beautiful wood, heads solid and well-carved after Pressenda. Faultless purfling and elegant sound-holes. Back is usually made from one piece of attractively flamed maple-wood. Excellent varnish of yellow, red, brown or red-brown tint. Powerful and resonant tone. Instruments with the date 1831 are mostly fakes.

Price 50.000—80.000 Kč. The sizes of a violin built by G. R. in 1850 are as follows; length of back 357 mm, upper width 167.5 mm, centre 110.5 mm, lower width 208.5 mm.

Joseph Rocca Taurini 1830.

Joseph Rocca fecit O R.
Premiato di Medaglie alle Esposizione
di Torino, Genova, Londra e Parigi I H S
Taurini anno Domini 18 .

JOSEPH ROCCA fecit
Premiato di Medaglie alle Esposizioni
di Torino, Genova, Londra e Parigi.
Taurini, anno Domini 185 IHS

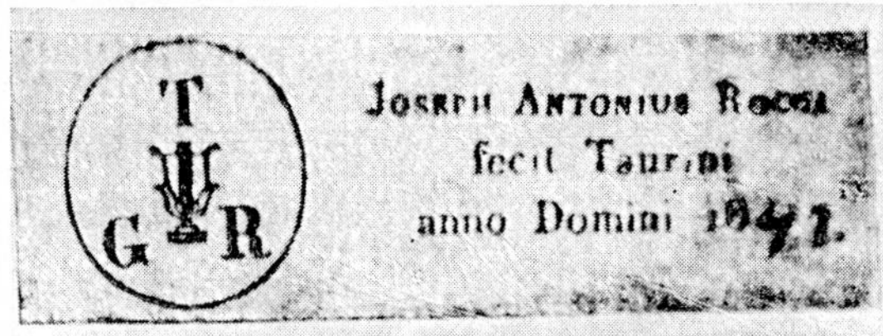
T G R
Joseph Antonius Rocca
fecit Taurini
anno Domini 184

Joseph Rocca fecit
Taurini anno Domini 1843

Roche Sebastian, Venice. 1620. Lute maker.

Rocchi Sesto, S. Paolo d'Enza (Reggio Emilia). B. Oct. 4, 1909. Pupil of Gaetano Sgarabotto, followed Stradivari and Guarneri and applied a yellow or red varnish. Exhibited a violin and a quartet at Cremona 1937.

Sextus Rocchi +
Regiensis fecit 1948 S R

Rocchi Sextus Regiensis — All
L. Bisiach Faciebat Anno 1935

Sextus Rocchi ✠
Regiensis fecit 1948 S R

Rocchi Sextus Regiensis-All.
L. Bisiach Faciebat Anno 1935

Roccus P. Domenico, Florence. Ca 1696. Worked in the style of Nic. Amati; transparent yellow varnish.

P. Roccus Dom.us de Bonis fecit
Florentia anno Salutis 1696

Rochi Christofilo, Padua, Venice. Lived in the early 17th century. Good craftsmanship. Best are his works of the year 1620. Rare.

Rodiani Giovita, Brescia, Bologna. Born about 1545, died after 1624. Worked on the pattern of Gasparo da Salò, whose helpmate he had been for a long time. His creations of later years are in the style of Maggini. He applied an amber-yellow varnish. Historically valuable instruments if not too much damaged by age. Price about 20.000 Kč.

Giouita Rodiani in Brescia.

Rogeri Giovanni Battista, Brescia. Born in Bologna about 1650, died in Brescia in 1730. He soon came to Cremona, where he was, along with Stradivari, initiated in the craft by N. Amati. In 1680, he left Cremona for Brescia where he worked until his death. He built instruments on the large model of Amati which he imitated with excellent skill. There are, however, also instruments of small pattern with middle arching. He selected wood of excellent quality. Beautifully finished scrolls, long sound-holes, purfling finely executed, sometimes, however, only engraved on the back of the instrument. His 'cellos and contrabasses are admired instruments. He applied a fine golden-red, bright red or golden-brown varnish. The tone of his instruments is sweet and mellow. The labels he used are red and bear an inscription printed in black letters. The backs of the 'cellos are occasionally of maple-wood. The price of the violins is according to Fuchs-Möckel 50—80.000 Kč, 'cellos more: according to Hamma up to 200.000 Kč. The dimensions of a violin of 1704 are as follows: length of back 354 mm, upper width 162 mm, centre width 107.5 mm, lower width 201.5 mm; sizes of a 'cello of the year 1700: length of back 733 mm, upper width 364 mm; lower width 443 mm, upper sides 112 mm, and lower sides 118 mm. Violin of 1699: length 355, upper width 169, centre width 109, and lower width 207 mm. Violin of 1700: length of back 351, upper width 159, centre width 106 and lower width 197 mm.

Jo: Baptista Rugerius Nicolai Amati
Cremonae alumnus Brixiae fecit anno 1709.

Io: Bapt. Rogerius Bon: Nicolai Amati de Cremona alumnus Brixiæ fecit Anno Domini 1705

Rogeri Pietro Giacomo, Brescia. Born about 1680, died after 1730. Son of Giambattista Rogeri, keeping on the whole his model (of a more slender shape), but lacking the careful craftsmanship of his father. He used good wood, made the purfling nearer the edge, cut the scrolls and sound-holes with taste and skill. Applied a beautiful golden-yellow varnish. His speciality were instruments of small pattern. The excellent tone of his creations, particularly of the 'cellos and violas, is reflected in the price of a large 'cello, once owned by Paganini, which was sold at the price of 400.000 Kč. Contrabasses by him are also outstanding. Price of violins 65—80.000 Kč, even more.

Violin of 1713: length of back 354 mm, upper width 168 mm, centre width 108, lower width 207 mm.

Petrus Jacobus Rogeri
fecit Brixiae 1709.
Petrus Jacobus Rogerius de Nicolai
Amati Cremonensis Fecit Brixiae 1700.

Rogieri Domenico, San Valentino, Cremona, until 1750. Very careful workmanship on the pattern of Amati. He selected very good wood, enhanced the beauty of his instruments with double purfling, and applied a golden yellow varnish of excellent quality. Instruments by him are said to be of exquisite tone, but there is little evidence for the identity of the maker and the spelling of the name is doubtful (Rogeri — Ruggieri?).

Rolla Ferdinando, Fiesole. ?

Rollini Giambattista, Pesaro. 1471. Lute maker.

Romagnoli Francesco, Bologna. 1821. Guitar and mandolin maker.

Romani Giulio Cesare, Rome. 18th century.

Romanini Antonio, Cremona. 1705, 1740. Good violas d'amore and violins.

Antonio Romanini fecit
Cremonensis anno 1740

Romano Clemente, Como. Died 1949. Stradivari pattern.

Romano Pietro, Pavia 18th century.

Pietro Romano in Borgo di Pavia

Romarius Antonio, Cremona 1703. Known only from a viola d'amore preserved in the Museum of Stockholm.

Romarius Antonio, Cremona 1703

Antonius Romarius 1703

Rondani Ernesto, Turin. 1884. Violin maker of no particular merit.

Ronchetti Domenico, S. Valentino (Reggio). 1689, 1769. Said to have been successor of Dom. Rogieri. Inferior workmanship. Dark-red varnish.

Ronchini Raffaelle, Fano. 1851. Worked on the patterns of Stradivari and C. G. Testore. Good wood, yellow-brown varnish. Very good repairs.

Rafaele Ronchini, Fece
in Fano, Nummero, 4
del 1851

Rosa Agostino, Rome. 1795. Son of Nicola Rosa of Naples. Produced mandolins.

Rosa Nicola, Naples. 1680—1720. Lute maker.

Rosadoni Giovanni, Pavia. B. June 14, 1905. Self-dependent since 1949. Stradivari pattern, golden-yellow varnish.

Costruito dal Liutaio Rosadoni Giovanni
in Pavia anno 194.

Rosario P. and son, Catania. 1898. Mandolin makers.

Roselli Antonio, Sassuolo (Modena). Born Jan. 17, 1798, d. Feb. 22, 1870. Violin maker. Instruments and repairs by him are below standard quality. He was a Jack-of-all-trades, made wind instruments, painted pictures, was a good musician, a barber, and finished as beggar.

Rossi Domenico, Piacenza. D. 1910. Imitations and repairs.

Domenico Rossi
fece in Piacenza
Anno

Rosiero Rocco, Cremona. 1730. Good workmanship. Instruments modelled on Stradivari, otherwise little-known.

Rosio Paolo, Verolanuova. 1857. Contrabass maker.

Rossani Salvatore, Milan. 1920.

Rossi fu Domenico, Piacenza, Via Castello 66. Exhibited one violin at Cremona in 1937.

Rossi Emilio, Piacenza. B. Feb. 14, 1895. Son and pupil of Domenico R. Emilio exhibited a violin at Cremona in 1937.

ROSSI EMILIO — LIUTAIO
PREMIATO CON MEDAGLIA D'ORO
TECNICO PER RIPARAZIONI
A STRUMENTI A CORDA
PIACENZA — Via Castello — Piacenza

Rossi Enrico, Pavia. Born in March 1848 at Pavia. Son and pupil of Giovanni Rossi. Good craftsmanship modelled on Guarneri, Stradivari, Guadagnini and Testore. He worked with his son Guglielmo and applied good golden-yellow varnish.

Enrico Rossi
Fabbricante d'instrumenti a
corde
Pavia Piazza del Carmine
1888.

Rossi Ferdinando, Modena. 1880. Highly skilled in repairing instruments by old masters, but his original creations lack quality. Golden-yellow varnish.

Rossi Gaetano, Milan. 1870—1880. Perhaps son and pupil of Nicola Rossi. Good craftsmanship, particularly his violoncellos, double-basses, mandolins and guitars are very good. He applied thin coating of red varnish. Expert repairs.

Rossi G., Milano

Rossi Giovanni, Pavia. 1847—1858. A pupil of P. Pallota Perugia. Among his instruments the contrabasses are the best.

Rossi Giuseppe (Cte), Rome. Born in Florence in 1869. His parents, descendants of a titled family, were from Venice. Rossi worked on the patterns of all the great masters, but his favourite model was Stradivari. He applied a rosy-yellow oil or spirit varnish of beautiful lustre. He was many times awarded prizes and other distinctions at various exhibitions for his careful workmanship. He used different labels.

Rossi Guglielmo, Pavia. 1875—1949. Was son and pupil of Enrico Rossi.

Rossi Nicola, Milan. 1842, 1844. Good workmanship on the patterns of old masters, excellent contrabasses. Red varnish (dragon's blood).

Nicola Rossi
Fabbricatore e ristauratore
d'instrumenti a corde armoniche
Abita in Milano
Contrada S. Mattia alla Moneta
al civico 3137
Fece nell Febrairo del
1844

Rossi Guglielmo, Pavia. Born about 1875. Son, pupil and collaborator of Enrico Rossi. Skilful violin maker.

Rosilli Salvatore, Rome. Ca 1797. A violin maker, unknown until recent time. Only one violin by him is known, a specimen of wonderful perfection, coated with yellow-brown varnish. The instrument has a peculiar shape of its own, most pleasing to the eye; the sound-holes are gracefully cut. It is unknown whether he was a violin maker or a self-taught fancier of the craft, but his workmanship shows the assured touch of a master.

Rossini Giovanni, Battista Maria, Ravenna. 1765—1777. Skilful violin maker who made violins with low arching.

Iohannes Maria Rossini fecit
Ravena A. D. 1775.

Rossio Giovanni, Rome. 1901. His repute is not yet established.

Rota Giovanni, Cremona. Instruments built between 1770—1810. Very careful workmanship. He applied a fat yellow-brown or red varnish. Price 15.000 Kč. and more.

Joannes Rota fecit
Cremona anno 17..

Joannes Rota
Cremonese Anno 1808.

Rotta Giuseppe Antonio. See Rocca G. A. Fictitious label; a violin maker of this name has never lived.

Rotella Bernardino, Spoleto, 1815—1827. A master, whose instruments did not owe their success to any particular quality.

Rovati Christoforo, Bazzano. 1789—1795.

Rovescalli Azzo, Milan. B. 1880, d. 1941. Followed Stradivari.

Rovescalli Tullio, Varese. B. 1906 in Milan. Son and pupil of Azzo Rovescalli.

Rovetta Antonio, Bergamo, Milan. 1840—1884. Worked very carefully in the style of old Cremonese masters. Copies by him are very good both in finish and in tone. Brown varnish.

Rovetta Felice, Brescia. 1880—1900.

Rubini or Rubis Aug. or Ang., Viterbo. 1763—1771. Skilful self-taught violin maker. Surviving labels are damaged and illegible.

Aug. de Rub ad animi delectationem
Fecit Viterbi 1763.

Rubini, Bologna. 1880. Devoted himself to the production of guitars.

Rubino Gennaro, Naples. 1899. Mandolin maker.

Ruggeri Antonio, Cremona. 1723. Son of Giacinto Ruggeri. Little known member of the family. Paul de Witt (Geigenzettel alter Meister) reproduced a label of his from an isolated specimen.

Antonio Ruggieri figlio
del fu Giacinto fece
in Cremona 1723

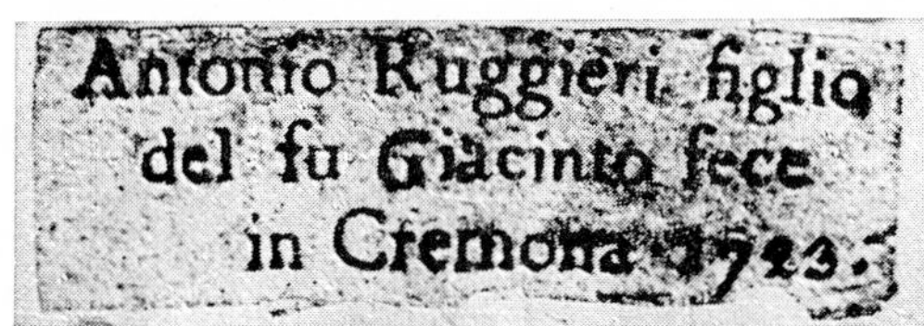
Antonio Ruggieri figlio
del fu Giacinto fece
in Cremona 1723.

Ruggeri Francesco, Cremona. 1645—1700. The oldest and best violin maker of the family (not to be mistaken for the Rogeri family). He was a pupil of Nic. Amati. He selected fine wood, but made the backs of the 'cellos (on which he specialized) often of maplewood. The pattern is long, rather broad, of beautiful shape, pleasing to the eye; the arching is somewhat higher, the scrolls bigger than those designed by his teacher. Faultlessly modelled instruments; sound-holes rather short, tastefully cut; broad, yet handsome purfling; typical long middle bouts. He applied a lustrous brilliant and transparent varnish deep red, dark-yellow-red, bright-yellow-red or orange. The 'cellos, which are more powerful in tone than his violins (the latter are more mellow than strong), belong to the best in general and are in great favour. He built more 'cellos than violins and violas. Price 150—200.000 Kč. and more. Francesco Ruggieri was the father of Giacinto (1666—1698) and Vincenzo (1690—1735). Antonio, who worked in Cremona ca 1723, was a son of Giacinto Ruggieri.

Violin of 1672: length 357 mm, upper width 165 mm, lower width 203 mm.

Dimensions of 'cellos built in 1667:

	Large pattern:	Small pattern:
Length of back	767 mm	729 mm
Upper width	377 mm	360 mm
Lower width	465 mm	446 mm
Height of upper sides	114 mm	110 mm
Height of lower sides	117 mm	112 mm

Francesco Rugier detto il Per
Cremona 16.

Francesco Ruggieri detto il Per
fece in Cremona l'anno 1676

Francesco Ruggieri detto
il per Cremona 1673

Francelco Ruger detto il Per
Cremona 1697

Francesco Ruggeri detto il Per
in Cremona 1696

Ruggeri Giacinto (Giovanni Battista), Cremona. 1666—1698. Son of Francesco and probably his pupil, for he worked in the same manner as his father, lacking, however, to some extent the latter's skill. According to Lüttgendorff, Giacinto was not identical with Gio Battista, but they were two different violin makers. (We incline to the same opinion, but without definite evidence. Giacinto may have been a nickname. Our efforts to throw more light on the lineage of the Ruggeri and Roggeri families have been hampered by Nazism, war and the unsettled conditions afterwards. We hope, however, to succeed later.) Giacinto Ruggeri built his instruments on a large, broad model with a still higher arching than that designed by his father. The shapely scrolls are rather large, the delicately cut sound-holes longer and more upright than those of his father. The dark-brown varnish he applied is of good quality. He devoted most of his time to the building of 'cellos which are very good, although they are not finished with such care as those of his father. The tone of his instruments is outstanding. Price 120—160.000 Kč.

Gio Battista Rugier detto il per
fecit Cremonae Anno 1666/7.

Giacinto figlio di Francesco
Ruggerie detto il Per 1696.

Giacinto filio di Francesco
Rugier detto il per 1692.

Giacinto figlio di
Francesco Rugger detto il Per
16..

Ruggeri Guido, Milan, Cremona. 1680, 1720. His existence has not been proved and there are reasons to think that he never lived and is mistaken for someone else.

Ruggeri Vincenzo, detto il Per, Cremona. 1690—1735. Second son of Francesco Ruggeri. Instruments by him are not characterized by particularly careful workmanship, but inasmuch as their tone is concerned, they are good. The wood is, with but few insignificant exceptions, fine; the scrolls and the small sound-holes are gracefully cut; the carefully finished purfling is near the edge. His 'cellos are excellent. He applied a beautiful yellow-brown, brown or red varnish. Price 65—80.000 Kč.

Vincenzo Rugier detto il per
in Cremona 17..

Vincenzo Ruger il Per
In Cremona 1711.

Vicenzo Ruger detto il Per.
InCremona 1735

Ruscheri Georgius, 1680. Works marked with this name are fakes made about the end of the 18th or beginning of the 19th century. They are of German origin, for Ruggeri's name is written with "sch".

S

Sacconi Benigno, Milan. 1910. Skilful violin-maker of the 20th century. Golden-yellow varnish.

Sacconi Fernando, Rome. Born 1895. Pupil of Gius. Rossi. Worked very carefully on the pattern of Stradivari. Applied orange-yellow or brown varnish of beautiful lustre. Instruments by him are much in favour with active artists; they were played by the violinist Arrigo Serato and the 'cellist Arturo Bonucci.

Fernando Sacconi
fece. Roma, Anno 1925

Sacchetti Francesco, San Martino (Reggio Emilia). 1935.

Sacchetti Gianetto e Figli, S. Martino in Rio, Reggio Emilia, Via Facci 6. They exhibited one violin at Cremona in 1937.

Sacchini Sabattino, Pesaro. 1670—1686. Imitator and perhaps also a pupil of Antonio Mariani. Good workmanship. He specialized in making beautiful pochettes, i.e., narrow pocket-violins with thin tone for dancing-masters. Price of a violin 16.000 Kč.

Sabattino Sacchini
da Pesaro, 16..

Sebastiano Sacchini
de Pesaro, l'anno 16..

Sagliocco Ed. & Co., Naples. Musical instrument factory.

Saisione Giovanni, Rome. 1725. Excellent lutes and mandolins, but suspicious labels. Lüttgendorff admits the possibility of his being identical with the Venetian lute maker "Maestro Sansone" or of a fake, the real man being the Sicilian musician Bat. Sansone, who lived in Rome in the 16th century, or, finally, a misreading of the Roman violin maker's name Giov. Smorzone (see below).

Salavio, Bologna. 1760—1770. Used golden-yellow varnish.

Salerni Roberto. Salle. Died Aug. 2, 1960.

Salino Giov. Battista, Rome. Ca 1750—1760. Well built, high-arched instruments coated with dark-brown varnish. Price 10.000 Kč. and more.

J. B. Salino
fecit Roma anno 1760.

J. B. Salino fecit
Roma anno 17..

Saltinari Giacomo, Morano sul Parano (Modena). 1880. Devoted himself almost exclusively to repairs.

Salvadori Giuseppe, Pistoia. 1861, 1863. Maker of all stringed instruments, but mainly of guitars. Varnishes yellow, yellow-brown, red or red-brown.

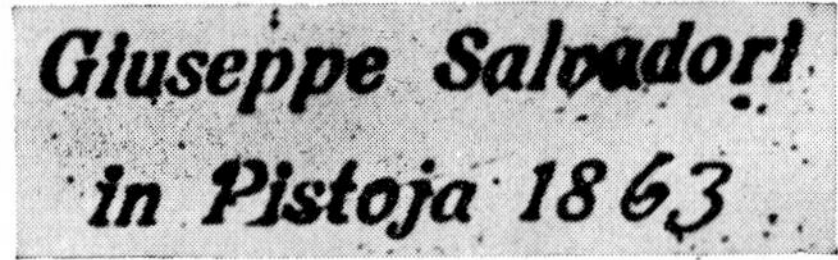
Giuseppe Salvadori
in Pistoja 1863

Salvaterra Francesco, Milan. 1609. Lute and mandolin maker.

Franciscus Salvaterra civis Mediolani
pro Solatio fecit Anno 1609.

Salviati Armando, Pavia. Pupil of Pietro Menenghesso.

Salviati Francesco, Verona, 19th century violin maker; brown varnish.

Sanazzo Santino. Milan. 1690—1740.

Sancino Joannes Carolus. Trieste. Born 1893 in Trieste. Studied Conservatoire in Steyer. He was also member of the Prague Zika Quartet. He worked after Stradivari and Guarneri using golden-yellow or red varnish.

Sangelia Lorenzo, Florence. 1777—1780. Instruments of fine finish, rare.

Sannino Vincenzo. Rome. Established himself in 1914 and worked after Stradivari and Guarneri. Some of his instruments are modelled on Gagliano. Golden-yellow or red varnish.

Sanoni Giovanni Battista, Verona. 1680—1740. His violins are predominantly high-arched, of a very characteristic shape, with rather upright sound-holes, large scrolls

303. Rogeri Giovanni Bapt., Brescia 1701
Photo Hamma & Co

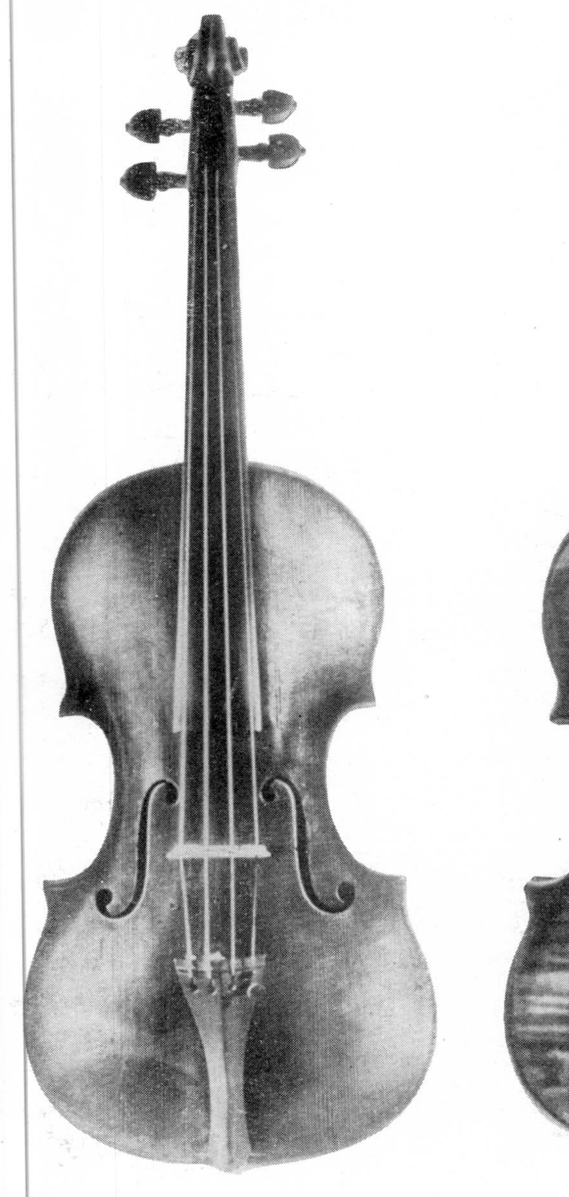

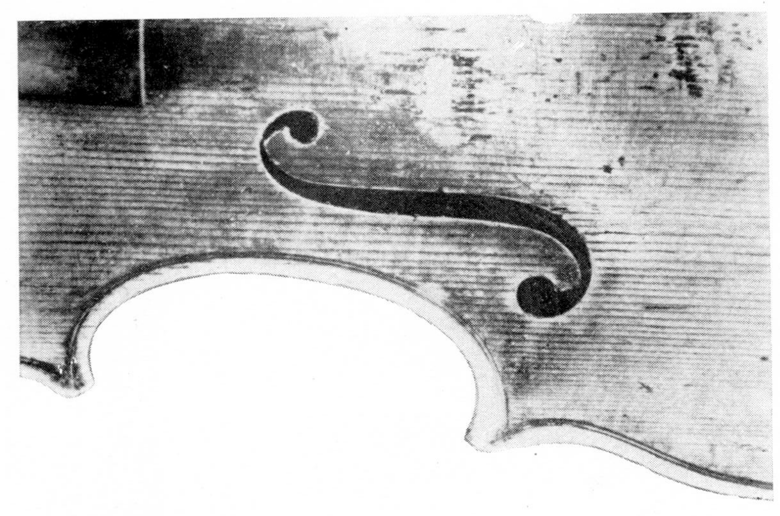

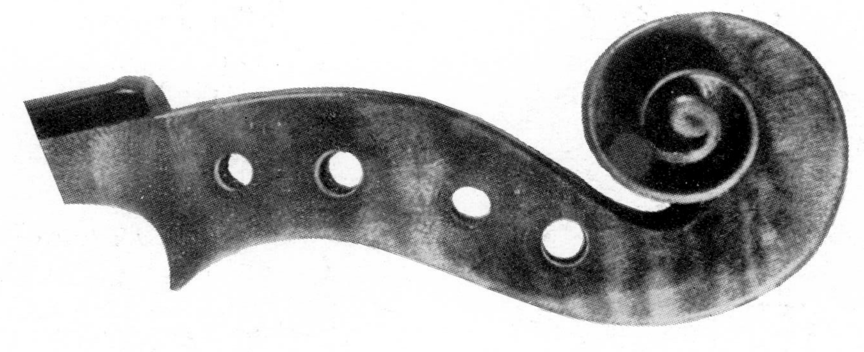

304. Rogeri Giovanni Bapt., Brescia 1712
Photo Hamma & Co

305. Rogeri Pietro Jacopo, Brescia 1713
Photo Hamma & Co

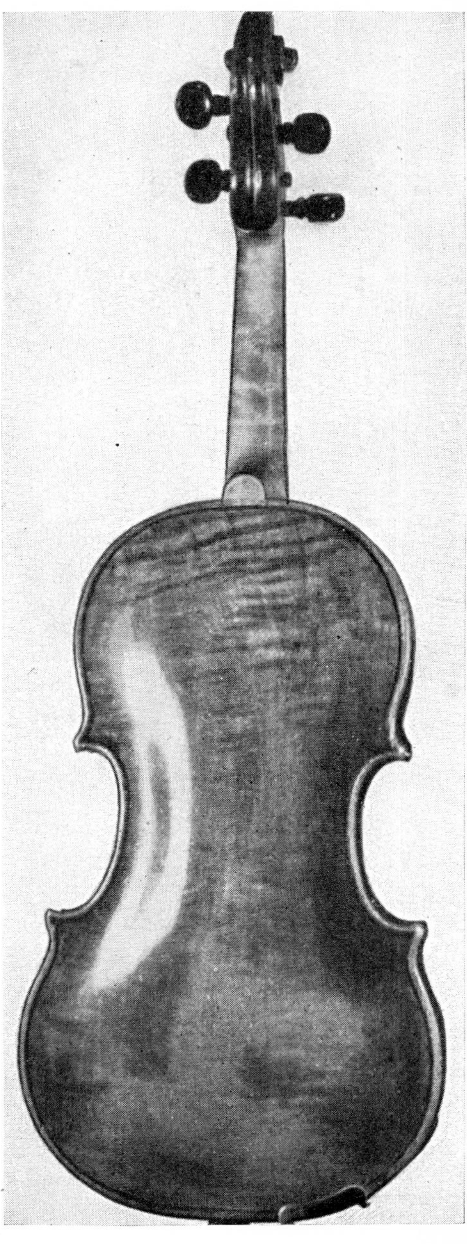

306. Ruggeri Antonio, Cremona 1723
Photo Hamma & Co

307. Ruggeri Francesco detto il Per, Cremona 1678
Photo Hamma & Co

308. Ruggeri Francesco detto il Per, Cremona 1698

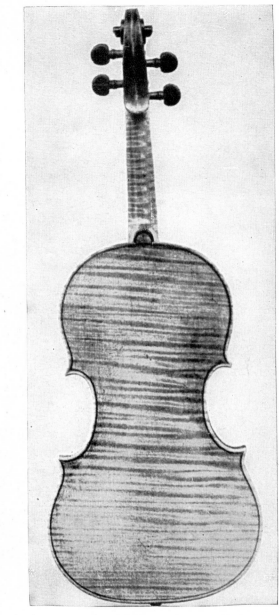

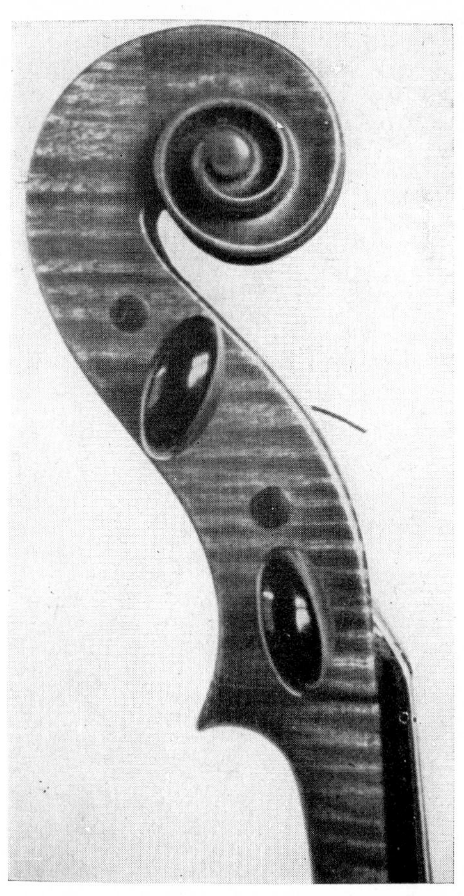

309. Ruggeri Francesco detto il Per, Cremona 1698

310. Ruggeri Francesco detto il Per, Cremona 1686
Photo Hamma & Co

311. Ruggeri Francesco detto il Per, Cremona 1690
Photo Hamma & Co

312. Seraphin Santo, Venezia

313. Seraphin Santo, Venezia 1725
Photo Hamma & Co

314. Seraphin Santo, Venezia 1732 (CELLO)
Photo Hamma & Co

315. Seraphin Santo, Venezia 1734
Photo Hamma & Co

316. Soliani Angelo, Modena 1790
Photo Hamma & Co

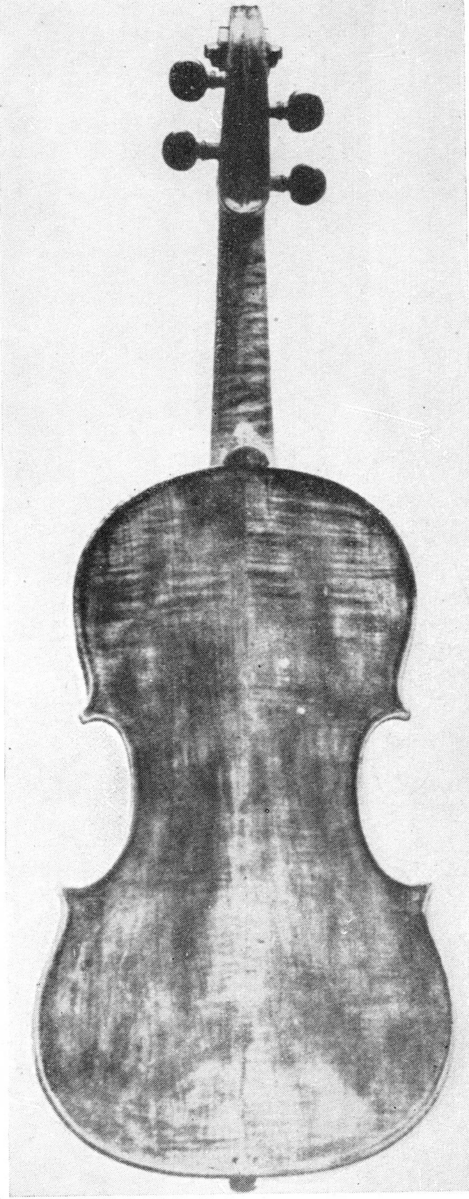

317. Soliani Angelo, Modena 1791

318. Sorsana Spirito, Como 1736

319. Storioni Lorenzo, Cremona

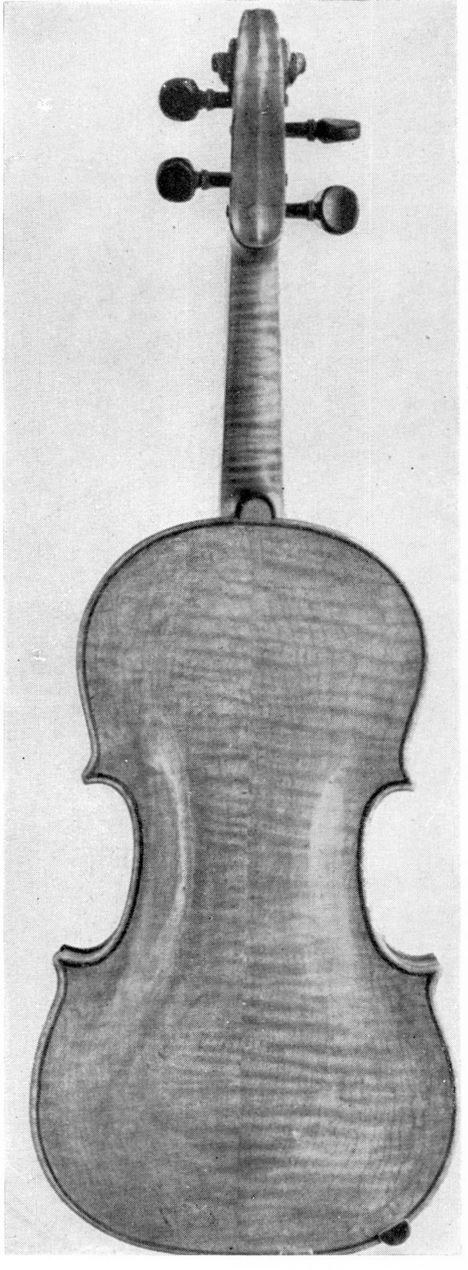

320. Storioni Lorenzo, Cremona

321. Storioni Lorenzo, Cremona 1776
Photo Hamma & Co

322. Storioni Lorenzo, Cremona 1780
Photo Hamma & Co

323. Stradivari Antonio, Cremona 1683

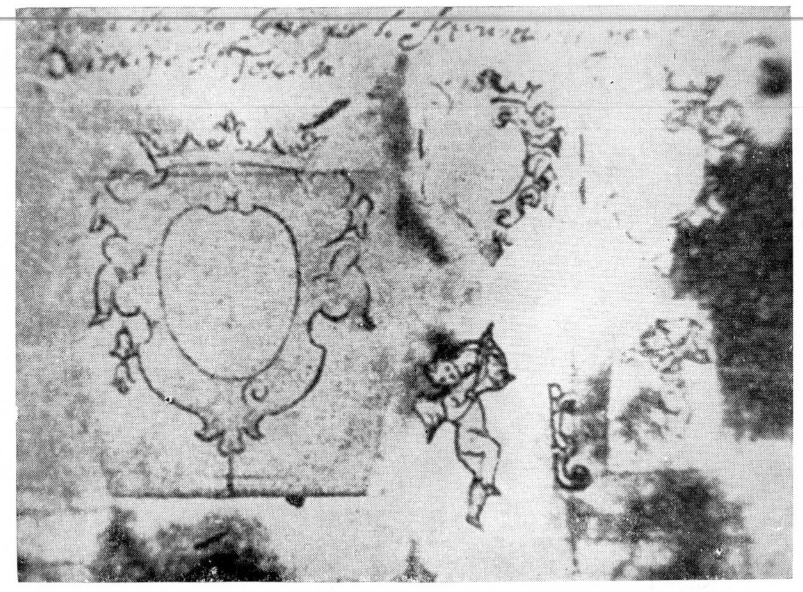

324. Stradivari Antonio, Cremona (DALLA VALLE)

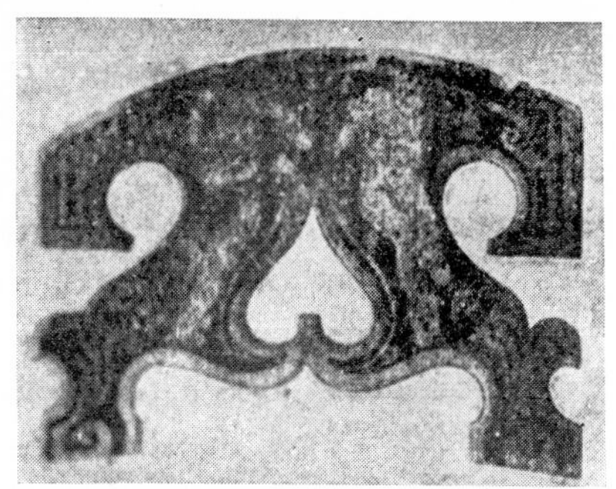
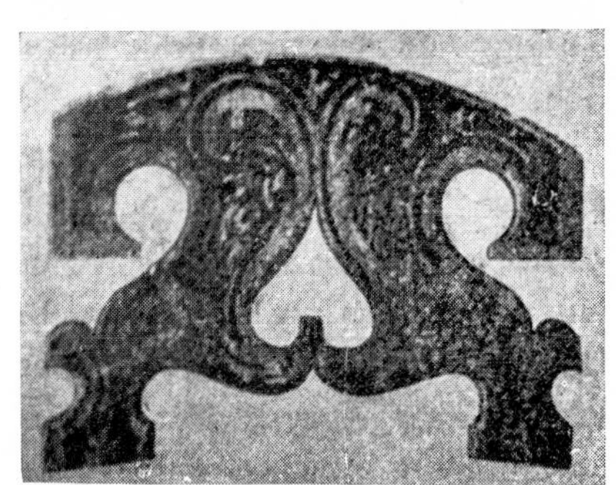
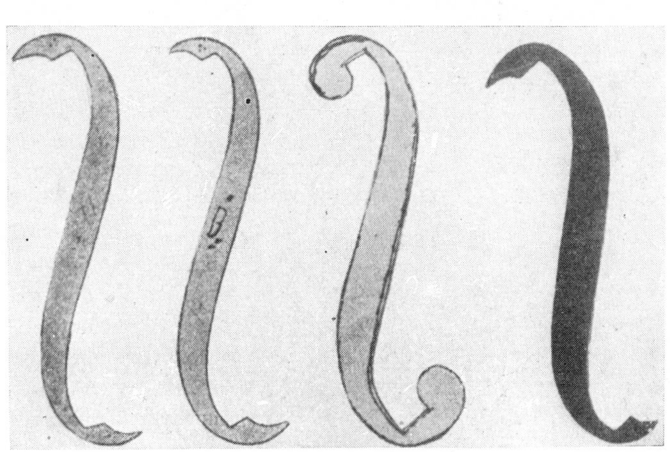
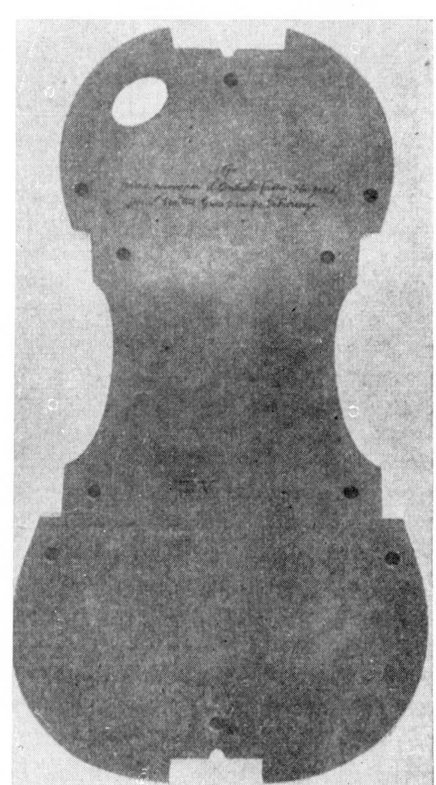

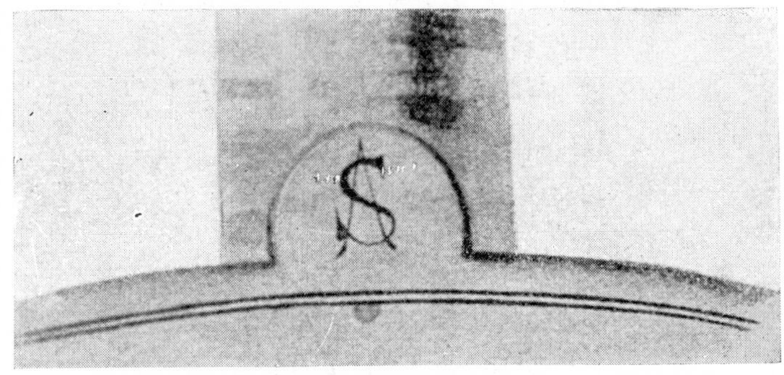

325. Stradivari Antonio, Cremona (DALLA VALLE)

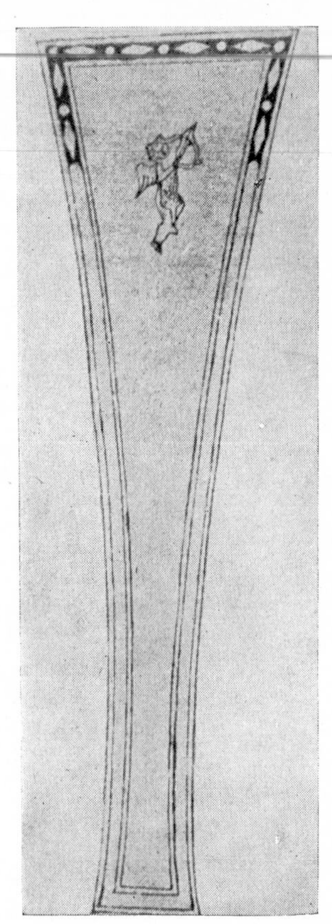

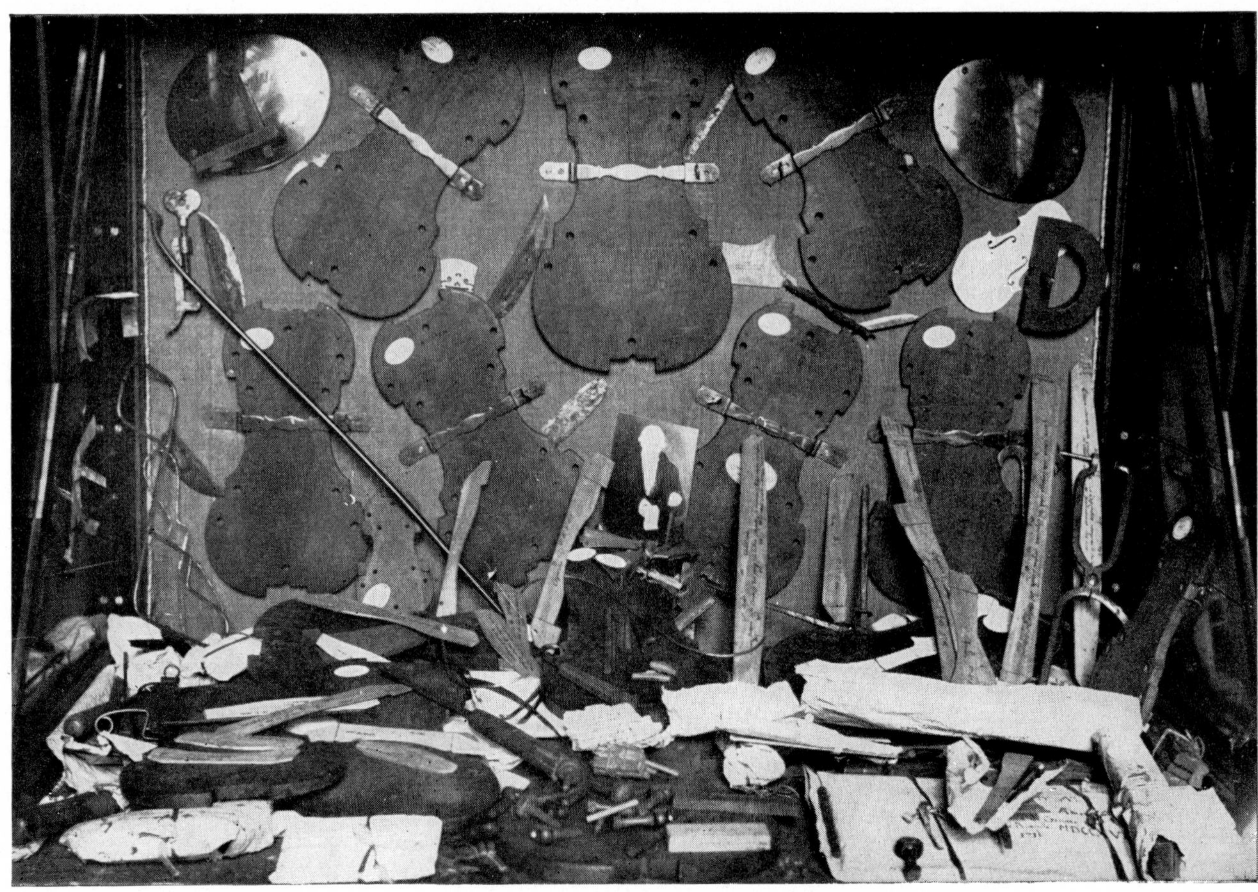

326. Stradivari Antonio, Cremona (DALLA VALLE)

Stradivari's work can be divided into four periods:

I. The *Amati period* or the years of growth, 1665—1685. All creations of that time are worked on the pattern of Nic. Amati. At a later stage, he carved the scrolls in his own fashion, cutting them deeper and widening their shape. For the belly he used light pine-wood with clear grain which is not of a particularly beautiful appearance, but has good tonal qualities. The backs are made of fine maple wood, showing the smooth sheen which is constituted by the grain of the maple. Stradivari reduced the arching to 14—15 mm, as compared with Amati who used to arch his violins up to 20 mm, for he was well aware that a lower arched instrument would have a more powerful tone than an instrument with high arching. He applied at this time a golden-yellow, golden-red or amber-coloured varnish.

From this period we know of the following instruments: 1665: "Santa Agata", earliest extant violin with a Stradivari label; 1666: violin with the label "Antonius Stradivari, Alumnus Nicolaj Amati, faciebat anno 1666; four violin from the year 1667; one violin from 1668; two violins from 1671: "Hellier" from 1679 inlaid ivory and ebony; "Seliere", exhibited in Cremona in 1937; five violins from 1683: "Da Ahna", "Bucher", "Petherick Horace", "Josef Suk", "Webster"; five violins from 1684, among them "Pressardi"; six violins from 1685, among them "Mackenzie"; and the well-known "Florentine" from 1684.

Three violas: "Mahler" from 1672, further from 1677 and 1685.

Three violoncellos: from 1677, "Bonjour" from 1684 and from 1685.

II. *The time of experiments:* 1686—1694. During this period Stradivari reduced the arching, modified the sound-holes and situated them in a slightly more reclining position. The bouts, between which the bridge stands, are broader, their corners longer. The resonance-box is enlarged, the scroll more worked in detail and appears bigger. The varnish coating violins whose back is made of one piece, is golden-yellow of various tints, darker or lighter. For violins whose back is made of two pieces, he often used a light-red varnish. The narrow purfling is beautifully finished. About 1693, Stradivari modified his pattern, reducing the width of his violins and making them a little longer. Thus the "allongé" pattern came into being. At the same time the colour of the varnish also changes, becoming amber-yellow or light-red, but always keeping its transparence and wonderful lustre. The "allongés" match in beauty of tone the other violins, having the same velvety blend of sounds and a clear tone with deep resonance underneath the G-string.

Notwithstanding the differences of the successive models, their tone is always good, which proves the greatness of this master's art. In 1687, Stradivari produced for the royal court of Spain, a quartet inlaid with mother-of-pearl and ivory. One violin of this quartet belonged later to the virtuoso Ole Bull. At the same time pochettes, adorned in a similar manner, came into being. This is the time when Stradivari's renown began to spread; he was working for the courts of Toscana, Spain, Modena, for King Augustus of Poland, for the Duke of Alba and others.

From this period we know of about 40 violins. "The Avery" from 1688; one violin from 1687 (first violin of Jan Kubelík); "Mercur" from 1688; "Tuscan" from 1690; "Medici", a violin with the inscription PRIMA 20 OTTOBRE 1690 PER S. A. DA FIORENZA; "Amatise" from 1689; "Ex Payne" from 1690; "Fetzer" from 1694.

Five violas: two of them from 1690 made for the Grand Duke of Tuscany, belonging to the quartet "Medici di Toscan".

Eleven violoncellos: from 1690 belonging to the "Medici" quartet; "May le Bon" from 1688; "L'Evique" from 1689; "The Marylebone" from 1688; "Bonjour" from 1692: and a violoncello for Cosimo of Medici with the inscription "*Mussure giusta per il Tenore de occhi fatt aposta per il Gran Principe de Toscana. Adi 4. Ottob. 1690*" ("Correct measure for sound-holes of a violoncello made especially for the Grand Duke of Tuscany on Oct. 4, 1690").

III. *The golden period* 1695—1725. With rich experience, after many experiments, the master, already 56 years old, attained what he had striven to achieve. He had succeeded in combining the powerful tone of the Brescian instruments with the enchanting, clear and sweet sound of the Cremonese Amatis.

His instruments now have widened outlines, the faultlessly regular arching forms elegant lines. The material is very carefully selected, the scrolls, less deeply carved than those of the previous period, but sufficiently large, are executed in a clean and delicate manner. The golden-yellow varnish is of matchless quality, of delicate, high lustre; it is often provided with a further coat of bright red varnish which appears a little brownish today. Some superb specimens are (or were) dark red. All instruments are finished with the same perfect workmanship, although deviations occur in the thickness of both back and belly, in the rounding-off of the shape and in the position of the sound-holes; as to the tonal quality they are always magnificent. It is the tonal quality that bears out Stradivari's sure judgment, musical insight and outstanding knowledge of materials. He now selected light wood with beautiful grain, and it is not a mere chance that both belly and back show thin lines which cross the joints, meeting there accurately, and are interlaced, thus forming a kind of natural design in the wood. The belly varies in thickness, which is mostly 2.4 mm — 2.8 mm, sometimes even less. The back is made of flawless maplewood; its thickness varies to a great extent, attaining as much as 6 mm. The arching of the back is 14—15 mm. The height of the sides measures usually, at the very least, as much as the archings of belly and back taken together, i.e., 28—30 mm. Greater care was often bestowed by Stradivari on the execution of the inside work than on finishing the outside of instruments, and with good reason he made the corners and the lining inside his violins of light willow wood. The bass-bar was originally thin and suited then the requirements. It has been replaced since, in order to stand the increased pressure, but some experts today are again in favour of a low bass-bar. The beautifully shaped sound-holes are cut with delicate taste and still show traces of Amati's school. Their upper parts are inclined towards each other reducing slightly the distance between the upper ends. The purfling, inserted at a distance of 4 mm from the edge, is finished in a masterly manner.

This model is characterized by the widening of the upper and lower parts and a slightly narrower middle part between the bouts, a most graceful design. The bouts are in their middle part only slightly curved and part of them appears almost as a straight line; consequently, the corners seem to protrude and are rather broad. The weight of the resonance body without neck and scroll is 260—280 grammes. In individual cases we observe slight deviations which, however, do not change the characteristic timbre of Stradivari's tone. It was to suit the quality of material that he adopted these modifications. The following violins are known from this period: "Vornbaum" from 1696; "Miss Crespi" 1699; "Loguet" 1699; "Lady Tennant" 1699; "Amatise" 1699; "Long Pattern" 1700; "Van Houten Kreutzer" 1701; "Montbel" 1703; "Emiliani" 1703; "The Irish" 1702; "Viotti" 1704; "Betts" 1704; "Fritz Hirt" 1704; "Marsick" 1705; "Castelbargo" 1707; "Rivaz" 1707; "Rubin" 1708; "Le Regent" 1708; "Greffuhle" 1709; intricately inlaid with ebony and ivory: "Ernst" 1709; "La Pucelle" 1709; "Nachez" 1709; "Camposelice" 1710; "Vieux temps" 1710; "Ries" 1710; "Parke" 1712; "Dancla" 1711; "Parke-Strad" 1711; "Le Brun" 1712; "Sancy" 1713; "Boissier" 1713; "Gibson" 1713; "Delphin" 1714; "Wandling" 1714; "Ex Joachim" 1714; "Budapester-Strad" 1715; "De Barnau" 1715; "Gillot" 1715; "Allard" 1715; "Lipinski" 1715; "Emperor" 1715; "Il Cremonese" 1715; "Le Messie" 1716, best instruments by Stradivari: "Geosol" 1716; "Goldmann" 1716; "De Duranty" 1716; "Medici" 1716; "Ex Fau" 1716; "Saserno" 1717; "The Park" 1717; "San Lorenzo" 1718; "Hegar" 1718; "Maurin" 1718; "Alba" 1719; "Zahn" 1719; "Monasterio" 1719; "Haupt" 1719; "Conte de Villares" 1720; "L'Eveque" 1720; "Jansa" 1721; "Rode" 1722; "De Chaponay" 1722; "Rolla" 1722; "Le Laurie" 1722; "Sarasate" 1724; "Paganini" 1724; "Brancaccio" 1725; "Il Portoghese" 1725; "H & J. Hammig" 1725.

Among his violas are: "Archinto" 1696; "Macdonald" 1701.

Violoncellos of this period are represented by: "St. Senoch" 1698; "De Kernadec Bläss" 1698; "Christiani" 1700; "Servais" 1701; "Duport" 1711; "Mara" 1711 and "Bata" 1714.

IV. *Old age works*. 1726—1737. In the last epoch of the master's life a decline of strength is evident, the steadiness of his hand was relaxing and his helpers' share in the work was probably greater. These works are still outstanding for their rich tone, but they lack the flawless perfection of those built in former times. The varnish of these instruments is more brownish and not quite so transparent as that applied before. Some instruments of this time are marked with the inscription "sub disciplina" or "sotto la disciplina di Antonio Stradivari", which points to the fact that the master knew these minor deficiencies of his works and made strenuous efforts to maintain, at any cost, the high level of his works. Some of his instruments, with original neck, bear the initials "A. S." or "P. S." on the neck-plate. The legitimacy of the first monogram is quite obvious; the second, however, was made on the order of Antonio's son, Paolo Stradivari, who inherited his father's estate and had his own monogram inscribed on the violins bequeathed to him.

From this period about 50 violins are known, a. o.: "Greville" 1726; "Derbrouq" 1727; "Ex Antonio di Barbaro" 1727; "Kiesewetter" 1731; "Hercules" 1732; "Arkwrights" 1732; "Nadaud" 1734; "Talbot" 1734; "Muntz" 1736; "Rousy" 1736; "Lord Norton" 1737; and "Swan Song" 1737.

Viola: "Gibson" 1731.

Violoncellos: "Murray" 1730; "Pavie" 1730; "Barjansky" 1736 and "Da Venezia" (no date).

After Stradivari's death, his sons Francesco and Omobono took the management of the workshop into their own hands. In matters of violin making they were probably aided by Carlo Bergonzi. After the death of the brothers, Carlo Bergonzi took their workshop on lease in 1746, and Paolo Stradivari, Antonio's son and heir, lent Bergonzi models, moulds, gauges and tools of his father. In 1774, Paolo Stradivari offered, besides a rather considerable number of tools of his father and his brother Francesco, the whole estate for sale to the town of Cremona. The town could not afford to pay the demanded sum, and this made Paolo so angry that he resolved not to leave the property to the town.

In 1775 he received an offer from the firm Giovanni di Anselmi Briatta e C., merchants of Casale Monferrato, who earlier had already bought ten violins by Antonio and Francesco. Of this transaction as well as of the character of Paolo Stradivari the style of a letter, preserved at the municipal museum of Cremona, gives proof; it reads as follows:

"Dispensing with formalities, I am writing to the point in a business-like way. I understand from your esteemed letter dated 13th ult. that you offer 5 ducats for all patterns and moulds which I hold in my possession as well as for those which were lent to Bergonzi, and for the iron tools from my late father's workshop; but it is too little. To show you, however, my goodwill to do you a good service, and because I wish that nothing of my late father's property should remain at Cremona, I am ready to let you have the whole lot for 6 ducats on condition that you pay at once to Messrs. Domenico Dupuis & Sons, silk-footwear makers, and I shall send you all the things quoted above, on the understanding that I am to receive 5 ducats, and shall use the balance to defray cash expenses, packing and custom duties incurred during the transport of the above-said goods; for any other expenditure I shall reimburse myself on Mr. Dupuis. On the other hand you shall pay Mr. Dupuis 7 ducats in return for my defraying all disbursements; in addition I shall hand over to him the bows which I have in my keeping."

The transaction was performed, but in 1776 the whole Briatta collection, including the violins, came into the possession of the well-known collector Count Cozio di Salabue. After the count's death the collection was inherited by Marquis Orlando Della Valle di Torino, who assembled many further items and provided them with historical and technical notes. This abundant material, known under the name Collezione Salabue, remained in the family until the year 1905.

The violin maker Fiorini, who was keenly interested in the collection, then offered Marchioness Della Valle 100,000 lire for it Feb. 6, 1920. The lady replied on Feb. 8th as follows:

"I have received your letter, and it is good that you have written. You will pay 100,000 lire and in return you will receive the whole collection which you know well and which we have discussed in our letters. As a guarantee that the transaction will be carried out in a fair manner, you will hand over to me (as you have promised in writing), 20,000 lire plus 80,000 lire in cheques payable at the Banca di Sconto of Turin at the time when you take over the collection, which I shall keep with me, as I have done heretofore, until the rooms in Florence are ready to receive it for sake-keeping. Yesterday I happened to receive an offer of 120,000 lire from a man with whom I had been discussing the sale of the violins, but who had not been heard of for some time. I replied, of course, that it was too late, and I do not regret the fact that this unrealized negotiation would have turned out more lucrative. The violins would have been taken to France and would not have remained in the school of violin making in Florence to which you have assigned them in accordance with Count di Salabue's wish."

Fiorini's plans to open a school for the art of violin building (first in Florence, then in Bologna) did not succeed. Affected with a serious eye-disease, he attempted to find room for the memorial relics in Rome and later in Turin, again in vain. At last he decided to present the whole collection to the museum of Cremona. The terms of the donation are contained in a letter he wrote to the Museum on June 4th, 1930:

"On the 2nd inst. I forwarded to your address, by railway, a parcel of 9,15 kg net weight, and yesterday, i.e., on the 3rd of this month, another parcel of 5,65, net weight by registered post. The first contains 20 patterns of instruments, further a packet of curves, and wooden models. The second parcel comprises 9 packets which I now specify: No. 1. old tools for violin making; 2. old iron compasses; 3. a wooden fork for fitting the sound-post; 4. models of bridges; 5. (not specified); 6. models of violin-cases; 7. (not specified); 8. wooden wedges (which Stradivari used in making violin-plates); 9. cardboard models for violas. I presume that the things will be in your possession by the 10th of this month and trust that they arrive in good condition. The rate charged for the conveyance of the consignment to destination has been prepaid and the custom-house should impose no duty as all these things are old. Should you, for all that, incur any expenses on receipt of the parcels, I shall refund them. These parcels comprise but a part of my collection of Stradivari treasures. The remainder I shall bring personally to Cremona about the 15th inst., unless there be some unforeseen hindrances."

The complete collection comprises 1303 items, i.e., 475 paper models, 410 wooden moulds, 13 models of mother-of-pearl, 10 wooden implements, 46 iron implements, 8 wax seals, 11 sheets of drawings designed for Count Cozio di Salabue, 4 strips of paper measures made by Cozio, 14 books of manuscripts by Cozio, among them an inventory of the instruments once owned by Count Cozio (some of these books rather bulky), 232 sheets of manuscripts and various autographs, among them letters of Paolo and Antonio Stradivari, son and grandson of the famous master, further letters to violin maker Giov. Battista Guadagnini of Cremona by Giovanni Antonio March of Bologna, Giuseppe Baccheta of Brescia, and other persons concerning the sale of stringed instruments and their construction, and finally 80 sheets of printed labels. In addition to these items donated by Fiorini, the museum has several hundred other pieces presented by heirs of the Cerutti family and other citizens of Cremona. The museum is located in the New Town Hall of Cremona.

We show photographs of show-cases where the treasures are kept, as well as a reproduction of Stradivari's portrait and a picture of S. Domenico Church, where Stradivari was buried. Now his earthly remains are entombed in a common vault, situated on the south-eastern side of Piazza Roma, where in 1937, on the 200th anniversary of Stradivari's death, visitors laid roses at the obelisk.

Dimensions of some violins of Antonio Stradivari:

Violin built in	Specimen	Length of belly & back	Upper width	Lower width	Middle width	Upper sides	Lower sides
1667		352	167	201	—	33	33
1667	(ladies' size)	350	160	183	—	29	31
1672		356	165	200	—	30	31
1677		350	163	205	—	28	30
1678		353	162	201.5	108	—	—
1679	Hellier	359	172	213	—	30	31
1684		351	160	199.5	105	—	—
1685		356	162	202	105	—	—
1687		351	165.5	208	110	—	—
1688		356	163.5	205	107	—	—
1690	Tuscan	355	166	207	—	28	30
1693		362	165	201	—	30	30
1694	Fetzer	357	160	201	105	—	—
1696		356	161	202.5	106.5	—	—
1697		356	162	201	106	—	—
1699		362	162	201	—	30	32
1700		355	167.5	207	109	—	—
1700		355	166	207	—	28	30
1700		355	169	210	—	30	31
1702		357	167.5	207.5	109	—	—
1702		357	169	210	—	30	31
1704	Betts	357	170	210	—	30	31
1704	Viotti	354	165	204	—	30	31
1705		353	167	206	108	—	—
1707		355	168	207.5	109	—	—
1707		357	170	210	—	30	30
1708		360	168	207.5	109	—	—
1708	Davidoff	360	171	210	—	30	31
1709		354	168	207	—	30	31
1710		535	168	208	110	—	—
1710		359	169.5	207.2	110	—	—
1710		355	169	210	—	30	31
1710	Vieuxtemps	357	170	210	—	30	31
1710		355	169	210	—	31	31
1711		360	168	207	109	—	—
1711		357	167.5	207	107	—	—
1711	Dancla	360	170	210	—	30	30
1713	Sarasate	355	165	206	—	30	31
1713	Sancy	355	165	206	—	30	31
1713	Boissier	358.5	169	210	—	30	31
1714		355	166	207	109	—	—
1714	Dauphin	356	170	210	—	30	30
1715	Messie	354	166	206	109	30	31
1716		357	167.5	207	110	—	—
1716		358	162	203	108	32	32
1716	Cessol	357	166	207	—	29	31
1718	Maurin	360	170	210	—	30	31
1719	Alba	356	168	206	108	—	—
1720		357	168	210	—	30	31
1720		358.5	170	210	—	30	31
1720		357	168	210	—	30	31
1721		360	168.5	209	110	—	—
1721		355	167	207	—	30	31
1722	Vollrath	356	167	208	109	—	—
1725	Brancaccio	354	168	208	—	29.5	31.5
1726	Greffuhl	354	167	206	—	29	30
1728		356	166	205	108	—	—
1728		357	167	208	110	—	—
1729		355	167	207	—	30	31
1732	Hercule	359	169	210	—	30	31
1732		360	170	210	—	39	31
1733	Menuhin	358	168	207	109	—	—
1734		357	167	207	109.5	30	31
1734		360	170	210	—	32	33
1734		360	170	210	—	32	32.5
1734		356	166	206	108	—	—
1736		357	168.5	209	—	32	32.5
1736		357	164	205	—	30	31
1737		357	164	205	—	30	31
	Violas:						
1690		478	220	273	—	40	43
1690		413	187	243	—	39	40
1691		480	220	273	—	40	43
1701		410	186	243	—	38	39
Period I		405	198	241	—	45	46
Period II		410	185	240	—	38	39
	Violoncellos:						
1689		760	352	450	—	120	120
1690		793	368	468	—	114	121
1691		797	368	471	—	121	121
1700		790	360	465	—	111	114
1701		792	366	456	—	125	125
1710		756	346	440	—	117	124
1720		756	346	437	—	124	127
1730		746	329	421	—	117	121
without date		750	340	440	—	118	119

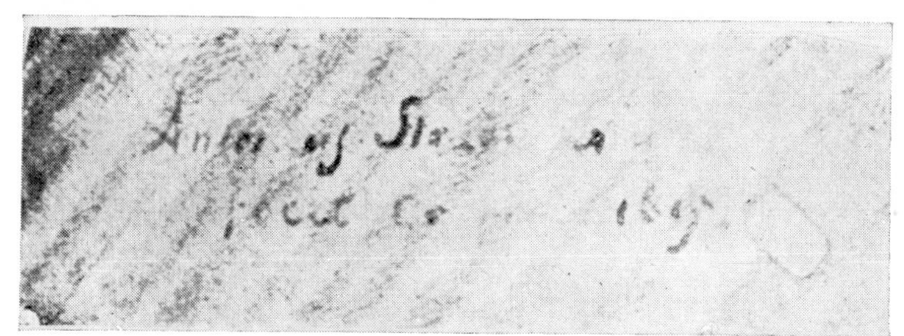

1672

1688

1689

1693

1700

1701

1703

1704

1708

1709

1711

1713

1714

1715

1716

1718

1722

1723

1727

Antonius Stradiuarius Cremonenſis Alumnus
Nicolaij Amati, Faciebat Anno 1666

Antonius Stradiuari
fecit Cremonæ 1693

Reuisto e Corretto da me Antonio
Stradiuari in Cremona 1701

Antonius Stradiuarius Cremonenſis
Faciebat Anno 1717

Antonius Stradiuarius Cremonenſis
Faciebat Anno 1719

Antonius Stradivarius Cremonenſis
Faciebat Anno 1736
D'Anni
D'ANNI 92

Sotto la Diſciplina d'Antonio
Stradiuari F. in Cremona 1737

Antonius Stradiuarius Cremonenſis
Faciebat Anno 1667

Antonius Stradiuarius Cremonenſis
Faciebat Anno 1699

Antonius Stradiuarius Cremonenſis
Faciebat Anno 1713

1714
Reuisto il Corretto da me
Antonio Stradiuari in Cremona

Antonius Stradivarius Cremonenſis
Faciebat Anno 1736
D'ANNI 92
92

Antonius Stradivarius Cremonenſis
Faciebat Anno 1737
D'Anni 93

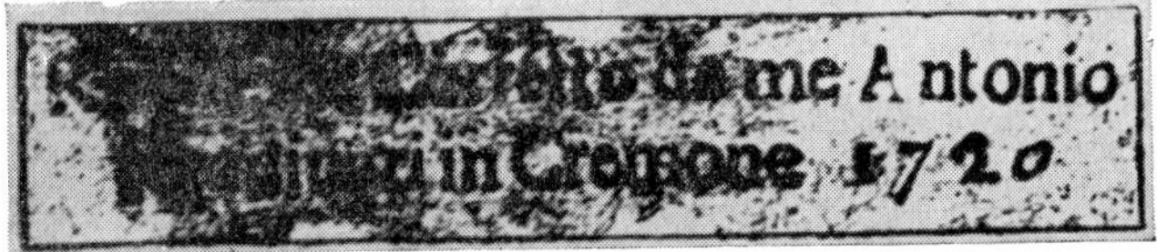

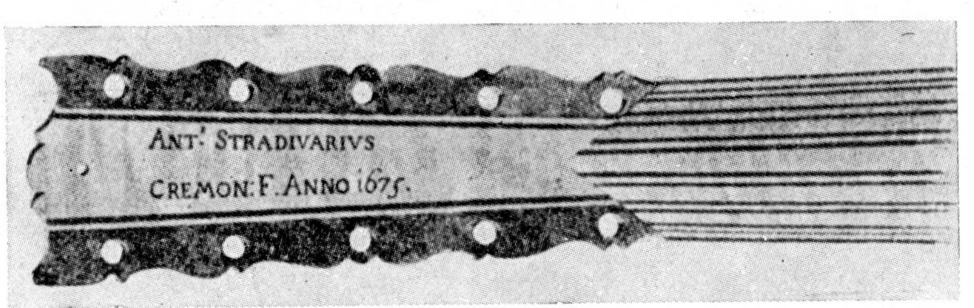

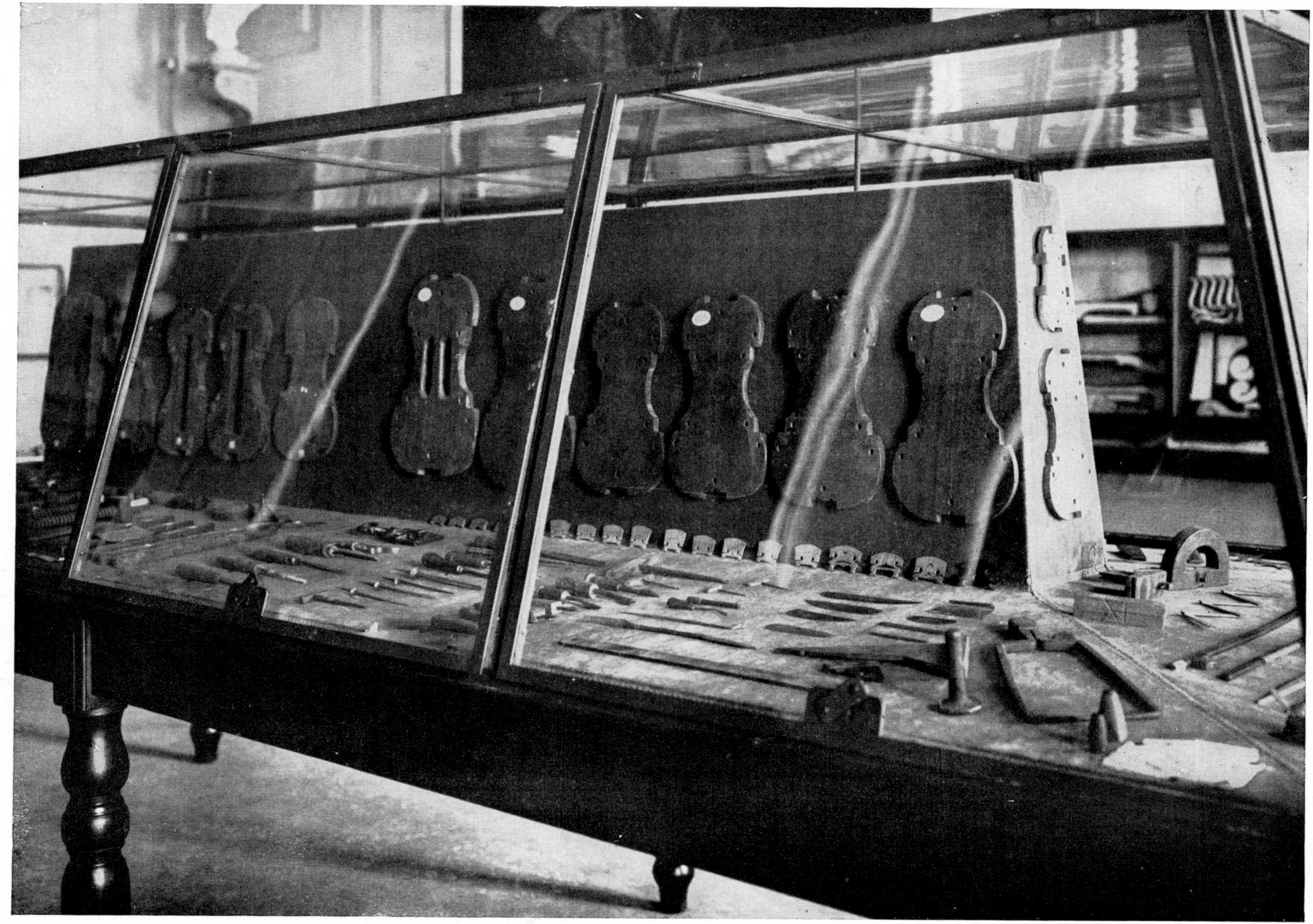

327. Stradivari Antonio, Cremona (DALLA VALLE)

Fr. Vincentius Maria Romanus Ordinis Predicatorum Miseratione Divina
Tituli S. Xysti S.R.E. Presbyter Cardinalis Ursinus S. Ecclesie Beneventane Archiepiscopus.

Considerantes fidelitatem servitutis, atque amoris sinceritatem quam Antonius Stradivarius
Cremonensis erga nos, ut occasio postulavit semper ostendit, eidem nos ipsi benevolentie
nostre minimam prestandam duximus significationem, ac nostros inter actuales familiares
eum connumerandum optamus, ut iisdem fruatur privilegiis, prerogativis, et exemptionibus,
quos ceteri apud nos nostro actualiter addicti servitio potiuntur. Ideoque hortamur
omnes, et singulos, ut eundem favoribus prosequantur, existiment, et debito donent
honore: nostram nos omnibus alacrem spondentes animi gratitudinem. In quorum
omnium, et singulorum fidem has presentes faciendas mandavimus, nostra propria
manu subscriptas, nostrique impressione sigilli munitas. Dat. Beneventi hac die
XXV mensis Junii M.D.C.LXXXVII

Fr. Vincentius Maria Cardinalis Ursinus Archiepiscopus

328. Stradivari Antonio, Cremona (DALLA VALLE)

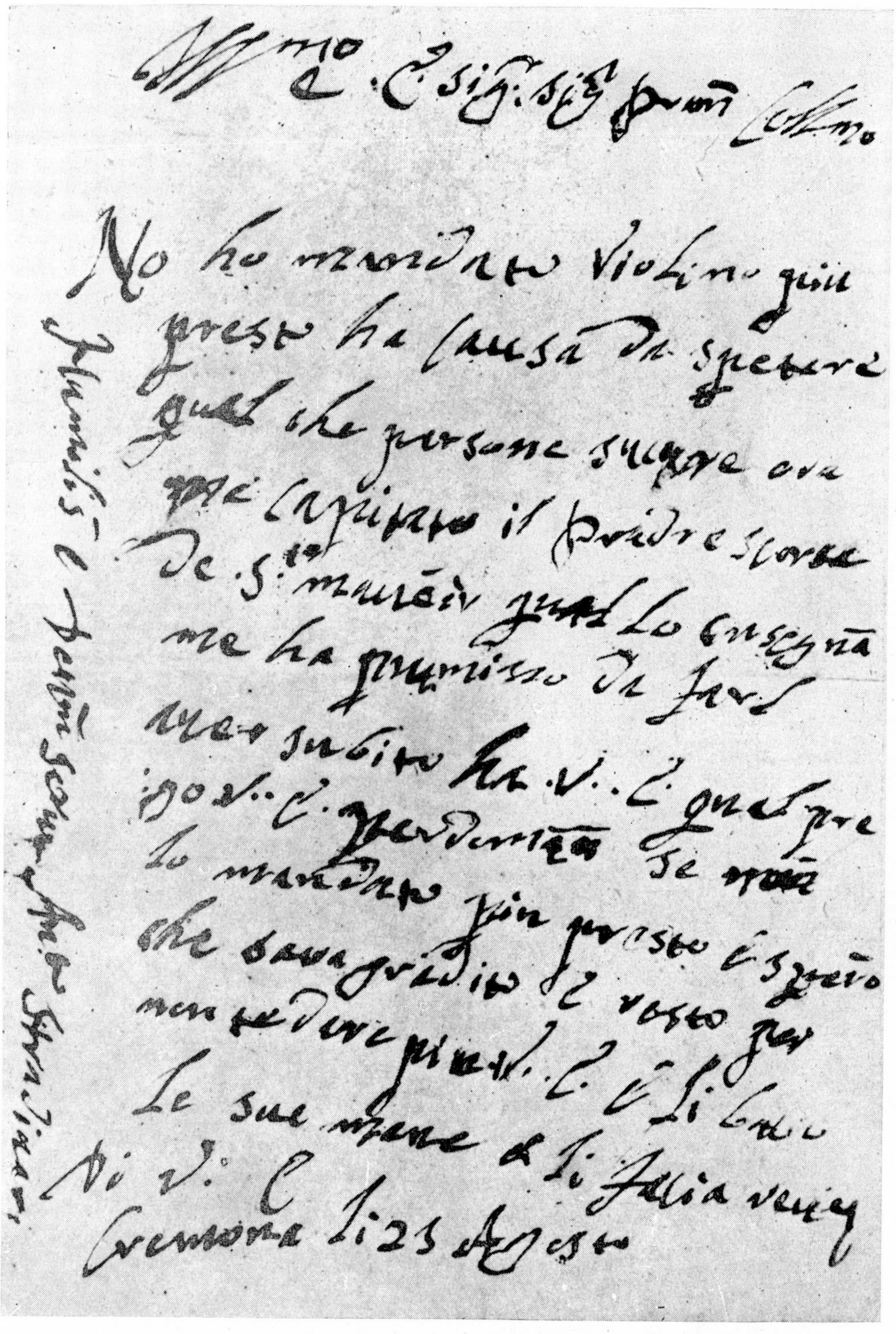

Ill.mo e R.mo Sig.r Sig.r Pron Col.mo

No ho mandato violino più
presto ha causa da spetare
qual che persone sicure ora
me capitato il Padre Scorsa
de S.ta Maria quale lo consegna
me ha promisso de fare
mettere subito ha V. S.
e V. S. perdonerà se non
lo mandato più presto
che sarà gratia e spero
non tediare più V. S. e li bacio
Le sue mane e li fatio reverenza
Di V. S.
Cremona li 23 Agosto

Humiliss.o e Devotiss.o Servitore Antonio Stradivari

329. Stradivari Antonio, Cremona (DALLA VALLE)

330. Stradivari Antonio, Cremona 1672 (VIOLA)
Photo Hamma & Co

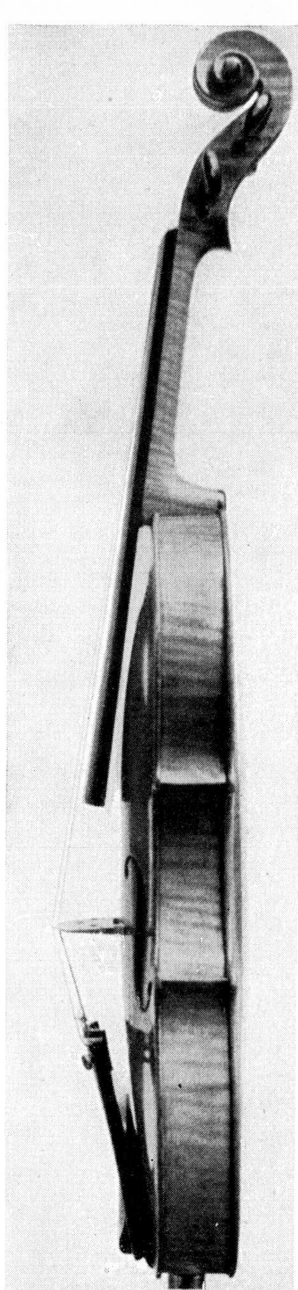
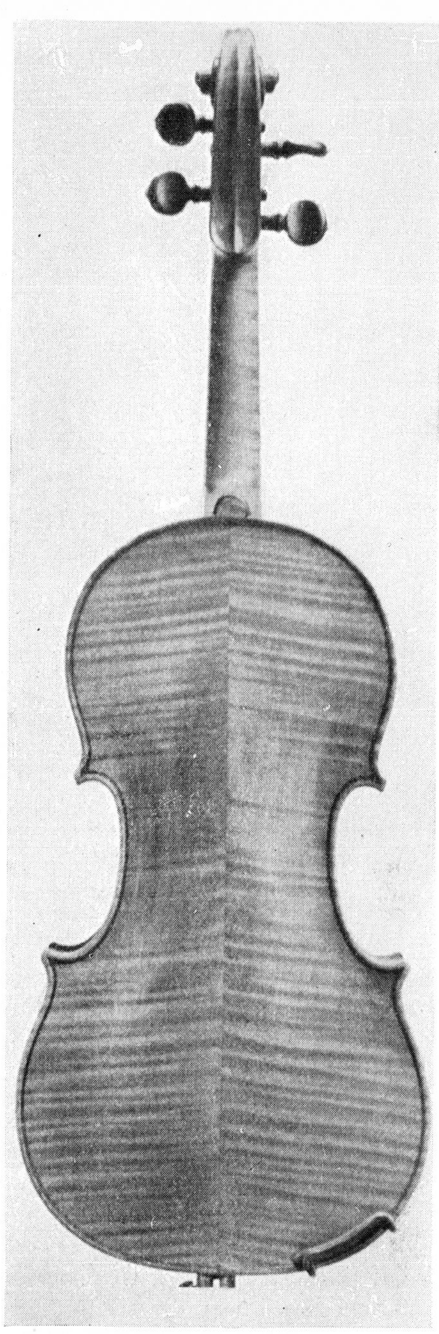
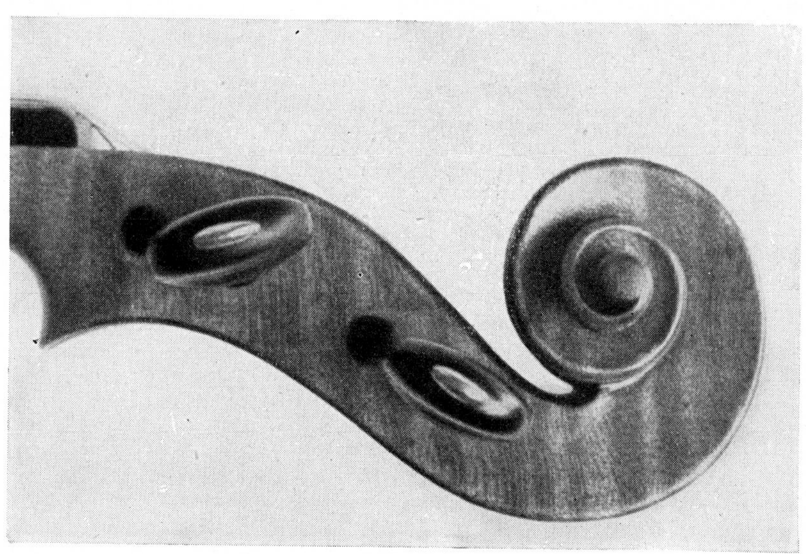

336. Stradivari Antonio, Cremona 1688

337. Stradivari Antonio, Cremona 1685
Photo Hamma & Co

338. Stradivari Antonio, Cremona 1691 (EX DANCLA)
Photo Hamma & Co

339. Stradivari Antonio, Cremona 1694 (EX FETZER)
Photo Hamma & Co

340. Stradivari Antonio, Cremona 1697
Photo Hamma & Co

341. Stradivari Antonio, Cremona 1702
Photo Hamma & Co

342. Stradivari Antonio, Cremona 1702 (LORD BORWICK)
Photo Hamma & Co

343. Stradivari Antonio, Cremona 1704 (VIOTTI)
Photo Hamma & Co

344. Stradivari Antonio, Cremona 1704 (LIEBIG)
Photo Hamma & Co

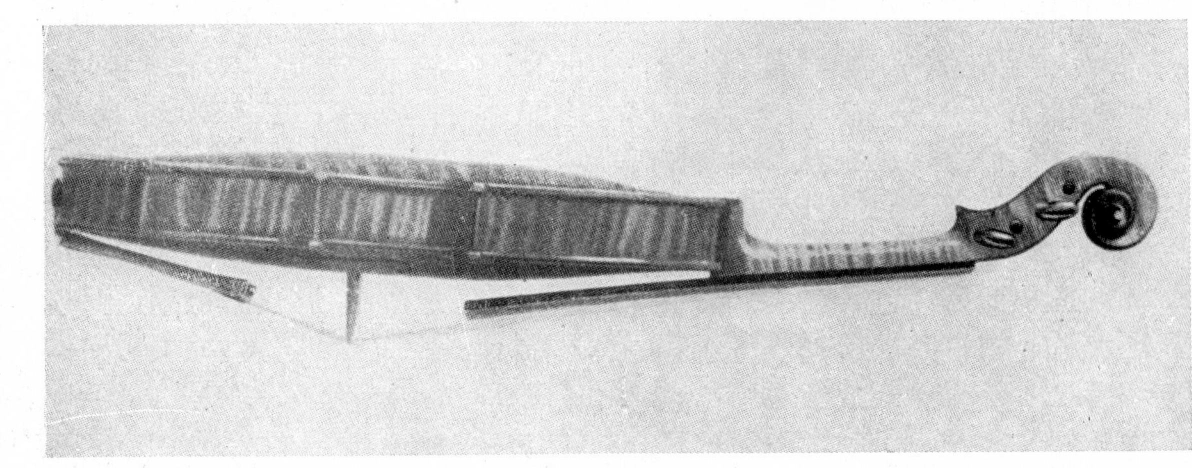

345. Stradivari Antonio, Cremona 1704 (BETTS)

346. Stradivari Antonio, Cremona 1707 (CASTELBARCO) CELLO
Photo Hamma & Co

347. Stradivari Antonio, Cremona 1709 (RIES)

348. Stradivari Antonio, Cremona 1709 (ARTOT)
Photo Hamma & Co

349. Stradivari Antonio, Cremona 1709
(MARKEWITSCH) CELLO
Photo Hamma & Co

350. Stradivari Antonio, Cremona 1710 (CAMPO SELICE)
Photo Hamma & Co

351. Stradivari Antonio, Cremona 1711
(VOGELWEIT)
Photo Hamma & Co

352. Stradivari Antonio, Cremona 1714
Photo Hamma & Co

353. Stradivari Antonio, Cremona 1715 (EX PROVE)
Photo Hamma & Co

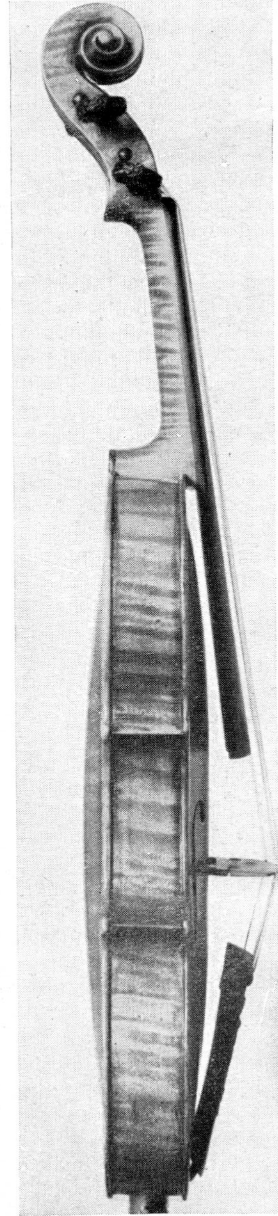

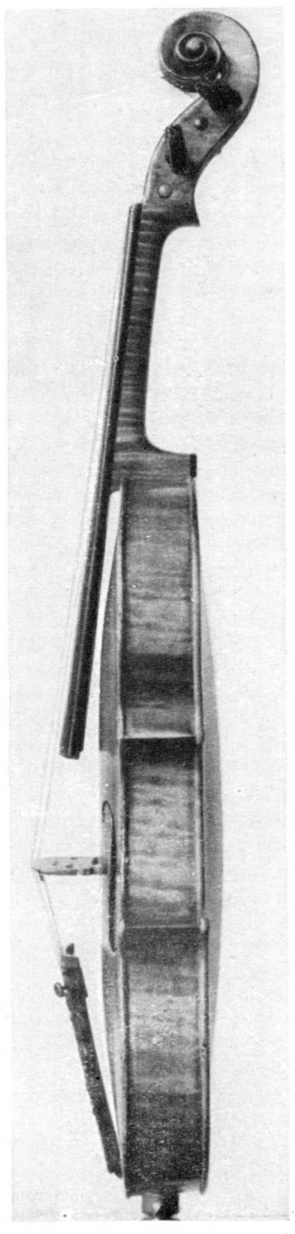

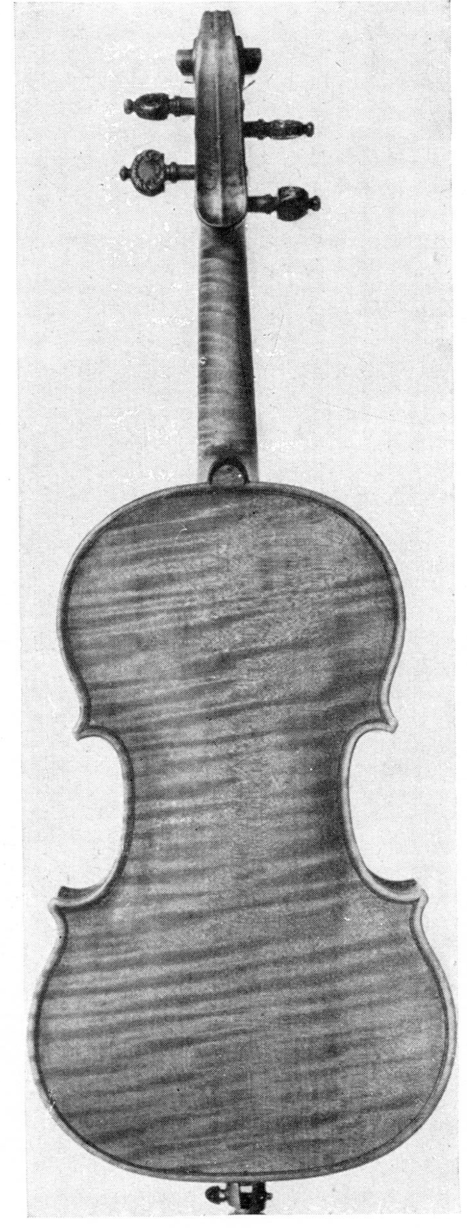

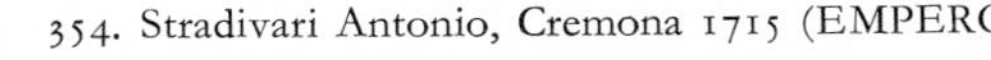

354. Stradivari Antonio, Cremona 1715 (EMPEROR)

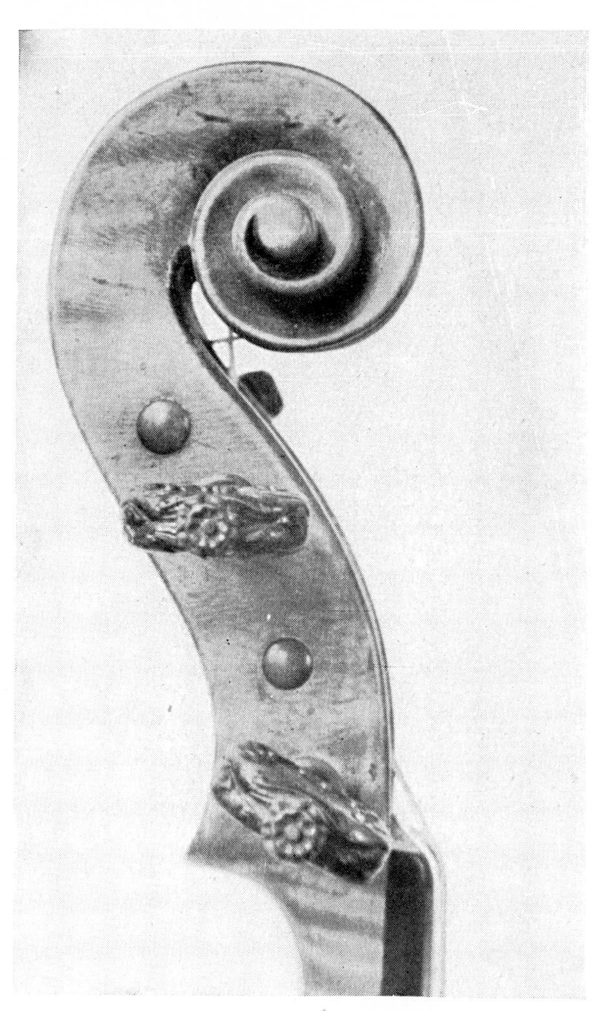

355. Stradivari Antonio, Cremona 1715 (EMPEROR)

356. Stradivari Antonio, Cremona 1715 (EX VESCEY)
Photo Hamma & Co

357. Stradivari Antonio, Cremona 1716 (EX FAU)
Photo Hamma & Co

357. Stradivari Antonio, Cremona 1716
(EX BUSCH — EX STUCKI)
Photo Hamma & Co

358. Stradivari Antonio, Cremona 1716
(BARON KNOP)

359. Stradivari Antonio, Cremona 1718
(EX PROF. HEGAR)

360. Stradivari Antonio, Cremona 1719 (HERZOG ALBA)
Photo Hamma & Co

361. Stradivari Antonio, Cremona 1728 (PERKIN)
Photo Hamma & Co

362. Stradivari Antonio, Cremona 1720 (EX BOCKERATH)
Photo Hamma & Co

363. Stradivari Antonio, Cremona 1721 (LADY BLUNT)
Photo Hamma & Co

364. Stradivari Antonio, Cremona 1722 (RODE)

365. Stradivari Antonio, Cremona 1725
Photo Hamma & Co

366. Stradivari Antonio, Cremona 1721 (JANSEN)
CELLO
Photo Hamma & Co

367. Stradivari Antonio, Cremona 1722 (EX VOLLRATH)
Photo Hamma & Co

368. Stradivari, Antonio Cremona 1724
(PAGANINI — EX BEUTINCK)

369. Stradivari Antonio, Cremona 1725 (EX CHACONNE)
Photo Hamma & Co

370. Stradivari Antonio, Cremona 1725 (PORTUGIESE)
Photo Hamma & Co

371. Stradivari Antonio, Cremona 1728
Photo Hamma & Co

372. Stradivari Antonio, Cremona 1728
Photo Hamma & Co

373. Stradivari Antonio, Cremona 1731
Photo Hamma & Co

374. Stradivari Antonio, Cremona 1731 (FETZ)
Photo Hamma & Co

375. Stradivari Antonio, Cremona 1733 (MENUHIN)
Photo Hamma & Co

376. Stradivari Antonio, Cremona 1734 (NADAUD)
Photo Hamma & Co

377. Stradivari Antonio, Cremona 1737 (CHANT DU CYGNE)
Photo Hamma & Co

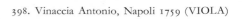

397. Vinaccia Antonio, Napoli 1782

398. Vinaccia Antonio, Napoli 1759 (VIOLA)

399. Vinaccia Gaiectanus, Napoli
Photo Hamma & Co

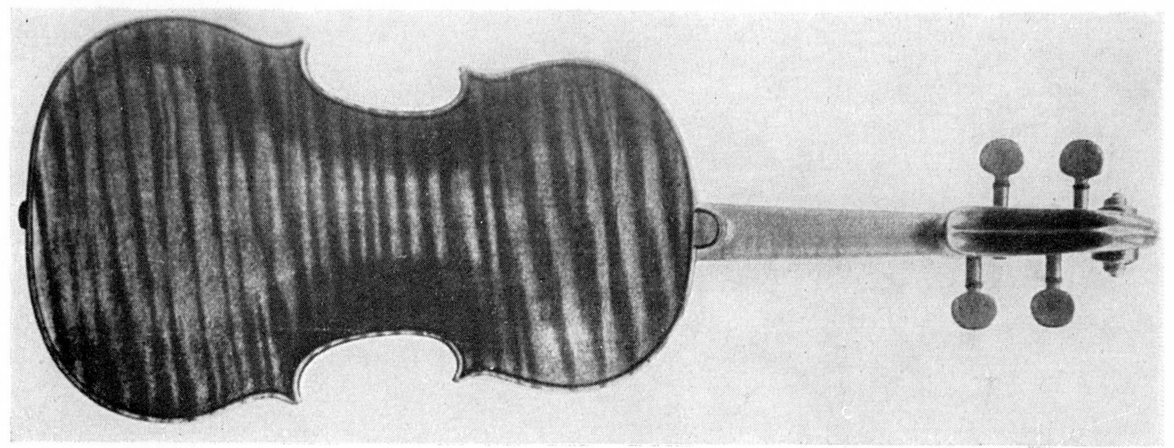

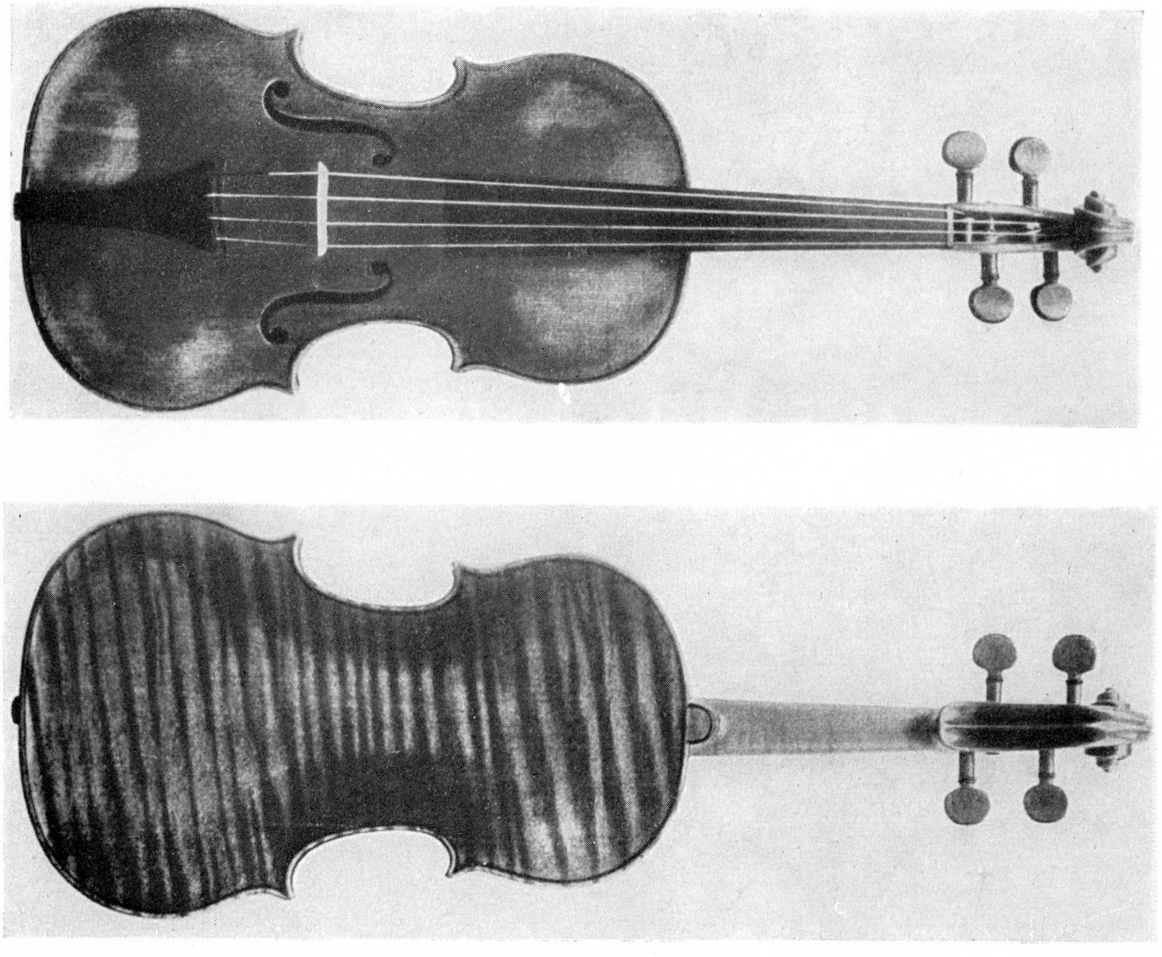

400. Vinaccia Giovanni, Napoli 1754
Photo Hamma & Co

401. Zanioli Giacomo, Venezia 1737
Photo Hamma & Co

402. Zanioli Giacomo Bapt., Verona

403. Zanetto Peregrino, Brescia 1581 (CELLO)

404. Zanetto Pietro, Brescia 1686 (CELLO)

Stradivari Francesco, Cremona. Born Feb. 1, 1671, died May 11, 1743. Son and pupil of Antonio Stradivari. After his father's death he continued to run the shop in company with his brother Omobono. His works are imitations of the large violin model of his father in 1708; they have a very good, powerful tone, though lacking the careful finish of instruments built by his father. Violins by Francesco have broad edges, their purfling is not so handsome, the sound-holes are upright, rather open after the Amati brother's fashion and the right sound-hole is in a more inclined position. He applied orange-yellow varnish, of fairly good quality, but falls short of that used by Antonio. The scrolls of his instruments are beautifully carved. Even without Antonio, Francesco would have become very famous. Price 160.000 Kč; some of his instruments fetched, however, as much as 320.000 Kč.

Franciscus Stradivarius sub disciplina
A. Stradivari 1700

Franciscus Stradivarius Cremonensis
Filius Antonii faciebat Anno 1740

Stradivari Omobono, Cremona. Born at Cremona Nov. 14, 1679, died at the same place on June 8, 1742. The Hill Brothers stated in their great work that they had never seen a violin by Omobono Stradivari, inferring that Omobono had not been a violin maker at all. We are inclined to share this view, because neither correspondence nor bequests mention any instruments by Omobono. They constitute most reliable documents, for some of them come from the time when the sons of Stradivari were still alive. Paolo, the most agile businessman, though not the most prudent member, of the family, did not mention anywhere instruments by Omobono, although he wrote about sales of violins and bows of his deceased father and brother Francesco. It is improbable that there should not have been left a single instrument by Omobono, although he died a year earlier than his brother Francesco; or is it to be supposed that Francesco provided them with his own name?

It is generally stated that he was Antonio's son and pupil. The brothers Francesco and Omobono are alleged to have assisted their father and, after the latter's death, to have continued working together. Omobono is said to have built instruments far inferior to those created by the former two and to have devoted more of his time to repairing work than to the making of new instruments. The arching of his instruments (which Hill considers as fakes, although they are marked with Omobono's name) is imperfect, the sound-holes are of no particular beauty, the rather deep cut scrolls, however, are well done. The instruments are coated with a golden-yellow varnish of a quality inferior to that applied by his father and brother. As for the tone, these violins also do not meet demands associated with the name. The price of 120.—150.000 Kč is, therefore, certainly exaggerated.

Homobonus Stradivarius
sub disciplina A. Stradivari 1725

Omobonus Stradivarius Filius Antonij
Cremone Fecit Anno 1740

Omobonus Stradivarius figlij Antonij
Cremone Fecit Anno 1740

Strati Michael, Verona. Ca 1792. He imitated, with careful workmanship, Guarneri, Stradivari and the French school, used good wood and applied yellow varnish. The edges of his instruments are sharply bevelled, the gracefully cut sound-holes designed in a slanting position.

Michael Strati
Verona 1792.

Straub Michael, Venice. 1670—1680. Little known violin and lute maker.

Michel Straub
in Venezia 1680.

Strauch Matteo, Modena. 1640. Little known lute maker; probably a German settled in Italy.

Suover Giovanni, Florence. 1637. Lute maker.

T

Tacconi Enrico, Rome. 1884. Mandolin maker.

Tadolini Giuseppe, Modena, Bologna. Born about 1796, died 1870. Probably a music master teaching 'cello and contrabass; later maker of stringed instruments who built chiefly 'cellos and contrabasses.

Tachinardi, Cremona. Ca 1690. His instruments remind one of Andrea Amati's works.

Tadolini Ignazio, Modena. Born 1797, died 1873. — Brother of Guiseppe Tadolini. Maker of guitars, pianos and good bows.

Taffelli Alessandro, Mantua. 1619. Lute maker.

Talevius Antonio, Ancona. 1820—1830.

Tanegia Carlo Antonio, Milan. 1725—1731. Worked on the pattern of Grancino, but with less skill. Golden-yellow varnish. Price 16.000 Kč.

Carolus Antonius Tanegia
fecit in Via Lata Medio-
lani Anno 1730

Tanigard (Tanigardi) Giorgio, Rome. 1735—1750. Worked, very skilfully, on the outlines designed by Tecchler, making the archings like Jacob Stainer. The wood is good, the purfling delicately finished, the scrolls carved in a graceful manner. He applied a fine golden-yellow and red-brown varnish. Best are his 'cellos. Price 20.000 Kč, 'cello more.

Giorgius Tanigardus
fecit Romae anno 1735

Giorgio Tanigardi
fecit Romae anno 1745

Giorgio Tanigardi
fecit Romae 17..

Gio Giorgio Taningard
fecit Romæ Anno 1745

Tantino Constantino, Modena. 15th cent. Known only as teacher of his son Giovanni Tantino.

Tantino Giovanni. 1475. Ancient lute maker, son and pupil of Costantino Tantino.

Tantino Sesto, Modena. 1461—1490. Brother of Giovanni.

Tarasconi Carlo, Rome. 1900—1910. An amateur. Yellow varnish.

Carolus Tarasconi
No. 36 fecit Romae 1903

Tarasconi Giuseppe, Milan. 1888—1920. He chiefly traded in violins. His own instruments lack the sure touch of the master. Yellow and orange varnish.

Giuseppe Tarasconi
Saronno - Milano Anno

G.T.
S-M

Tarasconi Mirco, Milan, Paris. 20th century. Son of Giuseppe Tarasconi and pupil of Bernard of Liège, E. Laurant of Brussels and Ornati of Milan.

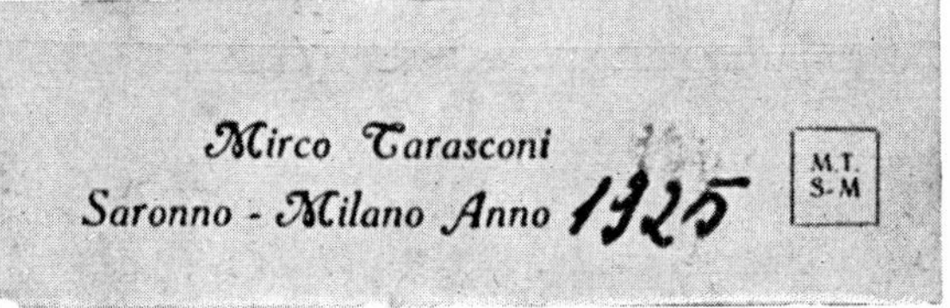
Mirco Tarasconi
Saronno - Milano Anno 1925
M.T.
S-M

Targhetta Carlo, Mantua. 16th — 17th centuries. Little known violin maker.

Tarotanus Antonius, Novara. Ca 1623. The maker of an orange-coloured violin, adorned on the back with French lilies, with the belly flatter than the back, was a monk, a good amateur, equalling in tone and workmanship good Italian masters.

Tartaglio Francesco, Stroppiana, Biella (Modena). Lived about the end of the 19th century. Good instruments.

Tassini Bartolomeo, Venice. 1740—1756. Worked on the large, broad model of Stradivari as well as in the style of Carlo Antonio Testore, but in a less skilful manner. Instruments of graceful outlines, arching executed in a beautiful manner, sound-holes carefully cut, excellent resonant wood. The back is often made of one piece. He used varnish to suit the model he imitated. Price 40.000 Kč.

Opus Bartholomæi
Tassini Veneti.
1754.

Opus
Bartholomæy Tassini
1750

Taus Andreas, Siena. Ca 1621. Little known violin maker.

Tecchler Andreas, Rome, 1742—1748. Son of David Tecchler. Worked very carefully. The wood of his instruments, especially on the back and sides, is fine. He applied a golden-yellow varnish. The sizes of a 'cello by him are as follows: length 764 mm, upper width 340 mm, middle width 240 mm, lower width 430 mm. Price 30—40.000 Kč.

Tecchler Antonio Hieronymus, Rome. 1730—1745. Very good workmanship. Chestnut-brown varnish. In the collection of the Prague Loreto Church, there is a violin labelled as follows:

Antonius Hieronymus Tekler
Davidis Nepos Lautaro fecit 1735

Tecchler David, Venice, Rome. Born about 1666, died 1743. Built instruments on the large pattern of Amati, the arching is made, however, in the fashion of Stainer. The corners are elongated in a characteristic way, the scrolls gracefully carved: the rather broad purfling is well finished; the small, adequately open sound-holes are designed according to Stainer. He selected wood of fine appearance, applied a wonderful yellow or yellow-red varnish of excellent quality; the 'cellos are red-brown or dark red. His broad contrabasses are likewise very good. He was an assiduous master and left a considerable number of instruments. Singular is a viola which is rather broad, with the arching of the belly spreading in a graceful manner over the whole surface of the plate, the sides glued to the very edges of the tables (as it is usual in contrabasses), the short sound-holes gracefully rounded off, while the back is flat, without arching, made up of 9 strips like that of a guitar. This instrument does not sound like a viola, but has a deep bass tone. Price of violins 50—80.000 Kč, 'cellos far more.

David Tecchler Liutaro fecit
Romae 1703

David Techler
fecit Romae 1710

David Techler fecit
an Dni 1743
aetatis suae 77

David Techler Liutaro
fecit Romae An. D. 17..

David Dechler fecit
Rom 1710

David Dechler fecit
Rom 1710.

Tedesco Leopoldo il (i.e. Leopold the German), Rome. Born about 1625, no works after 1658. Pupil of Nic. Amati, worked on the latter's pattern but fell short of his master's art. Price 20.000 Kč.

Telesi Senofonte, Ostiglia (Mantua). Exhibited a violin at Cremona in 1937.

Tenzel Benedict, Naples, 1717. Little known master.

Teodoti Giovanni, Rome. 1690—1712. Probably the father and teacher of Girolamo Teodoti. Violin and lute maker. Worked on the pattern of Stainer and repaired stringed instruments.

Teodoti Girolamo, Rome. 1711. A follower of David Tecchler.

Termanini Giuseppe, Modena. 1755—1773. He worked well, but did not attain the quality of the instruments built by Pietro Termanini. The tone of his instruments is soft, but without power. Probably Pietro's brother and collaborator.

D. Joseph Termanini
fecit Mutinae a: 1755. opus No 5

Termanini Pietro, Modena. 1755—1773. Developed his own model; his violins are of a long shape, rather high arching, have long bouts, short corners. Very fine wood, medium quality workmanship. He applied a hard yellow-brown varnish. With regard to the tone his instruments are fairly good, decidedly better than those of Giuseppe Termanini.

Price 12—16.000 Kč.

Terrana Gerlando, Milan. B. Feb. 26, 1909 in Naples. Instruments with yellow or orange varnish.

T Gerlandus Terrana
G Neapolitanus Mediolani
fecit MCMXLVII

Testator, called "Il Vecchio", Milan. 16th century. Little known, said to have made small instruments (certainly not violins).

Testore Carlo Antonio, Milan. Born about 1688, died after 1764. Son and pupil of Carlo Giuseppe Testore. His works differ from those of his father by their larger pattern and higher arching. He worked on the models of Nic. Amati, Guarneri del Gesù and occasionally on that of Stradivari. The wood he used is very good. He applied a golden-yellow varnish. The tone of his instruments is powerful and of good quality. Valued instruments. Price 45—50.000 Kč.

Carlo Antonio Testore figlio maggiore
del fu Carlo Giuseppe in Contrada lar
ga al segno dell'Aquila Milano 1710

Carlo Antonio Teſtore figlio maggiore
del fù Carlo Giuſeppe in Contrada lar
ga al ſegno dell'Aquila Milano 1710

Carlo Antonio Teſtore figlio maggiore
del fu Carlo Giuſeppe in Contrada
larga al ſegno dell' Aquila. 1740

Testore Carlo Giuseppe, Milan. Born 1660, died 1737. Pupil of Giovanni Grancino. Worked on the models of Nic. Amati, Guarneri, Gofr. Cappa and Ant. Stradivari. Each specimen, however, is distinguished by a peculiar touch of its own; the arching reminds of Nic. Amati. The wood is not always fine-looking; the back is often of pear wood, but always finished with care. The purfling is rather broad, the delicately carved scrolls often too small. The faultlessly applied varnish is golden-yellow, brown-yellow or red-yellow. As far as the tone is concerned, his works constitute outstanding concert instruments, particularly his contrabasses and 'cellos which are coated with a red-brown or hard red varnish. Price 40—75.000 Kč. Length of violin with neck 588 mm, length of belly and back 355 mm, middle width 109 mm, height of sides 29 mm. Another violin of his making has a table length of 356 mm, upper width 168 mm, middle width 110 mm, lower width 205 mm, length of head 105 mm. (The Testore family is headed by Carlo Giuseppe (1660—1764) whose sons were Carlo Antonio (1688—1737) and Paolo Antonio (1690—1750). Giovanni Testore was a son of Carlo Antonio and Gennaro son of Paolo Antonio. All of them lived in Milan.)

Carlo Giuseppe Testore in Con
trada Larga di Milano
Segno dell'Aquila 1690

Carlo Giuseppe Testore, allievo
di Gio Grancino in contrada
larga di Milano 1690

Carlo Giuseppe Testore in Contrada larga di Milano al
segno dell aquila 1700

Carlo Giuseppe Teſtore in Con
trada Larg di Milano
Segno dell' Aquila 1690

Testore Gennaro, Milan. 1767. Son of Paolo Antonio Testore. Conscientious master. The wood he used is, however, not of best quality; the backs are for the most part of poplar wood. His instruments possess high sides and are coated with a dark-brown varnish. Dimensions of one of his violas: length with neck 690 mm, length of belly and back 425 mm, upper width 195 mm, width of centre 135 mm, lower width 235 mm, top sides 43 mm, bottom sides 41 mm. It is characteristic that he made the top sides higher than the bottom sides, whereas with other Italian masters it is always the other way.

Genaro Testore figlio
del fu Paolo 1767

Testore Giovanni, Milan. 1760—1770. Son of Carlo Antonio Testore. His instruments are of very good finish and have a sweet, well-balanced tone. He modelled his instruments on Guarneri.

Carlo Antonio e Giovanni Padre e figlio
Testori, il qual Carlo e figlio Maggiore
del fu Carlo Giuseppe Testore, abitanti
in Contrada larga al segno dell aquila
Milano 1764

Testore Nicolo, Venice. 1755—1765. Flat Testorian model and golden-brown varnish.

Testore Paolo Antonio, Milan. Born about 1690, died after 1750. Son of Carlo Giuseppe Testore. Produced cheaper instruments in company with his brother, somewhat on the pattern of Gius. Guarneri del Gesù. He was a prolific craftsman and a real master, but only a few specimens have a fine finish. The arching of his instruments is beautiful. He applied a light yellow, golden-yellow or brown-yellow varnish. With his brother he worked up to the year 1710. Some of his instruments have, nevertheless, an excellent tone. Price 25.000 Kč at least.

Paolo Antonio Testore
Milano 17..
Paolo Antonio Testore figlio
di Carlo Giuseppe Testore
in Contrada Larga di Milano al Segno dell Acquila. 1759

Paolo Antonio Teſtore figlio
Carlo Giuſeppe Teſtore in
Contrada Larga di Milano al
ſegno dell' Aquila. 1736

Paolo Antonio Teſtore figlio
di Carlo Giuſeppe Teſtore
in Contrada Larga di Milano al Segno dell' Acquila.
1759

Theodoti Giovanni. See Teodotti Giovanni.

Theoditi Hieronymus. See Teodoti.

Thir Tommaso, Trevi-Foligno. 1692. A violin maker, perhaps from Vienna, who is known only from one viola.

Thomas Thir Trebiano
in Italia 1692

Tiburtinus Giuseppe Centurio, Padua. Ca 1780. Worked in the style of Nic. Amati.

Jos. Centurio Tiburtinus in Padua 1780

Tiefenbrucker Jacomo, Milan. 18th century.

Tieffenbrucker Leonard, Venice. 1590. Perhaps son of Vendelius, according to E. G. Baron (author of a German book on lutes) probably a pupil of Leonardo Tieffenbrucker.

1551
In. Padoua Vvendelio Vene
de Leonardo Tiefembrucke

Gorizia:
Comel Stefano, 1937.
Franchi Galliano, 1937.
Michetti Gio Battista, 1764.
Pellizon Antonio, 1759—1850.
Pellizon Antonio, 1815—1869.
Pellizon Carlo, 1811—1891.
Pellizon Filippo, 1817—1897.
Pellizon Giuseppe, d. 1874.
Gradisca (Gorice):
Guargnal Rodolfo, 1937.
Guastalla (Mantova):
Lauzza Mateo, 1918.
Mellini Giovanni, 1768.
Polli Francesco, 1616.
Gubbio (Perugia):
Lepri Luigi, 1880.
Naffisi Carlo, 1867.
Nardelli Michelangelo, 1850.
Nastesi Valento.
Pieroni Luigi, 1833—1847.
Pierotti Luigi, 1787—1823.
Guiglia (Modena):
Pianazzi Domenico, 1760—1780.
Chiaggio (Arezzo):
Giacomo, 1346.
Giacomo, 16th century.
Wagner Dom. Casp., 1725.
Chiavari (Genoa):
Castagnino Giuseppe, 20th century.
Chieti (Abruzzio):
Maviglia Francesco, b. 1902.
Muzio Francesco di, 1830, 1838.
Iddiano (Modena):
Cornia Giuseppe, 1884—1894.
Imola (Bologna):
Berati, 1760—1784.
Contavalli Luigi, b. 1862.
Contavalli Primo di Luigi, b. 1899.
Ivrea:
Pietti Lorenzo, 1935.
Jesi (Ancona):
Giombini Egio, b. 1907.
Langres:
Raynaldi Antonio, 1517.
Lauria (Potenza):
Alagio Nicola, b. 1879.
Lavagna (Genoa):
Ravena Giovanni Battista, 19th cent.
La-Valetta (Island of Malta):
Tonna, 1850.
Lecce:
Genovese Ricardo, b. 1883.
Milella Giuseppe.
Milella Vito, 1870—1880.
Legnano (Milano):
Franchi Ernesto, 1940.
Lentigione di Brescello:
Vaccari Raffaelle, b. 1908.
Livorno:
Bastogi Gaetano, 18th cent.
Becchini Renzo, b. 1911.
Compare Vittorio, 1898.
Dulfenn Alexander, 1689—1700.
Giraniani (Gragnani?), 1730.
Gragnani Antonio, 1740—1800.
Gragnani Gennaro, 1730.
Gragnani Jacopo, 1743.
Gragnani Onorato, 1785—1799.
Livorno Vincenzo, da 1862.
Locchi Gius, Bern., b. 1895.
Magri Francesco, 1766—1784.
Meiberi Francesco, 18th century.
Lodi:
Baroncini Michele.
Zanotti Antonio, 1709—1740.
Lonigo:
Chiavellati Domenico, 1780—1796.
Lovere:
Amighetti Giacomo, 1914.
Lucca:
Campetti Lorenzo, 1833.
Cicognani Umberto, 1945.
Davini Giusto, 19th century.
Faustino, 17th cent.
Gentile Michele, 1883.
Giovanetti Leonardo, b. 1816, d. 1884.
Giovanetti Luigi, 1840.
Giusti Giovanni Battista, 1682—1693.
Maffei Lorenzo, 1767—1787.
Palma Paolo, 1760.
Peregrino Giovanni, 1689.
Spelta Osvaldo, 1937.
Storino Giovanni, 1725.
Lucignano:
Dini Giovanni Battista, 1700—1707.
Lugano:
Andina Francesco, b. 1891.
Lubino, 1750.
Vistoli Luigi, b. 1890.
Lugo:
Rasura Vincenzo, 1785.
Stefanini Giuseppe, b. 1908.
Vistoli Luigi, b. 1890.
Macerata near Ancona:
Finoravanti Andrea, 1741—1747.
Norfi Floriano, b. 1922.
Spalletti Antonio, 1865.

Macerone:
Milandri Galiano, 1930.
Malo (Vicenza):
Boriero Alfonso, 19th cent.
Mancasale (Reggio):
Gallingani, 19th cent.
Mantua:
Albani Nicolo, 1763—1770.
Bachetta Giuseppe, 1780.
Baccani Stefano, 19th century.
Balestrieri Tommaso, 1720—1790.
Barbieri Francesco, 1695—1750.
Barbieri Pietro, 1821—1864.
Bonoris Cesare, 1568.
Camilli Camillos, 1704—1754.
Coppi Sante de, 1800—1817.
Dalla Costa Pietro Antonio, 1700—1768.
Dall Aglio Giuseppe, 1723—1775.
Dall Aglio Giuseppe, 1795—1840.
Dardelli Fra Pietro, 1497—1500.
Dionelli Gaetano, 1865—1869.
Gadda Gaetano, b. 1900.
Grancino Giovanni Battista, 1727.
Guarneri Pietro, b. 1655, d. 1728.
Legnamaro Pietro, d. 1569.
Luppi Giovanni, 19th cent.
Martini Oreste, b. 1893.
Morella Morglato, 1545—1602.
Mutti Vittorio, b. 1903.
Pesseti Giovanni Battista, 1674.
Raccoris Nicolo, 1760.
Scarampella Stefano, b. 1843, d. 1927.
Simonis Loreto, 1800.
Smith Domenico, 1647.
Solferini Remo, b. 1882.
Soliani Angelo, 18th cent.
Stefanini Carlo, 1764—1790.
Stelluto Lorenzo, b. 1886.
Taffelli Alessandro, 1619.
Targhetta Carlo, 16th—17th cent.
Virchi Giovanni Paolo, b. 1552, d. 1612.
Zanotti Antonio, 1709—1740.
Zanti Alessandro, 1765—1819.
Marano sul Parano (Modena):
Obici Prospero, 1880.
Saltinari Giacomo, 1880.
Mariano Comense (Como):
Erba Carlo, b. 1905.
Erba Paolo, b. 1874, d. 1927.
Usuelli Eraldo, b. 1879.
Marina di Ravena:
Dolcini Renato, 1903.
Massa:
Chericoni Carlo, 1935.
Medolla:
Pellacani, b. 1900.
Mercato Cilenico:
De Luccia Gennaro, b. 1901.
Messina:
Chiarelli Andrea, b. 1675, d. 1699.
Gastono Antonio, 1890, 1896.
Grinaldi Carlo, 1681.
Ionata Luigi, b. 1883.
Lazzaro Giov., b. 1913.
Pettinato Pietro, b. 1883.
Spadaro Bertuccio, 19th—20th cent.
Milan:
Airaghi Cesare, 1883—1915.
Albani Giuseppe, b. 1684, d. 1712.
Albani Nicolo, 1763—1770.
Alberti Fernando, 1730—1769.
Albertini Carlo, b. 1866, d. 1940.
Allegri Giovanni, 1714.
Angiollo Luigi fu Giacinto, 20th cent.
Antolini Francesco, 19th cent.
Antoniazzi Riccardo, b. 1858, d. 1910.
Antoniazzi Romeo, b. 1862.
Arassi Erezzo, b. 1889.
Arienti Carle Giuseppe, 1810—1863.
Artalli Giuseppe Antonio, 1765.
Artioli Antonio, 1880.
Auciello Luigi, b. 1881.
Auria Fratelli.
Bajoni Luigi, 1838, d. 1878.
Balcaini, 18th cent.
Barnia Fedele, 1760—1780.
Bassi Leandro, 1910—1920.
Batiazza Antonio Maria, 1707.
Battaglia Antonio, 1757—1766.
Ballone Pietro Antonio, 1691—1708.
Bendini Pietro Antonio, 1691—1708.
Bendini Giambattista, 1668.
Benettini, 1868.
Benito Antonio, 1664.
Bisiach Andrea, b. 1890.
Bisiach Giacomo, b. 1900.
Bisiach Leonardo, I, b. 1864, d. 1946.
Bisiach Leandro II, b. 1904.
Bobi Giuseppe, b. 1891.
Borgia Antonio, 1765—1772.
Bozzolo Pietro, b. 1830, d. 1907.
Bortolotti Luigi, 1810—1830.
Bortolotti Luigi, 1860—1875.
Bozzi Raffaelo, b. 1905.
Bresa Francesco, 1700—1708.
Briani Cipriano, d. 1920.
Broga Brossa Francesco, 1710—1740.
Cabroli Lorenzo, 1716.

Capo, 1717, 1718.
Carlo, Giuseppe 1769.
Catignoli Giuseppe, 1850.
Colombo Camillo, 1937.
Compostano Antonio, 1699—1710.
De Peccati Umberto, 1937.
Farotti Celeste, b. 1864, d. 1928.
Farotto Celestino, b. 1905.
Farotto Salvatore, b. 1875.
Finolli Giuseppe, 1750, 1755.
Fiscer Carlo Vincenzo, 1770.
Fiscer Giuseppe, 1760, 1764.
Flarotti Celeste, 20th cent.
Galbusera Carlo Antonio, 1813—1833.
Galimberti Luigi, b. 1888.
Gatti Angelo, 1937.
Gerardi Marco, 1920—1950.
Giacinti Celeste, 20th cent.
Gianoli Domenico, 1731.
Giulietti Armando, b. 1903.
Giulietti Tullio, b. 1873, d. 1933.
Gramino Giovanni, 1722, 1724.
Grancino Andrea, 1646.
Grancino Francesco, 1690—1746.
Grancino Giovanni, 1675—1737.
Grancino Giovanni Battista, 1669—1710.
Grancino Giovanni Battista, 1697—1735.
Grancino Gramino, 1722.
Grancino Paolo, 1665—1692.
Guadagnini Giovanni Battista I., b. 1683, d. 1768.
Guadagnini Giovanni Battista, b. ca 1711, d. ca 1786.
Guadagnini Giuseppe, b. 1736, d. ca 1805.
Isep Carlo Giuseppe, 1800.
Landolfi Carlo Fernando, b. 1714, d. ca 1787.
Landolfi Pietro Antonio, 1750—1800.
Lavazza Antonio Maria, 1703—1722.
Lavazza Santino, 1634.
Lavazza Santino, 1718—1780.
Laviguetta Antonio, 1900.
Leoriporri Giovanni Francesco, 1755, 1759.
Luppo Francesco Antonio, 1716.
Malagutti Arminio, b. 1914.
Manfredini Eros, 1940.
Mantegazza Carlo, 1760.
Mantegazza Francesco, 1747—1760.
Mantegazza Giovanni, 1760—1790.
Mantegazza Pietro. Giovanni, 1750—1790.
Manzone Giovanni, 1624.
Marafi Ambrogio, 18th cent.
Marchetti Abbondio, 1815—1840.
Martineghi Marcello, 1937.
Mazzochi. A, 1901.
Meloni Antonio, 1690—1694.
Menticasia.
Merighi Antonio, 1800.
Mezzadri Francesco, 1700—1758.
Milani Francesco, 1742—1751.
Milani Giuseppe Carlo, 1769.
Montanari Luigi, d. 1908.
Montani Costante.
Monzino Antonio, 1725—1800.
Monzino Antonio, 1799—1872.
Monzino Antonio, 1847—1930.
Monzino Antonio, 1885—1918.
Monzino Antonio, b. 1909.
Monzino Giacomo Antonio, 1772—1845.
Monzino & Figli.
Moretti Antonio, 1730.
Mussolessi Giuseppe, 1940.
Novelli Natale, b. 1908.
Ornati Giuseppe, 1937.
Pacherele Vincenzo, 1885.
Pasta Bartolomeo, 1681.
Pedrazzini Giuseppe, b. 1879.
Poli Giovanni, 1850—1882.
Ponzi Giulio, 1850.
Posta Cristofano, 1666.
Presbler Francesco, 1730—1773.
Presbler Giuseppe, 1760—1801.
Ravenna Luciano, 1919.
Ravizza Carlo, b. 1882.
Ricordi Giovanni, d. 1853.
Riva Severino, 1917.
Rivolta Giacomo, 1800—1834.
Rossani Salvatore, 1920.
Rossi Gaetano, 19th cent.
Rossi Nicola, 1842, 1844.
Rovescalli Azzo b., 1880, d. 1941.
Rovetta Antonio, 1840—1884.
Saconi Benigno, 1910.
Salvaterra Francesco, 1609.
Sanazzo Santino, 1690—1740.
Santo Santino, 1684—1700.
Sassi Alessio, 1784.
Schiavoni Tullio, 1939.
Scoti Antonio, 1733—1747.
Scrosati Giovanni Domenico, 1775.
Sgarabotto Gaetano, Caval., b. 1878.
Sironi Ambrogio, b. 1901, d. 1934.
Smit Giovanni, 1646.
Tanegia Carlo Antonio, 1725—1731.
Tarasconi Giuseppe, 1888—1908.
Tarasconi Mirco, 20th cent.
Terrana Gerlando, b. 1909.
Testator Vecchio il., 16th cent.
Testore Carlo Antonio, b. 1688, d. 1764.
Testore Carlo Giuseppe, b. 1660, d. 1737.
Testore Gennaro, 1767.

Testore Giovanni, 1764.
Testore Paolo Antonio, 1690—1750.
Tiefenbrucker Jacomo, 18th cent.
Ullmann Georg, b. 1879.
Vascallo Giovanni, 18th cent.
Vecchio Testator il, 1520—1560.
Ventura Annibale, 1740.
Ventura Antonio, b. 1910.
Ventura Enrico.
Vimercati Gasparo, 1766.
Worschel Antonio, 1697.
Zanardi Giuseppe, 1937.
Zerboni Antonio, 1829.

Mirandola:
Ferri Primo, 1848—1850.

Modena:
Abbati Giambattista, 1755—1795.
Adani Pancrazio, 1770—1820.
Baraldi Alfonso, 1879—1891.
Baldi Giovanni, 1760.
Belcioni Antonio, 1663—1673.
Bertani, 19th cent.
Bonardi Domenico, 1728.
Borghi Pietro, 1893—1921.
Braglia Antonio, 1790—1820.
Braidi Geminiano, 1790—1805.
Braidi Giovanni, 1766.
Calori-Stremiti Eugenio, 1840.
Cassini A., 1630—1710.
Cristoni Eusebio, 1847—1883.
Despines G., 1770—1780.
Dodi Giovanni, 19th cent.
Dodi Fratelli, 19th cent.
Faustino Luca, 17th cent.
Fiori Andrea, b. 1796, d. 1870.
Fiori Gaetano, 1798—1872.
Gavoni Antonio, 1777.
Gianni Alessio, 1793.
Gibertini Giuseppe, 1800.
Guerra Giacomo, 1810.
Heisele Jacob, 1614, 1619.
Jori Ensa, b. 1891.
Jori Orlando, b. 1915.
Lancilotto Jacopino, 1507—1551.
Lecchi Enrico, 1885.
Lucci Giuseppe, b. 1910.
Maccari Antonio, 1885—1890.
Malagoli Eleuterio, d. 1827.
Malagoli Folgenzio, 1856.
Manfredi Francesco, b. 1902.
Mani Paolo, 1809, 1811.
Manni Pietro, 1827.
Mantelli, 18th cent.
Manzini Lodovico, b. 1804, d. 1878.
Martinelli, 17th cent.
Marverti A., 1834.
Messori Pietro, b. 1870.
Modeni Antonio, 1831.
Montanari Enrico.
Mucchi Antonio, 1800, d. 1883.
Muzzarelli Demetrio, 1880.
Parmeggiani Romolo, b. 1888.
Pasio Lodovico, 1506.
Piccagliani Antonio, b. 1914.
Piccagliani Armando, 1879—1945.
Picciotto, 1930.
Piva Giovanni, 1860—1880.
Pollastri Antonio, 1765—1800.
Pollastri Giuseppe, 1764—1783.
Richter, 1808.
Righi Antonio, 1817.
Rinaldi Celeste, 1878.
Rossi Fernando, 1880.
Saratelli Carlo Antonio, 1913.
Segizo Girolamo Maria, b. 1503, d. 1553.
Seraphin Giorgio, 1841—1887.
Sgarbi Giuseppe, 1818—1905.
Soliani Angelo, 1752—1810.
Strauch Matteo, 1640.
Tadolini Giuseppe, b. ca 1796, d. 1870.
Tadolini Ignazio, b. 1797, d. 1873.
Tantino Constantino, 15th century.
Tantino Giovanni, 1475.
Tantino Sesto, 1461—1490.
Termanini Giuseppe, 1755—1773.
Termanini Pietro, 1755—1773.
Tomasi Carlo Gasparo, 17th or 18th cent.
Valdastri, 1805.
Vecchi Orazio, 1880.
Verini Andrea, 1884.
Zanfi Giacomo, b. 1756, d. 1822.
Zanotti Christofano, 1685.
Zoccoli Pietro, 1753.

Molina di Fiemma (Rovereto):
Cavada Fortunato, 1937.

Molise (Campobasso):
Jorio Giorgio fu Luigi, 1937.

Montagnana:
Degani Domenico, 1820, d. 1887.

Montebello:
Piotti, 19th cent.
Saretta Giuseppe, b. 1894.

Montegno (Sondrio):
Gerosa Giovanni, 1937.

Mont - Orsello:
Bertucci D. Giuseppe, 1741—1777.

Mont Orso (Modena):
Cioni Emilio, 1884—1894.

Scarabelli Agostino, 1884, 1894.
Soncini Luigi, 1831.
Monzino:
Riva Sever., 1917.
Morciano di Romagna:
Arcangeli Udelrico, b. 1889.
Naples:
Abbate Alessandro, 1890—1899.
Abbate Alfonso, 1845.
Abbate Luigi, 1860.
Achille Vinaccia, See Vinaccia Ach.
Amati Pietro, 1581—1627.
Ambrosio d'Antonio, 1870—1896.
Angelin Domenico, 1625—1630.
Arezzo Nicolo, 20th cent.
Avellano e figlio, 1894.
Avenia Carlo, 1780—1810.
Avenia d'L., 1888.
Bairhoff Giorgio, 1757—1786.
Bellarosa Vittorio, b. 1907.
Blasio Raffaele di, 1780.
Bolli, 1897.
Bora Eugen, 1905.
Borani A., 1873.
Botello Angelo, 1857.
Calace Antonio, 1828—1875.
Calace Giuseppe fu Raffaele, 20th cent.
Calace Nicola, 1881—1903.
Calace Raffaele, b. 1863, d. 1934.
Cardillo Luigi, 1790—1799.
Carone Giuseppe, 1883.
Celentano Michael.
Christophori Pietro, 1790—1800.
Circapa Tommaso, 1730, 1735.
Contino Alfredo, b. 1890.
Coppo Armando, 1608.
Coppo Raffaele.
Costa Alfonso della, 1876.
Cristofaro E. de, b. 1870.
Curatoli Alfredo, 1885.
Curatoli Antonio, 1900.
Dalla Corte Alfonso, 1828—1882.
D'Ambrosio Antonio, 1817.
D'Avenia Carlo, 1788.
D'Avenia L., 1888.
De Blosij Nicolo, 1795.
De Luccia Matteo, 1819—1877.
De Luccia Michele, b. 1924.
Desiato Giuseppe, 1890—1906.
Desiato Luigi, 19th cent.
Desiato Vincenzo, 1855.
Dinacci Antonio, 19th cent.
Donozetto Pietro, 1789.
Eberle Tommaso, 1760—1792.
Enrico Giovanni di, 1590—1608.
Esposito Giosue, 1890, 1900.
Fabricatore Gennaro, 1773—1832.
Fabricatore Giovanni Battista, 1780—1811.
Fabricatore Pietro, 1780—1799.
Fabricatore Vincenzo, 1770.
Ferrer Antonio, 1481.
Filano Antonio, 1787.
Filano Donato, 1763—1783.
Filano Giuseppe, 1785—1797.
Filano Luigi, 1821, 1832.
Follis Carlo, 1790—1810.
Gagliano Alberto, 1877.
Gagliano Alessandro, b. 1660, d. 1725.
Gagliano Antonio, b. 1728, d. 1795.
Gagliano Antonio, b. ca 1794, d. 1860.
Gagliano Fernando, b. 1724, d. 1781.
Gagliano Gaetano, b. ca 1770, d. 1824.
Gagliano Gennaro, 1700—1770.
Gagliano Giovanni, 1800—1867.
Gagliano Giuseppe, 1725—1793.
Gagliano Joannes (Giovanni I), 1740, d. 1806.
Gagliano Nicola, fil. Alessandro, b. 1670, d. ca 1740.
Gagliano Nicola, 1770—1826.
Gagliano Nicolo, 1780—1795.
Gagliano Raffaele, b. 1790, d. 1857.
Gagliano Vincenzo, 1870—1886.
Galiani Alexander.
Galieri Filippo, 18th cent.
Gamboni, b. 1724, d. 1814.
Garani Nicola, 1700.
Gardelli Federico, 1880—1900.
Gerani N., 1790—1830.
Grado Gaetano, da.
Grossi Gualterio de.
Jorio Vincenzo, 1780—1849.
Kasermann Giovanni, 1937.
Legnani Luigi, 1765.
Locicero Luciano, 1830.
Lolij Jacopo, 1727.
Loveri Carlo, 1881—1898.
Loveri Diego, b. 1884.
Loveri Giuseppe, 20th cent.
Magnus Antonio, 18th cent.
Man Hans, 1710—1750.
Mango-Longo, 1749.
Maratea Domenico, 1887—1900.
Maratea Michele, 19th cent.
Maratea Michele e Domenico e figli.
Maria Giuseppe da, 1770, 1779.
Micle Gennaro, 1823.
Monachini Francesco, 1725.
Moreno Arturo, 29th cent.
Moro Vito, 1883.

Obbo Marco, 1712—1727.
Obbo Marco, 1803.
Odani Giuseppe Morello, 1738.
Panirillo Pasquale, 1805.
Paolo Luigi, b. 1903.
Pardino Francesco, b. 1906.
Pellecchio Francesco, b. 1890.
Picino Giuseppe, 19th cent.
Pistucci Giovanni, b. 1864.
Popella, 17th cent.
Postiglione Vincenzo, b. 1835.
Postiglione Vincenzo, 19th cent.
Ranaldi Antonio, 1898.
Ricci Luigi, 1898.
Rinaldi Enrico, 1895—1905.
Rosa Nicola, 1680—1720.
Rubino Gennaro, 1899.
Sagliocco Ed. & Co.
Santo Giovanni, 1700—1740.
Seraphine, G., 1900.
Serosati Domenico, 1710—1775.
Steger Lucas, 17th cent.
Tenzel Benedict, 1717.
Tolino Giuseppe, 19th cent.
Tonelli Pietro, 19th cent.
Trapani Raffaele, 1800, 1826.
Valenzano Pietro, 1810—1825.
Ventapane Giuseppe, 19th cent.
Ventapane Lorenzo, 1809—1828.
Ventapane Pasqual, 1740—1801.
Ventapane Vincenzo, 1750—1799.
Verzella Francesco, b. 1864.
Vinaccia Antonio, 1734—1781.
Vinaccia Antonio, 1754—1781.
Vinaccia Domenico, 1780.
Vinaccia Gaetano, 1779—1821.
Vinaccia Gaetano, 1914.
Vinaccia Gennaro, 1755—1778.
Vinaccia Giovanni, 1767, 1777.
Vinaccia Giuseppe, 1914.
Vinaccia Mariano, 1796.
Vinaccia Nicolo, 1715.
Vinaccia Nicolo, 1775.
Vinaccia Pasquale, b. 1806, d. ca 1881.
Vinaccia Vincenzo, 1769—1785.
Vinaccia Fratelli (Gennaro & Achile),.

Necetto (Parma):
Scrollavezza Renato, b. 1927.

Nomi (Trento):
Vinotti Gesualdo, b. 1911.

Novara (Milan):
Gerardi Marco, 1920—1950.
Mombelli Giacomo, b. 1846.
Tarotanus Antonius, 1623.
Torossi Cesare, 1841—1846.

Novellara (Modena): Rizzoti Nicola, 1880.

Osimo (Ancona): Giacco Antonio, 1928.

Ostia (Brescia):
Geroni Domenico, 1800—1820.

Ostiano (Cremona):
Regonini Domenico, b. 1929.

Ostiglia (Mantova):
Telesi Senofonte, 1937.

Padua:
Attore Michele, 1583—1620.
Bagatella Antonio, b. 1755, d. 1829.
Bagatella Pietro, 18th cent.
Bagoletto A., 1782.
Bargazo Francesco, 17th century.
Barrata Ermentoli, 17th cent.
Bergamo Domenico, fu Giacoma, 20th cent.
Borrerio Francesco, 1834.
Branzo Francesco, Barbaro, 1620—1660.
Calzavara Santo, 1764.
Centurio Giuseppe, 1750—1780.
Chiocchi Gaetano, b. 1814, d. 1880.
Dall'Oglio Domenico, b. 1700, d. 1765.
Danieli Giovanni, 1745—1785.
Deconeti Michele, 1752—1795.
Dinumerato Giovanni, 1661.
Galieri Giuseppe, 1753.
Giovanni Antonio, 1744.
Gorrieri Antonio, 1802.
Harton Michael, 1602—1624.
Jansen Andrea, 1629.
Kayser Georgio, 1595.
Krebar Andrea, 16—17th cent.
Krebar Giovanni, 1629.
Lanaro Luigi, b. 1920.
Linarolo Ventura, 1577—1591.
Longo Mangno, 1599.
Mancini Ventura, 1678.
Martino 1572.
Meneghesso Pietro, d. ca 1939.
Meneguzzi Carlo, 1884.
Moro Bartolomeo, 1678.
Mosca-Cavelli C., 1726.
Muratori Rocco, 1704.
Obizzi Tommaso Marchese degli, 1769.
Oglio Domen. dall, 1700—1765.
Palmerio Matteo, 1743—1759.
Picino Carlo, 1726.
Railich Giovanni, 1672—1678.
Railich Pietro, 1644—1670.
Rochi Christofilo, 1620.
Spilman Dorigo, 1591.
Tiburtinus Giuseppe, 1780.
Tieffenbrucker Leonardo, 16th cent.

Tieffenbrucker Vendelino, 1572—1611.
Trentin Gregorio, 1768—1854.
Valenciano Maria, 1764.
Verle Francesco, 1590, 1600.
Wenger Ben Delio, 1622.
Zanoli Giacomo, 1740—1757.

Palermo:

Agostini Sante, 1822.
Agostino Nicolo d', 19th cent.
Albani Michele, 18th cent.
Albani Paolo, 1630—1695.
Averna Alfonso.
Averna Alfredo, 1937.
Averna Enrico, 20th cent.
Casiglia Casimoro, 1869.
Di Leo Camillo, 20th cent.
Di Leo Domenico, b. 1878.
Di Leo Domenico.
Liverani Ettore, 1937.
Megazzi Enrico, 1830.
Panormo Vincenzo, b. 1734, d. 1813.
Pedrazzi Pietro, 1870.
Perollo Luigi, 1894.
Ragona Pietro, 1840.
Selva Giuseppe, b. 1904.
Sgarbi Antonio, b. 1866.

Parma:

Albani Paolo, 1705—1720.
Borelli Andrea, 1720—1746.
Borelli Antonio, Cesare, 1792.
Broschi Carlo, 1730—1744.
Carboni Gius. & Eugen, 1890—1942.
Costa Felice Mori, 1802, 1812.
Donati Frederico, 1765—1775.
Galli Domenico, 1687—1691.
Garsi Ant., 1875—1914.
Ghidini Carlo, 1746—1773.
Gibertini Antonio, 1797—1866.
Gisalberti Andreas, 1716, 1721.
Guadagnini Giovanni Battista, 1685—1770.
Guadagnini Giovanni Battista, 1711—1786.
Guadagnini Giuseppe, 1736—1805.
Leoni Fernando, 1816.
Leoni Giovanni, 1870.
Mancini Ventura, 1678.
Mantovani, 16th cent.
Mantovani Alessandro, 1853—1858.
Merighi Pietro, 1770.
Pellegri, 19th cent.
Realli Cosma Battista, 1667.
Sgarabotto Gaetano b. 1878.
Sgarabotto Pietro, b. 1903.
Sgarbi Antonio, b. 1866.
Ventura Giovanni, 1622.

Zillioli Domenico, 1792.

Pavia:

Alberti Adalberto, 1920.
Carboni Gius. & Eugen., 1890—1942.
Catenaro Gaetano, 1639—1670.
Guadagnini Giuseppe, 1736—1805.
Gusnasco Lorenzo, 1500.
Lorenzo Laurentius, 1497—1510.
Romano Pietro, 18th cent.
Rosadoni Giovanni, b. 1905.
Rossi Enrico, b. 1848.
Rossi Giovanni, 1847—1858.
Rossi Guglielmo, 1875—1949.
Rossi Guglielmo, b. 1875.
Salviati Armando.
Sneider Joseph, 1701, 1718.
Vigoni A., 19th cent.

Pergola:

Fiorani Vincenzo, 1855.

Perugia:

Gavelli Giacomo, 1797.
Palla Vincenzo, 1790.
Pallotta Pietro, 1788—1831.
Pierotti Luigi, 1787—1833.

Pesaro:

Assalone Gasparo d', 1690—1740.
Bertucci.
Bertucci Costantino, b. 1860, d. 1930.
Brandini, 1660.
Carlo da Pesaro, 1682.
Cortesi Carlo, 1612.
Del Coradel, 1860—1870.
Domenico, 1522—1548.
Felipuci Pier Lodovico, 1660.
Forni Stefano, 1666.
Mariani Antonio, 1636—1680.
Mariani Fabio, 1679.
Mariani Lodovico, 1692.
Orselli Enrico, b. 1891.
Rollini Giambattista, 1471.
Sacchini Sabattine, 1670, 1686.
Sante, 1670.
Spadari Francesco, 1603—1670.
Spadari Giovanni Battista, 1721.

Pescara:

Palumbi Bernardino, b. 1921.

Pescia:

Fracei Pietro, 1816.

Pescina:

Campi Giuseppe, 1760, 1762.

Piacenza:

Benedetti Giuseppe, 1700.
Comuni Antonio, 1820—1823.
Galieri Giuseppe, 1753.

Guadagnini Giovanni Battista, 1711—1786.
Guadagnini Lorenzo, 1695—1760.
Leb Matias, 1775.
Lorencini Gasparo, 1750.
Lorencini Giov. Bat., 1848—1878.
Nadoti Josef, 1757—1789.
Riva Giovanni, 1884.
Rossi Domenico, d. 1910.
Rossi fu Domenico, 1937.
Rossi Emilio, b. 1895.
Zanotti Giuseppe, 1700.

Piadena:
Bertasio Luigi, 19th cent.
Bertassi Ambrogio, 1730.

Piedmont:
Ceruti Sebastiano, 1615.
Galerzena, 1790.

Pienza: Drinda Giacomo, 18th cent.

Pieve San Stefano:
Lorenzi Giov. Bat., 1848—1878.

Piperno: Visco Bruto, 1600, 1608.

Pisa:
Badalassi Pietro Valentino di, b. 1915.
Belluomini Maurizio, 19th cent.
Bottari Fernando, 1849.
Brandini Fausto, 1777.
Brandini Jacopo, 1789—1807.
Chericoni Carlo, 1935.
Chiochini Pietro, 1740—1760.
Del Senna A., b. 1845, d. 1940.
Grandi Luigi, 1874.
Imperio Annibale, 1750.
Meleandri Adolfo, 1940—1945.
Turchi Gian Martino, 1606.

Pistoia:
Baroncini Giuseppe, 19th cent.
Boccaccini Giuseppe, b. 1836.
Salvadori Giuseppe, 1861, 1863.

Piumazzo:
Monturri Giuseppe, 1840.

Pive di Cento (Bologna):
Carletti Carlo, b. 1873, d. 1941.
Carletti Genuzio, 1949.
Carletti Natale, b. 1904.
Carleti Orfeo, 1873—1944.
Gamberini Claudio, b. 1895.
Gotti Orsolo, b. 1867, d. 1922.
Govoni Guglielmo, b. 1911.

Poggio (Mantova):
Barbieri Giuseppe, 1880.

Polcenigo (Udine):
James Mario, 1809—1839.

Polpenazza:
Bertolotti Francesco, 16th cent.
Bertolotti Santino, 16th cent.

Pontedera:
Lanini Loris, b. 1902.

Pontremoli:
Zara Gaspare, 1896, 1902.

Pordenone: (Udine):
Pera Gerolamo, 1846, 1847.

Quistello: Morselli Arturo, 1862.

Rafallo:
Banni Giuseppe, 1940.

Ravena:
Cavalazzi Ant., b. 1905.
Cavazza Sandro, b. 1903.
Franchi Celso, b. 1905.
Legnani, b. 1790, d. 1877.
Miani Domenico, 18th cent.
Mingazzi Luigi, b. 1859, d. 1933.
Rossini Giovanni Battista Maria, 1765—1777.
Vasi Marco, 1830.

Reggio Emilia:
Bedocchi Mario, 19th cent. 1880.
Belondi Odoastro, b. 1906.
Bertolini Angelo, b. 1881.
Finicchio Bibbiano, 17th cent.
Guastala Alfr., 1949.
Guastala Dante, 1893.
Martani Antonio, b. 1804, d. 1866.
Simonazzi Amedeo, b. 1891.
Simontazzi Riccardo, b. 1929.
Sancini Fernando, b. 1891.
Zani Francesco, 1724—1765.

Rimini (Forli):
Ballarini Santo, 1740—1781.
Capicchioni Marino, b. 1895.
Diotallevi Michelangelo, 1820.
Gori Pietro, 1820.
Lombardi Giulio, 1789.
Paolini, Luigi, b. 1875, d. 1942.
Rinaldi Lodovico 1804.
Sombaldi Giuseppe, 1741.

Ripa (Ascoli):
Desideri Pietro, 1793—1837.
Desideri Raffaele, b. 1797, d. 1871.

Ripa Saravezza (Lucca):
Bertozzi Alfredo, fu Giuseppe, 29th cent.

Ripatrasone (Ascoli):
Capriotti Pacifico, 1884.

Riva:
Desideti Pietro.
Floriani Pietro, b. 1787, d. 1870.

Rolo:
Caprari Francesco, 1846.
De Luca Ant. Di Mateo, 1937.
Fifo Pagliano del, 1840.

Guadagnini Gaetano, 1775—1831.
Guadagnini Gaetano, 1835—1852.
Guadagnini Giovanni Antonio, 1750.
Guadagnini Giovanni Bapt., b. 1685, d. ca 1770.
Guadagnini Giovanni Battista, b. 1711, d. 1786.
Guadagnini Giuseppe, 1884—1900.
Guadagnini Giuseppe, 1890—1900.
Guadagnini Lorenzo, 1790.
Guadagnini Paolo, 20th cent.
Guerra Evasio, b. 1880.
Lione Francesco, 1790.
Marengo-Rinaldi Romano, b. 1866.
Marchetti Edoardo, 1890—1910.
Marchetti Enrico, 1855—1930.
Marchetti Vittorio, 1894.
Massrelli Giuseppe, 1847—1855.
Medard Henri, b. 1629.
Melegari Enrico, 1860—1888.
Melagari Pietro, 1855—1893.
Menighetti Martino, d. 1940.
Michetti Plinio, b. 1891.
Miglini Carlo, 1937.
Mongel A., 1820, 1830.
Morano Arnaldo, b. 1911.
Moruto Carlo, 19th cent.
Moruto Marcelo, 20th cent.
Oddone Carlo Giuseppe, b. 1866.
Oliveri Felice, 1870—1904.
Oliveri Vincenzo, 1878—1889.
Orzero Tommaso, 19th cent.
Pacherle Pierre, b. 1803, d. 1871.
Politi Fernando, 1882—1928.
Pratasini Giovanni, 1780.
Pressenda Gianfrancesco, b. 1777, d. 1854.
Pressenda Raffaele, ca 1790.
Prochet Enrico, 1900.
Ramusio Giovanni, 1779.
Rinaldi Gofredo Benedetto, 1850, d. 1888.
Rinaldi Marengo Romano, b. 1866.
Rocca Giovanni Domenico, 1809.
Rocca Giuseppe Antonio, b. 1807, d. 1865.
Rondani Ernesto, 1884.
Senta Fabricio, 1664.
Senta Felicio, 18th cent.
Spampinato Giuseppe b., 1916.
Torrano, 1700.

Udine:
Gofriller Francesco, 1660—1740.
Moretti Egidio, b. 1894.
Muschietti Renzo.
Muschietti Umberto, b. 1875, d. 1937.
Nonini Giuseppe, b. 1897.
Puppati Francesco, b. 1838.
Seraphin Giorgio, 1841—1887.
Seraphin Santo, b. 1668, d. 1748.
Vaccari...
Veronesi Enrico, b. 1875.
Zugolo Frederico, 19th cent.
Zugolo Pietro. d. 1888.

Umbria:
Tomassuci Cigno, b. 1912.

Urbino:
Costa Lodovico, 1786.

Valenza:
Valenzano Giovanni Maria, 1771—1825.

Valtezze (Bergamo):
Lolio Giovanni Battista, 1740—1750.

Varese (Como):
Giudici Antonio, b. 1860, d. 1931.
Giudici Carlo, b. 1894.
Morilli Mauro, 1937.
Rovescalli Tullio, b. 1906.

Venerio (Reggio Emilia):
Giaroni Elviro, 20th cent.

Venice:
Aceldero Giov. Tonio, 1870—1876.
Alessandro "il Veneziano", 1540.
Amatis Giambattista, 1677.
Castro, 1680—1720.
Andrea Pietro, 1650—1700.
Andreae Joannes, 1511.
Andreolo, 1359.
Angeloni Sigism., 1846—1859.
Anselmo Pietro, 1730—1760.
Antonio Maestro, 16th cent.
Attore Michele, 1583—1620.
Baffo Antonio, b. about 1490.
Barbi Michele, 1748.
Barnia Fedele, 1760—1780.
Bellosio Anselmo, 1715—1789.
Bellosio Giovanni, 1730—1740.
Belosi Antonio, 1734.
Birlotti Giovanni, d. 1920.
Bartoli Giuseppe, 1899.
Bodeni Luigi, 1719.
Bodio Gennaro, 1740.
Bodio Giambattista, 1790—1832.
Bono Gaetano 18th cent.
Bonozzatti Gerolamo, 1899.
Busan Domenico, 1740—1780.
Caspan Giovanni Pietro, 1658—1670.
Cecco Christoforo, 1654.
Cerin Marco, 1610.
Cerin Marc Antonio, 1780—1824.
Chely Francesco, 1742—1753.
Chiericato Luigi, 1912.
Chiocchi Antonio, 1770—1790.
Ciochi Antonio, 1790.

Cliricato Luigi, 1899.
Cocks Christoforo, 1654.
Corara Giacomo, 1775.
Corbucci Domenico, 1775.
Cordano Pietro, 1913.
Cornelli Giorgio, 1797.
Cosetto Giuseppe, 1760—1790.
Costa Giovanni Battista, 1765—1778.
Cozzi Battista, 19th cent.
Dalla Porta Marc Antonio, 1601.
Dall'Ongaro Ignazio, 1747—1783.
Deconetti Giovanni Battista, 1720—1742.
Deconetti Michele, 1752—1795.
Degani Eugenio, b. 1840, d. 1900.
Degani Giulio, b. 1875.
De Luccia Matteo, b. 1819, d. 1877.
De March Carlo, d. 1904.
Domenico, 1522—1548.
Donato Serafino, 1411.
Ebert Enrico, 1655.
Erthel Leopoldo, 1710.
Fabris Luigi, 1838, d. 1873.
Farinato Paolo, 1695—1725.
Faruzi Francesco, 1853.
Fontana Nicolo, b. 1499, d. ca 1557.
Chirardi Giovanni Battista, 1791.
Gobetti Francesco, 1690—1732.
Gofriller Antonio, 1730.
Gofriller Francesco, 1660—1740.
Gofriller Matteo, 1690—1742.
Guarneri Pietro I, 1655—1728.
Guarneri Pietro II, 1695—1762.
Gusnasco Lorenzo, 1500.
Hesin Giacomo, 1566.
Hieber Giovanni, 1560—1590.
Hoch Christian, 17th-18th cent.
Indri Antonio, 1781—1864.
Kaysser Georgius, 1595.
Kaysser Martino, 1609—1632.
Linarolo Francesco, 1540.
Linarolo Giovanni, 1622.
Linarolo Ventura, 1577—1591.
Lorenzo Giovanni Battista Cavaliere de, 1862—1878.
Luglioni Giuseppe, 1777.
Maler Sigismondo, 1460—1526.
Malta Simone, ca 1499.
Marco Antonio, 1700.
Mezzano Frederico, 1695.
Molinari Antonio, 1672—1703.
Molinari Giuseppe, 1737—1763.
Montagnana Domenico, 1690—1750.
Morella Morglato, 1544—1602.
Novello Marco, 1720.
Novello Marc Antonio, 1780—1795.
Novello Pietro Valentino, 1790—1800.
Ongaro Ignazio viz Dall'Ongaro.
Paganoni Antonio, 1750.
Pandolfi Antonio, 1710—1740.
Pietri Pietro, 1690.
Railich Pietro, 1644—1670.
Rechardini Giovanni (Zuane), 1605—1609.
Rechardini Pietro, 1617.
Roche Sebastiano, 1620.
Sansone Maestro Battista, 1540.
Santagiuliana Giacinto, 1770—1830.
Santo Bartolomeo di, 1536.
Sardi, 1649.
Schwarz Giovanni, b. 1865, d. 1937.
Sellas Giorgio, 1624—1680.
Sellas Matteo, 1600—1627.
Seraphin Giorgio, 1742—1747.
Seraphin Santo, b. 1668, d. 1748.
Settin Giuseppe b. 1893.
Siciliano Antonio, 1630—1660.
Siciliano Giacchino, 1670—1680.
Siega Ettore, b. 1860, d. 1936.
Siega Iginio, b. 1903, d. 1936.
Sigismondo, Maestro, 1514.
Stanza Giuseppe, b. 1660, d. 1684.
Steger Magnus, 17th cent.
Straub Michael, 1670—1680.
Tassini Bartolomeo, 1740—1756.
Tecchler David, 1666, d. 1743.
Testore Nicolo, 1755—1765.
Tieffenbrucker Leonard, 1590.
Tieffenbrucker Magnus, 1557—1621.
Tieffenbrucker Moises, 18th cent.
Tieffenbrucker Ulrich, 1521.
Tonide Carlo, 1730.
Tononi Carlo Antonio, 1721—1768.
Tononi Giovanni, 1689—1740.
Tosselli Enrico, 1880—1890.
Unverdorben Max, 1515.
Valonini Zanoli, 1765—1783.
Varangoli Ferrucio, 1885—1916.
Ventura Francesco.
Venturi Leonello, 16th cent.
Vicenardi Paolo, 18th cent.
Vimercati Paolo, 1660—1710.
Vimercati Pietro, 1640—1660.
Violcete Giov. G., 1655.
Zamberti Giuseppe, 1937.
Zanoli Giacomo, 1730—1763.
Zanoli Valentino, 1783.
Zuzzi Vittorio, 20th cent.

Venie: Mercolini Pietro, 1821—1891.

Verica (Frigano):
Bortolotti Giovanni, 1884—1894.

Verucchio (Pesaro):
Vignali Giuseppe, b. 1888, d. 1918.
Verolanuova:
Rosio Paolo, 1857.
Verona:
Andreae Joannes, 1511.
Barbieri Francesco, 1695—1750.
Bastiano, 15th — 16th cent.
Campoy J., 1854—1860.
Capsoni Giovanni & Leopoldo, 1920.
Cardi Luigi, 1857—1886.
Carletti Giovanni, 20th cent.
Carlomordi Carlo, 1650—1670.
Costa Agostino di, 1600—1622.
Daniele, 18th cent.
Dominichino Giuseppe, 1700, 1709.
Foradori Giovanni, 1855, 1860.
Lucca Antonio, 1905—1923.
Maratti Giambattista, 1690, 1700.
Mariatti (Maratti?) Giambattista, 1700.
Obici Bartolomeo, 1665—1685.
Obici Bartolomeo, 1750—1755.
Palazolli Giovanni Battista, 1605.
Rabaglietti Antonio, 1652.
Rauser Sebastian, 1590—1605.
Salviati Francesco, 19th cent.
Sanoni Giovanni Battista, 1680—1740.
Scotto, 1511.
Strati Michael, 1792.
Torelli, 1625.
Zanoli Giacomo, 1740—1757.
Zanoli Giacomo, 1730—1763.
Vescovato near Cremona:
Beltrami Giuseppe, 1870—1881.
Vevey:
Radrizzani Angelo, b. 1870.
Viadana:
Ventura Annibale, 1740.
Viareggio (Lucca):
Giannini Fabricio, b. 1912.
Mei Giovanni Ranieri, b. 1863.
Vicegnano (Pavia):
Ferrari Oreste, 1930.
Vicenza:
Bausaterra Mariano, b. 1927.
Busan Domenico, 1740—1780.
Gerardi, 1810—1820.
Lazzaretti Francesco, 1852—1900.
Lorenzo Giov. Bat., 1862—1878.
Santagiuliana Gaetano, 1804.
Santagiuliana Giacinto, 1770—1830.
Sgarabotto Gaetano Cavaliere, b. 1878.
Vetorazzo Giovanni, 1793.
Vignate:
Travi Erminio.
Villafranca (Piedmont):
Bombirio Domenico, 1720—1730.
Villa Minozza (Modena):
Chiari Francesco, 1880, 1883.
Razzoli Felice, 1880.
Viterbo:
Rubini or Rubis Aug., or Ang., 1763—1771.
Zentis Girolamo de, 1633—1680.
Vittoria (Ragusa): Cinino Angeli, 1900.

SCALE PLANS OF INSTRUMENTS

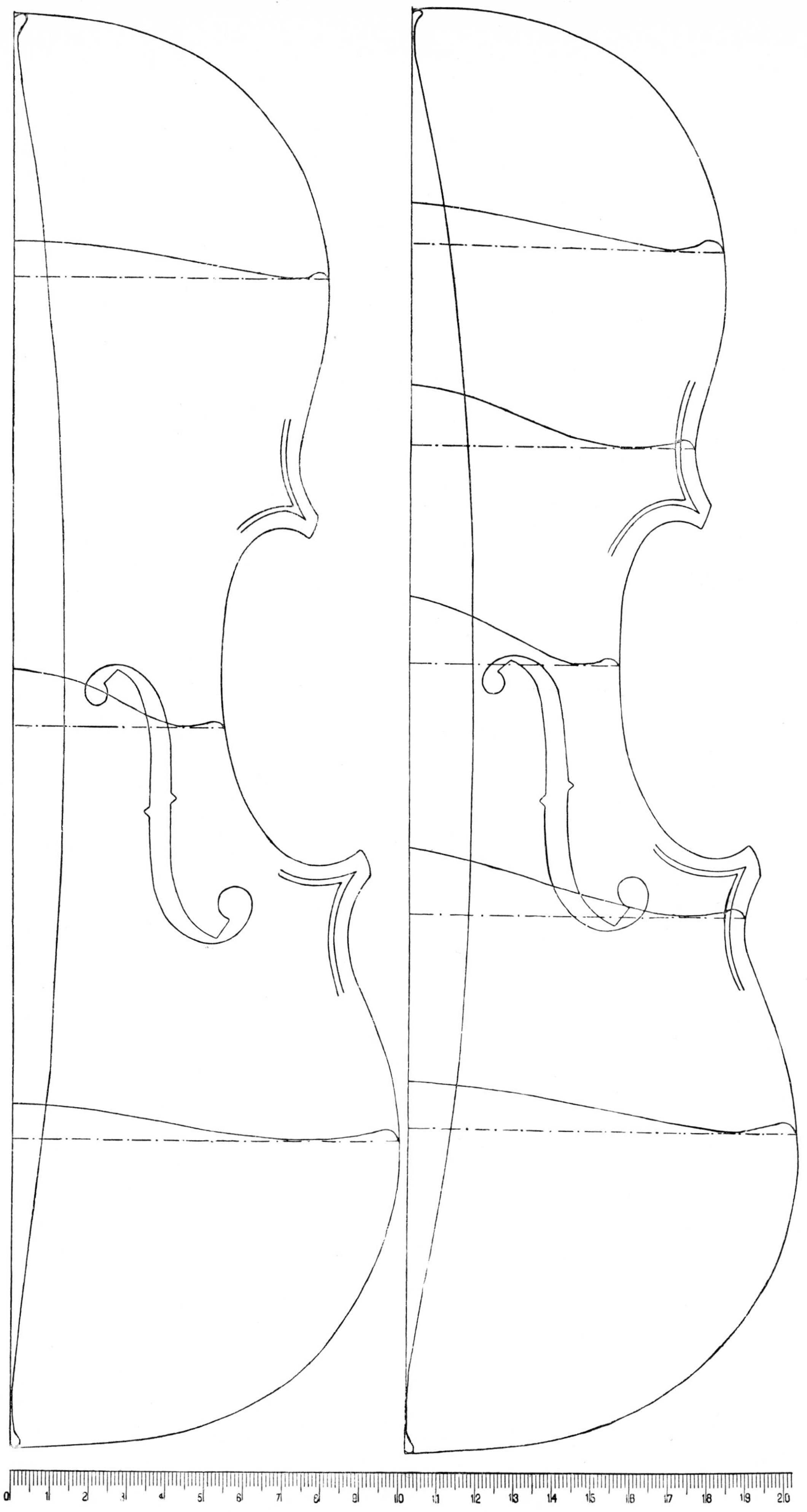

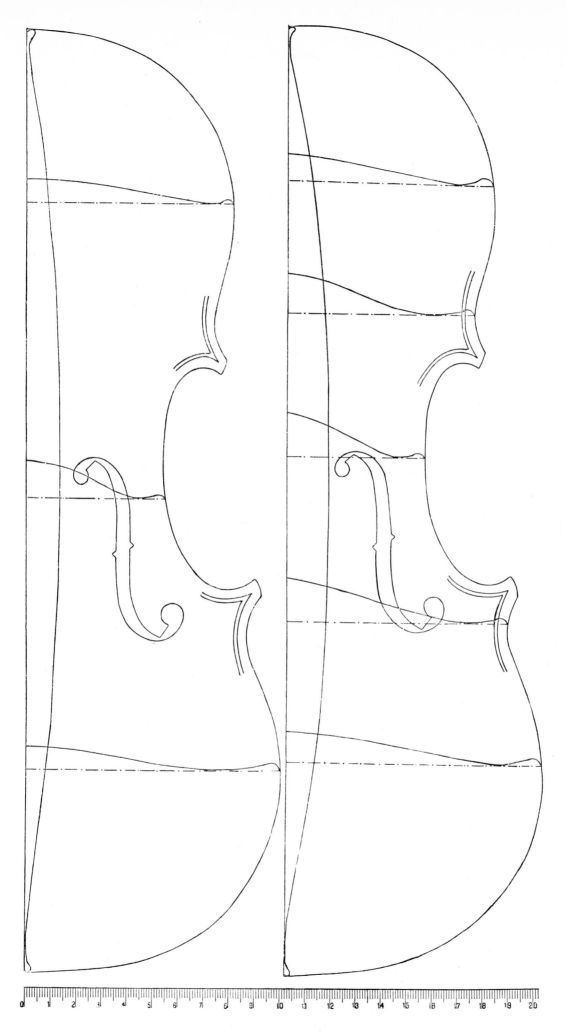

Nicolo Amati, Cremona, 1663

Nicolo Amati, Cremona, 1658

Nicolaus Amatius Cremonica Hieroni-
mi Filius Antoni Nepos fecit 1676

Nicolo Amati, Cremona, 1676

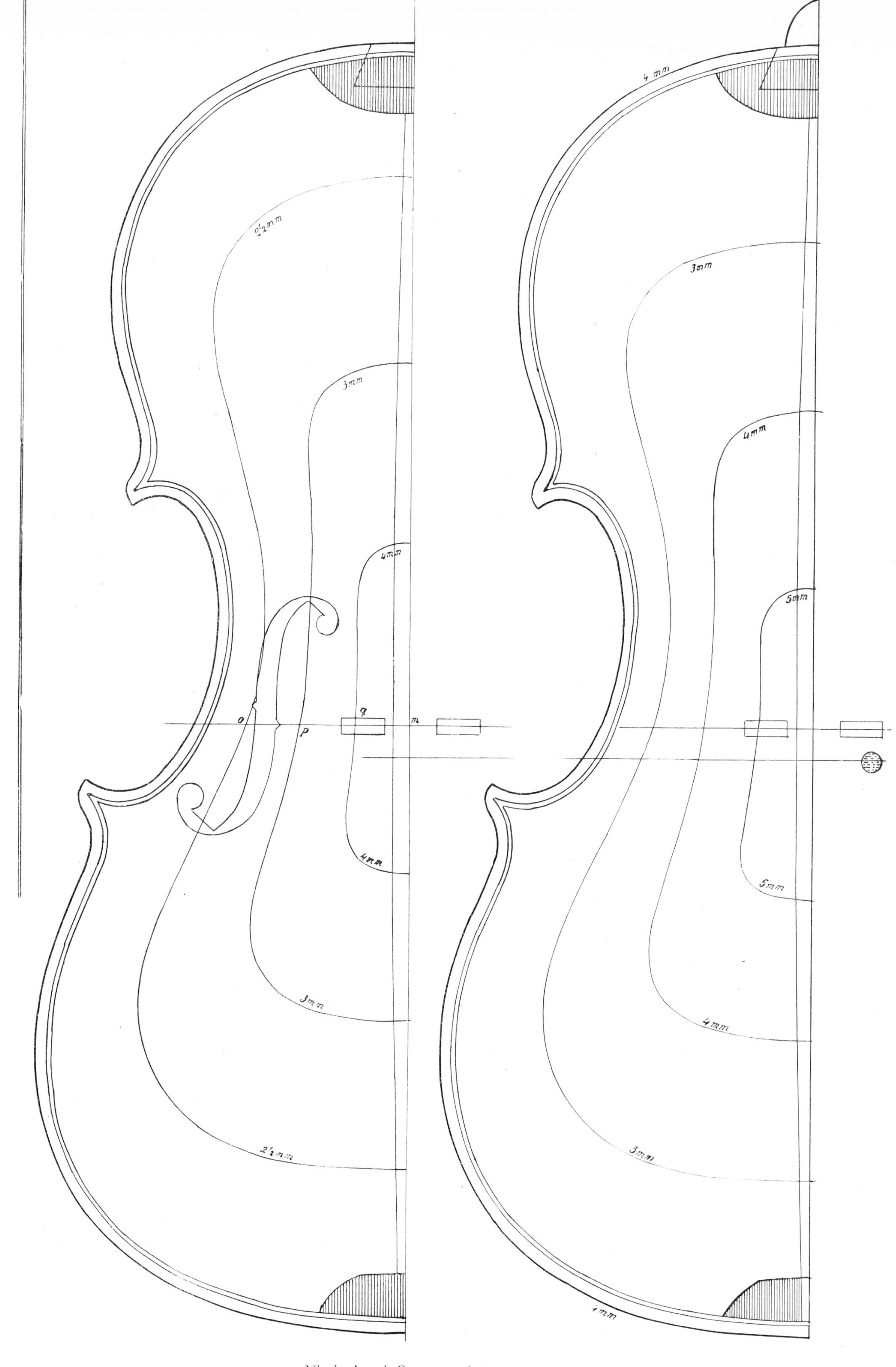

Nicolo Amati, Cremona, 1678

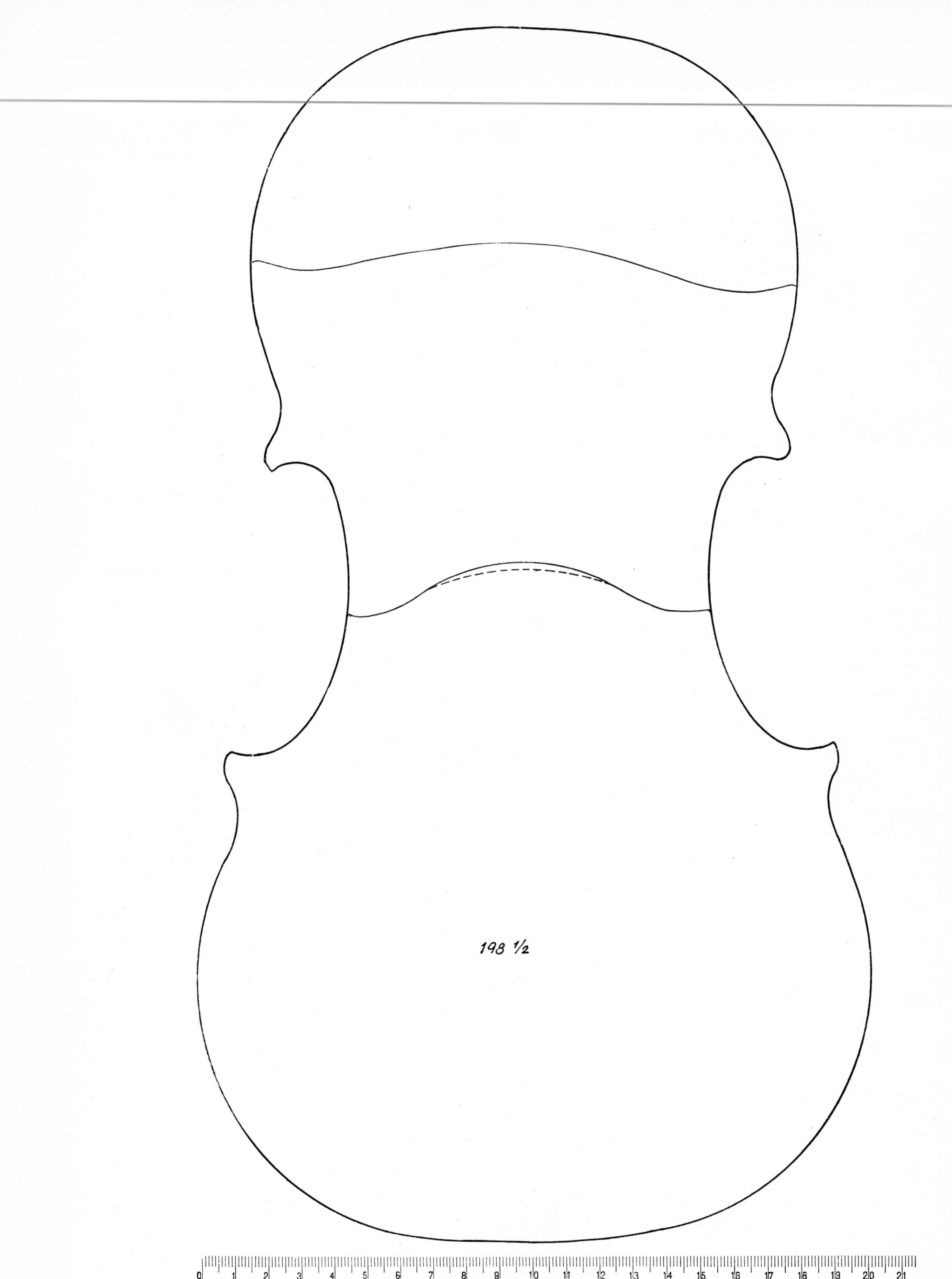

Nicolo Amati, Cremona

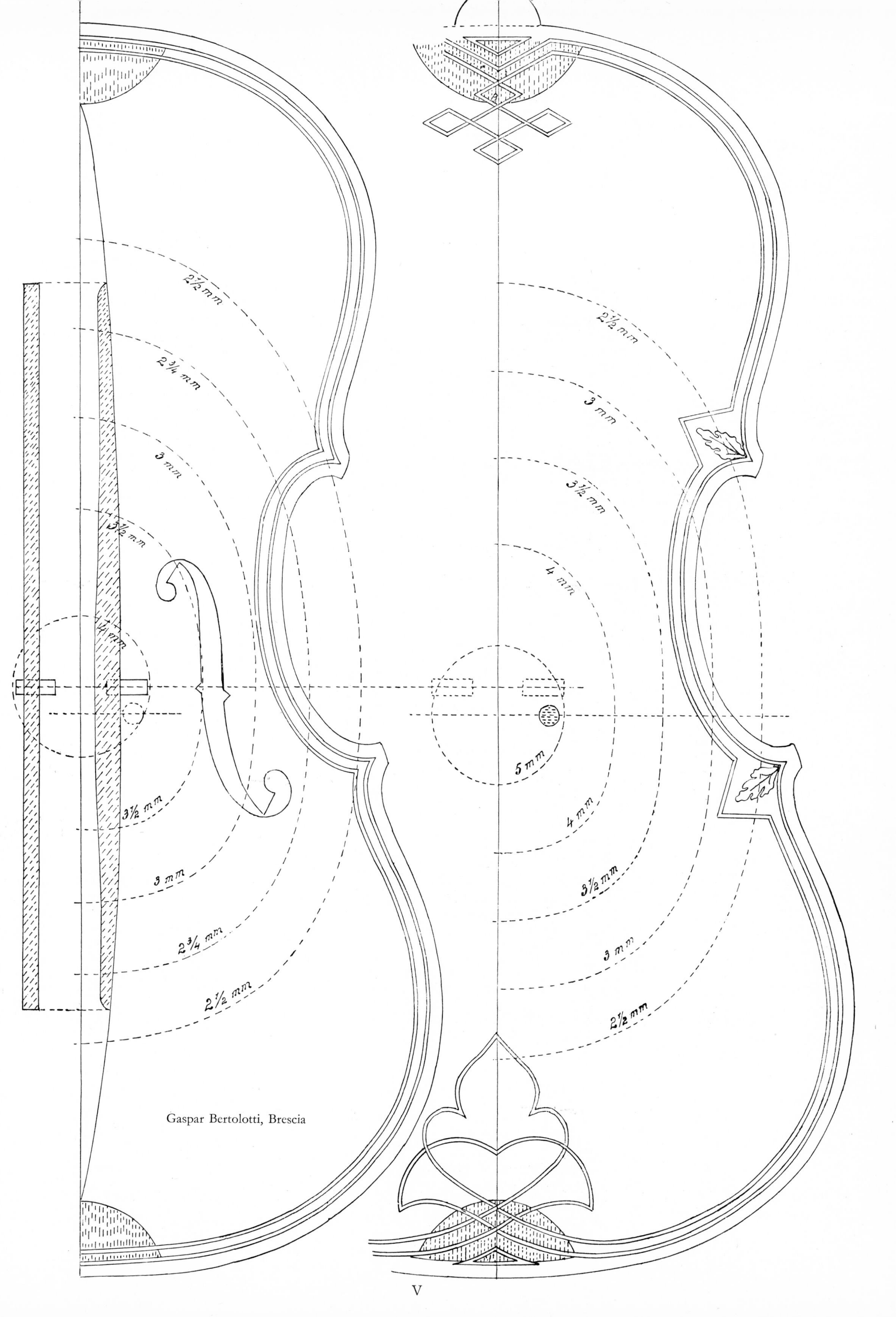

Gaspar Bertolotti, Brescia

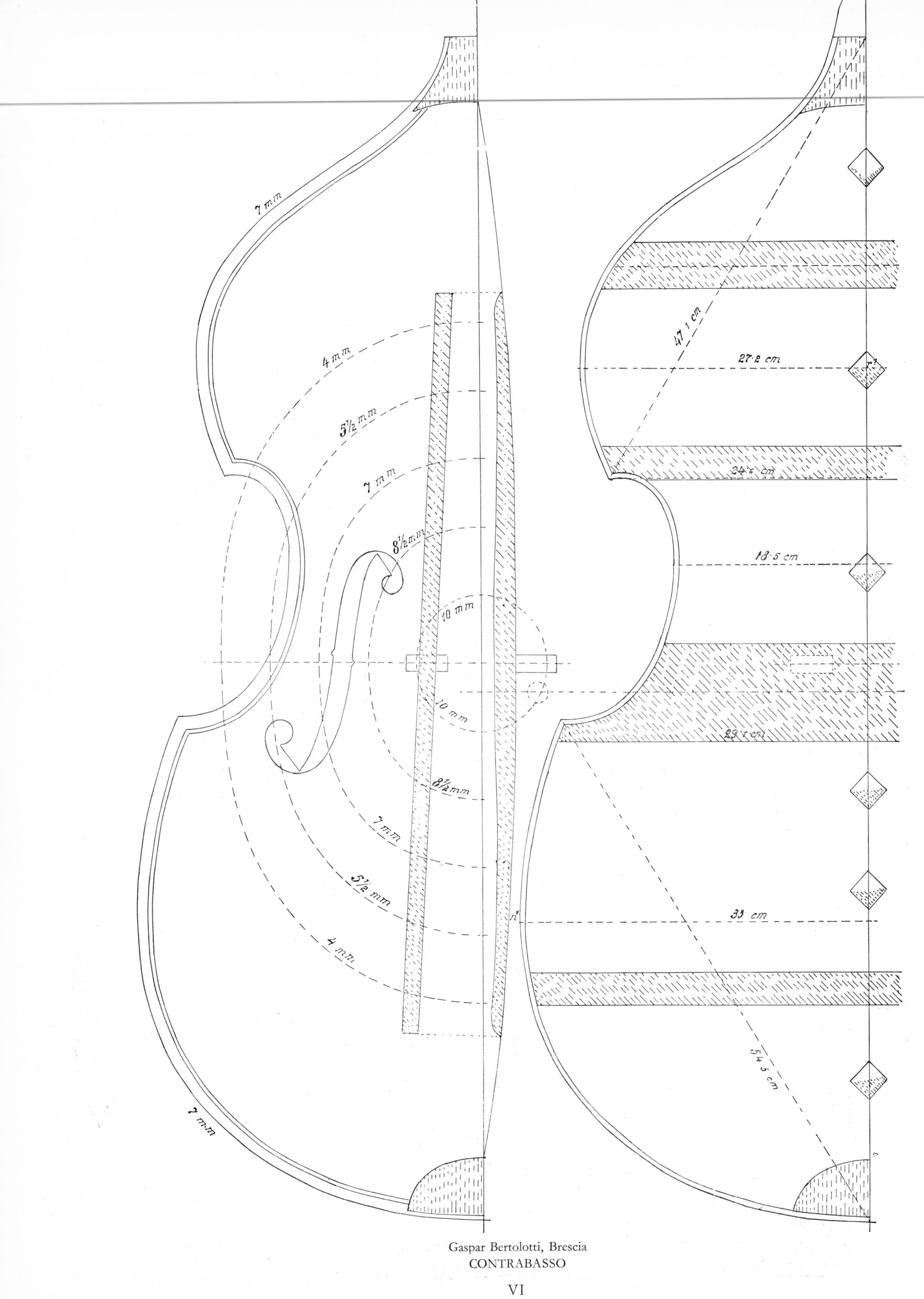

Gaspar Bertolotti, Brescia
CONTRABASSO

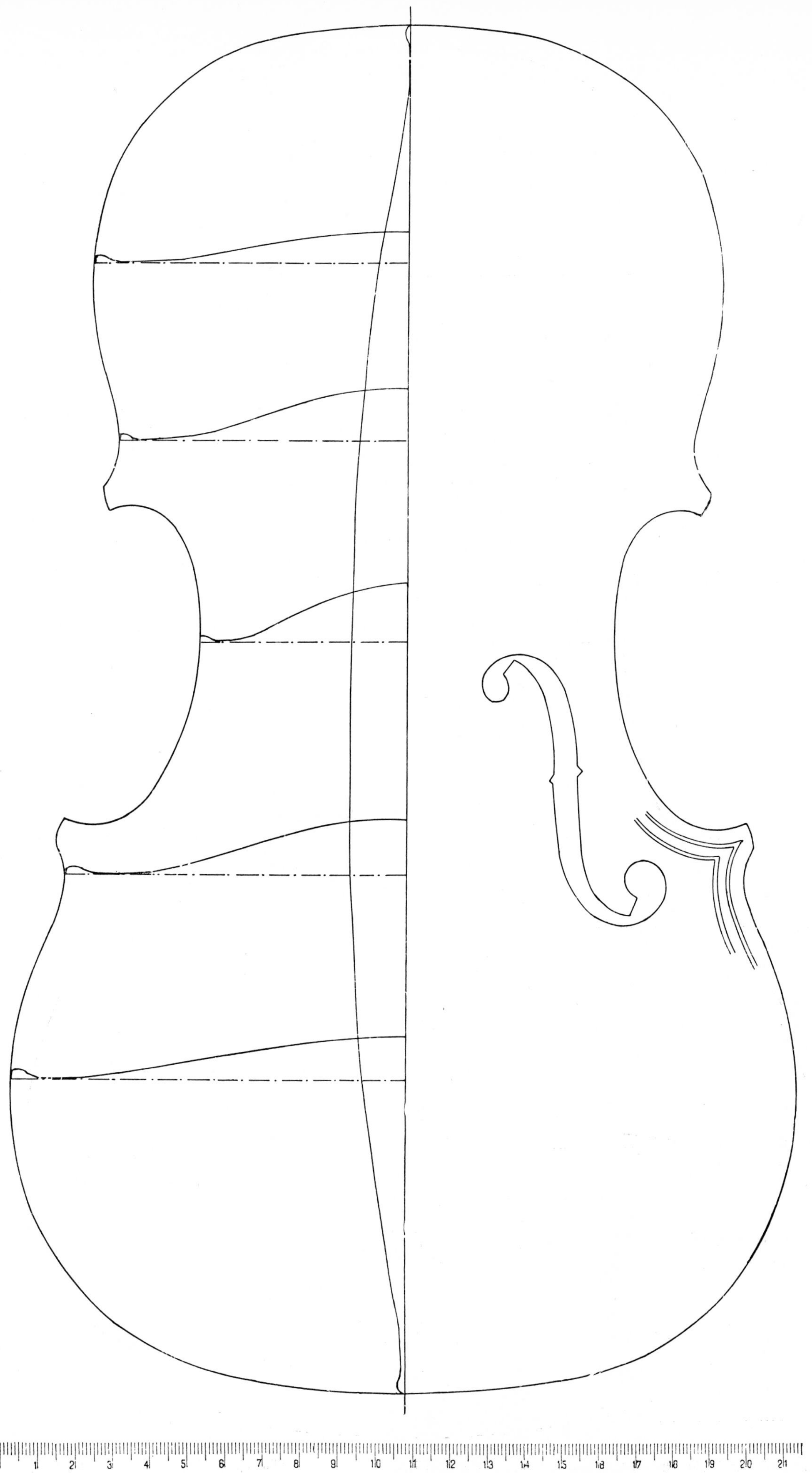

Andrea Guarneri, Cremona, 1635

VII

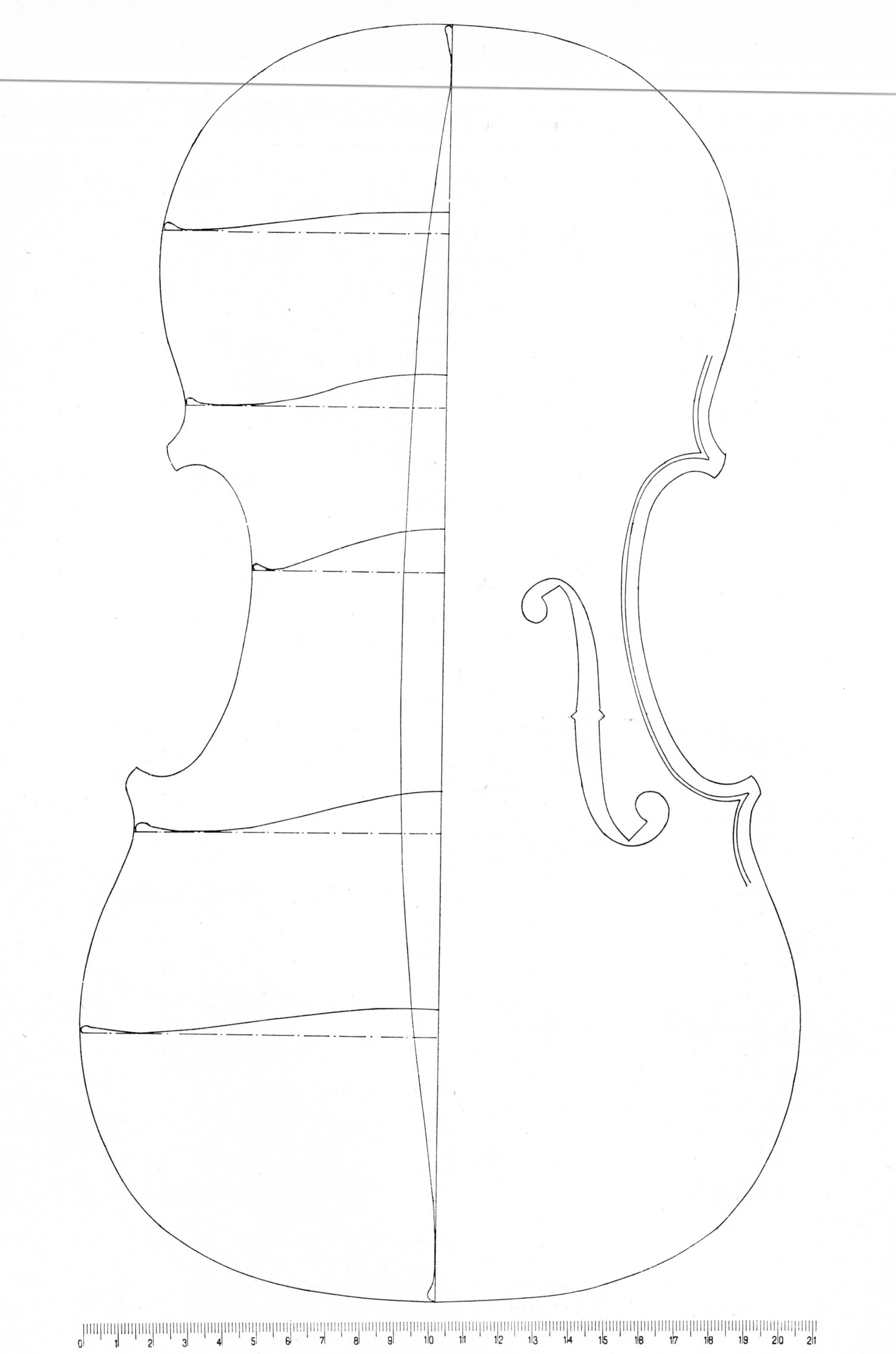

Joseph Guarneri, fil. Andreae, 1735

VIII

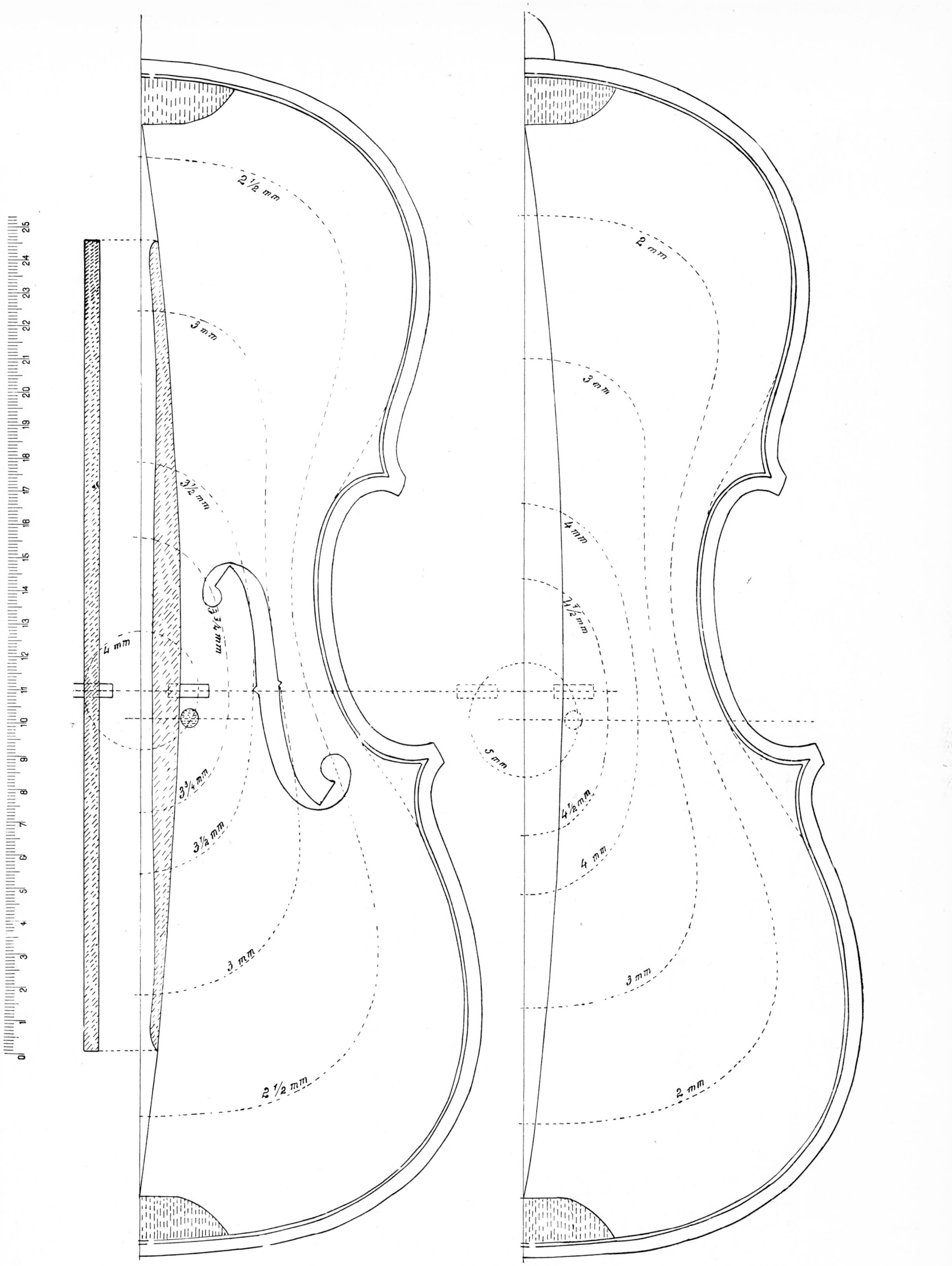

Giuseppe Guarneri del Gesù, Cremona, 1739

0 1 2 3 4 5 6 7 8 9 10 11 12 13 14 15 16 17 18 19 20 21

Giuseppe Guarneri del Gesù
YSAY

Giuseppe Guarneri del Gesù, Cremona, 1734

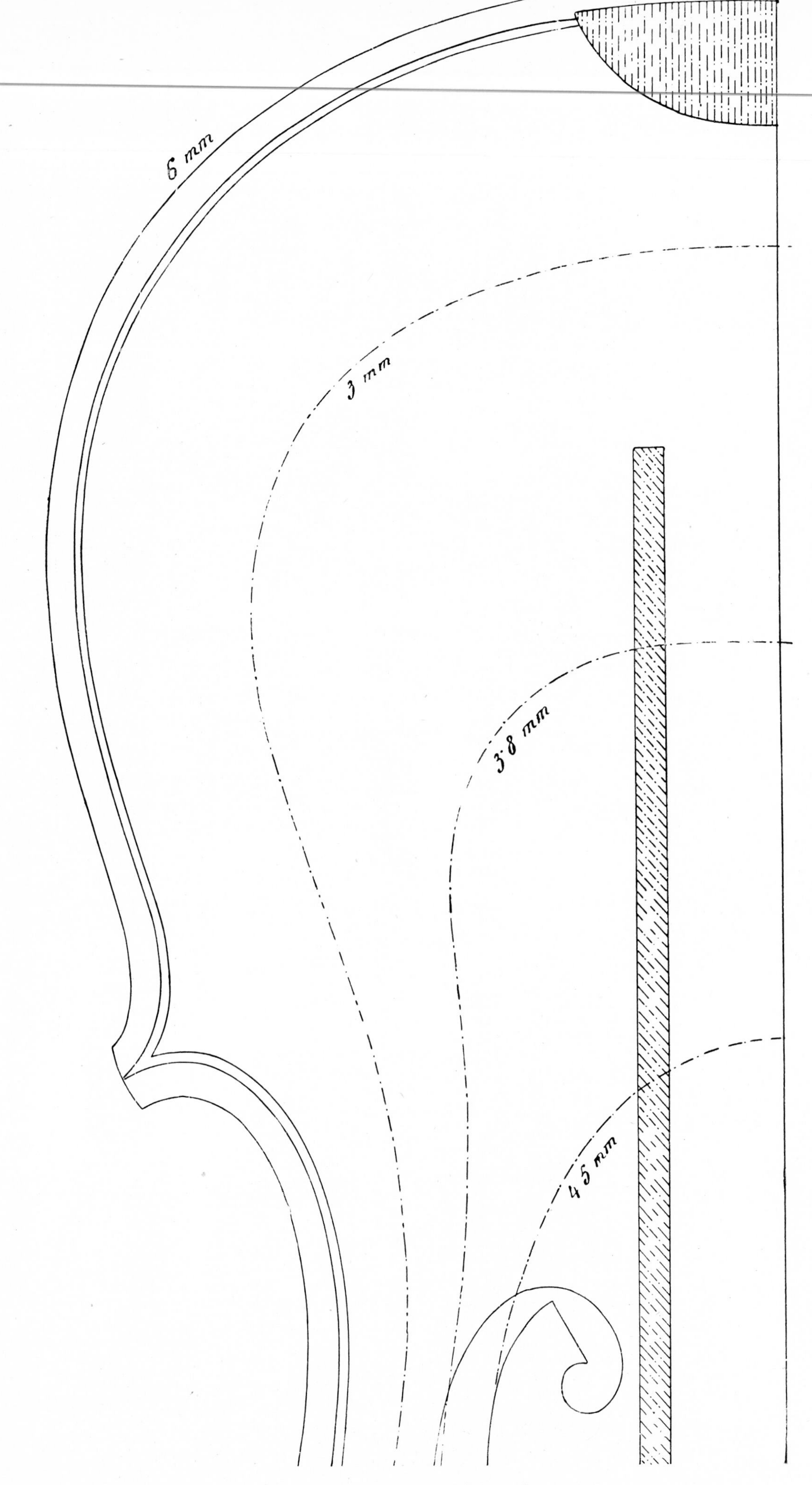

Giuseppe Guarneri del Gesù, Cremona, 1739
CELLO

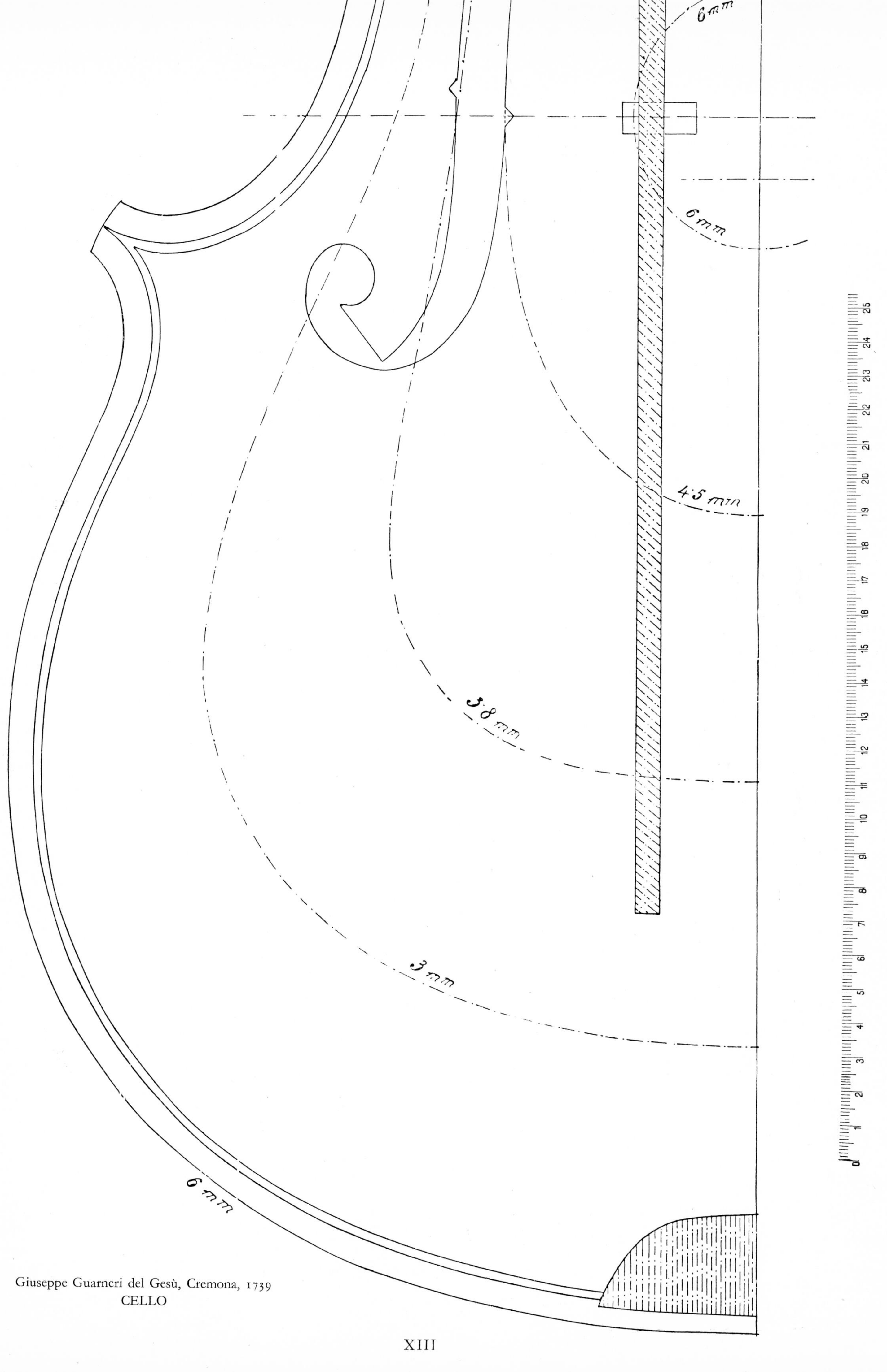

Giuseppe Guarneri del Gesù, Cremona, 1739
CELLO

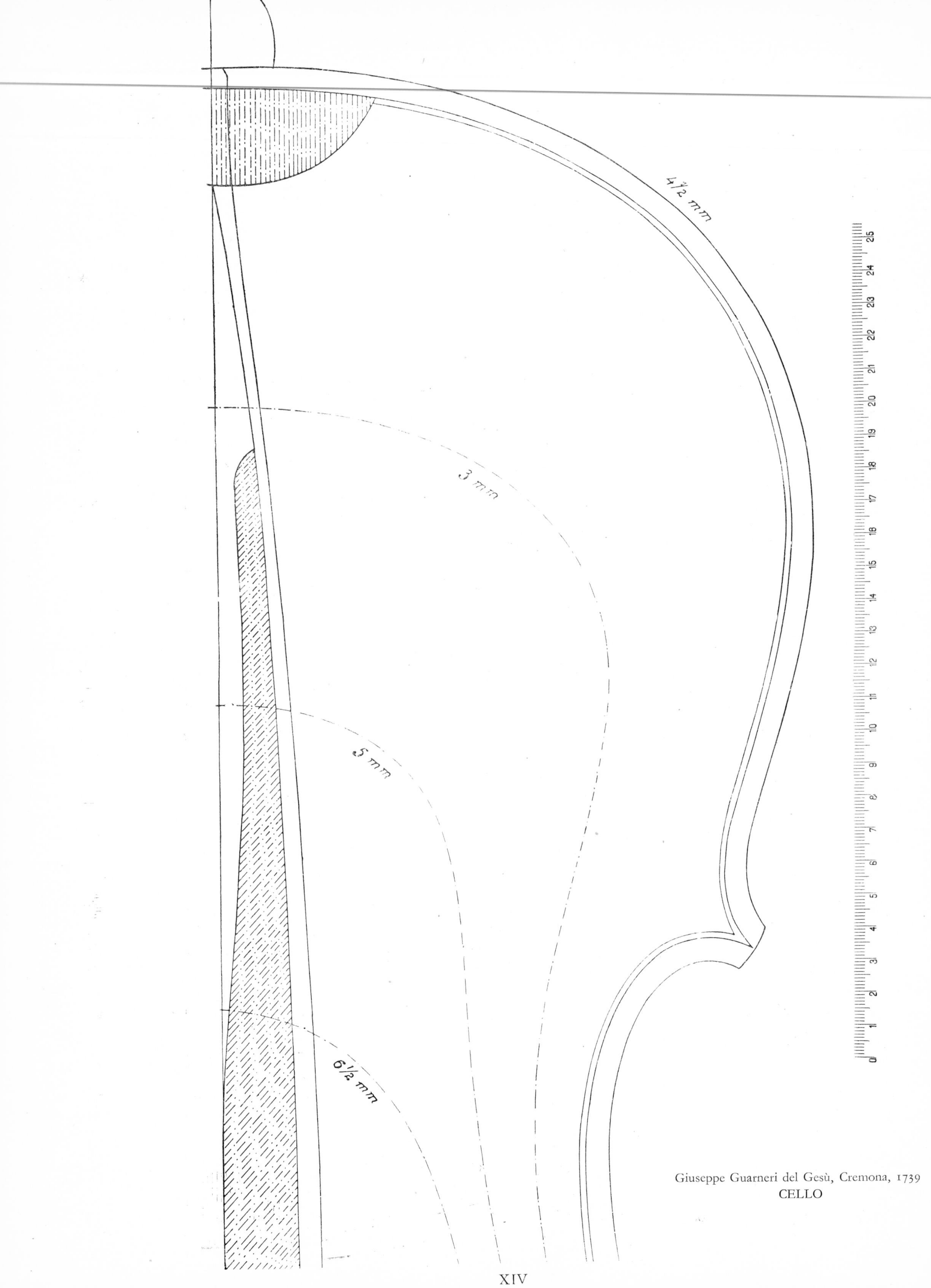

Giuseppe Guarneri del Gesù, Cremona, 1739
CELLO

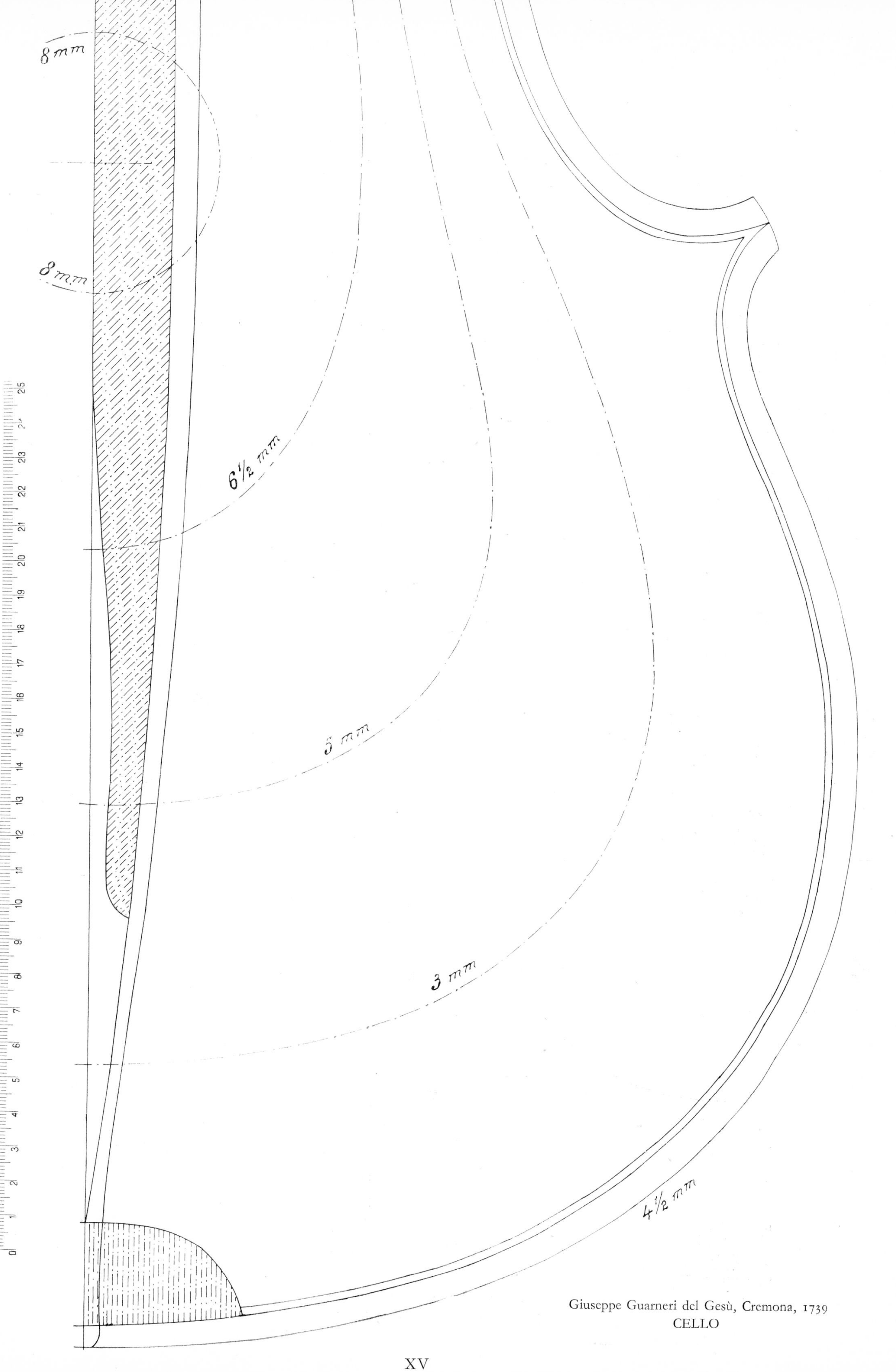

Giuseppe Guarneri del Gesù, Cremona, 1739
CELLO

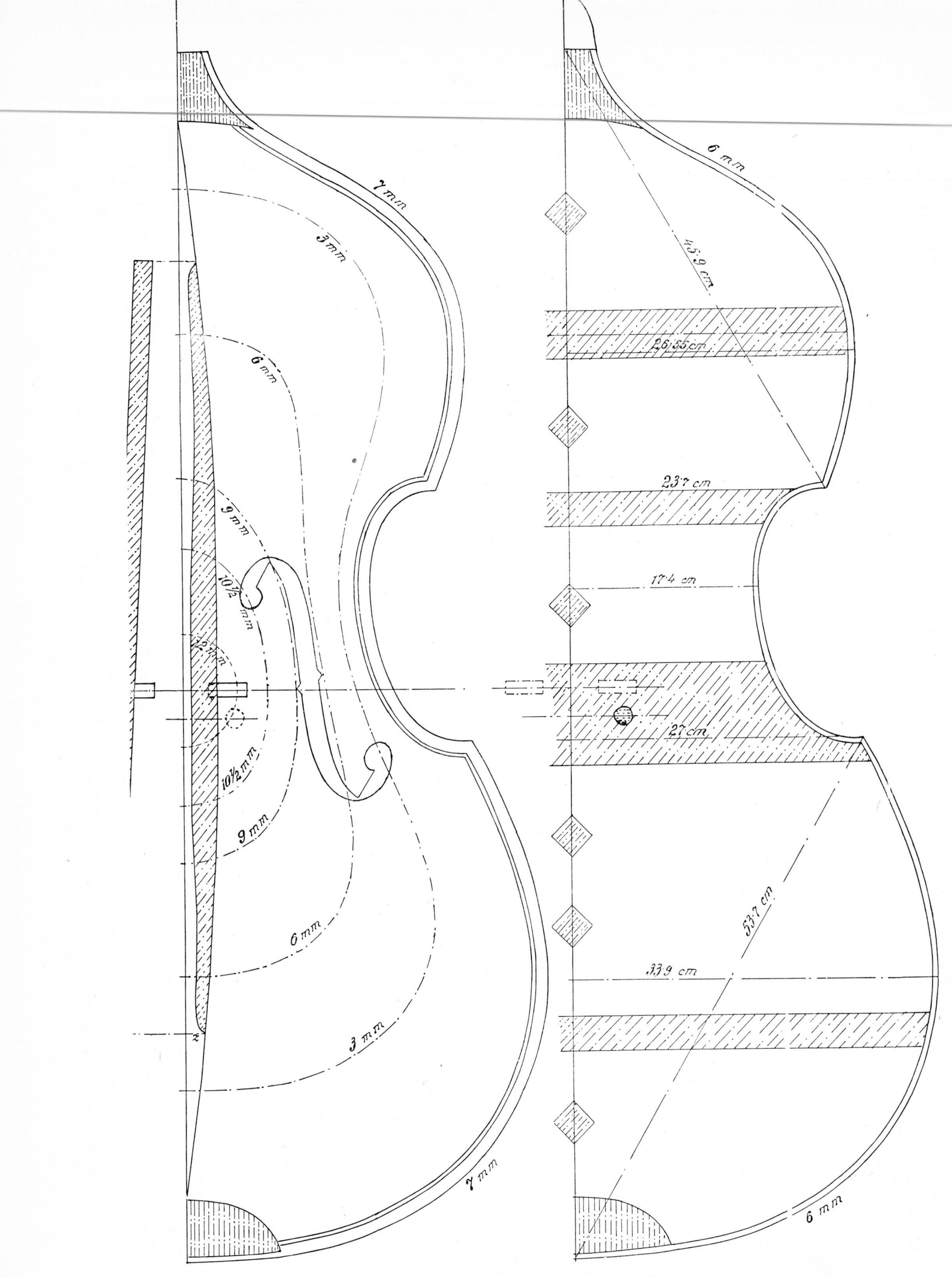

Giuseppe Guarneri del Gesù, Cremona, 1742

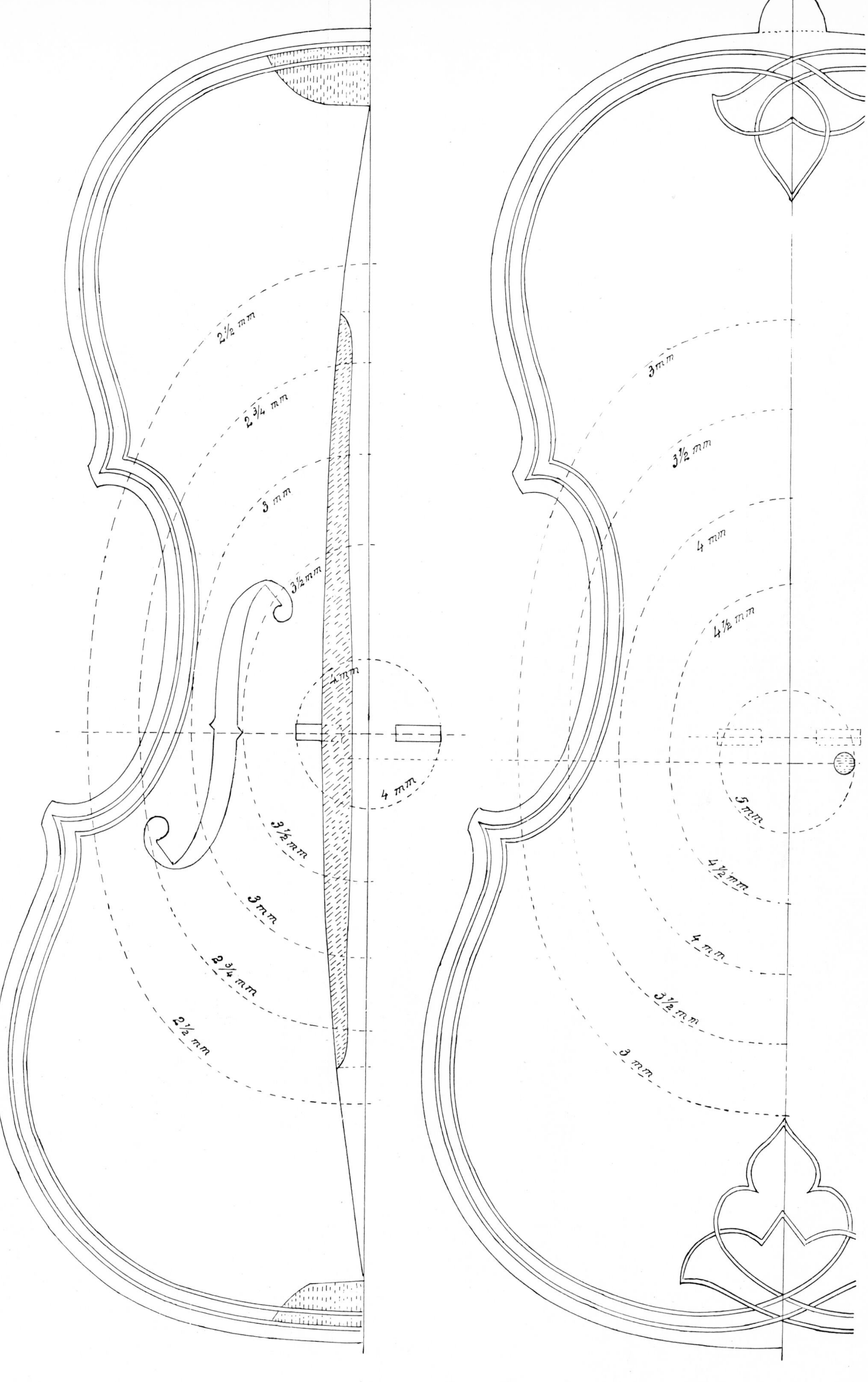

Paolo Maggini, Brescia

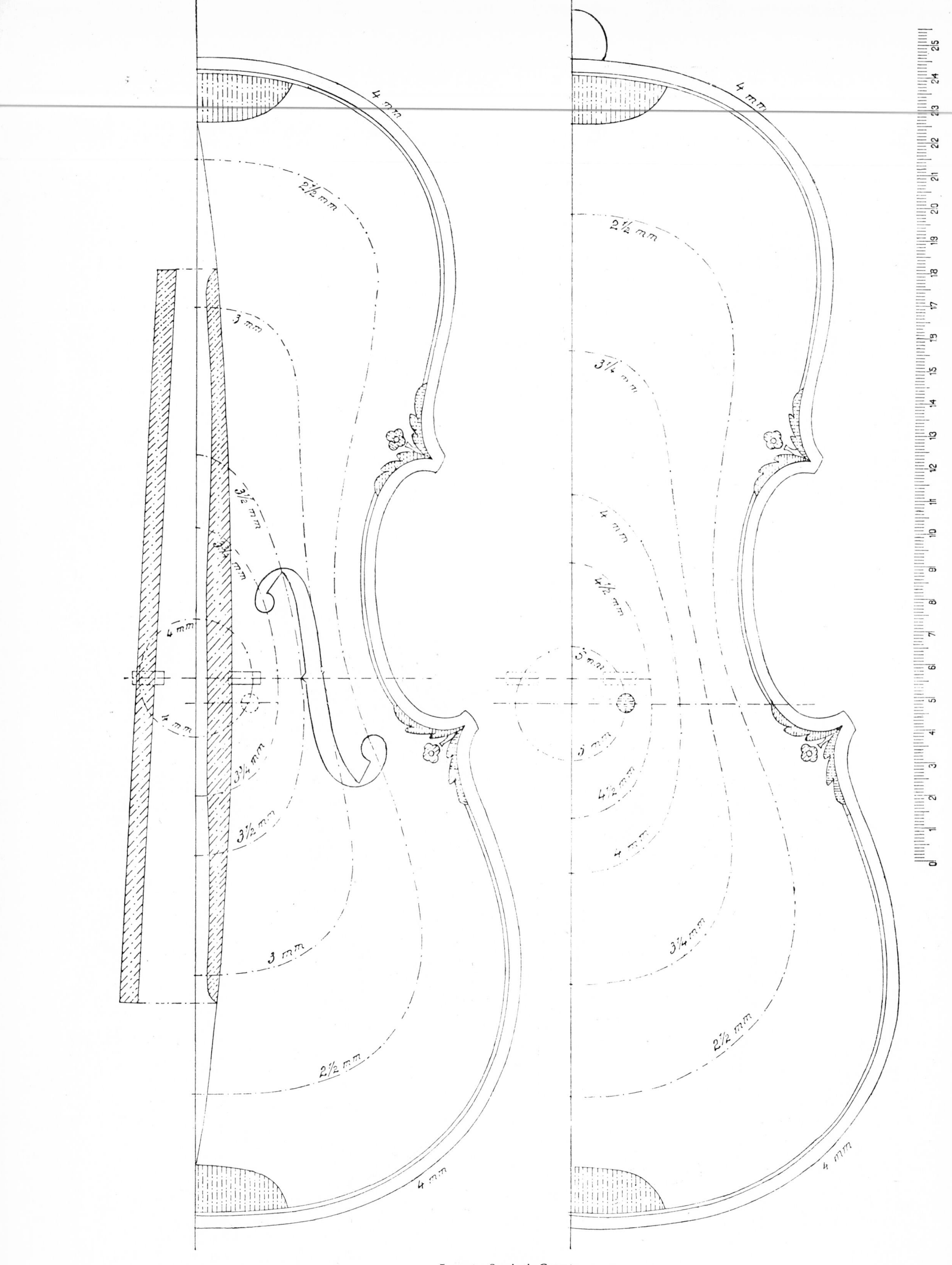

Lorenzo Storiani, Cremona, 1795

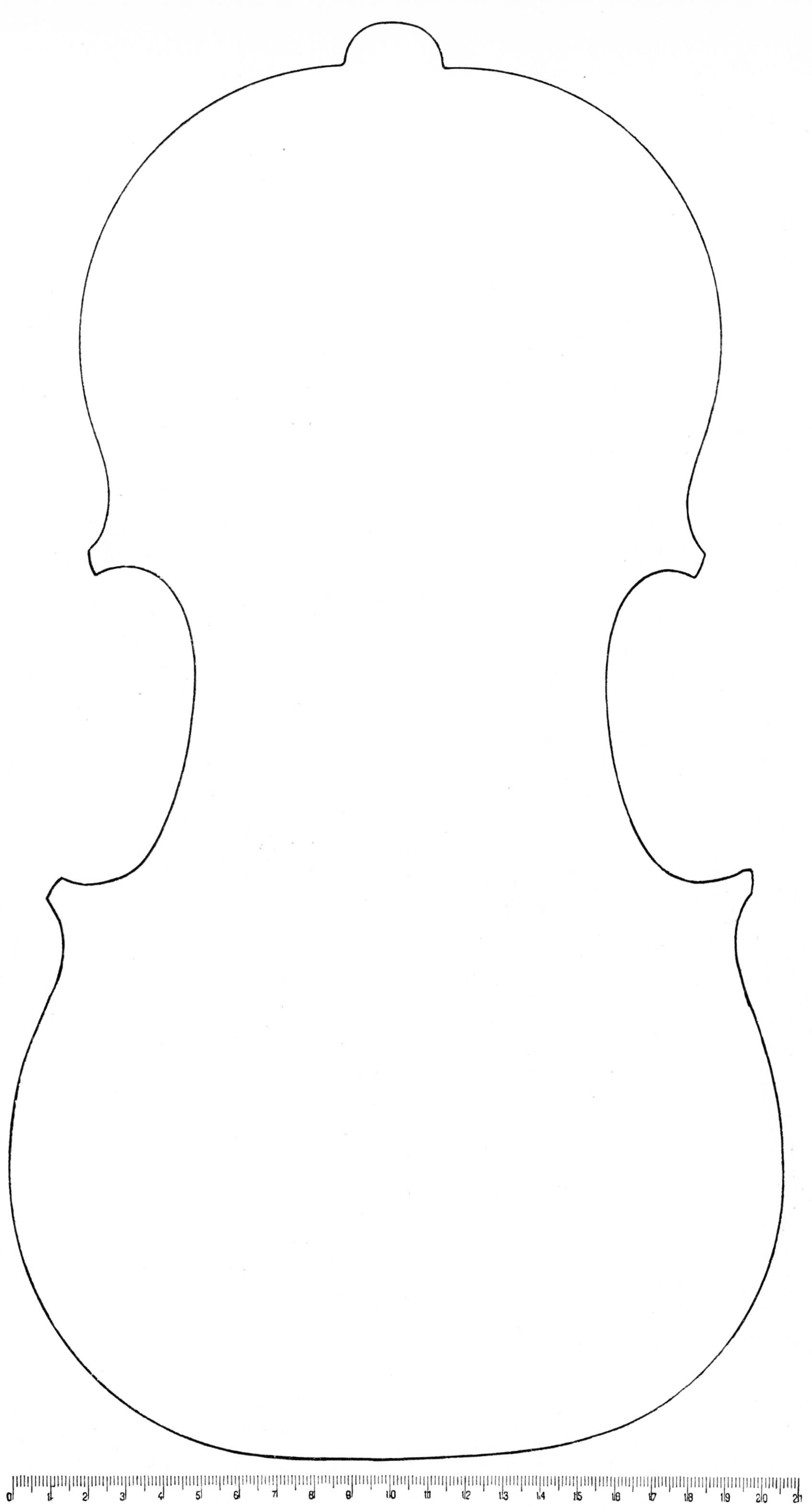

Antonio Stradivari, Cremona, 1688

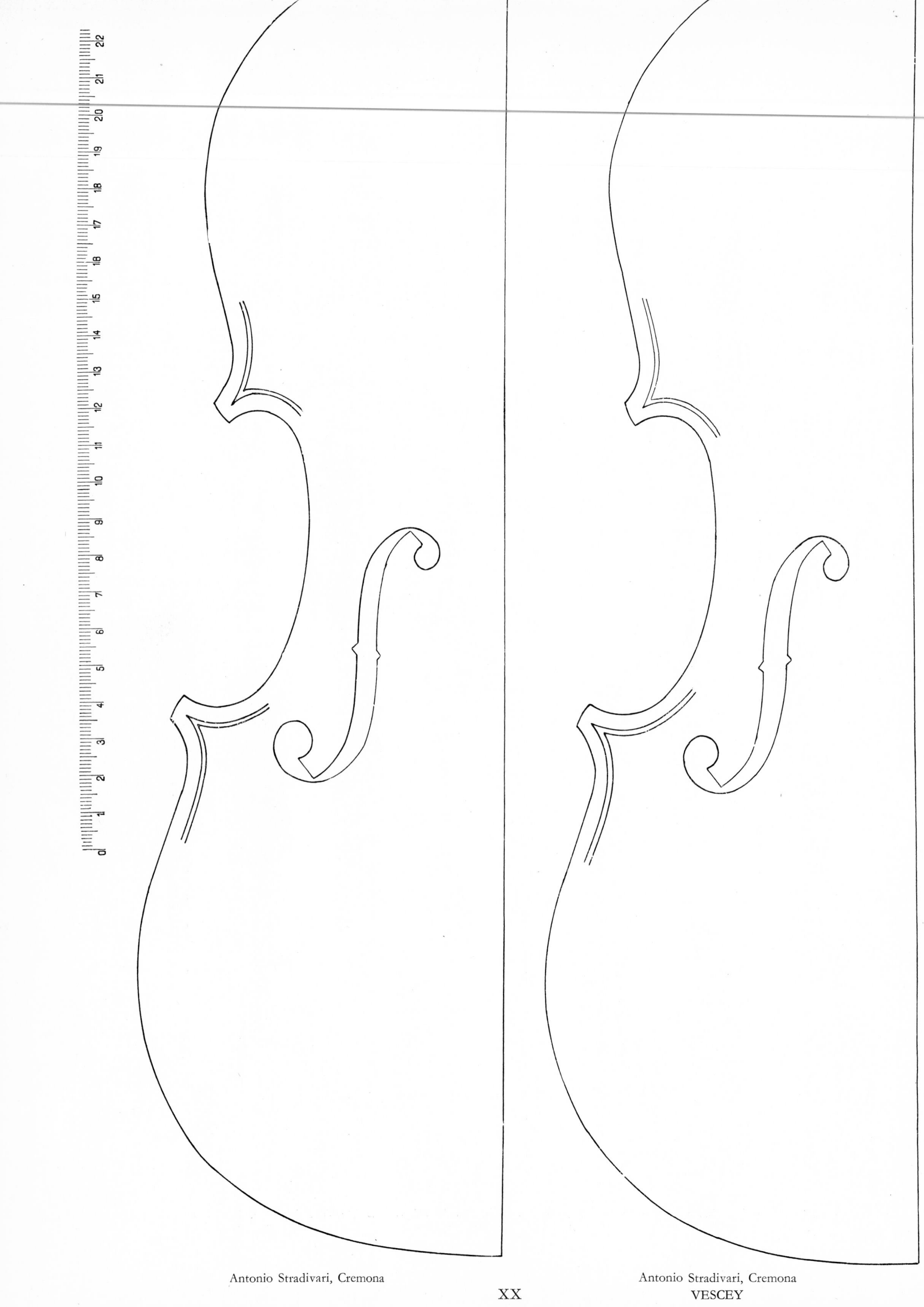

Antonio Stradivari, Cremona

Antonio Stradivari, Cremona
VESCEY

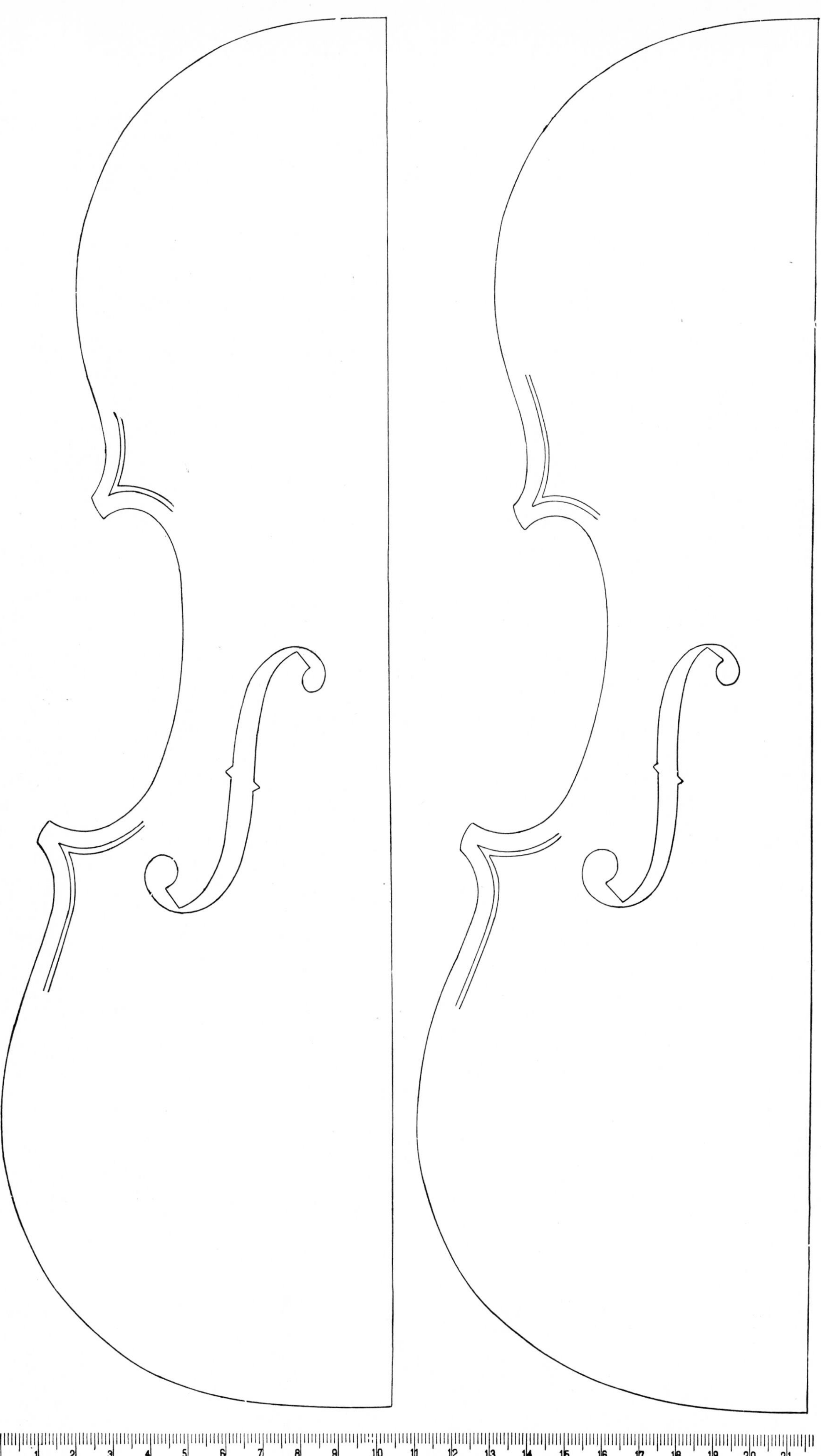

Antonio Stradivari, Cremona, 1688

Antonio Stradivari, Cremona, 1700

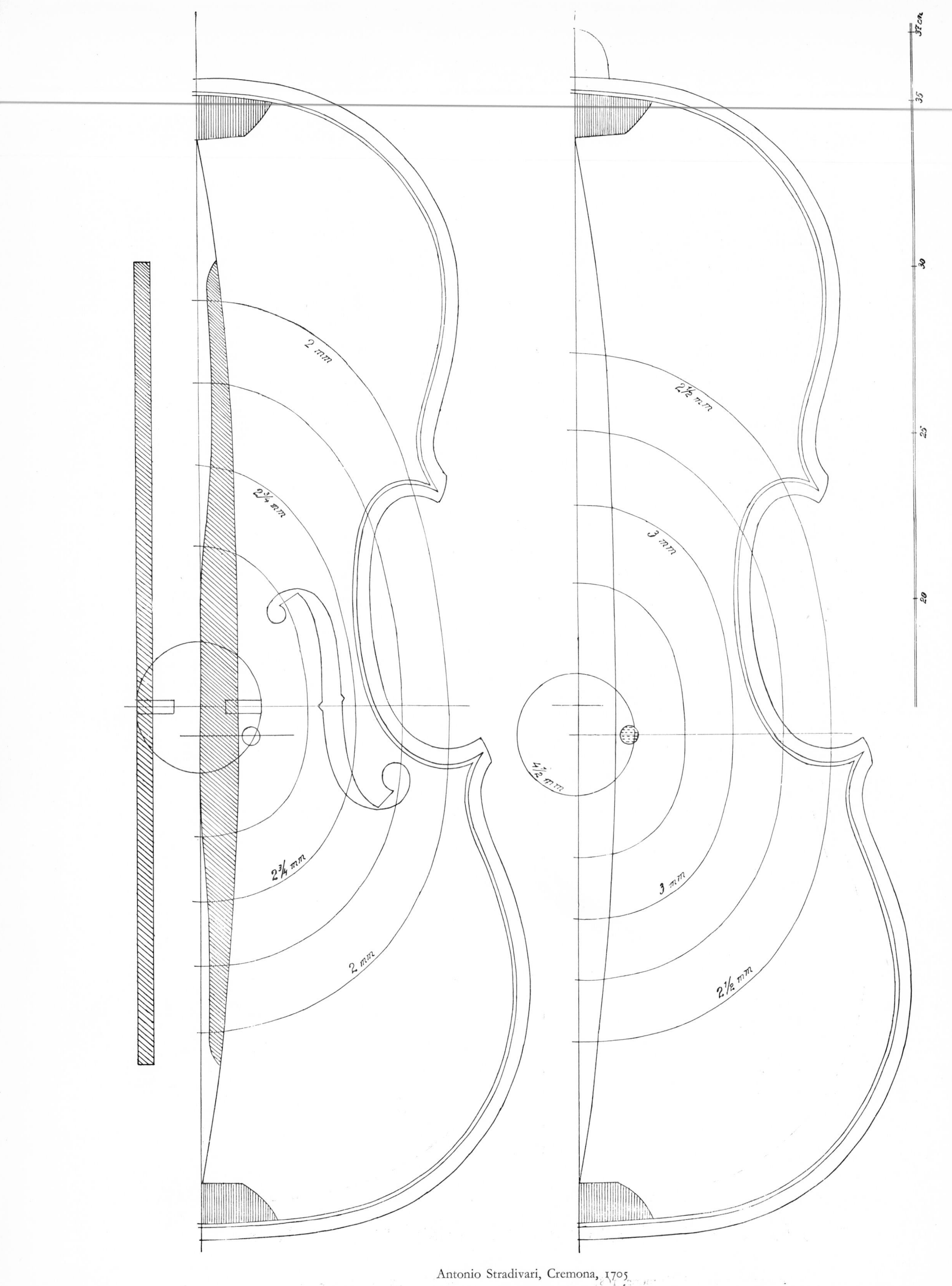

Antonio Stradivari, Cremona, 1705

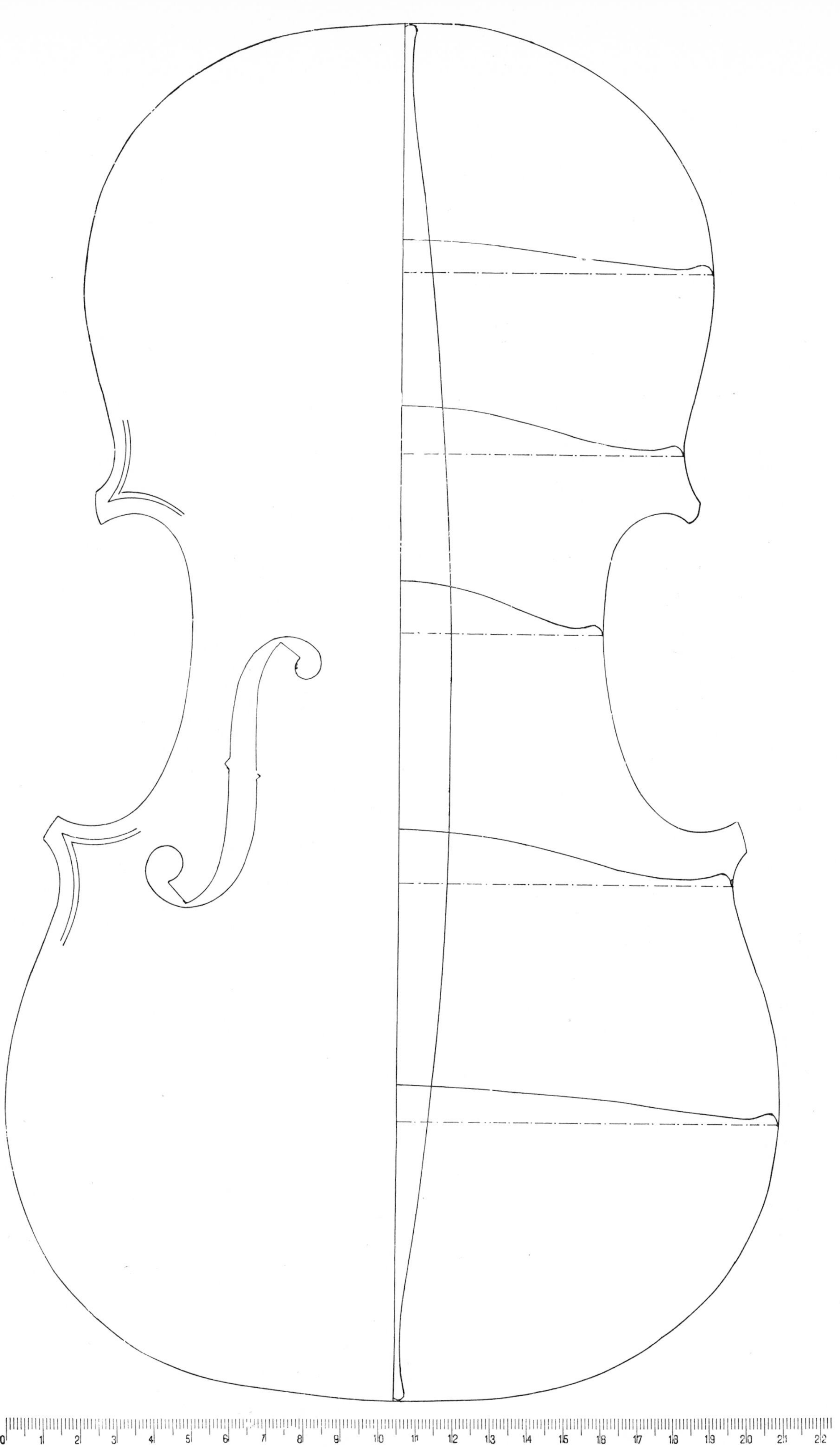

Antonio Stradivari, Cremona, 1710
VIEUXTEMPS

XXIII

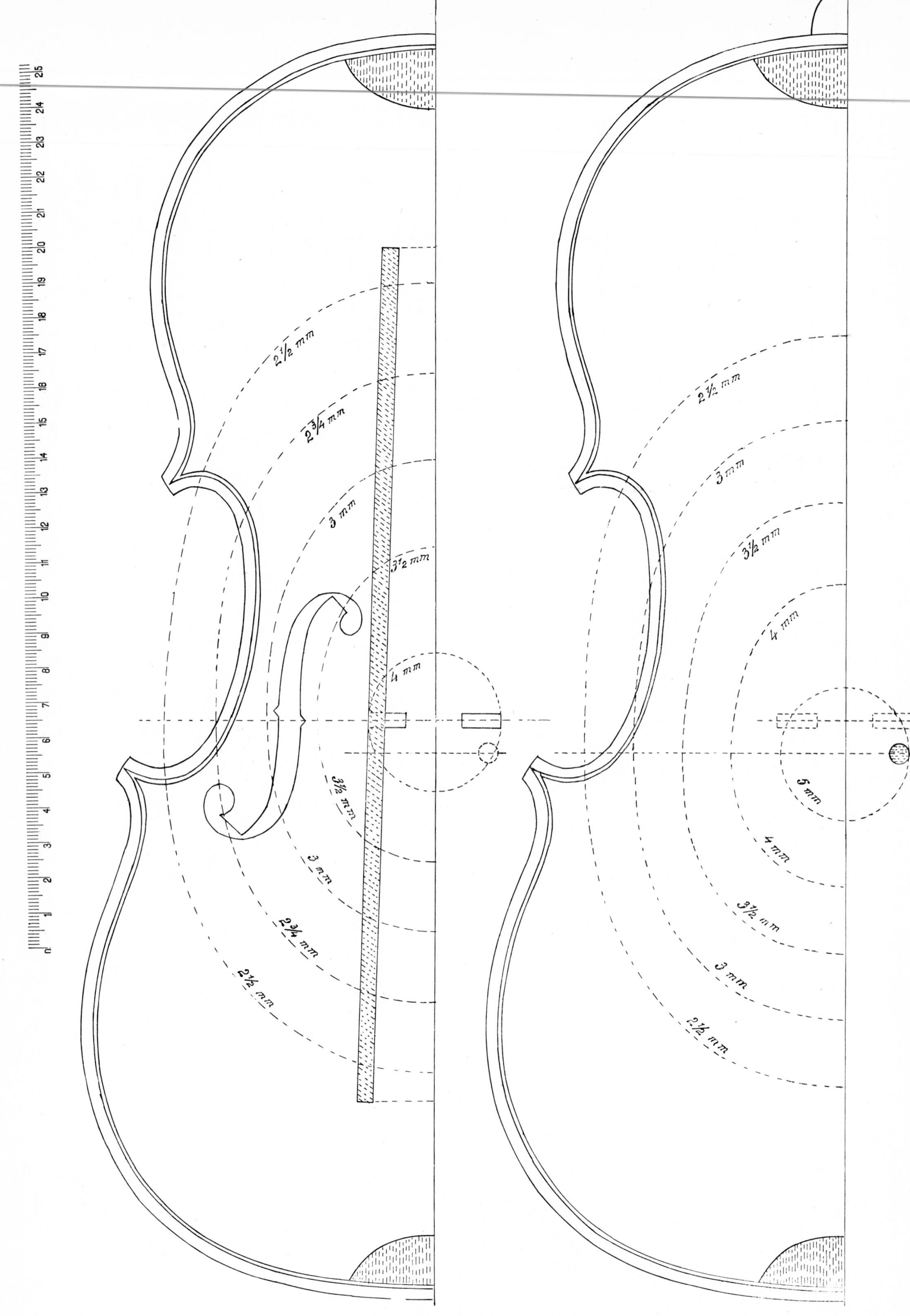

Antonio Stradivari, Cremona, 1708

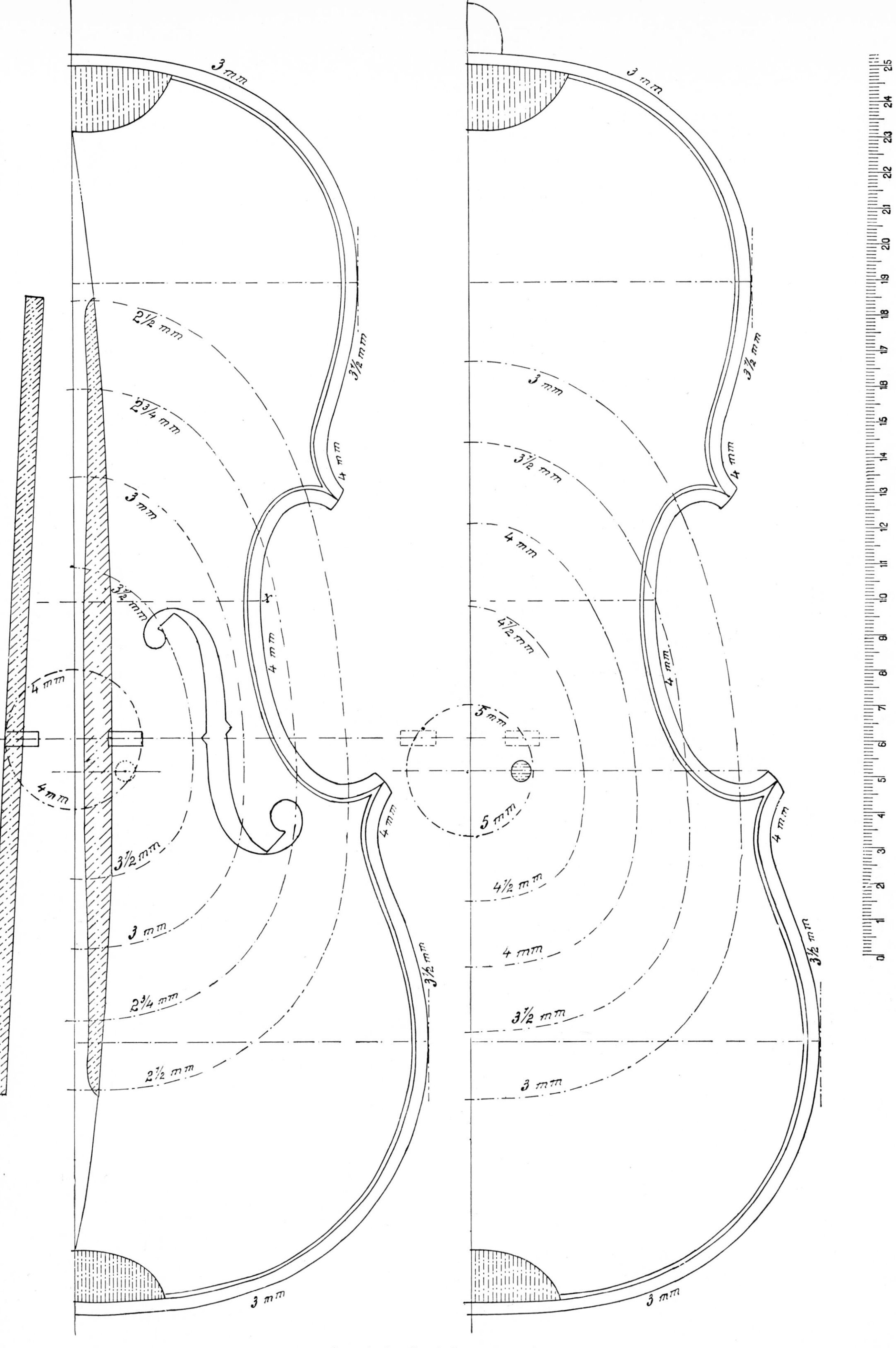

Antonio Stradivari, Cremona, 1716

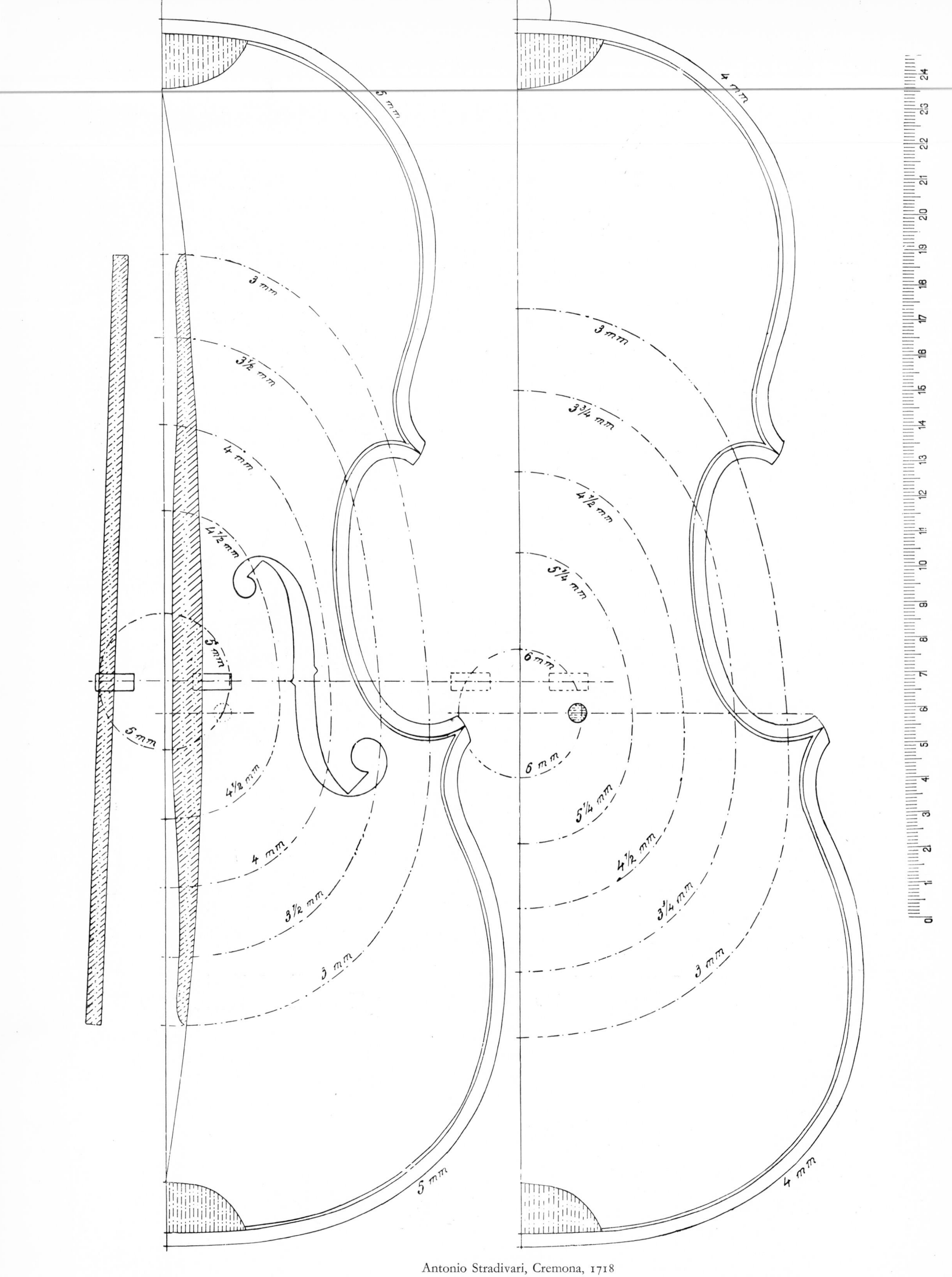

Antonio Stradivari, Cremona, 1718

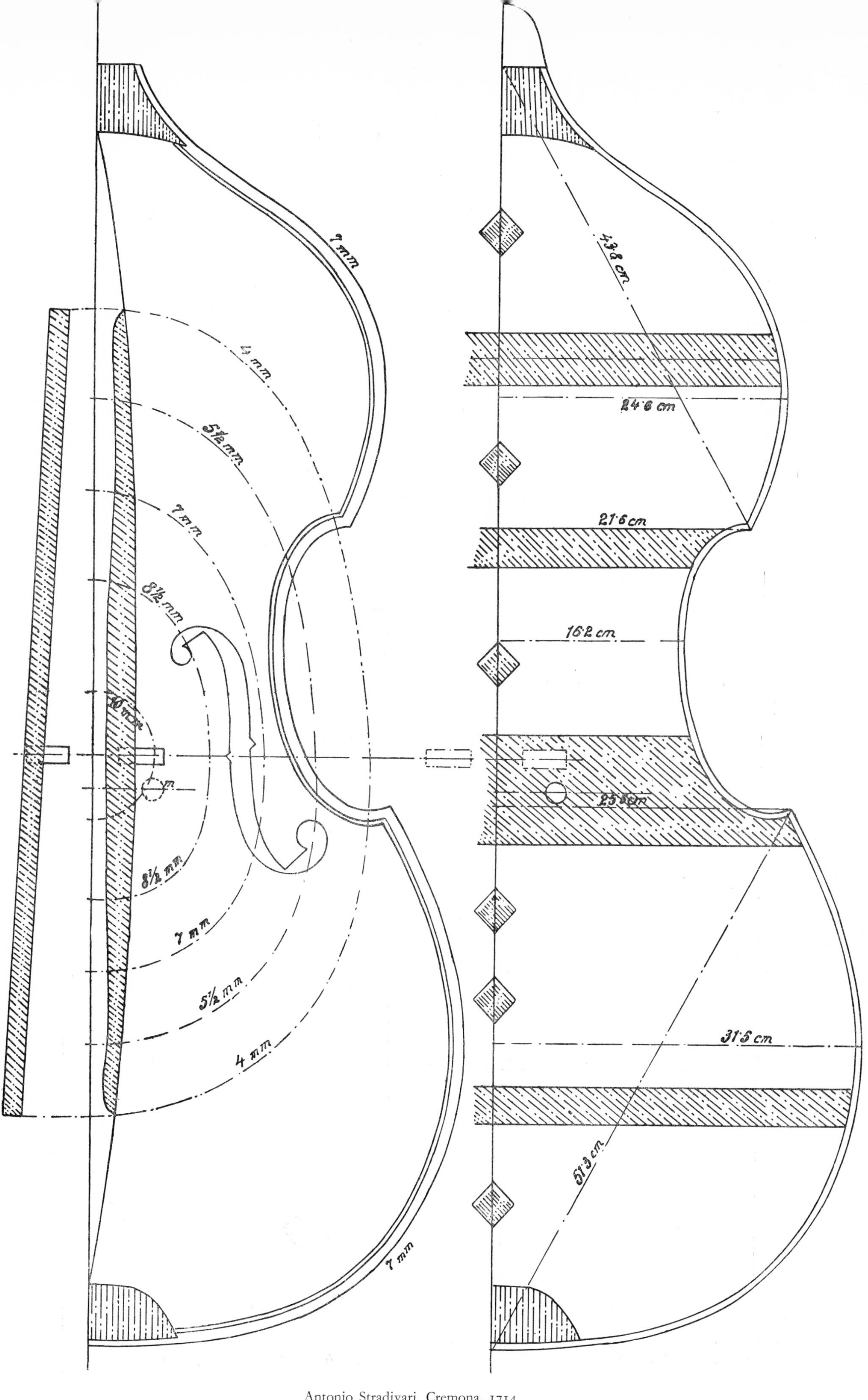

Antonio Stradivari, Cremona, 1714
CONTRABASSO

XXVII

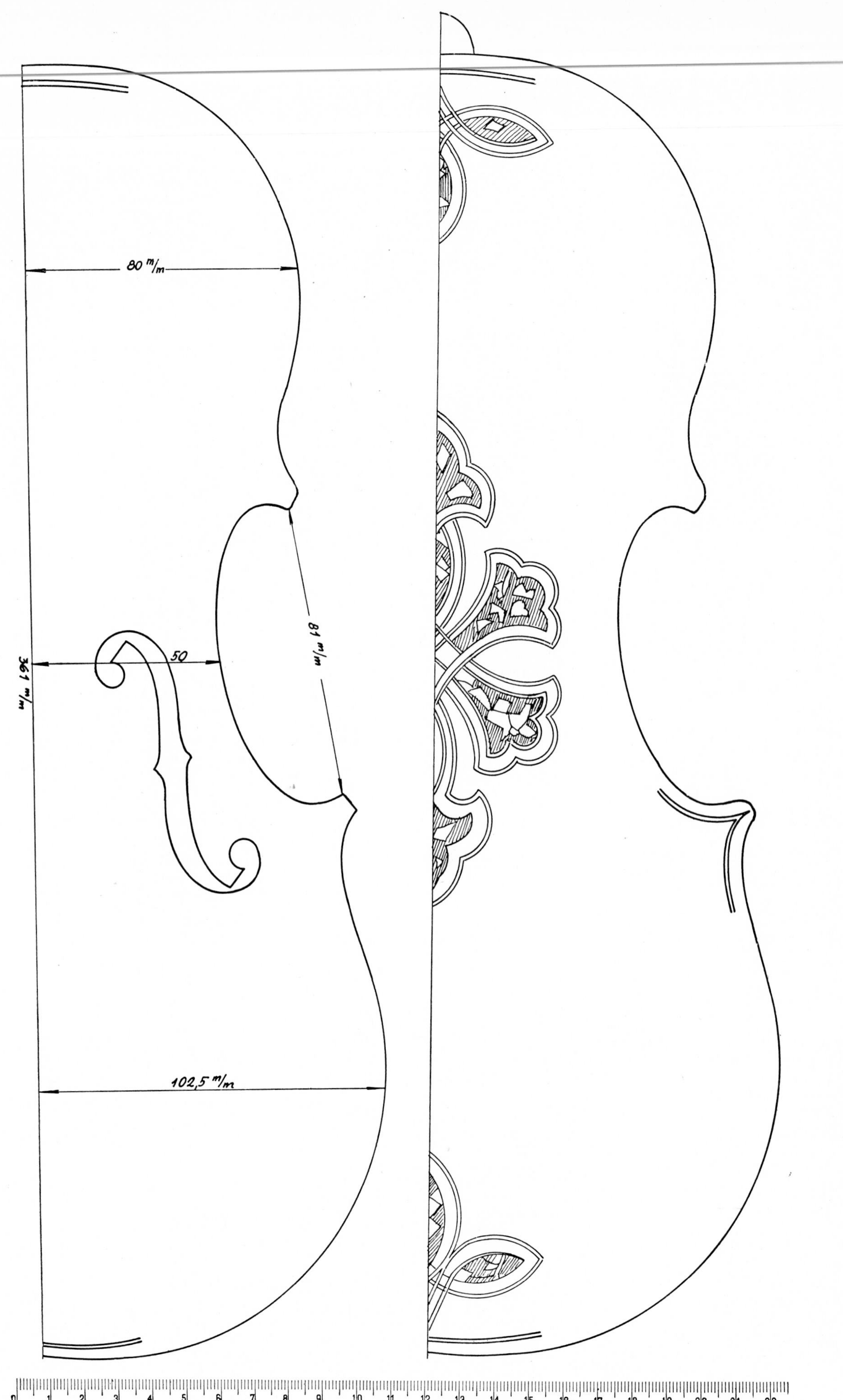

Carlo Antonio Tononi, Venezia

XXVIII

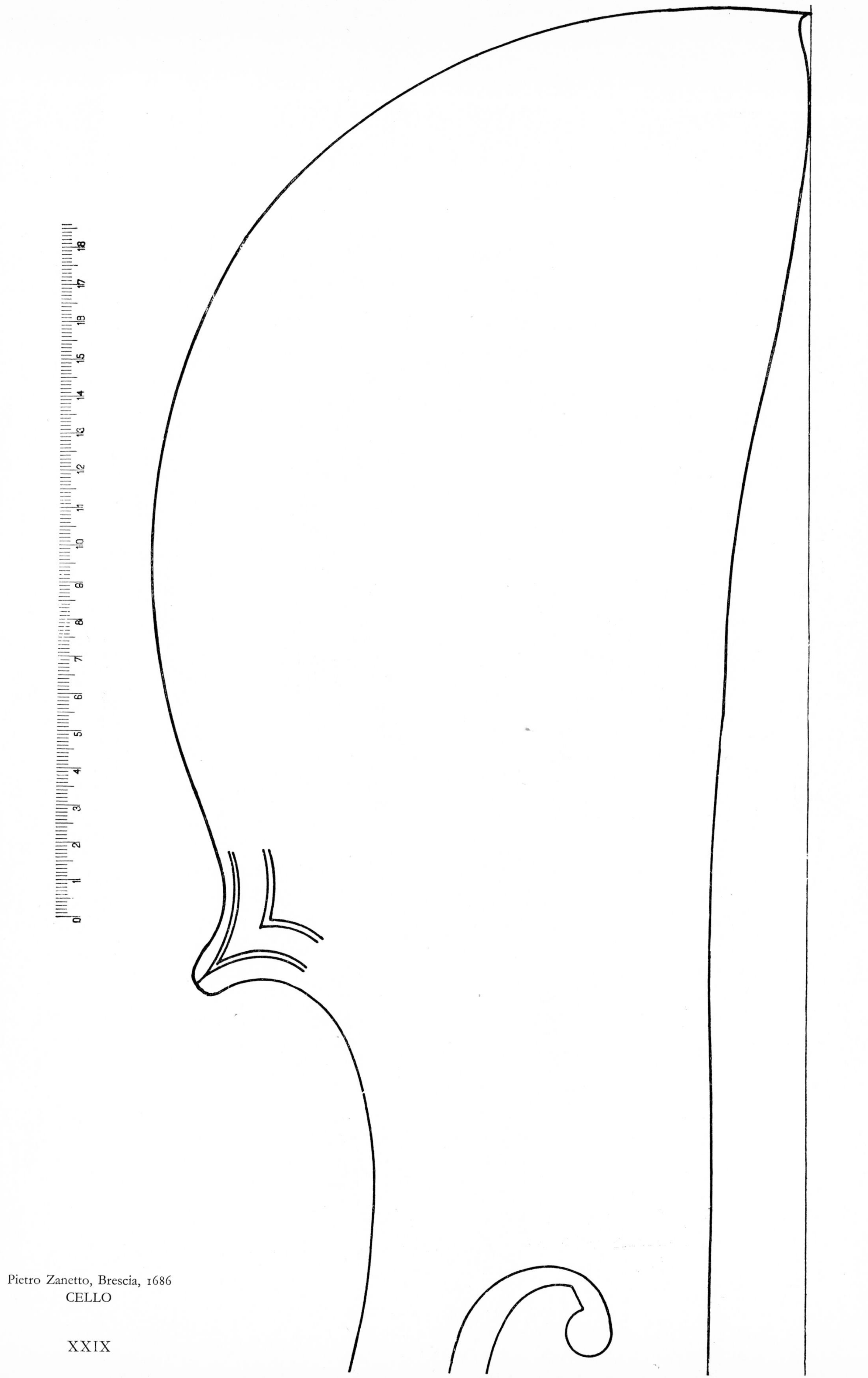

Pietro Zanetto, Brescia, 1686
CELLO

XXIX

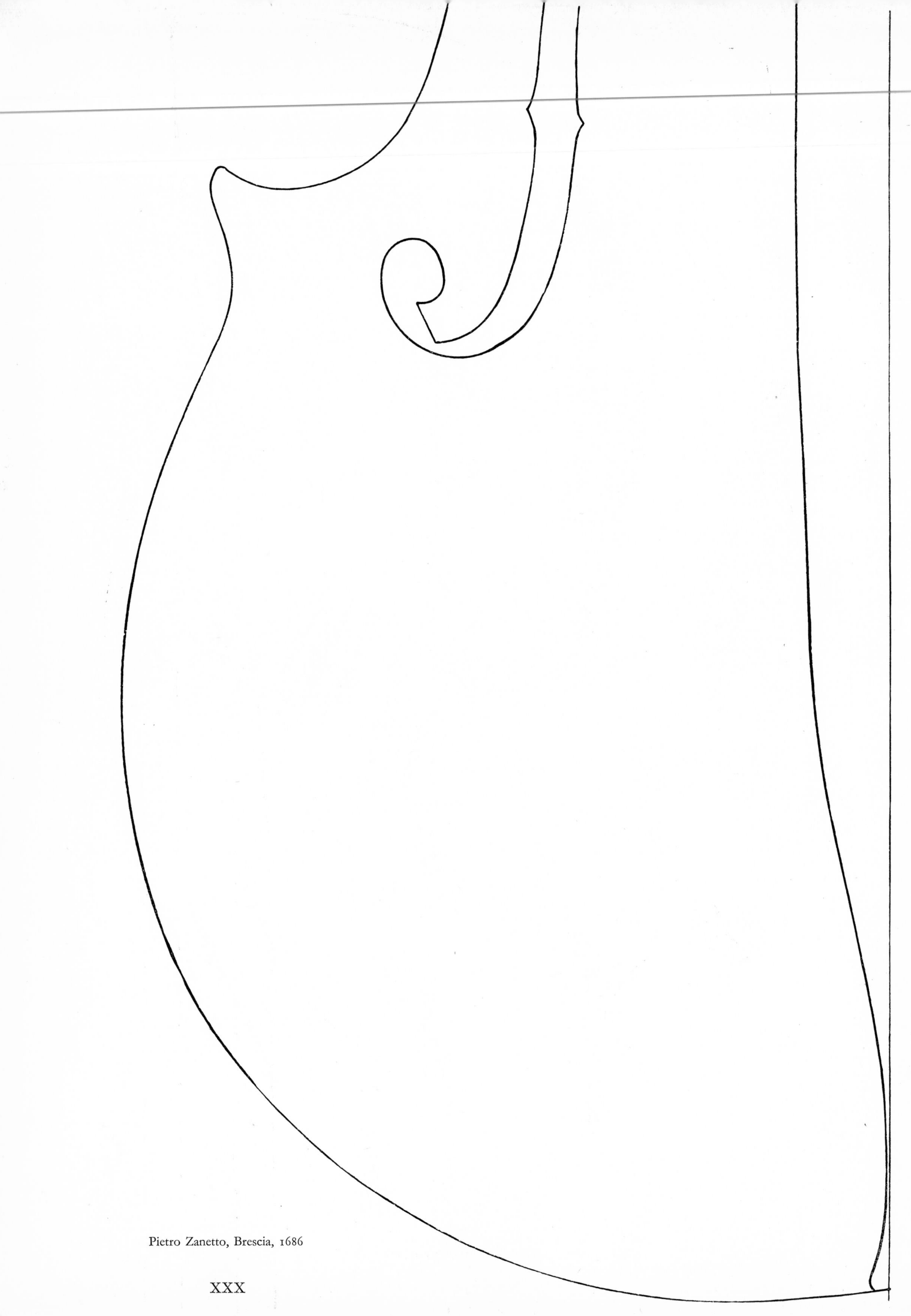

Pietro Zanetto, Brescia, 1686

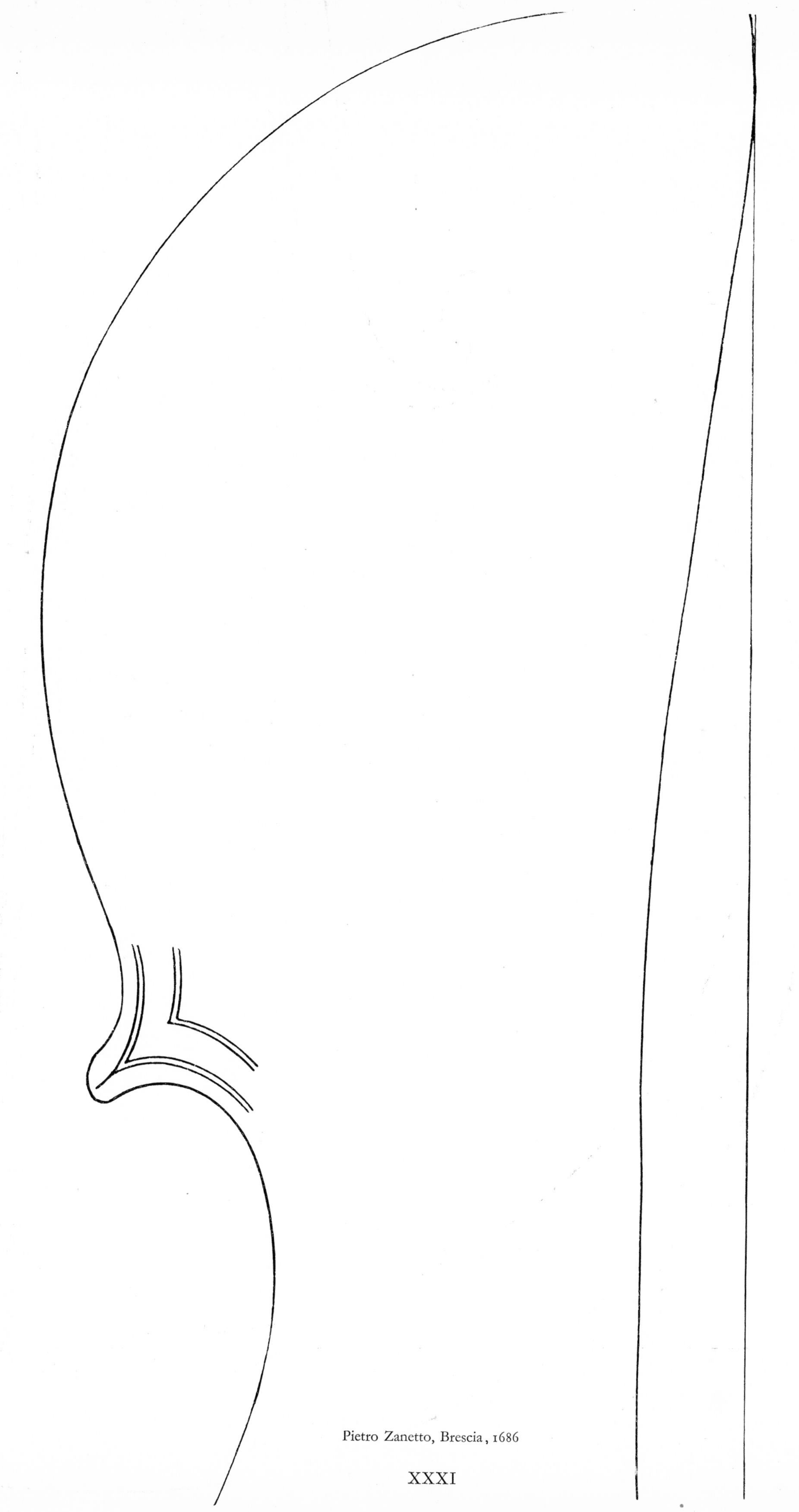

Pietro Zanetto, Brescia, 1686

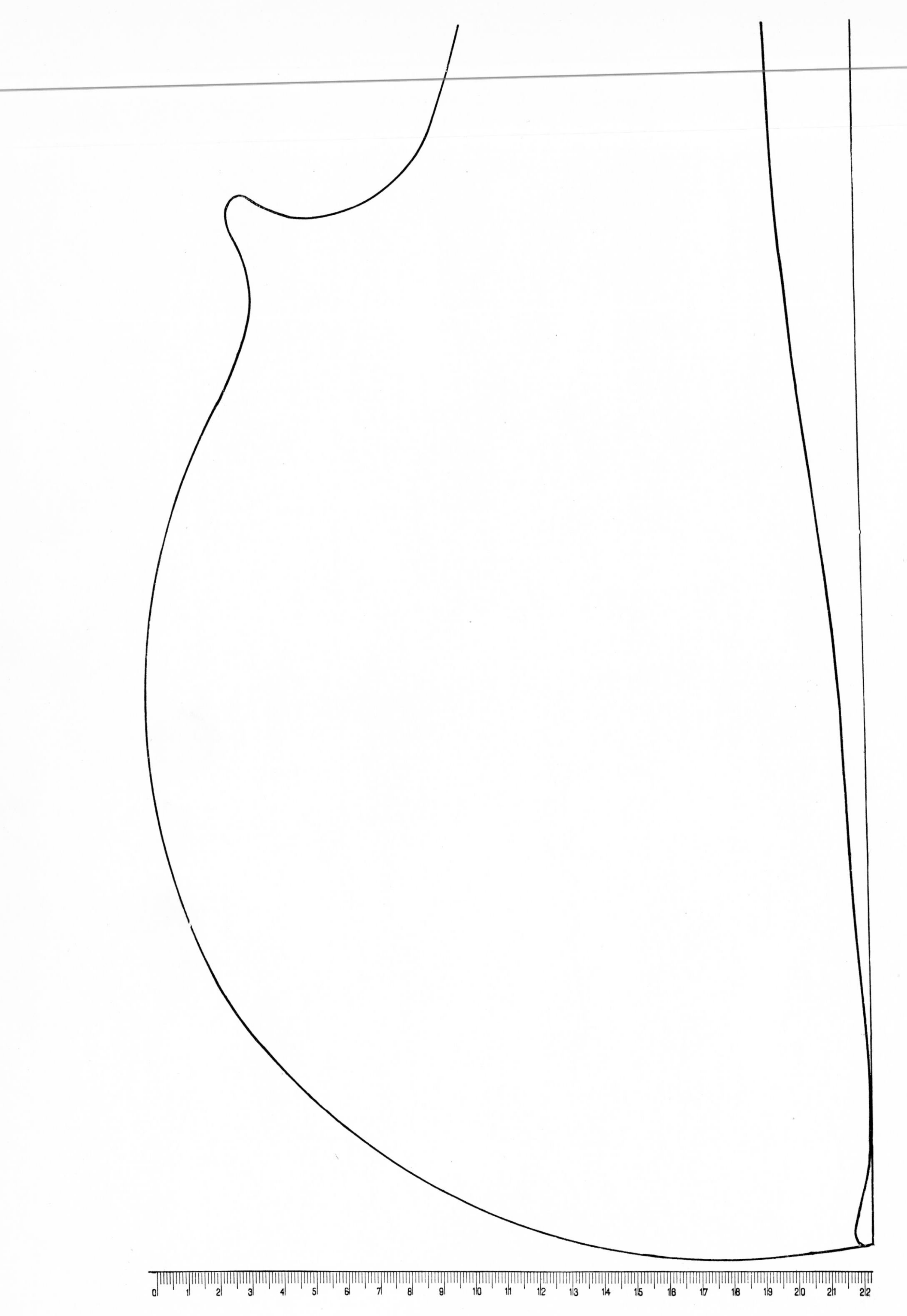

Pietro Zanetto, Brescia, 1686
CELLO

XXXII